PROGRAMMING COMPONENTS WITH MICROSOFT® VISUAL BASIC® 6.0

Guy Eddon and Henry Eddon

Microsoft Press

PUBLISHED BY
Microsoft Press
A Division of Microsoft Corporation
One Microsoft Way
Redmond, Washington 98052-6399

Library of Congress Cataloging-in-Publication Data
Eddon, Guy, 1974-
    Programming Components with Microsoft Visual Basic 6.0 / Guy Eddon,
Henry Eddon.
        p.   cm.
    Includes bibliographical references and index.
    ISBN 1-57231-966-6
    1. Microsoft Visual BASIC.   2. BASIC (Computer program language)
I. Eddon, Henry, 1945-   .   II. Title.
QA76.73.B3E34   1998
005.26'8--dc21   98-30228
                                                           CIP

Printed and bound in the United States of America.

3 4 5 6 7 8 9   QMQM   3 2 1 0 9

Distributed in Canada by ITP Nelson, a division of Thomson Canada Limited.

A CIP catalogue record for this book is available from the British Library.

Microsoft Press books are available through booksellers and distributors worldwide. For further information about international editions, contact your local Microsoft Corporation office or contact Microsoft Press International directly at fax (425) 936-7329. Visit our Web site at mspress.microsoft.com.

Macintosh is a registered trademark of Apple Computer, Inc. Intel is a registered trademark of Intel Corporation. ActiveX, Authenticode, Developer Studio, FrontPage, IntelliMouse, JScript, Microsoft, Microsoft Press, MS-DOS, MSN, Outlook, PowerPoint, Visual Basic, Visual C++, Visual FoxPro, Visual InterDev, Visual J++, Win32, Windows, and Windows NT are either registered trademarks or trademarks of Microsoft Corporation in the United States and/ or other countries. Other product and company names mentioned herein may be the trademarks of their respective owners.

The names of example companies, products, people, characters, and/or data mentioned herein are fictitious and are in no way intended to represent any real individual, company, product, or event, unless otherwise noted.

Acquisitions Editor: Eric Stroo
Project Editor: Alice Turner
Technical Editor: Dail Magee Jr.

Table of Contents

Table of Contents

Preface

This book is written for everyone interested in learning about building component software with Microsoft Visual Basic 6. We worked hard to make this a great book. We hope you read it, enjoy it, and learn a lot from it. In this book, you will learn about the Component Object Model (COM) from the perspective of Visual Basic, as well as how to build various types of COM-based components. In most chapters, interspersed within the text are numerous exercises that enable you to experiment with the various concepts presented. The accompanying CD contains solutions to all the exercises.

In writing this book, we are indebted to many others. We thank our friends at Microsoft Press, including Eric Stroo, who entrusted us with the project and provided moral support in times of need, and Alice Turner and Dail Magee Jr., who did a great job editing the book. Thanks to Eric Maffei, Joanne Steinhart, Joe Flanigen, Joshua Trupin, Laura Euler, and the rest of the gang at *Microsoft Systems Journal* and *Microsoft Interactive Developer*.

Guy thanks the people at Learning Tree International for fostering a stimulating working environment. David Collins, Eric Garen, John Moriarty, Francesco Zamboni, Mindy Robbins, and David Barkley deserve special mention. Henry thanks his fellow UPSers for their ideas on component software. In particular, Laynglyn Capers, Sherri Berman, Dave Karlson, and Rudy Vossen all contributed their unique views on COM. Laynglyn believes the Interface Definition Language (IDL) is a COM programmer's best friend; Sherri insists that type libraries have low fidelity because they do not include IDL attributes such as *size_of*; Dave sees COM as a better C++; Rudy thinks connection points are a hack. Thanks to our family and friends; without their support and understanding, this project would never have been possible.

Guy Eddon
Henry Eddon
guyeddon@msn.com

Part I

Introducing Component Development

Chapter 1

Understanding Component Software

Software development processes have not changed that much over the years. Most software development efforts are beleaguered by cost and time overruns, and the results are often bug-ridden and not maintainable. A number of different paradigms and methodologies, from flow charts to object orientation, have been offered and sometimes accepted for varying lengths of time as a panacea for the problems inherent in software development. However, all of these purported solutions have failed to meet expectations; no reliable substitute has been found for the success achieved by small groups of individuals working on one project at a time. This isn't to say that flow charts are unhelpful or that object-oriented designs are flawed, but simply that they do not reduce software development to a formula that guarantees results. The time has come to realize that software development is inherently difficult and fraught with many problems that have no single solution.

Software developers and technical managers alike have long dreamed of a day when software would be assembled from prebuilt components, in much the same way that circuit boards are assembled primarily from existing components. With the advent of the Component Object Model (COM), that day has arrived.

Component-based software development brings the advantage of consistency to the software development process. Since most software shares common elements, component software enables developers to easily integrate thoroughly tested and proven components into an application. In addition, developers can build as a software component the functionality that is unique to a specific application, to facilitate integration of the functionality with the larger system.

In this chapter, we first explore the developments in object-oriented programming that preceded component software. Second, we focus on the advantages that building component software in Microsoft Visual Basic 6 has over object-oriented programming techniques.

OBJECT-ORIENTED PROGRAMMING: A BRIEF HISTORY

Object-oriented programming is one of the recent paradigms to enjoy a long and somewhat favorable reception by the software industry. This acceptance is reflected in the popularity of object-oriented programming languages such as Ada, Smalltalk, Java, and C++. These languages each carry the object-oriented flag at varying heights depending on the areas of expertise of the designers, the problems they set out to solve, and the limitations with which they had to contend. C++, for example, takes a pragmatic view of object-oriented programming, although this view can mostly be traced to the roots that C++ has in C and its stringent compatibility requirements with C. While Microsoft Visual Basic isn't fully object-oriented, object-oriented ideas have permeated its design and it continues to evolve toward a more complete object-oriented language.

What Is Object-Oriented Programming?

In a nutshell, the goal of object-oriented programming techniques is to write software in a way that reflects how individuals think in the real world. This is in contrast to procedural languages, such as C, in which programming is done in a procedural and logically organized manner intended to mimic the logic of a computer. Object-oriented programming methods recognize that most software attempts to model things (objects) that people work with every day. Rather than reducing these objects to a procedural set of steps, object-oriented programming languages allow developers to express more easily and effectively the existence of objects directly in the code. The hope is that this will lead to more expressive code that will be easier to develop and less costly to maintain.

Most object-oriented programming languages maintain a distinction between a *class* and an *object*. A class is a template that defines its members. An object is an instance of that class and can actually do things. For example, compare a cookie cutter with a cookie. A cookie cutter is a template (class) that defines various attributes of cookies, such as shape and size. A cookie is an instance based on the cookie cutter and is analogous to an object.

The object-oriented paradigm expounds three major characteristics of an object-oriented programming language:

- *Encapsulation*   The ability to hide an object's implementation details.

- *Inheritance*   The ability to reuse existing objects in the creation of new, more specialized objects.

- *Polymorphism*   The ability to exhibit multiple behaviors depending on the object being used.

Encapsulation

In most standard procedural languages, such as C, code is written in modules of functions that operate on data. Encapsulation specifies that code be combined with related data to define an object. This combination of code and data is called the *implementation*. The implementation is private to the object that is defined, which means that the object's internal implementation is nobody's business but its own; the object is a sort of black box.

The object also exposes a public *interface* through which the data can be accessed; this interface constitutes the contract between the object and its clients (applications or other objects that need the services provided by the object). We are not talking about end-user interfaces here, but rather programmatic interfaces that enable one piece of software to talk to another. The idea behind an encapsulated design is that it allows the internal implementation of an object to be modified, improved, and expanded, so long as the public interface exposed by the object isn't compromised.

Properly done, encapsulation imposes a slight performance penalty on software due to the extra layer of the public interface. For efficiency reasons, it's sometimes necessary to allow certain users of an object to bypass this public interface and access your private implementation directly. In these cases, it's appropriate to specify these special users as friends, thereby giving them access. If abused, the friend concept ruins the whole idea of encapsulation, so it should be used only when necessary.

Inheritance

Code reuse is the Holy Grail of object-oriented programming. If you consider the time and effort expended developing and debugging code that has been written countless times before, you will recognize that code reuse is a tantalizing promise. Inheritance reuses code within an application by creating an object that inherits functionality from another object. Inheritance techniques are especially useful when an existing class has the basic functionality you need but doesn't behave exactly as you want. In this situation, the new class is a superset of the existing base class, which allows you to reuse the functionality available in the base class and at the same time to add functionality to the derived class. Using inheritance almost always requires that developers have access to the source code so that they can copy the code of a base class member function into an override function in the derived class and then modify it slightly.

Class libraries

The ability to inherit functionality from existing classes has given rise to *class libraries* such as the Microsoft Foundation Class library that is to be used in conjunction with Microsoft Visual C++ to develop applications for Microsoft Windows. These class libraries provide much of the default code needed to create a standard Windows-based application, allowing you to create classes that inherit the default functionality. This technique makes it easy to begin writing Windows-based applications, as most of the common drudgery has been done for you. All you need to do to create your own application is add your own customizing code and possibly override default code in the base classes—the "just add water and mix" approach to Windows application programming.

Multiple inheritance

Another feature available in some object-oriented programming languages such as C++ is *multiple inheritance*. Multiple inheritance allows developers to inherit code from two or more base classes at a time. For example, imagine that you have a TextEdit class that provides text editing capabilities and a Window class that provides a windowing system. If you want to create one class consisting of a text editor in a window, you can use multiple inheritance.

In theory this sounds great, but in reality things don't always turn out quite so rosy. If, by unlucky coincidence, both the TextEdit and Window classes were originally built by inheritance from some other class—for instance, a Display class—you will now have two sets of identical data members colliding in the new multiple-inheritance class. While C++ provides a workaround to this problem in the form of virtual base classes, you can legitimately question the maintainability of such complicated designs. (As an interesting aside, the Java programming language avoids such problems by not supporting multiple-class inheritance. Java gets around this limitation by supporting multiple inheritance from interfaces that have no data members and therefore won't have duplicate data members colliding.)

Polymorphism

With inheritance of the sort offered by C++, many classes in the inheritance hierarchy will implement identical methods, with each method overriding its base class implementation. Polymorphism enables developers to write relatively general code for the base class that works properly with more specialized derived objects by permitting code to adapt to a wide variety of situations that might not have been initially planned for. Suppose that you have written a Vehicle class containing a Go method. Sometime later in the life of the project, you add an Airplane class and a Car class, both of which inherit characteristics from the Vehicle base class. In the Airplane class, you override the Go method with a function that causes the plane to fly, and in the Car class you override the Go method with a function that causes the car to drive. Polymorphism says that if you call the Go method on a Vehicle object that is actually an Airplane object, the Airplane object's Go method is called, causing the plane to fly, whereas a Car object's Go method would cause it to drive.

As a more realistic example for Visual Basic, let's consider a package shipping company. A generic Package class would probably have a Ship method that knows how to ship the package. The NextDayAir and all other package types would also have Ship methods of their own. Each package type would require a special Ship method that takes into account when the package needs to arrive, how it will be shipped (air or ground), special precautions (insured packages), and so on. Now suppose you write a shipping application to be run from the company's shipping counter. You want this application to deal with any type of package that comes along, including future package types that don't currently exist. The application knows about the generic Package class, but you would like to keep this class nonspecific—you would rather the application knew nothing detailed about any derived package types. Nevertheless, when the application invokes the Ship method on whatever package type it has on hand, the application uses that specific package's Ship method.

This ability to take on many shapes is polymorphism. Developers can write code for a basic type of object, but at run time the code might in fact be working with an object that is derived from the base object. It's as if the code is sending a generic message to an object that then has the ability to interpret the message in the context of what the object is capable of doing. The ability to write relatively general code that can then work correctly with specialized types of objects is a clear benefit of polymorphism.

CODE SHARING AND REUSE

Object-oriented programming became as popular as it did in large measure due to its promise of allowing developers to share code among entirely different projects. As we have already mentioned, the redevelopment of code and algorithms occurs all the time, resulting in an incredible waste of time, effort, and money. While code sharing and reuse is considered to be a primary benefit of a well-implemented object-oriented design, the percentage of code actually being shared is still small. Until recently, even applications in suites such as Microsoft Office each had different code to implement standard shared features such as toolbars, status bars, and spelling checkers. In Windows 98 and Micro-soft Windows NT, many of these standard graphical user interface (GUI) controls have been built into the operating system, allowing all applications to share them. If you think about it, an operating system is a great (if not tremendously flexible) example of code reuse.

Code reuse seems to be one of those things that everyone sort of assumed would happen spontaneously. This turned out to be a lot of wishful thinking, as code reuse needs to be planned for and its implications carefully thought through. If you write some code and then give it to friends so that they can use it, is that code reuse? What about linking code libraries into applications? While these are examples of code reuse, each has its problems. If you give your code to your friends and they don't like some aspects of it, they might go into your source code and make modifications. This tinkering isn't in keeping with the idea of code reuse. Modifying someone else's source code is like breaking a figurine in a china store—the hapless browser becomes the proud new owner.

If something doesn't work after someone changes the code you passed on, you are not obliged to support the code anymore. In addition, when you later update your own code and then make available the new version, your friends will have to go through it and integrate their changes anew. The code is then manifestly not reusable. If you purchase a class library and you don't like the way it works, that's too bad unless you also bought the source code so that you can alter it, and that brings you back to the previous problem. To better understand code reuse, a more solid definition is needed: true code reusability is the ability to use code written in a general enough manner for reuse in your software to build something larger, while still being able to customize the way the code works and what it does.

Another problem with most types of code reuse is that they normally require both the original developers of the software and the person who wants to reuse the code to be working in the same programming language. If a class library is written in C++, for example, it is basically impossible to reuse that code in an application written in any language other than C++. By the same token, a

Java class can be used only in a Java program. So although you often get more code reuse using an object-oriented programming language than not, there are still limitations.

How, then, can we apply what everyone agrees to be the great idea of code sharing and reuse to practical, real-life programming? While object-oriented programming has long been advanced as a solution to the problems at hand, it has yet to reach its full potential. No standard framework exists in object-oriented programming through which software objects created by different vendors can interact with one another in the same address space, much less across address spaces or network and machine boundaries. According to the COM specification, the major result of the object-oriented programming school has been the production of islands of objects that can't talk to one another in a meaningful way across the sea of application boundaries.

COMPONENTWARE ENTERS THE SCENE

As developers, we tend to have a natural bias against high-level tools that confine us to the features that the designers of those tools provide. The worst of these tools envelop you in a kind of black box that hides the errors that are likely to occur in low-level programming languages such as C. The best of these tools allow you to create simple applications or impressive prototypes easily, as long as you stay within a restrictive set of features. However, the moment you need to do something that in C would be relatively straightforward, using the high-level tool often becomes a nightmarish experience of finding workarounds to subvert the tool's sophistication.

For many developers accustomed to lower-level programming languages such as C, the conversion to programming in Microsoft Visual Basic has been slow and hampered by skepticism. Visual Basic is obviously a well-thought-out development tool and is great for prototyping, but at first these features served only to confirm the bias against it as a real application development tool. Over time, however, developers have discovered some of the more advanced features provided by Visual Basic, such as the ability to make calls easily to the Windows API by using Visual Basic's *Declare* statement. This feature initially came with a limitation: Visual Basic didn't allow calls to Windows API functions that use callback addresses directly because it didn't provide function pointers. However, developers soon realized that by writing a dynamic-link library (DLL) in C or C++ that uses callbacks they could circumvent this limitation since Visual Basic lets you call a DLL written in any language using identical *Declare* syntax. If you're a Win32 API aficionado, you might be interested to know that Visual Basic no longer limits you when making Windows API calls that require callback addresses.

Soon it became apparent that any limitation encountered in the Visual Basic world had already been anticipated by the designers of Visual Basic and that a straightforward workaround had been devised. In addition, developers discovered that by writing a DLL in C they could overcome potential performance problems of Visual Basic. Since GUI programs spend most of their time waiting inside the Microsoft Windows operating system for user action, Visual Basic performance is often not a problem. However, when an application needs to do processor-intensive work, developers can write modules in C and then call them from Visual Basic. One would not want to calculate a fractal from within a Visual Basic program, for example.

Visual Basic Extensions

Developers discovered something far more exciting than the ability to call DLLs from Visual Basic: Visual Basic extension controls (VBXs). Microsoft initially thought that only Microsoft developers would be writing VBXs and that these controls would perhaps be sold as an add-on pack separate from Visual Basic. Microsoft nevertheless released the Control Developers Kit, which provided some bare-bones sample code demonstrating how to create your own VBXs in C. No one was more surprised than Microsoft when, over the several years following the initial release of Visual Basic, the VBX interface sprouted a cottage industry of small companies producing add-on VBXs for Visual Basic. Suddenly, for the first time, a claim could be made that code reuse actually existed. No one could deny that VBXs were general-purpose software components that could be written by one person and used in a Visual Basic project by another person. This was the birth of componentware.

From OLE to ActiveX

Meanwhile, back in its Redmond, Washington, headquarters, Microsoft was regretting that it had not initially invested more thought in the VBX interface, because it was being used for all sorts of purposes they had never envisioned. In addition, Visual Basic 4 was going to be available in a 32-bit version, and VBX controls had been designed for a 16-bit environment. Microsoft decided to revamp the VBX interface and base it on object linking and embedding (OLE). Since VBXs were software components, it was only logical to base VBXs on Microsoft's component technology. These new and improved OLE controls supported both 16-bit and 32-bit environments, had a well-thought-out programming interface, and could be written in Microsoft Visual C++ utilizing the Microsoft Foundation Class library.

The OLE controls specification had another major advantage over VBXs: writing an OLE control container became a legitimate and documented strategy.

An *OLE control container* is any application that is capable of hosting or containing OLE controls. Originally, the only environment supporting VBXs was Visual Basic. Microsoft realized that other development tools and applications besides Visual Basic would benefit from being able to use all the diverse controls being developed by independent software vendors. As part of the OLE controls specification, Microsoft therefore documented the interfaces an application would need to support in order to host OLE controls. Developers using tools such as Delphi, PowerBuilder, Microsoft Access, and Microsoft Visual C++ could now take advantage of the wide variety of OLE controls available. The ability to call OLE controls from various applications encouraged more companies to invest in creating OLE controls, since there was suddenly a much broader market of developers who could use such controls. Many sizable software companies existed solely on the revenue of their OLE controls. Developing OLE controls had moved to the big time.

With the advent of the Internet, Microsoft renamed OLE controls to ActiveX controls, signifying a new concentration on creating interactive Web content. In addition to the renaming job, Microsoft also refined the control specification, giving thought to how these controls would work over the Internet. Because of this, the major design goals of ActiveX controls were that they be smaller, faster, and have less overhead than OLE controls. This revised interface is called the ActiveX Controls '96 specification. The enhancements defined by the ActiveX Controls '96 specification include optimizations that allow objects and controls to stay inactive most of the time, that provide optimizations and enhancements for drawing graphics, and that support windowless, nonrectangular, and transparent controls.

Building Components

COM is an extension of the object-oriented paradigm. The COM specification proposes a system in which application developers create reusable software components. The breakdown of a project into its logical components is the essence of object-oriented analysis and design. That's also the basis for *componentware*, which is software composed of building blocks. A component is a reusable piece of software in binary form (as opposed to source code) that can be plugged into other components from other vendors with relatively little effort. These reusable software components present their functionality through a defined set of interfaces—a crucial concept in COM. With COM, operating systems as well as software components built by us ordinary folk can make an interface available (sometimes called publishing, or exposing, an interface). In this context, an interface is simply a defined set of methods (member functions) that are grouped together under one name. For now, this will be our working definition of an interface.

Components created using COM can fall into a variety of categories, including visual components such as buttons or list boxes and functional components such as ones that add printing capability or a spelling checker. For example, a spelling checker component from one vendor can be plugged into several word processing programs from other vendors. This capability can hold many advantages for the end user. You might love the word processor produced by company A but hate the spelling checker it comes with. So you can go off and buy the spelling checker you like from company B, which specializes in spelling checkers, and specify that your word processor use the component spelling checker. This enables each software developer to specialize in what he or she does best.

A good analogy can be found in the automobile industry. Many car manufacturers buy individual car parts, such as engines and transmissions, from various manufacturers and assemble cars from all these components. The key point about componentware is that the pieces can be used as they are—they don't need to be recompiled, developers don't need the source code, and the components aren't restricted to using one programming language. The term for this process is *binary reuse* because it is based on binary interfaces rather than on reuse at the source code level. While the software components must adhere to the agreed-upon interface, their internal implementation is completely at the discretion of component developers. For this reason, the components can be built using procedural languages as well as object-oriented languages, although the latter provide many advantages in the component software world.

Interoperability

The main goal of COM is to promote *interoperability*. Interoperability is one of those buzzwords in the computer field that means different things to different people. COM supports interoperability by defining mechanisms that allow applications to connect. The designers of COM tried their best to give a fresh look to the process of software development. When they recognized areas in which software seemed to be forced together unnaturally, the designers tried to break up the software into components.

Let's use the example of controls. In the good old days of Windows-based programming, if you needed a new widget for your application, you wrote it. If your program needed a toolbar, you would simply write the toolbar code directly into the main part of the application. This example has two inherent problems: First, your goal isn't to create a cool toolbar but a great application that has a toolbar. Second, now that you have consumed many precious hours developing a toolbar, perhaps somebody else in your company would like to use that toolbar in his or her project. How is that possible if the toolbar code is sprinkled throughout your program, responding to *Load*, *Paint*, and *MouseDown* events?

COM's designers would take this case, in which you can easily spot software being grouped together unnaturally, and say that we should turn the toolbar into a component. The problem is how the toolbar component and the application should interact. This is the whole issue of interoperability and that's where COM comes in. COM can define the interface between the component and the application using the component. As long as both sides follow the interface, interoperability results. In the toolbar example, the application developers can concentrate on the software and simply purchase the toolbar component from some other developer who specializes in making great toolbars, thus saving development, debugging, and maintenance time. (Of course, this solution will deprive developers of the opportunity to create a toolbar on company time, but that is a different issue altogether.)

While this type of architecture has many obvious advantages, developers are often concerned (and rightly so) with the overhead involved in separating software into components. There is no doubt that architecture built on components imposes overhead. COM attempts to minimize this overhead by staying out of the components' way as much as possible. For example, COM is heavily involved in helping components to connect, but once the connection is established COM drops out of the picture. COM serves to connect a client and an object, but once that connection is established the client and object can communicate directly without suffering added overhead. COM isn't a prescribed way to structure an application. Rather, it is a specification that makes the programming, use, and independent evolution of binary objects possible.

Object-oriented programming concepts used in conjunction with COM allow developers to build flexible and powerful objects that can easily be reused by other developers. One important principle of object-oriented programming, discussed earlier, is encapsulation. Remember that encapsulation specifies that the implementation of an object is of concern only to the object itself and is hidden from the clients of the object. The clients of an object have access only to the object's interface. Developers who use prebuilt objects in their projects are interested only in the promised behavior that the object supports. COM formalizes this notion of a contract between an object and a client. By implementing certain interfaces, each object declares what it is capable of. Such a contract is the basis for interoperability.

THE THREE FACES OF COM

What is COM then? When we sat down to answer this question, we came up with the following answers:

- COM is a specification.
- COM is a philosophy of modern software development.
- COM is a binary standard for building software components.

COM as a Specification

First, COM is a specification. By this, we mean that COM is a document that can be printed and read. Our copy of the COM specification is stained with blood, sweat, and tears. The complete COM specification can be downloaded from the Microsoft Web site (*http://www.microsoft.com/com/*) and is included on this book's companion CD. (For the sake of completeness, we should mention that this COM specification includes some system code implemented by Microsoft.)

COM as a Philosophy

Second, COM is a way of thinking about modern software development. The COM specification describes a world in which applications are built from components. In contrast, most software projects are still designed around the idea of producing a monolithic behemoth that encompasses all the features a user might ever want. The trouble with this model of software development is that applications become more fragile as they grow. It is difficult to have a complete understanding of an application containing 100,000 lines of code, and all but impossible with 1,000,000 lines. Even a small modification in an application of that size requires extensive retesting of the entire system. Often what appears to be an innocuous modification in one section of code does damage in many other locations.

But the days of the monolithic application are over. The dinosaurs are extinct, and in the brave new COM world developers create compact, well-defined components that work together. These components can then be reused in many environments. For example, a particular business component can be used in a desktop application, as well as by a Web application running in Microsoft Internet Information Server or by a back-end server running Microsoft Transaction Server.

Building a system based on interoperable components doesn't mean that the user can't have an icon on the desktop to launch the application. As an example, let's examine the architecture of Microsoft Internet Explorer. The shell is a simple Active Document host, and the actual parsing and rendering of HTML is done by an Active Document component that loads whenever the user navigates to a Web site. If that Web site contains an ActiveX control component, the control is downloaded and installed. This COM-based architecture keeps every part of the shell focused on a specific job. Different teams using different programming languages can develop components and, so long as everyone plays by COM rules, they will work together seamlessly.

COM as a Binary Standard

Third, COM is the name of the specification for Microsoft's basic object technology; it defines what it means to be a COM object and how a COM object is called. The role of COM is that of the connecting "glue" between components, enabling unrelated software objects to connect and interact in meaningful ways. To put it succinctly, COM is a binary standard for integration between components.

To further explain the reason for COM's existence, let's review some of the challenges faced by the software industry that led Microsoft to develop COM. As everyone knows, the continuous evolution of computer hardware and software has brought an ever-increasing number of sophisticated applications to users' desktops and networks. As discussed in the COM specification, with such complex software have come a commensurate number of problems for both developers and users:

- Modern software applications are large and complex—they are time-consuming to develop, difficult and costly to maintain, and risky to extend with additional functionality.

- Applications continue to be developed in a monolithic style—they come prepackaged with a range of static features. No features can be added, removed, upgraded independently, or replaced with alternatives.

- Applications do not lend themselves to integration—both the data and the functionality of one program are not readily available to another program.

- Programming models are like religions that reflect the provider's upbringing—they vary widely depending on whether the service is coming from a provider in the same address space, in another address space on the same machine, in another machine running across the network, or in the operating system.

Will COM fix all this? As the nature of the difficulties described here suggests, no one piece of software can single-handedly solve all these problems. However, software built on COM architecture can better meet these challenges.

COM INTERFACES

As stated in the COM specification, COM defines standards for creating components and for controlling the communication between these components and their clients. Unlike traditional programming environments, these standards are independent of both the applications that use the components and the programming languages used to create the objects themselves. COM therefore defines a binary interoperability standard rather than a language-based standard. With COM, applications interact with each other and with the system through collections of function calls known as interfaces. In COM, an interface is a strongly typed contract between a software component and a client. The interface provides a relatively small but useful set of semantically related operations; it is an articulation of an expected behavior and expected responsibilities, and it gives programmers and designers a concrete entity to use when referring to the component. Although not a strict requirement of the model, it's a good idea for interfaces to be factored in such a fashion that they can be reused in a variety of contexts.

Multiple Interfaces

The use of COM interfaces is instrumental in creating adaptable component software. COM provides applications with the ability to evolve over time. One of the major problems with previous attempts at component-based software was *versioning*. Versioning of software components can be problematic when a component relies on some external code that is modified. This was a common problem with DLLs in Windows-based applications, because a program that depended on a particular DLL could fail if it encountered a newer or older version of the DLL than it was expecting. Similar problems face component software. As the developers of a component continue to make changes to it and modify its interface, the applications dependent on that component are affected.

COM addresses this issue by dictating that COM-based components are never permitted to change their interface. For this reason, developers must be careful when designing a component's interface. After a component product is released, the interface can't be changed; at that stage the only choice is to publish a new interface. Client applications aware of this new interface can take advantage of it, while older applications will work with the updated software through the old interface.

The ability for a single object to support multiple interfaces simultaneously is an important feature of COM. This feature enables successive versions of an object to introduce new interfaces that support added functionality, while at the same time retaining complete binary compatibility with applications that depend on the object. In other words, revising an object by adding new or even unrelated functionality won't require recompilation on the part of any existing client. Because COM allows objects to have multiple interfaces, an object can express a number of interface versions simultaneously.

The rule that COM interfaces are never changed might raise some questions. For example, we have said that updating an existing interface requires a new interface to be created. Suppose the time has come to update your great ICool interface. What is to be done? For starters, you can create a new interface named ICoolEx that contains the desired modifications. But what happens when it comes time to update ICoolEx? Would you name the new interface ICoolExEx? To avoid confusion, it is better to use numbers in interface names to indicate versions. In our example, the ICool3 version would follow ICool2.

When you design ICool2, do you now have to implement the code for ICool twice, once for the old ICool and once for the new ICool2? Not necessarily, because COM allows objects to have a single internal implementation of the common capabilities exposed through two or more similar interfaces. Immutable interfaces combined with the support of multiple interfaces effectively solve the problem of versioning components.

Calling COM Objects

With all this talk of calling interfaces, you might be wondering exactly how to call a COM-based component. Well, every COM object must support at least one interface: *IUnknown*. This is the most fundamental interface. When a client initially gains access to an object, the client will receive at minimum an *IUnknown* interface pointer through which it can control the lifetime of the object and invoke *QueryInterface*. *QueryInterface* is the basic function in COM through which one piece of software determines what interfaces are supported by a component. This high-level handshaking enables the client to determine whether a component supports a particular capability. If a word processor encounters a component it wants to use as a spelling checker, it might ask the component via *QueryInterface* whether it supports a predefined spelling checker interface. If the answer is yes, *QueryInterface* will return a pointer to the interface through which the word processor can call any of the functions contained within that interface.

COM interfaces enable fast and simple interaction among in-process objects. Once a client establishes a connection to an object via *IUnknown* and *QueryInterface*, calls to that object's interface functions are simply indirect function calls through pointers. As a result, the overhead of interacting with an in-process COM object is negligible.

Interfaces do not define any implementations, meaning that interfaces do not contain code. An object can be said to implement an interface only when the object implements each and every member function. The interfaces implemented by a COM object are exposed to outside clients through the *QueryInterface* method of the *IUnknown* interface. Every interface has a unique identification number known as a Globally Unique Identifier (GUID) that eliminates any chance of an identification collision between interfaces. (A GUID looks like this: {13198125-998D-11CE-D41203C10000}.) Component developers assign a GUID to each interface and must consciously support that interface—confusion and conflict among interfaces do not happen by accident.

TYPES OF COMPONENTS

Components come in one of three flavors in the COM world—in-process, local, or remote—depending on the structure of the code module and the code module's relationship to the client process.

In-Process Components

In-process components are loaded into the client's process space because they are housed in DLLs. As you might know, DLLs are code libraries that are loaded at run time (dynamically) by the operating system on behalf of programs that want to call functions in the DLLs. DLLs are always loaded into the address space of the calling process. This is important because Windows 98 and Windows NT load each program (process) into its own private 32-bit address space for security and stability reasons. Since it isn't normally possible to access memory locations beyond this private address space, DLLs need to be loaded in-process. The Windows operating system is itself implemented in numerous DLLs, the most famous being User (the user interface), Kernel, and GDI (Graphics Device Interface).

The main advantage of in-process components is their speed. Since the objects are loaded in-process, no context switching is necessary to access their services, as is the case with .EXE files. The single potential disadvantage to an in-process component is that, since an in-process component is in fact a DLL and not a complete executable application (EXE), an in-process component can be used only in the context of a calling program and can't be run as a stand-alone application. ActiveX controls are implemented as in-process components.

Local Components

A local server runs in a separate process on the same machine as the client. This type of server is an executable application of its own, thus qualifying as a separate process. Local servers are significantly slower for clients to access than are in-process components because the operating system must switch between processes and copy any data that needs to be transferred between the client and the server applications. Local components have one advantage over other types of components: since they are executable files, users can run local components as stand-alone applications without an external client. An application such as Microsoft Internet Explorer is an example of a local component. You can run Internet Explorer to surf the net, or you can call Internet Explorer's objects from another application, such as Visual Basic.

Remote Components and DCOM

A remote component runs on a separate machine connected to the client via a network. A remote component therefore always runs in another process. This functionality can be implemented using Distributed COM (DCOM). The beauty of DCOM is that it doesn't require any special programming to enable remote functionality. Without the network support for communication that DCOM provides, programmers face several daunting tasks. They must write a large number of procedures, each of which has been specialized for communicating with a different type of component; and they must perhaps recompile their code depending on the other components or network services with which their code needs to interact.

Visual Basic developers might have heard of Remote Automation, a precursor of DCOM that was included with Visual Basic 4, Enterprise Edition. Remote Automation allows components to be called across the network in a manner similar to DCOM. Visual Basic supports both Remote Automation and DCOM, but Remote Automation is no longer recommended unless you have 16-bit clients. DCOM is supported only on 32-bit platforms.

As mentioned previously, DCOM supports distributed objects—that is, it allows application developers to split a single application into a number of different component objects, each of which can run on a different computer. DCOM works by using a proxy to intercept an interface call to an object and then issuing a remote procedure call to the real instance of the object that is running in another process on another machine. A key point is that the client makes this call exactly as it would for an in-process object and that DCOM performs the interprocess and cross-network function calls transparently. While there is, of course, a great deal more overhead in issuing a remote procedure call, no special code is required. Since DCOM provides network transparency, these applications do not appear to be located on different machines. In a properly implemented system, the entire network can appear to be one large computer with enormous processing power and capability.

A major goal of COM is to insulate the developer who is using a component from the differences between in-process, local, and remote components. It is apparent that different mechanisms are used to call code in a remote component on another computer than are used to load an in-process DLL. However, COM hides those differences from users of an object so that all these types of components appear identical. Obviously, depending on the type of component employed, there will be differences in operating speed.

THE COM LIBRARY

It should be clear by now that COM isn't just a paper specification. COM also involves some system-level code—that is, some implementation of its own. The COM implementation is contained in the COM library. This implementation is provided through a DLL that includes the following elements as described in the COM specification:

- A small number of fundamental API functions that facilitate the creation of both client and server COM applications. For clients, COM supplies basic object instantiation functions; for servers, COM supplies the facilities to expose their objects.

- Implementation locator services that enable COM to determine from a class identifier which server implements that class and where the server is located.

- Transparent remote procedure calls when an object is running in a local or remote server.

- A standard mechanism to allow an application to control how memory is allocated within its process.

COM AS A FOUNDATION

COM is an underlying architecture built on the concept of binary standard interfaces that enable various software components to interact intelligently. The basic elements of COM we have been discussing up to now form the foundation on which the rest of the COM and ActiveX technologies are built. However, COM provides more than just the fundamental object creation and management facilities described previously. It also builds an infrastructure of three other core operating system components: *persistent storage, monikers,* and *uniform data transfer,* as described in the COM specification.

Persistent Storage

Persistent storage is a set of interfaces and an implementation of these interfaces that together create structured storage, otherwise known as a *file system within a file*. Information in a file is in a hierarchical structure of *storages* (similar to directories) and *streams* (similar to files). This structure enables sharing storage between processes, incremental access to information, transaction support, and the ability for any code in the system to browse the elements of information in the file. COM defines standard persistent storage object interfaces that support the ability to save their state to permanent (persistent) storage devices, so that the state of the objects can be restored at a later time.

Monikers

Monikers enable a specific instantiation of an object to have a unique name so that at a later time a client can reconnect to that same object instance with the same state (not just another object of the same class). Monikers also enable developers to assign a name to a specific operation, such as a query, that can be executed repeatedly using only that name to refer to the operation. This level of indirection allows developers to make changes to an operation without requiring any changes to the client code that uses the name of the operation. Since all monikers are polymorphic, any client that uses the *IMoniker* interface can use any moniker implementation.

Uniform Data Transfer

Uniform data transfer refers to standard interfaces through which data is exchanged between a client and an object and through which a client can ask an object to send notifications (call event functions in the client) in case of a data change. The uniform data transfer standards include powerful structures used to describe data formats as well as the storage mediums on which the data is exchanged.

ACTIVEX ON TOP OF COM

Microsoft's ActiveX technology supersedes what used to be known as OLE, as we discussed previously. ActiveX is a collection of additional higher-level technologies that build on COM and its infrastructure. All the features of ActiveX are implemented by means of specific object interfaces and defined sequences of operation in both clients and servers. Their relationships and dependencies on the lower-level infrastructure of COM are shown in Figure 1-1 on the following page.

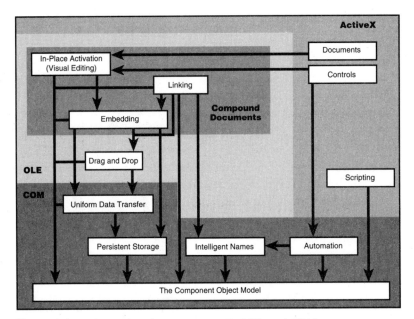

Figure 1-1. *Relationships between ActiveX, OLE, and COM.*

ActiveX has three important areas of functionality: Automation, Active Documents, and ActiveX objects. *Automation* (formerly called *OLE Automation*) is the ability to create programmable applications that can be driven from an external script running in another application, in order to automate common end user tasks. Automation enables cross-application macro programming.

Active Documents provide the ability to embed information in a central document, encouraging a more document-centric user interface. OLE introduced in-place activation (or visual editing), a user interface improvement to embedding whereby the end user can work on information from different applications in the context of the compound document, without having to switch between applications. Active Documents allow an application to open a document window from within another application. Internet Explorer, for example, supports applications that contain the Active Document interfaces necessary to open documents within Internet Explorer windows.

The ActiveX controls specification defines the interfaces that must be implemented by a component to qualify as an ActiveX control that can be used in Visual Basic and other environments such as Internet Explorer. The ActiveX controls specification also defines the interfaces necessary to create a control container such as Visual Basic.

Chapter 2

The Component Object Model

Creating components requires an in-depth understanding of the two most primitive Component Object Model (COM) interfaces: 00000000-0000-0000-C000-000000000046, otherwise known as *IUnknown*; and 00000001-0000-0000-C000-000000000046, otherwise known as *IClassFactory*. Although Microsoft Visual Basic hides most of the details of COM programming, a thorough understanding of the internal workings of COM is essential to building efficient component software. In addition, since Visual Basic is often used to connect components built in other languages such as C++, Java, and Delphi, understanding how Visual Basic works with COM will help you to integrate components built in other languages. In this chapter, we blaze a trail from these fundamentals to a full-fledged component. Along the way, we'll encounter the Interface Definition Language (IDL), the starting point for programming COM.

Let's begin by defining a custom interface, ISum, that an in-process component might implement. As we established in Chapter 1, an interface is defined as a semantically related set of methods. Interfaces defined by Microsoft, such as *IUnknown* and *IClassFactory*, are called *standard interfaces*; interfaces that developers define are known as *custom interfaces*. On the following page is the Visual Basic definition of the ISum interface.

```
VERSION 1.0 CLASS
BEGIN
    MultiUse = -1  ' True
    Persistable = 0  ' NotPersistable
    DataBindingBehavior = 0  ' vbNone
    DataSourceBehavior  = 0  ' vbNone
    MTSTransactionMode  = 0  ' NotAnMTSObject
END
Attribute VB_Name = "ISum"
Attribute VB_GlobalNameSpace = False
Attribute VB_Creatable = True
Attribute VB_PredeclaredId = False
Attribute VB_Exposed = True
Public Function Sum(x As Long, y As Long) As Long

End Function
```

As you can see, the ISum class has only one public method, Sum. Notice that the Sum method doesn't provide implementation code because we are defining only an interface. Visual Basic inserts the address of each method into a special binary structure called a *virtual function table* (v-table, sometimes abbreviated as vtbl). This structure forms the basis of COM interfaces and was adopted because most C++ compilers produce this memory layout for objects. For language such as Visual Basic to integrate with COM, the language must use the same memory layout as does COM. At run time, every COM interface actually exists in memory as a v-table, as demonstrated by the following equation:

COM interface = virtual function table

Implicit to every COM object built in Visual Basic is the *IUnknown* interface. Because all COM objects must implement the *IUnknown* interface, any object that implements the ISum interface will have to implement *IUnknown* as well.

From this examination of ISum, you can see that a COM interface is simply a contract that requires all implementations of an interface to adhere to the defined specifications. A COM interface doesn't contain code. A *COM class* is a named implementation of one or more interfaces. In Visual Basic, a COM class is implemented as a class module, although the two are not synonymous. In C++, for example, a COM class is usually implemented as a C++ class. One or more COM classes are contained in a *component*. A component is a sort of housing for COM classes and can be built as either a .DLL file or an executable (.EXE) file.

THE INTERFACE DEFINITION LANGUAGE

One of the most important aspects of COM is its language independence. A COM component can be written in any language and then seamlessly called from any other language. In the previous section, we defined the ISum interface using Visual Basic code. In Java, the definition of the same ISum interface would look like this:

```
public interface ISum extends com.ms.com.IUnknown
{
    public abstract int Sum(int x, int y);
}
```

And in C++, ISum would look like this:

```
class ISum : public IUnknown
{
public:
    virtual HRESULT __stdcall Sum(int x, int y, int* retval)=0;
};
```

These three language-based definitions of the ISum interface expose the fallacy of our assertions. How can we claim to have a language-independent architecture and then define a single interface differently in every programming language? This would lead to chaos, since a single interface could have multiple correct definitions. The answer to this problem lies in IDL.

The Open Software Foundation originally developed IDL for their Distributed Computing Environment's Remote Procedure Call (RPC) package. IDL helps RPC programmers to ensure that both the client and the component sides of a project adhere to the same interface. IDL is not a programming language; it is a language used only to define interfaces. For this reason, Microsoft decided to adopt IDL for use in defining COM interfaces. Standardizing in one special language for defining interfaces does away with the confusion generated by having multiple languages each define the same interface differently. The implementation of an interface defined in IDL can still be coded in any language you want.

> **NOTE**   IDL plays an important role in the development of COM objects, but it isn't part of COM. IDL is simply a tool used to help programmers define interfaces.

The .IDL File

The .IDL file for the ISum interface as defined in IDL is shown in listing 2-1 on the following page.

COMPONENT.IDL

```
import "unknwn.idl";

[ object, uuid(10000001-0000-0000-0000-000000000001) ]
interface ISum : IUnknown
{
    HRESULT Sum([in] int x, [in] int y, [out, retval] int* retval);
};
```

Listing 2-1.   *The IDL file for the* ISum *interface.*

The .IDL file quickly betrays its C-language roots. A cursory examination reveals a construct rather like a header file that provides forward declarations for functions. Several additional aspects of this interface definition immediately attract attention.

First, the definition begins with the *object* attribute, a Microsoft extension to IDL that is used to identify a COM interface. Any interface definition not beginning with the *object* attribute describes an RPC interface rather than a COM interface.

Second, following the *object* attribute is the *universally unique identifier (UUID)* assigned to this interface that distinguishes it from all other interfaces. A UUID is a 128-bit hexadecimal number that is guaranteed to be unique across space and time. Two different developers might define an interface named ISum, but so long as both interfaces have different UUIDs no confusion between the two interfaces will result.

Third, the ISum interface as defined in the IDL file derives from *IUnknown*, the root of all COM objects. The interface definition of *IUnknown* is in turn imported from the UNKNWN.IDL file, where it is defined as follows:

```
[
    local,
    object,
    uuid(00000000-0000-0000-C000-000000000046),
    pointer_default(unique)
]

interface IUnknown
{
    typedef [unique] IUnknown *LPUNKNOWN;

    HRESULT QueryInterface(
        [in] REFIID riid,
        [out, iid_is(riid)] void** ppvObject);
    ULONG AddRef();
    ULONG Release();
}
```

Directional Attributes

Let's look again at the ISum interface definition. Notice that each argument of the *Sum* method is preceded by the *[in]* or *[out]* directional attribute. Since the interface defines the communication between a client and a component that might end up running on separate machines, the interface definition specifies the direction in which each parameter needs to travel.

In this interface definition, the first two parameters of the *Sum* function are passed only to the component; they are not passed back to the client because their value won't have changed. (The *[in]* attribute isn't required because it is the default when you don't specify a directional parameter attribute.) The third parameter is flagged with the *[out, retval]* attributes, indicating that the parameter is a return value and thus needs to pass back to the client from the component. Visual Basic insulates the developer from the returned HRESULT value and transparently makes the *[out, retval]* parameter appear to be the value the function returns.

GLOBALLY UNIQUE IDENTIFIERS

A UUID is equivalent to a *globally unique identifier (GUID),* the term more commonly used in COM. Normally, developers create GUIDs by using the GUIDGEN.EXE utility. (GUIDGEN.EXE is available with Microsoft Visual C++ and the Microsoft Platform Software Development Kit.) Alternatively, an application can generate a GUID at run time by calling the *CoCreateGuid* API function. Visual Basic uses this method internally to dynamically generate the GUIDs applied to components.

You might wonder why a simple 32-bit value couldn't have been used to identify interfaces. After all, a 32-bit value gives us 2^{32} (4,294,967,296) possible unique identifiers. The issue isn't so much the total number of possible interfaces as how that space is divided to guarantee uniqueness. Witness the problems encountered with Internet Protocol (IP) addresses that use 32-bit identifiers. There are currently fewer than 4 billion computers connected to the Internet, but a lot of the IP addresses are wasted because of the allocation method that IP uses.

The 128-bit interface identifier used by COM gives us the theoretical possibility of creating approximately 340,282,366,920,900,000,000,-000,000,000,000,000 unique interfaces. That's enough to create one trillion new interfaces every second for the next 10,782,897,524,560,000,000 years. The algorithm used to generate GUIDs limits the total number to significantly fewer unique interfaces, but it still provides plenty for the foreseeable future.

The Microsoft IDL Compiler

Once an interface has been defined in IDL, you can use the Microsoft IDL compiler (MIDL.EXE) to translate the interface into several C-language source files. But using the Microsoft IDL compiler to generate C or C++ code brings us back to a language-dependent interface definition, the point where we began. If the Microsoft IDL compiler could generate Visual Basic and Java code in addition to C and C++ code, language-specific interface definitions generated from IDL code would be acceptable. However, you would be wrong to assume that the Microsoft IDL compiler contains a magic command-line parameter that generates code other than C or C++ code.

To avoid having to update the Microsoft IDL compiler's code generation engine for every new language that comes along, Microsoft decided that a more extensible mechanism was needed. The solution is for the Microsoft IDL compiler to generate interface definitions in a single, universal format that all languages, including Visual Basic, Java, and C++ (arguably a broad range of languages with quite different goals), can understand.

Recall that COM is a binary standard for component implementation and integration, and therefore the language used to build or call COM objects is irrelevant. In view of this, why is anything special required to make COM-based components accessible to developers using different languages? The answer is that to make a component accessible to developers working in other languages, a *type library* must be built.

Eureka! Type Libraries

In most cases, Visual Basic programmers do not deal directly with IDL. Instead, Visual Basic automatically produces interface definitions for components in the form of type libraries. A type library is best understood if thought of as a binary version of an .IDL file. It contains a binary description of the interfaces exposed by a component, defining the methods along with their parameters and return types. Many environments support type libraries. Visual Basic, Microsoft Visual J++, Visual C++, Delphi, Microsoft Visual FoxPro, and Microsoft Transaction Server all understand type libraries.

Microsoft has defined the COM interfaces needed to build (*ICreateTypeLib* and *ICreateTypeInfo)* type libraries and to read (*ITypeLib* and *ITypeInfo)* type libraries. Few programs other than the Microsoft IDL compiler have any need for the interfaces used to build type libraries, but Visual Basic, Visual C++, and Visual J++ are all capable of reading type libraries. What is the advantage of describing interfaces in a type library? A type library provides complete information about interfaces so that sophisticated modern programming tools can read this information and present it to programmers in an accessible format. This makes COM programming a breeze.

Visual Basic's Auto List Members feature, shown in the Code window in Figure 2-1, retrieves all the information it needs to list statement options from the type libraries of available components. Microsoft Visual C++ 6 and Microsoft Visual J++ 6 offer a similar feature.

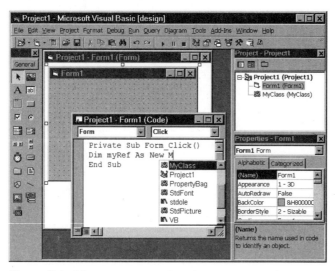

Figure 2-1. *The Auto List Members feature in Visual Basic.*

Visual Basic automatically generates a type library for a component built in Visual Basic and then stores it in the component's .EXE or .DLL file. As a result, Visual Basic programmers typically do not need to use either IDL to define custom COM interfaces or the Microsoft IDL compiler to generate type libraries. Nevertheless, it's useful to understand that Visual Basic generates interface definitions in the form of a type library for every public class module. Type libraries are especially helpful when you want to integrate a component built in Visual Basic with a component developed in another language.

Instantiating Objects

In Visual Basic, COM objects are instantiated either by calling the standard *CreateObject* function or by means of the *New* operator. Either of these methods results in a call to the COM function *CoCreateInstance*. In this section, we will discuss how *CoCreateInstance* works; this will help you to understand better what *CreateObject* and *New* do under the covers provided by Visual Basic.

The class identifier parameter

The *CoCreateInstance* function takes several parameters, including a *class identifier (CLSID)*. A CLSID is a GUID that is associated with the COM class we want to instantiate. The *CreateObject* function obtains a CLSID by searching the HKEY_CLASSES_ROOT section of the Microsoft Windows registry for the program identifier. The program identifier contains the component's CLSID as a subkey. *CoCreateInstance* locates the component by searching for a match to the CLSID in the HKEY_CLASSES_ROOT\CLSID section of the registry. HKEY_CLASSES_ROOT\CLSID is undoubtedly the most fundamental COM-related key in the registry. *CoCreateInstance* fails if no match is found. Assuming that *CoCreateInstance* locates an entry for the CLSID, the various subkeys provide COM with information about the component.

> **DEFINITION**   Once instantiated, a COM class is called a *COM object*.

As you may know, a component can contain multiple objects. A component that supports multiple objects needs to register a unique CLSID for each supported class of objects. A client must call *CoCreateInstance* once for each object it wants to create. If some of the objects coexist in the same component, that's all right with COM. Each object is listed in the registry by its CLSID, and the CLSID entry contains information specifying the component that contains the object. Figure 2-2 shows two calls to *CoCreateInstance* for two different objects that turn out to be housed in the same component. Using an object's CLSID, *CoCreateInstance* looks in the registry for the component; in this case, both Object1 and Object2 exist in COMPONENT.DLL.

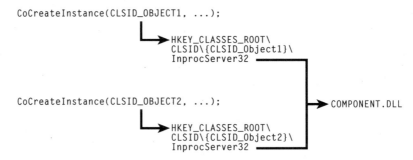

Figure 2-2. *Two COM classes that live in the same component.*

The component type parameter

Another parameter of *CoCreateInstance* enables you to specify the class context in which the component will run. As we discussed in Chapter 1, COM provides support for building three types of components: in-process, local, and remote. Sometimes a particular component may be implemented in several flavors. For example, a component might be available as an in-process version and as a local and remote version. In such cases, you can select the version that best meets your needs. If you aren't particular about the component type, you can use a generic component type parameter option that retrieves the first available in-process, local, or remote component by looking in that order.

The following table shows the HKEY_CLASSES_ROOT\CLSID\{*YourCLSID*} subkeys that identify the different component types available for a particular COM class.

Subkey	Description
InprocHandler32	Full path to a 32-bit DLL component handler.
InprocServer32	Full path to a 32-bit DLL component; specifies the threading mode.
LocalServer32	Full path to a 32-bit local .EXE component.
AppID	Information for remote components is stored in the HKEY_CLASSES_ROOT\AppID\{YourAppID} section of the registry.

The interface identifier parameter

When you instantiate a component using *CoCreateInstance*, you must also use a parameter that specifies the *interface identifier (IID)* of the interface you want. (An IID, like a UUID, is equivalent to a GUID.) *CoCreateInstance* will return a pointer to this interface. Visual Basic typically retrieves the *IUnknown* interface pointer first; using this *IUnknown* interface, later calls can locate other interfaces.

The *IUnknown* Interface

Assuming that all has gone well, *CoCreateInstance* returns to the client a pointer to the *IUnknown* interface of the requested COM object. The name *IUnknown* highlights the fact that at this stage the true capabilities of the object are unknown. At this stage, the only thing known is that we are dealing with a COM object. By using this pointer, the client can call any of the three *IUnknown* methods: *AddRef*, *Release*, and *QueryInterface*. Although Visual Basic automatically provides a standard implementation of *IUnknown* for all objects, it is worthwhile for you to understand the purpose of *IUnknown* because this is where the core concepts of COM can be found.

The *AddRef* and *Release* methods

The *AddRef* and *Release* methods of the *IUnknown* interface are designed to perform reference counting for each interface. The object uses reference counting to determine when it can free itself from memory. For every interface pointer, a client must call *AddRef* prior to calling any other methods and a client must call *Release* when it has finished using the interface pointer. Once we have a pointer to the desired interface, we no longer need the *IUnknown* pointer that was originally returned by *CoCreateInstance*.

Note that calling *Release* on an interface pointer doesn't necessarily destroy the object providing the implementation. *Release* simply decrements the reference counter for the interface. If the interface's reference count falls to zero and no other interfaces of this component are in use, the component is freed from memory.

To make things more efficient, and somewhat more confusing, convention dictates that an object must call *AddRef* when *CoCreateInstance* returns an interface pointer. For this reason, the client can skip the call to *AddRef* and proceed directly to the most interesting *IUnknown* method: *QueryInterface*.

The *QueryInterface* method

Every COM object is guaranteed to support the *IUnknown* interface, a pointer to which can be obtained by means of the COM function *CoCreateInstance*. Aside from the *IUnknown* interface, however, COM offers no guarantees that an object can return pointers to other interfaces. The purpose of the *QueryInterface* method is to determine what interfaces other than *IUnknown* an object supports. We like to call this the "discovery phase" of the relationship between the client and the COM object, since the client calls *QueryInterface* to discover the capabilities of a particular object. *QueryInterface* requires a parameter indicating the IID of the interface the client is looking for. If the object supports the desired interface, *QueryInterface* returns a pointer to that interface. Convention dictates that the object has already called *AddRef* for any interface pointer returned by *QueryInterface*.

The *IUnknown* interface pointer is the most fundamental pointer to an object that you can have—it establishes the identity of a COM object. You can always determine whether two pointers are pointing to the same COM object simply by comparing their *IUnknown* interface pointers; if they both point to the same address, they refer to the same object. This might seem obvious, but understanding the implications of interface identity in COM will help you to understand the entire architecture that has been built on a few fundamental ideas.

As a consequence of the need to preserve identity in COM, developers must adhere to several rules regarding their implementations of the *IUnknown* interface. Specifically, the five requirements for implementations of the *IUnknown::QueryInterface* method are:

■ If a client retrieves an interface pointer from a call to *QueryInterface*, subsequent *QueryInterface* calls for the same interface must return the same pointer value.

■ The set of component interfaces accessible through *QueryInterface* must be static rather than dynamic. If a call to *QueryInterface* to request a pointer to a specific interface succeeds the first time, it must succeed again; and if it fails the first time, it must fail on all subsequent attempts.

- *QueryInterface* must be reflexive. If a client holds a pointer to an interface and queries for that same interface, the call must succeed.

- *QueryInterface* must be symmetric. If a client holding a pointer to one interface queries successfully for a second interface, the client must be able to call *QueryInterface* through the second pointer for the first interface.

- *QueryInterface* must be transitive. If a client holding a pointer to one interface queries successfully for a second interface and through that pointer queries successfully for a third interface, a query for the first interface through the pointer for the third interface must also succeed.

Figure 2-3 shows the effects of the reflexive, symmetric, and transitive rules of *QueryInterface*.

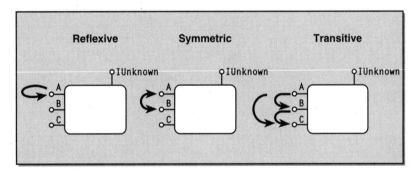

Figure 2-3. *The reflexive, symmetric, and transitive rules of* QueryInterface.

The V-Table Situation

Figure 2-4, on the following page, shows the mechanism through which a client program holding an interface pointer is able to call methods in a component.

Here you can see that for every class module containing public methods, Visual Basic automatically creates a v-table structure containing pointers to all the class's methods. Note that a v-table is built for each class, not for each instance of the class. A pointer to the v-table is stored in the object's memory structure, followed by the other properties of the class. What we refer to as an interface pointer is actually a pointer to a pointer to a table of method addresses—which is a rather inconvenient way to describe the mechanism by which a client calls an object.

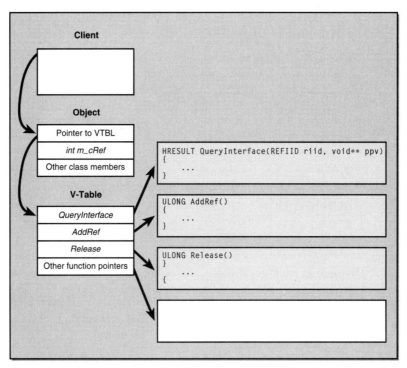

Figure 2-4. *This figure shows that an interface pointer is really a pointer to a pointer to a v-table containing method addresses.*

CoCreateInstance (Again)

Perhaps you're wondering what really happens when a client calls the COM function *CoCreateInstance*. How does *CoCreateInstance* return that first pointer to an object's *IUnknown* implementation? This is an excellent question, but unfortunately the answer is a bit complicated.

CoCreateInstance needs only to create an instance of a class that implements ISum. This technique could be as simple as allocating memory for the new object. However, here is the place to recall that one of the central tenets of COM is the concept of *location transparency*. Location transparency postulates that clients should be able to reach objects easily, regardless of whether they are contained in in-process, local, or remote components. Assuming that our object is housed in an in-process component, the *New* operator could simply and easily be used to create an instance of a class. But what if that component was running in a separate process address space or on a remote computer? The client can't directly allocate memory in a remote address space. COM's answer to this issue is the *IClassFactory* interface.

DEFINITION   A *COM class object* is an object that typically has no behavior except to create new instances of some other class. COM class objects normally implement the *IClassFactory* interface and thus are often referred to as *class factories*.

The *IClassFactory* Interface

IClassFactory is an interface implemented by class factory objects that are designed especially to manufacture other COM objects. The name *IClassFactory* is a misnomer; a much more descriptive name would be *IObjectFactory*. Be that as it may, every COM class must have an associated class factory object implementing the *IClassFactory* interface, to enable clients to instantiate the class using a function such as *CoCreateInstance*. In fact, *CoCreateInstance* calls *IClassFactory* internally.

The *IClassFactory* interface has two methods: *CreateInstance* and *LockServer*. It's the job of the *CreateInstance* method to actually instantiate a COM object.

The *CreateInstance* method

Who calls *IClassFactory::CreateInstance*? The client does, of course. When the client calls *CoCreateInstance* to instantiate an object, COM does some work that results in a call to *CreateInstance* in the component.

The *LockServer* method

The client calls the *LockServer* method to keep a component open in memory, thus allowing instances to be created more quickly. Most clients do not need to call *LockServer*; this method is provided only for those clients that require special performance in creating multiple instances of classes.

A client might call *LockServer* if it knew that it wanted to create some objects, use them, free them, and then do it all over again at a later time. Without the ability to call *LockServer*, the class factory's reference counter would go to zero and, assuming there were no other clients, the component would exit and be unloaded. When the client wanted to use the services of the component again later, the component would have to be reloaded. With *LockServer*, the client can force the component to sit tight in memory, waiting to be called. This can result in a performance improvement for clients that create and release multiple objects over a period of time.

Exported DLL Functions

We've almost completed our journey through the code required to build a COM object, but there is one last decision to make on how to package the object. A component can be packaged as an executable .EXE file or as a .DLL file.

Executable components require a *main* or *WinMain* function; DLL components require the two helper functions *DllGetClassObject* and *DllCanUnloadNow*. For now, let's explore creating an in-process (DLL) component.

The *DllGetClassObject* function

As you know, each class factory creates only one type of object and a useful component might contain multiple objects. The purpose of *DllGetClassObject* is to direct us to the correct class factory for the type of object we want to create. *DllGetClassObject* first checks to see whether the client has requested the COM class. If the client has not, the object simply returns an error. If the client requests a class object supported by the particular component, *DllGetClassFactory* instantiates a class factory.

You might be wondering why *DllGetClassObject* even bothers with the *IID* parameter of the *IClassFactory* interface. After all, if all objects are instantiated by a class factory, why not simply hard-code *IID_IClassFactory* and rename the *DllGetClassObject* function to *DllGetClassFactory*? The answer is that some objects might have special requirements not met by *IClassFactory* and instead will want to implement a custom activation interface. (A *custom activation interface* is a custom interface implemented by a class object with the purpose of allowing the instantiation of objects.) A custom activation interface is useful when a standard implementation of *IClassFactory* just won't do. For example, say that you wanted to support licensing to restrict use of your component to those machines on which it was properly installed. *IClassFactory* doesn't offer this functionality, but luckily an improved version of the interface, named *IClassFactory2*, does.

In those rare cases in which neither *IClassFactory* nor *IClassFactory2* is sufficient, a custom activation interface might be the only solution. The client will then pass the *IID* parameter of the custom activation interface to *GoGetClassObject*. Keep in mind that if either *IClassFactory* or *IClassFactory2* isn't supported by a component, clients can no longer instantiate objects using *CoCreateInstance* because *CoCreateInstance* automatically queries for the *IClassFactory* interface.

In Windows applications, DLLs are primarily controlled by three Win32 API functions: *LoadLibrary*, *GetProcAddress*, and *FreeLibrary*. Windows applications use *LoadLibrary* to load a DLL into the caller's address space. *GetProcAddress* retrieves pointers to the DLL's exported functions so that the client can call those functions in the DLL. When a client has finished with the DLL, it frees the DLL by calling *FreeLibrary*. *FreeLibrary* decrements the internal Windows usage counter and unloads the library if the counter is zero.

One of the main reasons COM exists is to move applications to an object-oriented world of components and to have applications work with components in a consistent manner. However, it isn't possible for COM to entirely shed ties to earlier paradigms because underneath the shiny COM veneer is just a plain old DLL. To be able to call the methods of a COM object housed in a DLL, we need their memory addresses. *IUnknown::QueryInterface* is designed to give us these pointers, but how do we get that first pointer to the *IUnknown* interface? We don't call *LoadLibrary* or *GetProcAddress*—which is what *CoCreateInstance* is for. This is where *DllGetClassObject* comes in. The *DllGetClassObject* function isn't a member of any class; it is a fossilized exported function that gives us that first pointer.

The *DllCanUnloadNow* function

The last function we need to complete a component is *DllCanUnloadNow*. This function is used to determine whether the DLL is in use. If the DLL isn't in use, *DLLCanUnloadNow* returns *S_OK* and the caller can safely unload the DLL from memory. Otherwise, *DLLCanUnloadNow* returns *S_FALSE* to indicate that the DLL should not be unloaded. Client applications do not have to call *DllCanUnloadNow* directly—COM calls it automatically when a program exits.

CoCreateInstance (The Truth)

With all this discussion, you might be interested to know how the *CoCreateInstance* function actually works its magic. *CoCreateInstance* actually calls another function, *CoGetClassObject*, which in turn provides an interface pointer to the requested object associated with a specified CLSID.

The *CoGetClassObject* function

Figure 2-5, on the following page, shows how the *CoGetClassObject* function works. If necessary, *CoGetClassObject* dynamically loads the executable code required to return the pointer, even if that code happens to be on a remote machine. Normally, *CoCreateInstance* asks *CoGetClassObject* to retrieve a pointer to an object's implementation of the *IClassFactory* interface. Retrieving an interface pointer to *IClassFactory* enables *CoCreateInstance* to call *IClassFactory::Create-Instance* to manufacture a COM object. Once *CoCreateInstance* has finished creating the object using the class factory, COM can release the class factory.

Figure 2-5 illustrates the functions and the order in which they are called when a client instantiates an in-process COM component.

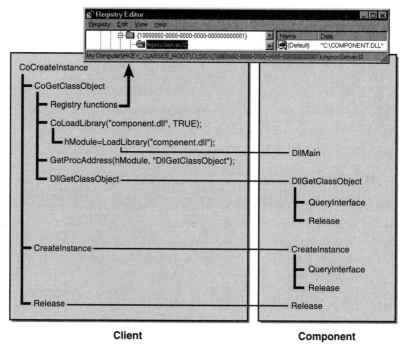

Figure 2-5. *A client calling* CoCreateInstance *to instantiate an in-process COM object.*

The Service Control Manager

In reality, *CoGetClassObject* delegates the task of locating and loading the component to the Service Control Manager implemented by the RPCSS.EXE process. After the Service Control Manager locates and loads the requested component, the COM library and the Service Control Manager drop out of the picture, allowing the client and the component to communicate directly. COM doesn't insert a mediator between in-process components and their clients that could hurt performance.

When an object is invoked on a remote machine, the Service Control Manager on the local machine contacts the Service Control Manager on the remote machine to request that it locate and load the component. (The DCOM Service Control Manager is not to be confused with the Microsoft Windows NT Service Control Manager used to manage services.)

COMPONENT SELF-REGISTRATION

Registration files are a useful and relatively easy way to automate the addition of items to the Windows registry. Most commercial software vendors, however, prefer their software packages to have as few unneeded files floating around as possible. Registration files are also not terribly flexible. For example, they don't offer a ready-made solution for when a developer wants an application's setup program to create different registry settings for different computer configurations. A better way to register a component is to create what is known as a *self-registering component,* which doesn't need the help of an external registration file to be properly registered. Like mountain climbers who register their projected climbing routes with the local park ranger, self-registering components carry with them all the code required to create the desired registry entries.

REGISTRATION USING CONTEXT MENUS

To make the self-registration of components even easier, use the following registry script. When added to your registry, this script will provide context menus that let you register and unregister components simply by right-clicking on a .DLL or an .EXE file and selecting Register Component or Unregister Component. For in-process components, this script simply launches the RegSvr32 utility.

```
REGEDIT4

[HKEY_CLASSES_ROOT\.dll]
@="dllfile"

[HKEY_CLASSES_ROOT\dllfile\shell\Register Component\command]
@="regsvr32 \"%1\""

[HKEY_CLASSES_ROOT\dllfile\shell\Unregister Component\command]
@="regsvr32 /u \"%1\""

[HKEY_CLASSES_ROOT\.exe]
@="exefile"

[HKEY_CLASSES_ROOT\exefile\shell\Register Component\command]
@="\"%1\" /regserver"

[HKEY_CLASSES_ROOT\exefile\shell\Unregister Component\command]
@="\"%1\" /unregserver"
```

The self-registration mechanism varies slightly from an in-process .DLL component to a local .EXE component. For an in-process component to be self-registering, the component needs to export two additional functions: *DllRegisterServer* and *DllUnregisterServer*. A setup program can call these functions to instruct the component to register itself. The RegSvr32 utility that comes with Windows can also call these exported functions, as shown here:

```
C:\WINDOWS\SYSTEM>regsvr32 c:\component.dll
```

When you are working in Visual Basic, any components you develop will automatically be registered on the development machine.

Self-registering local .EXE components don't export the *DllRegisterServer* and *DllUnregisterServer* functions. Instead, .EXE components examine their command-line parameters for the *-RegServer* or *-UnregServer* flag when they are executed. Local .EXE components built in Visual Basic automatically reregister themselves each time they are executed.

CONTAINMENT

Containment is a mechanism developed to enable reuse of COM-based components. Since COM is a binary standard, inheritance at a source-code level isn't possible. Instead, developers can have one object reuse another object at run time to implement some of the first object's own interfaces. For example, suppose you have designed a custom interface that inherits from another custom interface designed and implemented by someone else who works in your organization. There are two ways to implement the new interface: implement the entire interface again, including the methods belonging to the base interface; or simply delegate the new interface methods to the existing implementation. The basic idea of containment, in which one object completely contains another, is shown in Figure 2-6.

The technique of containment simply follows through on the idea that any COM object can be a client of another object. With containment, we see that one object pretends to support an interface when it is really acting only as a mediator by passing along the client's request to a third party. The IMultiply interface works similarly to the ISum interface, except that instead of adding two numbers it returns their product. In the usual fashion, the container object actually implements the IMultiply interface using its Multiply method. As part of its construction sequence, the container object also instantiates the inner object, as shown in the following code:

```
Dim myRef As InnerObject

Private Sub Class_Initialize()
Set myRef = New InnerObject
End Sub
```

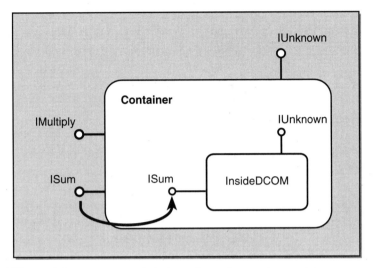

Figure 2-6. *Reusing a COM object through containment.*

Now when the client calls a method, the container object simply delegates the call to the inner object, as shown here:

```
Public Function Sum(x As Integer, y As Integer) As Integer
{
    ' Delegate this call to our contained object.
    Sum = myRef.Sum(x, y)
}
```

This code demonstrates the simplest kind of containment—it does nothing but delegate to another object. More sophisticated uses of containment might add code before and after delegating the call to the internal object, which could allow the container object to modify the behavior of the internal object in some way. The container object might even decide not to delegate to the internal object under some circumstances. In such cases, the container object is expected to provide the entire behavior necessary to satisfy the client.

THREADING MODELS

While Visual Basic offers only limited threading options, components built in Visual Basic often must interact with components built in other languages that might offer a wider range of threading possibilities. For this reason, it is important to fully grasp COM's threading options, including those that are currently beyond the reach of Visual Basic. COM and its predecessor, OLE, were developed at a time when Windows did not support multithreading, and thus COM initially provided no support for multithreaded components. Later, as threading became ubiquitous throughout Windows-land, the COM specification was expanded to include threading support. Today COM provides support and interoperability for components that use threads to any extent.

A QUICK REVIEW OF THREADS

A *thread* is a path of execution through a process. Every process has one or more threads of execution. The system executes threads only, never processes. Threads enable an application to perform (or appear to perform) several tasks concurrently, which can lead to a higher degree of functionality in an application and improved responsiveness in the user interface. On machines with multiple processors, different threads can execute concurrently on different processors, yielding improved overall performance.

One of the biggest problems associated with the safe use of threads is proper synchronization. Any unprotected access to data shared by multiple threads is an access violation waiting to happen. For example, if two threads manipulate an unprotected data structure, the probability of that data becoming corrupted is high. It is easy to envision a scenario in which one thread might begin to read some data only to be preempted by the scheduler. The scheduler might then decide to execute another thread that will begin to modify the data in the shared structure. When execution focus eventually returns to the first thread, the data might no longer be consistent. This scenario will likely end in an error.

This type of synchronization problem is difficult to detect and difficult to correct because it may happen infrequently, seemingly at random, making it very difficult to reproduce the error. Win32 offers several options for thread synchronization: events, critical sections, semaphores, or mutual exclusion objects can be used. Since data can't in itself be protected against concurrent access by different threads, the developers must write intelligent code that prevents this from happening. Developers can use the Win32 thread synchronization objects to guarantee that only one thread at a time executes a particular section of crucial code. Note that only data shared by multiple threads are at risk. Automatic variables located on the stack of a particular thread pose no difficulties because they are allocated on a per-thread basis.

Fundamentally, COM now supports two primary threading models: one for user-driven graphical user interface (GUI) applications and another for worker components that do not display a user interface, both of which utilize the threading infrastructure provided by the operating system. The threading model designed for GUI applications is synchronized with message queues used by windows, which makes it much easier for user-driven applications to work robustly with COM. The threading model designed for worker components, on the other hand, doesn't use window message queues to deliver COM method calls. This model works well for those components that need the best possible performance and that don't have to worry about synchronizing COM calls with a user interface.

APARTMENTS

Over the past decade, Windows has evolved from a cooperatively multitasked 16-bit environment into a preemptively multitasked 32-bit operating system. As Windows has evolved, threads have slowly but surely found their way into nearly all aspects of the operating system. This transition has at times been painful, but the overarching advantages have far outweighed the temporary inconveniences caused by the integration of threading. Because COM arrived to the threading game rather late, there has been more than a little consternation on the part of developers as threading support has been added.

Around the time multithreading support was added to COM (in Microsoft Windows NT 3.51), many design decisions made by Microsoft were affected by the amount of thread-unsafe legacy code that existed. Microsoft felt that it was crucial to enable existing threaded unsafe components to interoperate seamlessly with the new multithreaded components. Thus, several levels, called *threading models,* of thread safety were defined.

The basic unit of thread safety in COM is called an *apartment*. Two types of apartments are defined: single-threaded apartments (STAs) can have only one thread executing per apartment, and multithreaded apartments (MTAs) can have more than one thread executing per apartment. Aside from the number of threads executing in an apartment, method calls to objects in an STA are automatically synchronized and dispatched using window message queues, whereas calls to objects in an MTA are not. The STA and MTA models can be combined in a single process. A process can contain any number of or no STAs, but it can contain at most one MTA.

Until the advent of the MTA model, COM had not entirely shed its seedy, message-based past. In fact, to this day the STA model notifies an object of method calls by posting messages to a window message queue. Any component supporting the STA model must contain a message loop or nothing will happen. Why does a component architecture with as much finesse as COM rely on message queues? Because by relying on message queues to dispense method calls, COM effectively has hooks into every object in an STA. In this way, COM can serialize method calls to each STA to ensure that thread safety isn't compromised. The MTA model doesn't rely on message queues because COM doesn't provide thread synchronization for such objects.

In the past, different combinations of STAs and MTAs in a single process have been dubbed with the terms single, apartment, free, or mixed threading models. This terminology should be avoided, as it only causes additional confusion. The following table translates what you might know about these named threading models into the vocabulary of STAs and MTAs. A good way to think of these threading models is to remember that they all rely on the basic unit of an apartment. Some of those apartments can have only a single thread (STAs), while others support multiple threads (MTAs).

Old-Fashioned Threading Model Terms	Number of STAs	Number of MTAs
Single (legacy)	1	0
Apartment	1 or more	0
Free	0	1
Mixed (both)	1 or more	1

The threading models in COM provide the mechanism for clients and components that use different threading architectures to work together. From the perspective of a client, all objects appear to be using the client's threading model. Likewise, from the perspective of an object, all clients appear to support the object's threading model. A component built in Visual Basic declares its threading model at startup and then lets COM handle concurrency.

The Single-Threaded Apartment Model

The current STA model descended from the original thread-oblivious model used by COM. In the thread-oblivious model, COM objects could be accessed only from a single thread in the process. The STA model evolved to overcome this limitation; it introduces the ability for a single process to contain multiple STAs. Since each STA has only one thread associated with it, the ability for multiple STAs to exist in a single process means that several threads might actually be using COM objects concurrently. Under current implementations of COM, legacy components written prior to the advent of the COM threading models actually run in a single STA.

The STA owns any COM object instantiated by its thread, and henceforth all method calls on the object will be executed by the thread that created it. The fact that the same thread that created an object will be used to execute its methods is very important to objects that have thread affinity. A particular thread must execute an object that suffers from thread affinity.

Window message queues

As mentioned previously, COM dispatches method calls on objects running in an STA by using window message queues. During the startup of a component, COM calls the Win32 *RegisterClass* function to register the *OleMainThreadWndClass* window class. COM then automatically calls the Win32 *CreateWindow* function to create a hidden window of the *OleMainThreadWndClass* window class for each STA. COM uses the message queue of this hidden window to synchronize and dispatch COM method calls on this object. Therefore, the thread associated with an STA must retrieve and dispatch window messages.

This hidden window can be displayed using a utility such as Microsoft Spy++ (which comes with Visual C++), as shown in Figure 2-7 on the following page. A method call is received as a message to this hidden window. When the component retrieves the message and then dispatches it, the hidden window's window procedure will receive the message. This window procedure, implemented as part of COM, will then call the corresponding interface method of the object.

This message queuing architecture solves the problem of multiple clients making concurrent calls to an object running in an STA. Since all the calls are submitted as window messages posted to the message queue, the calls are serialized automatically. The object receives method calls when the message loop retrieves and dispatches the messages in the queue. Since COM serializes the calls in this manner, the object's methods don't need to provide synchronization. The dispatched method calls will always be made on the thread that instantiated the object. This is easily verified using the *App.ThreadID* property to retrieve the thread identifier in each method of an object. The thread identifier will always be the same for objects running in an STA.

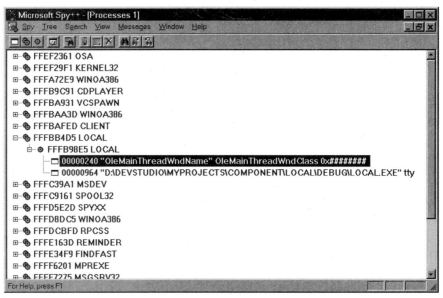

Figure 2-7. *The hidden STA window created by COM and displayed using Microsoft Spy++.*

Under some circumstances, it is possible for an object to be reentered by the same thread, in a manner similar to the way a window procedure can be reentered. If a method of the object processes window messages, another call to a method might be dispatched. This problem is most easily avoided by not processing window messages during a method call. An object may also be reentered if a method makes an outgoing call using COM and the outgoing method then calls back into the object. COM doesn't prevent these types of reentrancy but only guarantees that the calls won't execute concurrently.

STAs on a network

The message-based method invocation mechanism of an STA is used even when a network separates the client and the component. Figure 2-8 shows how the STA model works. Each arrow indicates a separate thread of execution. In the first thread, the client calls the proxy, which in turn calls the *IRpcChannelBuffer::SendReceive* method. Here the second thread is created to actually send the data across the network using an RPC. Meanwhile, the first thread sits in a message loop waiting for a response.

Across the network, a server-side thread takes the received data packet and posts a message to the message queue of the hidden window. Omitted from this diagram is the component's *GetMessage/DispatchMessage* loop, which takes messages from the queue and dispatches them back to the window procedure. From within the component's main thread, the window procedure calls the stub's *IRpcStubBuffer:Invoke* method. Last, the stub unpacks the parameters and calls the actual method in the COM object. This process of packing parameters for transmission is called *marshaling* and is basically repeated in reverse order once the method has finished executing.

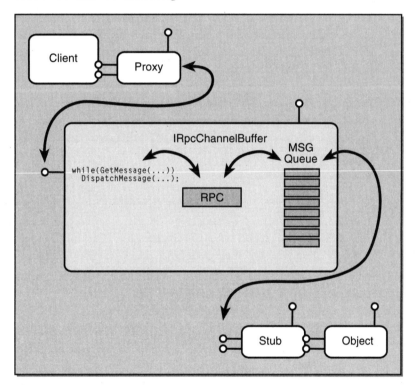

Figure 2-8. *The inner workings of the STA model.*

Observe that a total of four threads—two on the client side and two on the server side—are required to make the STA model work. An internal optimization of the STA model is possible when the client and the component are both executing on the same machine. In such cases, COM automatically uses only two threads: one thread in the client process and another thread in the component.

The Multithreaded Apartment Model

As mentioned previously, threads running in the MTA don't need to retrieve or dispatch window messages, because COM doesn't use messages to deliver method calls on objects running in the MTA. Since method calls are made directly through a v-table, COM doesn't impose any synchronization on objects running in the MTA. Therefore, these objects must provide their own synchronization by using critical sections, events, mutexes, semaphores, or other mechanisms, as dictated by their synchronization requirements.

Multiple clients can concurrently execute an object's methods from different threads, and thus threads of an MTA can't have any thread affinity whatsoever. An object running in the MTA will receive calls through a pool of COM-allocated threads belonging to the object's process. These threads are created by COM at run time and then reused as it sees fit. COM automatically spawns threads as necessary to enable concurrent access to the component. A utility such as Process Viewer (PVIEW.EXE), which is included with Visual C++, can be useful for dynamically spying on the threads created by COM.

The following table compares the various attributes of the STA and MTA models:

Feature	*STA*	*MTA*
Synchronization provided by COM	Yes	No
Can have multiple threads in one apartment	No	Yes
Uses window message queues	Yes	No

Threading models for in-process components

The functions *CoInitialize* and *CoInitializeEx* provide executable components with the ability to declare their support for a particular threading model. Clients use these functions to create apartments for use in calling components. In-process components work differently from executable components in that they do not call *CoInitialize[Ex]* on component startup because their client will already have initialized COM by the time they are loaded. Instead, in-process components declare their supported threading model by using registry settings. In the component's CLSID\InprocServer32 registry key, the named value *ThreadingModel* can be set to *Apartment*, *Free*, or *Both* to indicate support for one of those threading models. If no *ThreadingModel* value is specified, COM assumes the in-process component to be a thread-oblivious legacy component.

Note that the old-fashioned threading model names are used by the *ThreadingModel* value. The following table translates these names into the modern STA and MTA models.

ThreadingModel Values	Description
[No ThreadingModel value]	Thread-oblivious legacy component
Apartment	STA
Free	MTA
Both	Both STA and MTA models

NOTE It is legal for different COM classes provided by a single in-process component to have different *ThreadingModel* values. In other words, the *ThreadingModel* value is set on a per-CLSID basis rather than a per-DLL basis.

Threading concerns for Visual Basic components

Components built in Visual Basic can support either the thread-oblivious legacy model or the STA model. Visual Basic will automatically set the *ThreadingModel* registry value to *Apartment* for ActiveX controls or ActiveX DLLs supporting the STA model. Components built in Visual Basic 6 can't support the MTA model. To specify the threading model used by a Visual Basic application, choose Properties from the Project menu and then make your selection in the Project Properties dialog box, as shown in Figure 2-9.

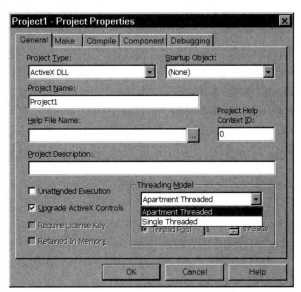

Figure 2-9. *The General tab of the Project Properties dialog box, showing the Threading Model drop-down list.*

Chapter 3

Object-Oriented Programming in Visual Basic

Is Microsoft Visual Basic an object-oriented language? Let's review what it means to be an object-oriented programming language, and then you can decide for yourself whether Visual Basic meets the requirements. As we discussed in Chapter 1, object-oriented programming languages are generally based on the three pillars of encapsulation, inheritance, and polymorphism.

Encapsulation means designing and writing your program in terms of objects, which contain both code (procedures) and data (property) members. This is considered to be a good design because the data and the code that operates on that data are stored and used together logically. Visual Basic allows you to create class modules that can contain both code and data and therefore meets this requirement.

Inheritance refers to the ability to create a new object based on another object, with the new object inheriting code and data members from the other object. Inheritance is best used when an obvious "is a" relationship can be recognized between objects. Visual Basic doesn't currently support inheritance.

You can use containment in Visual Basic to simulate, to a certain extent, a type of inheritance. Containment simply means building a new object by including existing objects within it. This is more easily understood by way of an example. Let's say you have a Door class defined, and you now want to define a Car class. Most sedans have four doors, so you simply put an array of four door objects within your Car class. Thus, your car *contains* four doors. This isn't a true example of inheritance because no "is a" relationship is present. It is correct to say that a car contains doors, but not that a car "is a" door.

Although Visual Basic doesn't currently support inheritance, it does support a special type of interface inheritance that allows one class to inherit the interface of another class. This is normally used to implement polymorphism.

Polymorphism means that many classes can provide the same property or method and that a client doesn't have to know what class an object belongs to before calling the property or method. Most object-oriented languages provide support for polymorphism through inheritance. Although Visual Basic doesn't support implementation inheritance (the inheriting of code), polymorphism is provided by means of interface inheritance (the inheriting of interfaces).

So, of the three basic requirements of a true object-oriented language, Visual Basic currently supports two: encapsulation and polymorphism. While perhaps not an object-oriented programming language for purists, Visual Basic is a language with very pragmatic features that is useful for applied object-oriented programming needs.

CLASS MODULES

In Visual Basic, class modules are used to define classes—the blueprints—of objects. To add a class module to a Visual Basic project, you simply choose the Add Class Module command from the Project menu. Class modules are a wonderful way to help you structure Visual Basic applications. If you design classes appropriate to the problems that you are solving with your software, the development and future maintenance of that software will be much easier.

A central tenet of object-oriented programming is that all data and procedures related to a particular object are kept together with the object itself. In Visual Basic, *code* is defined as methods and the *data* of an object is defined as properties. To define the interface of an object, you create your own properties and methods within the class module. Defining the properties and methods of class modules is very simple. The *Public Sub* and *Public Function* procedures in a class module become the methods of the class; the *Public* variables are the properties of the class. Class modules are similar to Visual Basic forms, except class modules have no visible user interface at run time. You can define only one class per class module.

All class modules have a *Name* property that defines the name by which the class will be identified. A class module should be assigned a meaningful name, because the name will identify the class to client programs. If you are creating a COM application, an *Instancing* property will be visible in the Properties window. The *Instancing* property determines if and how other applications are allowed to instantiate objects of this class. For now, we will simply accept the default value for the *Instancing* property; we will go into the various possibilities in Chapter 5.

ON YOUR MARKS: *LET*, *GET*, *SET*, *NEW*, AND *NOTHING*

Although Visual Basic has obviously evolved from original versions of the Basic programming language created over twenty-five years ago, some anachronisms have remained. While nobody writes code such as *Let X = 5* anymore—instead you can just write *X = 7*—this is still legal syntax because Visual Basic still supports the *Let* keyword. Although *Let* was almost relegated to the Basic recycle bin, it has recently been resurrected along with *Get* and *Set* in a whole new manner. *Set* is now used extensively in Visual Basic to set references. As you probably know, Visual Basic doesn't support pointers—references are the closest approximation. References provide a safe way of referring to an object without having the direct memory access that a pointer would provide. In Visual Basic, all object variables are only references that refer to a particular object. References are not an invention of Visual Basic—in fact, references have become a popular alternative to pointers in languages such as C++ and Java.

The *New* keyword, another idea borrowed from C++, allows Visual Basic applications to dynamically construct objects. *New* can be used in conjunction with the *Nothing* keyword. *Nothing* destroys objects and frees the memory used. The following snippet of code shows the use of the *Set* and *New* keywords:

```
Dim Thingy As New MyObject
Dim ReferenceToThingy As MyObject
Thingy.MyProperty = "TEST"

' Set the reference to the object.
Set ReferenceToThingy = Thingy

Print Thingy.MyProperty
Print ReferenceToThingy.MyProperty
' Delete the object?
Set Thingy = Nothing

Print Thingy.MyProperty
Print ReferenceToThingy.MyProperty
```

In this example, MyObject is an imaginary class module with a string property named MyProperty. Note in the code that Thingy is declared *As New MyObject*. This allocates memory, instantiates MyObject, and sets Thingy to refer to that object. Also interesting is that *As New MyObject* is simply a shortcut, as shown in this code snippet from the preceding longer code sample.

```
' This is a shortcut.
Dim Thingy As New MyObject

' For all intents and purposes is identical to:
Dim Thingy As MyObject
Set Thingy = New MyObject
```

THE *ADDRESSOF* OPERATOR

The *AddressOf* keyword is a unary operator that evaluates to the address of the procedure it precedes. This feature was added to Visual Basic 5 to let a program make Microsoft Windows API calls and to make calls to functions in other DLLs that expect to receive a function pointer as a procedure parameter.

Normally, when a procedure name appears in an argument list, the procedure is evaluated and the address of the procedure's return value is passed. *AddressOf* permits the address of the procedure, rather than its return value, to be passed to a Microsoft Windows API function in a DLL. The called function can then use the address to call the Visual Basic procedure. The automatic calling of functions by Windows in response to certain predefined events is known as a *callback*. Timer messages, window messages, dialog box messages, and font enumeration notifications, among others, are all supplied through callback functions in Windows-based applications. This means that you can write callback functions in Visual Basic.

Although you can use *AddressOf* to pass function pointers among Visual Basic procedures, you can't call a function through such a pointer from within Visual Basic. This means that a class written in Visual Basic can't make a callback to its controller by using such a pointer. When using *AddressOf* to pass a procedure pointer among procedures within Visual Basic, you must assign the parameter of the called procedure the *Long* data type. When using *AddressOf* to pass a procedure pointer to an API function, you must declare the procedure address argument *As Any* in the *Declare* statement. The *AddressOf* operator appears only in the call and not in the *Declare* statement.[1]

---

1. *AddressOf* works only on procedures stored in standard modules.

ReferenceToThingy, however, is declared only as an object variable of type MyObject, omitting the use of *New*. This means that ReferenceToThingy doesn't currently refer to an object of type MyObject but is instead only a variable that may refer to a MyObject object in the future. The following statement sets ReferenceToThingy as a reference to the Thingy object:

```
Set ReferenceToThingy = Thingy
```

This is known as aliasing, since the object referred to by Thingy is now equally accessible through either the Thingy or ReferenceToThingy references.

Here is a Visual Basic code example that uses a callback function. It calls the Win32 API function *EnumChildWindows* to display a list of all child window handles.

```
' Make Sub Main the startup, and put this code in a
' standard module.
Option Explicit

Declare Function GetActiveWindow Lib "User32" () As _
    Long

Declare Function EnumChildWindows Lib "User32" _
    (ByVal hWnd As Long, ByVal lpWndProc As Long, _
    ByVal lp As Long) As Long
Sub Main()
    Dim hWnd As Long
    Dim x As Long
    hWnd = GetActiveWindow()
    If (hWnd) Then
        x = EnumChildWindows(hWnd, AddressOf _
            EnumChildProc, 0)
    End If
End Sub

Function EnumChildProc(ByVal hWnd As Long, _
    ByVal lp As Long) As Long
    Debug.Print "Window: "; hWnd
    EnumChildProc = 1
End Function
```

Note that only one copy of the object actually exists, and that two variable names can now be used to access the one object. This is like a house with two doors, each of which allows you equal access inside. Later, this statement is executed:

```
Set Thingy = Nothing
```

The program displays *Thingy.MyProperty* and *ReferenceToThingy.My-Property* values after this statement executes. Assuming that ReferenceToThingy is a reference to the Thingy object and that the Thingy object has been freed using the *Nothing* keyword, you might expect these statements to cause runtime errors or at the very least to not print values. You might be surprised to learn, however, that while the attempt to print the value of *Thingy.MyProperty* will indeed not print anything, *Print ReferenceToThingy.MyProperty* will display the value "*TEST*".

How can this be? If only one copy of the object existed and this single copy was then destroyed by *Nothing*, how can ReferenceToThingy still display data? The answer lies in Visual Basic's implementation of the *Nothing* keyword.

Nothing will release the memory associated with an object only when there are no other open references to an object—in other words, when the object is no longer aliased. In our example, Thingy has been aliased by ReferenceToThingy, so setting Thingy to *Nothing* does not do anything. To actually free the memory associated with Thingy, you would also have to execute the statement *Set ReferenceToThingy = Nothing*. Since no reference to the object would be valid at that point, Visual Basic would free the object. In practice, the *Nothing* keyword is not used a great deal since an object variable that goes out of scope is automatically set to *Nothing*. Instantiating an object by using the *New* keyword is a relatively expensive operation, but creating a reference to an object is cheap. Realize that in Visual Basic we never really work with objects. Instead, we work with variables that contain references to objects.[2]

PROPERTY PROCEDURES

Programmers who are familiar with Visual Basic have been conditioned to think of objects as having methods and properties, but properties are really just a convenient abstraction. Properties are always implemented in terms of methods. In other words, suppose you write this statement:

```
Command1.Caption = "HELLO"
```

---

2. Accessing an object through a reference is safe, since we can access only the properties and methods exposed by the implementer of the class.

Visual Basic calls the Win32 API function *SendMessage*, which sends the *WM_SETTEXT* message to the command button's window procedure telling it to change the text in the Command1 command button. The command button then makes a couple of other API calls, culminating in *TextOut*, which actually displays the new text in the button. So, you can see that setting a *Caption* property might appear to be setting a data element, but in fact it always ends up calling code. For class modules created in Visual Basic, you can actually have properties in addition to methods. However, when creating a component, simple variable properties declared with a statement such as the following are usually not a good idea:

```
Public MyProperty As Integer
```

If you declare a property as public, any client of your class can read or modify this value directly. What would happen if in the future you decided to modify your internal implementation of MyProperty and declare it as a *Double* data type rather than as an *Integer*? That's something you wouldn't be able to do here without breaking the code that belongs to existing clients of your class. In this instance, a public property is restrictive because the interface and the implementation of the class are now one and the same, which isn't a good object-oriented design.[3]

Another problem with using public variables arises if you want to implement a property that enables an action. For example, let's say you want a control to have a *Caption* property, similar to the command button *Caption* property. When the client sets the *Caption* property, you want the new text to be displayed in your control. If you make your *Caption* property a *Public String* variable, how will you know when somebody has modified its value? Unless you write some polling code, you won't.

To solve this problem, Visual Basic enables you to create *property procedures*, which are procedures that masquerade as properties. Property procedures allow you to execute code when a client sets a property value or a component retrieves a property value. Property procedures come in three flavors: *Let*, *Get*, and *Set*. Consider this example of a Property Get procedure and a Property Let procedure:

```
Private ControlCaption As String

Property Get Caption() As String
    Caption = ControlCaption
End Property

Property Let Caption(NewCaption As String)
    ControlCaption = NewCaption
    Call InternalSubThatPaintsControlCaption(ControlCaption)
End Property
```

3. Although it's convenient for the client to think of the property as a public variable, the object should implement it as a property procedure.

Recall the MyObject class module we declared previously in this chapter. Let's say that the client runs this code:

```
Print MyObject.Caption
```

The component invokes the Property Get procedure to retrieve the value stored in the class module's private data member, ControlCaption. Now let's say that the client runs this code:

```
MyObject.Caption = "HELLO"
```

In this case, the component invokes the Property Let procedure. Although this sample Property Let procedure doesn't do this, the component could validate the new caption to make sure it was acceptable before repainting the control. This technique has the added advantage of enabling developers to modify the internal implementation of a class without affecting its clients. As an example, you might decide to add code to save the caption in a file. Clients of the class would not need to know about this or modify their code in any way.

The *Property Set* statement allows you to set a reference to an object in a property. *Property Set* is usually used in tandem with *Property Get*, just as *Property Let* is used in tandem with *Property Get* for properties whose values are not objects. You can also create a read-only property by implementing a Property Get procedure without a corresponding Property Let or Property Set procedure, giving the client no way to modify the property's value.

METHODS

Methods of an object are public procedures that perform some action. Either Sub procedures or Function procedures can be methods. The following code provides a simple method:

```
Public Function Sum(X As Integer, Y As Integer) As Integer
    Sum = X + Y
End Function
```

You can also design a method that accepts optional parameters, has default values, or has an indefinite number of parameters, as shown in these examples:

```
Public Function Sum1(X As Integer, Y As Integer) As Integer
    Sum1 = X + Y
End Function

Public Function Sum2(Optional X, Optional Y As _
  Integer) As Integer
    If IsMissing(X) Then X = -5
    Sum2 = X + Y
End Function
```

```
Public Function Sum3(Optional X As Integer = 5, Optional Y _
   As Integer = 2) As Integer
      Sum3 = X + Y
End Function

Public Function Sum4(ParamArray Guy() As Variant) As Integer
Dim Thingy As Variant
      For Each Thingy In Guy
            Sum4 = Sum4 + Thingy
      Next Thingy
End Function

Private Sub Form_Load()
      MsgBox Sum1(5, 3)   ' 5 + 3
      MsgBox Sum2         ' -5 + 0
      MsgBox Sum3         ' 5 + 2
      MsgBox Sum3(10)     ' 10 + 2
      MsgBox Sum3(, 9)    ' 5 + 9
      MsgBox Sum3(Y:=10)  ' 5 + 10    Using named arguments
      MsgBox Sum4(1, 2, 3, 4, 5, 6)  ' 1 + 2 + 3 + 4 + 5 + 6
End Sub
```

EVENTS

An *event* is an action recognized by an object; events make things happen. When an event is generated by a control it is called *firing* an event. The classic example of an event is the *Click* event. A command button control fires a *Click* event whenever an end-user clicks the command button. Control events inform the form that contains the control about things happening to the control. Events are by definition asynchronous, meaning that events can be fired at any time. To respond to the various events, Visual Basic allows programmers to write a type of Sub procedure called an *event procedure* that executes whenever a particular event is fired. For example, when a command button control named Command1 fires the *Click* event, Visual Basic calls the Command1_Click event procedure and runs any code contained in that procedure.

Class Module Events

All class modules support the *Initialize* event that Visual Basic fires when an object is first instantiated and the *Terminate* event that Visual Basic fires before the object is destroyed. The *Initialize* event is useful for allocating any memory that might be needed and initializing the state of the object so that it is prepared for client use. The *Terminate* event is useful for freeing resources and performing any general housekeeping necessary before the object is destroyed. Both the *Initialize* and *Terminate* events are optional, meaning that you do not have to implement them if you do not need them.

To further explore and understand the possibilities of class modules, let's try an exercise. This exercise walks you through the steps of adding a class module named Account to your project, creating Name and Balance properties, and writing a simple program that uses the Account class. The important thing to notice in this exercise is the use of the *New* and *Set* keywords. Everything generally works as you might expect until you reach this statement:

Set acctObject = Nothing

However, we don't want to give anything away.

Exercise 3-1

1. Open Visual Basic, and create new Standard EXE project.

2. Choose the Add Class Module command from the Project menu.

3. Select Class Module, and click Open.

4. Add the following code in the Code window:

    ```
    Option Explicit
    Public Balance As Double
    Public Name As String
    ```

5. In the Code window, select Class from the Object drop-down list.

6. Add the following code (shown in bold):

    ```
    Private Sub Class_Initialize()
        Form1.Print "Account Initialize"
    End Sub
    ```

7. In the Code window, select Terminate from the Procedure box.

8. Add the following code (shown in bold):

    ```
    Private Sub Class_Terminate()
        Form1.Print "Account Terminate"
    End Sub
    ```

9. In the Properties window, set the *Name* property to *Account*.

10. In the Project Explorer, double-click on Form1 (Form1).

11. In the Properties window for Form1, set the *AutoRedraw* property to *True*.

12. Place in the form a command button with the default name Command1.

13. Double-click the Command1 command button to open the Code window.

14. Write the following code:

```
Private Sub Command1_Click()
    Dim acctObject As New Account
    Dim acctReference As Account

    acctObject.Name = "YourNameHere"

    Print "acctObject.Name = " & acctObject.Name

    Set acctReference = acctObject

    Print "acctReference.Name = " & acctReference.Name

    acctReference.Balance = 7000

    Print "acctReference.Balance = " & _
      acctReference.Balance
    Print "acctObject.Balance = " & _
      acctObject.Balance

    Set acctObject = Nothing

    Print "acctObject.Name = " & acctObject.Name
    Print "acctObject.Balance = " & acctObject.Balance

    Print "acctReference.Name = " & acctReference.Name
End Sub
```

15. Press F8 to step through the code until the command button is displayed.

16. Click the command button.

17. Continue pressing F8 to step through the code.

In this exercise, we can see that an object dimensioned as *As New Account* works slightly differently than a standard reference dimensioned as *As Account*. Because of the way the object is dimensioned, Visual Basic doesn't report an error when the acctObject object is used after being set to Nothing. Instead, Visual Basic automatically creates a new Account object as evidenced by the second firing of the class *Initalize* event. Standard references dimensioned as *As Account* do not exhibit this behavior; in this case, Visual Basic returns an error if a reference is accessed after being set to *Nothing*.

Custom Events and the *WithEvents* Keyword

In addition to firing standard events, an object can fire *custom* events, which are events that developers define. This facility was developed for use by ActiveX controls created in Visual Basic because the ability to fire events is required to create controls. (Firing events from ActiveX controls will be examined in Chapter 6.)

Before a custom event can be fired, you must declare it by using the *Event* statement in the *Declarations* section of a class module. The *Event* statement defines the name of the event and any arguments that will be passed to the event procedure. Custom events are by definition public. For example, this statement defines a Test event with one string parameter:

```
Event Test(Message As String)
```

Once an event is declared, you can fire the event at any time by using the *RaiseEvent* statement. Here is the code to fire the Test event:

```
RaiseEvent Test("Testing RaiseEvent")
```

Thus, the code to declare and fire the Test event in a class module looks like this:

```
' Inside a class module named MyClass
Option Explicit
Event Test(Message As String)           ' Declare the event.

Public Sub MyMethod()
    RaiseEvent Test("Testing RaiseEvent") ' Fire it.
End Sub
```

Intercepting events that are fired from a class module is a bit trickier than firing the event.[4] If, after writing the previous code, you look for the Test event in the Code window of the form, you will be disappointed. Before Visual Basic can list Test in the Procedure box of the Code window, you need to inform Visual Basic about Test's existence. You do this by dimensioning a variable of the object's class using the *WithEvents* keyword. Try adding this line of code to the *Declarations* section of the form:

```
Dim WithEvents MyObject As MyClass
```

The *WithEvents* keyword specifies that this object reference will be used to intercept and respond to events fired from the class module. After adding the *WithEvents* statement (and pressing Enter), if you select MyObject in the Object box and then browse the Procedure box in the Code window, you will

---

4. There is a subtle difference between calling a procedure and firing an event. When firing an event, we don't direct it to anyone in particular and we don't care if someone intercepts it.

find the Test event listed. Selecting it automatically creates the following event procedure shell in which you can write code to respond to the Test event:

```
Private Sub MyObject_Test(Message As String)

End Sub
```

The *Dim WithEvents MyObject As MyClass* statement dimensions a variable that can refer to an object of type MyClass. For the event firing to work, you must set the reference to an actual instance of MyClass. This is usually best done in the form's *Load* event procedure so as to ensure that MyClass will refer to an actual object by the time an event is first fired:

```
Private Sub Form_Load()
    Set MyObject = New MyClass
End Sub
```

The last step to creating a custom event is to call the *MyMethod* method to cause the event to be fired within the class module. While it might seem silly to call a method simply to cause an event to be fired back to you, this is actually a very common tactic. Suppose the method has some arguments that give the class module information on the type of data that it should retrieve for the client. If enough information is supplied, the class module just goes out and retrieves the data. However, if the method requires additional information— say, a password—the method might fire an event back to the client requesting the additional data. The completed code that runs in the form module and calls the class module described earlier looks like this:

```
Option Explicit
    Dim WithEvents MyObject As MyClass

Private Sub MyObject_Test(Message As String)
    MsgBox Message     ' Displays "Testing RaiseEvent"
End Sub

Private Sub Form_Click()
    MyObject.MyMethod
End Sub

Private Sub Form_Load()
    Set MyObject = New MyClass
End Sub
```

> NOTE   To review the complete program, open the Events project in the \BK-SAMP\Chap03\EVENTS folder on the companion disc.

COLLECTIONS

Once you have defined a class by creating a class module and giving it properties and methods, in your program you can create any number of objects from that class. You could do this by declaring variables with the *New* keyword, as demonstrated earlier, but using this approach you could declare only as many objects as you had declared variables. In Visual Basic, you can easily create arrays of variables by using this syntax:

```
Dim ArrayName(100) As Integer
```

By the same token, you can create arrays of an object by using this syntax:

```
Dim ArrayName(100) As New Account
```

In this second example, Account is the name of a class module, as in the previous exercise.

Although arrays constitute a convenient formation in which to store a lot of data, they are not terribly flexible. Imagine for a moment that you are writing software for a bank, and you use an array of 100 Account objects to keep track of the bank's 100 accounts. If new customers want to open additional accounts or existing customers want to close accounts, you have a problem. Although increasing the array size with *ReDim Preserve* is possible, it isn't terribly efficient. When accounts are closed, you are left with empty objects in your array. These empty objects are also quite difficult to reuse efficiently. So, although you can keep multiple object references in an array, you will have to use *ReDim* and compress unused entries yourself.

A standard computer science algorithm used to solve these types of problems is called a *linked list*. A linked list consists of a list of objects that are linked to one another by means of their addresses in memory (pointers). If you need to add a new object, you can simply allocate it, and then point the previous object in the list to the new object and point the new object to the next object. If you need to remove an object, you can simply delete it and then set the previous object to point to the next one. Creating linked lists with Visual Basic isn't possible, because it doesn't support pointers. Visual Basic doesn't provide pointers because pointers enable developers to access memory locations directly without any sanity checks by the programming language. Although very powerful if used correctly, pointers are a major source of bugs in software. For this reason, most modern programming languages attempt to stay away from pointers. Even Java manages to keep pointers out of the language and instead supports only references.

Collection Characteristics

Microsoft introduced the concept of collections because linked lists are not an option in Visual Basic due to the lack of pointer support. Visual Basic provides a generic *Collection* object that you can use to keep track of the objects you create from your classes. A collection is a Visual Basic object that is built into the language for support of more flexible data structures. Basically, collections are for gathering objects together in a convenient and flexible manner. Internally, Visual Basic implements collections as linked lists by using pointers. Collections therefore provide a major piece of functionality otherwise available only by using pointers, without the difficulty and the danger associated with using pointers. Visual Basic collections have the following characteristics:

- A collection grows and shrinks automatically. When you remove an item from within a collection, no empty slot is left behind; when you add a new item to the end, you never get an out-of-bounds error.

- Collections have more flexible indexes than do arrays. Indexes will change as items are added and deleted. Keys can uniquely identify items within a collection regardless of their position.

- Collections are 1-based, meaning that the first item in a collection is the 1 item.

- Collections are unordered by default. Items are normally added to the end of a collection unless you specify otherwise.

- The *For Each...Next* statement in Visual Basic specifically supports looping through items in a collection.

The Visual Basic *Collection* object exposes its functionality by means of the following interface:

Item	Type	Description
Add	Method	Adds an object to the collection.
Item	Method	Returns an object in the collection by index or by key.
Remove	Method	Deletes an object from the collection.
Count	Property	Specifies the number of objects in the collection (read-only).

The *For Each...Next* Statement

A *For Each...Next* loop is similar to a standard *For...Next* loop, except that it repeats a group of statements for each element in a collection of objects or in an array of variants instead of repeating the statements a specified number of times. This is especially helpful if you don't know how many elements are in a collection. The following example creates a collection, adds two items, and then prints the *Name* property of both items in the collection using a *For Each...Next* loop:

```
Dim CollectionName As New Collection
Dim Thingy As Object

CollectionName.Add ObjectOne
CollectionName.Add ObjectTwo

For Each Thingy in CollectionName
    Print Thingy.Name
Next Thingy
```

Note that in this *For Each...Next* loop, Thingy is only a placeholder for a reference to the current object in the collection. For example, during the second iteration of the loop, Thingy is a reference to the second object in the collection. It is generally recommended that you choose a name for a collection based on the plural version of the type of object to be contained. For example, if you were creating a collection that would contain a collection of car objects, *Cars* would be the recommended name for the collection. However, keep in mind that collections can be heterogeneous, meaning that they can contain more than one type of object. For example, a collection could contain a mixture of cat and dog objects, although this is unusual.

The *TypeOf* operator can be used at run time to determine the class type of an object. This can be convenient in cases where more than one type of object has been added to a collection.

In the following exercise, you will create a class module named *Smile* and store it in a *Smiles* collection.

Exercise 3-2

1. Open Visual Basic, and start a new Standard EXE project.

2. Choose Add Class Module from the Project menu.

3. Select Class Module, and click Open.

4. Add the following code in the Code window:

```
Option Explicit
Public Name As String
```

5. In the Properties window, set the *Name* property to *Smile*.

6. In the Project Explorer, double-click on Form1.

7. In the Properties window for Form1, set the *AutoRedraw* property to *True*.

8. Double-click the form to open the Code window.

9. In the Declarations section of the form, enter the following code:

```
Option Explicit
Dim Smiles As New Collection
```

10. Switch to the Form window and place in the form a command button with the default name Command1.

11. Double-click on the Command1 command button to switch back to the Code window.

12. Write the following code:

```
Private Sub Command1_Click()
    Dim TheName As String
    Dim MySmile As Smile
    Do
        Dim OneSmile As New Smile
        TheName = InputBox _
          ("Please enter a name for this Smile object," _
          & Chr(13) & _
          "Press Cancel to see names in the collection.", _
          "Name the Smiles collection items")
        Let OneSmile.Name = TheName
        If OneSmile.Name <> "" Then
            Smiles.Add OneSmile
        End If
        Set OneSmile = Nothing
    Loop Until TheName = ""
    Print Smiles.Count & _
      " Smile object(s) in the Smiles collection"
    For Each MySmile in Smiles
        Print MySmile.Name
    Next MySmile
End Sub
```

THE *IMPLEMENTS* STATEMENT

As described in Chapter 1, inheritance refers to the ability to create a new object based on another object, copying its code and data members. Inheritance is best used when an obvious "is a" relationship between objects exists. For example, you might have a basic Tree class, from which a DeciduousTree class is derived. Then you inherit Oak and Maple classes from the DeciduousTree class. Inheritance would allow your code to express the fact that an Oak "is a" DeciduousTree.

Implementing Polymorphism

As we discussed earlier in this chapter, most object-oriented languages provide support for polymorphism through inheritance. Since Visual Basic doesn't currently support implementation inheritance (the inheriting of code), you might have assumed that Visual Basic can't support polymorphism. This is a common misunderstanding because, as developers, we are used to seeing polymorphism implemented as a by-product of inheritance. Visual Basic solves this dilemma in the same way COM does.[5] Implementation inheritance isn't supported in COM because the purpose of COM is to integrate objects. Polymorphism, however, lies at the heart of how COM works—you define an interface, and then any object can choose to implement it.

In Visual Basic, polymorphism is supported by means of interface inheritance. This type of inheritance is accomplished with the *Implements* statement. The best way to become familiar with a new language is to try it, so let's put *Implements* through its paces.

Exercise 3-3

Let's again use the example of the package shipper that we used in Chapter 1. As you may recall, in that example you are a consultant hired by a package shipping company to help them apply the new object-oriented features of Visual Basic to their software. Being bright, you quickly realize that the company's basic object is a package and decide to model it in Visual Basic with a class module that has a Ship method.

1. Open Visual Basic, and start a new Standard EXE project.

2. Choose Add Class Module from the Project menu.

3. Select Class Module, and click Open.

4. In the Properties window, set the *Name* property to *Package*.

---

5. In COM, two objects implementing the same contract (interface) are polymorphic.

5. Add the following code in the Code window:

```
Option Explicit
Public Function Ship() As Integer

End Function
```

You also remember that the package service has several different types of packages, such as next-day air, second-day air, and ground packages, so you decide to create class modules for all of these package types. Knowing about the *Implements* statement, you decide that all these new class modules should be implemented based on the generic Package class. After all, a next-day air package "is a" package—it's simply a more specialized type of package that needs to be delivered the next day. So, after you declare the Package class module, you complete the following steps:

6. Choose Add Class Module from the Project menu.

7. Select Class Module, and click Open.

8. In the Properties window, set the *Name* property to NextDayAir.

9. Add the following code in the Code window:

```
Option Explicit
Implements Package      ' Here we go!
```

Now click on the Object box in the Code window. Lo and behold, the Package class is peeking out at us. Select the Package class, and Visual Basic automatically declares the Ship method as a member of the Package class and lists it in the Procedure box. Note that when you use the *Implements* feature you inherit only the method signatures, and no code.

10. Fill in the implementation of the Package_Ship function so that it looks as follows:

```
Private Function Package_Ship() As Integer
    Package_Ship = 1 ' NextDayAir only takes one day.
End Function
```

NOTE Visual Basic requires that you implement the entire interface of the implemented class in the derived class, a requirement imposed by COM.

Repeat the same steps for the SecondDayAir class module—equate Package_Ship to "2". Follow the same steps for the Ground class module, except write the Ground class Ship method to look as shown on the following page.

```
Private Function Package_Ship() As Integer
    ' Between 1 and 10 days for a ground package
    Package_Ship = Int(10 * Rnd + 1)
End Function
```

Now let's write a test program that will exercise these classes.

11. In the Project Explorer, double-click on Form1.

12. In the Properties window for Form1, set *AutoRedraw* to *True*.

13. Place a command button in the form with the default name Command1.

14. Double-click on the Command1 command button to open the Code window for Form1.

15. Write the following code:

```
Private Sub Command1_Click()
    Dim MyNextDayPackage As New NextDayAir
    Dim MySecondDayPackage As New SecondDayAir
    Dim MyGroundPackage As New Ground
    Dim AnyPackage As Package     ' Only a reference!
    Dim Packages As New Collection

    Packages.Add MyNextDayPackage
    Packages.Add MySecondDayPackage
    Packages.Add MyGroundPackage
    For Each AnyPackage In Packages
        Print TypeName(AnyPackage) & _
          " package shipped in " & _
          AnyPackage.Ship & " day(s)."
    Next AnyPackage
End Sub
```

16. Now run and test the program. The result should look like this:

```
NextDayAir shipped in 1 day(s).
SecondDayAir shipped in 2 day(s).
Ground shipped in 8 day(s).
```

Now that you have the basic idea of how *Implements* works, let's experiment a bit to see what happens when we try something slightly less obvious. Add this statement anywhere in the Command1_Click procedure:

```
MsgBox MyNextDayPackage.Ship
```

Retest the program. When you receive the message "Compile error: Method or data member not found", it will dawn on you that Ship is not a method of the NextDayAir class even though it is implemented in that class. Instead, Ship is a method of the Package class and can only be called through a Package object variable. Now replace the bug-ridden line of code with the following code:

```
Set AnyPackage = MyNextDayPackage
MsgBox TypeName(AnyPackage)
MsgBox AnyPackage.Ship
```

The *TypeName* function in Visual Basic returns the data type of a variable. Since AnyPackage was declared as a Package, you might expect the message box to display Package. Instead, it displays NextDayAir. When you assign a NextDayAir object to a variable of type Package, Visual Basic asks the NextDayAir object whether it supports the Package interface.[6] If the answer is no, an error occurs. If the answer is yes, the object is assigned to the variable. Only the methods and properties of the Package interface can be accessed through this variable.

For experimentation purposes, let's add a GetLost method to the NextDayAir class that looks like this:

```
Public Function GetLost() As String
    GetLost = "Lost Package"
End Sub
```

Now, what happens if you assign the object variable to a generic object variable and call the GetLost method, as in the following code?

```
Private Sub Command1_Click()
    Dim MyNextDayPackage As New NextDayAir
    Dim AnyPackage As Package
    Dim MyObject As Object

    Set AnyPackage = MyNextDayPackage

    Set MyObject = AnyPackage
    MsgBox MyObject.Ship    ' Succeeds (member of Package)
    MsgBox MyObject.GetLost ' Fails (not a member of Package)

    Set MyObject = MyNextDayPackage
    MsgBox MyObject.Ship    ' Fails (not a member of NextDayAir)
    MsgBox MyObject.GetLost ' Succeeds (member of NextDayAir)
End Sub
```

To review the complete program shown in Exercise 3-3, open the ZIPPYPKG project in the \BK-SAMP\Chap03\EXER3-3 folder on the companion disc to this book.

As you can see, the interface last assigned to the object variable is the one that can be accessed. The important thing to be gleaned from these machinations is that while a class module in Visual Basic can define only one type of object,

---

6. The method used for asking this question is *QueryInterface*, as explained in Chapter 1.

by using the *Implements* statement you can create an object that has multiple interfaces. In our example, the NextDayAir object has two interfaces: the one defined in the NextDayAir class module and the interface inherited from the Package class. In Visual Basic, the default interface of every class is the one defined in the class module for that class. Thus, the NextDayAir class has a default interface called NextDayAir. Because NextDayAir also implements Package, the class has a second interface of that name. Underneath it all, however, the object is still a NextDayAir object.

Implementing COM Interfaces

In addition to the polymorphic behavior just described, you can also use the *Implements* statement to implement COM-based interfaces. Such interfaces are normally defined using the Interface Definition Language (IDL), as described in Chapter 2. By implementing specific, standard interfaces in a COM component that is built using Visual Basic, the component can plug into other applications that use those interfaces.

Web design-time controls are one good example of this type of component programming. The purpose of Web design-time controls is to help content developers author interactive HTML pages. Rather than having to manually code all the necessary HTML to include a Java applet, an ActiveX control, or some other advanced Web feature, a Web design-time control helps by generating HTML code. Basically, a Web design-time control is like a wizard or Visual Basic add-in. Wizards and add-ins, however, are generally tied to the development environment for which they were developed. For example, a developer can't use a Visual Basic add-in in Microsoft Visual C++. To make such utilities more flexible and reusable, Microsoft realized that it would be a good idea to define a new category of component. Thus were born Web design-time controls.

Technically speaking, a Web design-time control is a standard ActiveX control that also supports the *IActiveDesigner* interface. Since the standard ActiveX control you can build in Visual Basic doesn't support this interface, you might think that Web design-time controls can't be built in Visual Basic. Using the *Implements* keyword, however, it is possible to implement the *IActiveDesigner* interface in an ActiveX control written with Visual Basic and to have this manage the plug-and-play feature with any software that uses the *IActiveDesigner* interface.

To illustrate the concepts involved, let's use Visual Basic to implement this custom interface:

```
[
  uuid(2458D8A1-77B6-11d0-8F54-0001C80F4341),
  helpstring("Test interface built in IDL"),
  lcid(0x0409),
  version(1.0)
]
library TestIDL
{
    [object, uuid(2458D8A2-77B6-11d0-8F54-0001C80F4341),
        pointer_default(unique)]
    interface IDooHickey : IUnknown
    {
    HRESULT Greet(BSTR *Message);
    HRESULT Sum(long X, long Y, [out, retval]long *sum);
    };
};
```

Exercise 3-4

1. Create a file named TESTIDL.IDL, and enter the preceding sample IDL code.

2. Using the Microsoft IDL compiler, build a type library. A command line such as *MIDL TESTIDL.IDL* should do the trick. You might also need to set the *include* environment variable to point to the include directory of your development environment, as follows:

    ```
    set include=%include%;c:\msdev\include;
    ```

    If you do not have the Microsoft IDL compiler, a compiled version of the type library named TESTIDL.TLB is available in the \BK-SAMP\EXER3-4\Chap03 folder of the companion disc to this book.

    Now that we have defined the interface, let's implement it in a Visual Basic component.

3. Open Visual Basic, and create a new ActiveX DLL project.

4. Choose References from the Project menu, and then click the Browse button.

5. Go to the folder containing the type library that you compiled in step 2, and select the TESTIDL.TLB file.

6. Click Open, and then click OK.

7. Set the *Name* property of the class to *VBDooHickey*.

8. In the Code window, type *Implements IDooHickey* and press Enter.

9. From the Object box, select IDooHickey.

10. Write the following code (shown in bold), changing the function to a *Public* function:

```
Public Sub IDooHickey_Greet(Message As String)
    MsgBox Message, , "Hello from Visual Basic"
End Sub
```

11. Select Sum in the Procedure box.

12. Write the following code (shown in bold), changing the function from *Private* to *Public*:

```
Public Function IDooHickey_Sum(ByVal X As Long, ByVal _
    Y As Long) As Long
    IDooHickey_Sum = X + Y
End Function
```

13. Choose Project1 Properties from the Project menu.

14. In the Project Name box of the General tab, type *VBImplementation*.

15. In the Project Description box, type *DooHickey Component In Visual Basic*.

16. Click OK.

17. Choose Save Project from the File menu, and accept the default names for the class and the project.

18. Choose Make VBImplementation.dll from the File menu, and then choose OK.

    Now that we have implemented the IDooHickey interface in a Visual Basic component, let's create a project to test it.

19. Choose New Project from the File menu.

20. Click Yes when you are asked whether you want to save the VBImplementation project.

21. Select Standard EXE, and click OK.

22. Choose References from the Project menu.

23. Locate and check the DooHickey Component In Visual Basic entry.

24. Choose OK.

25. Choose Code from the View menu.

26. In the Object box, select the Form object; in the Procedure box, select the *Click* event.

27. Write the following code (shown in bold):

```
Private Sub Form_Click()
    Dim MyDooHickey As New VBDooHickey
    MyDooHickey.IDooHickey_Greet "Hey there"
    Print "3 + 4 = "; MyDooHickey.IDooHickey_Sum(3, 4)
End Sub
```

28. Choose Start from the Run menu.

29. Click on the form to test the code.

THE *FRIEND* KEYWORD

The *Friend* keyword is another object-oriented idea that Visual Basic has borrowed from other languages. Both C++ and Java support the *Friend* concept, although Visual Basic's version is closer to Java's version than to the C++ version. *Friend* allows other routines in a project to get access to the friendly function. Technically, *Friend* modifies the definition of a procedure in a class module, to enable the procedure to be called from modules that are outside the class but that are part of the project within which the class is defined. Let's say you create a class module that has a public interface and a private implementation. When your class is used by another application by means of COM interfaces, you want the object's clients to have access to only the public interface. However, you might decide that when your object is used from within another routine in the same project, it would be acceptable for the client to have access to some particular method that is declared as *Private*. In those cases, you can make that method a *Friend*, enabling the friendly functionality just described.

> **NOTE** You can use the *Friend* designation for *Sub* or *Function* methods, but never for data members such as variables. Also, a *Friend* procedure can't be late-bound.

Exercise 3-5
The following sample shows the correct usage of the *Friend* keyword:

1. Open Visual Basic, and create a new Standard EXE project.

2. Choose Add Class Module from the Project menu.

3. Select Class Module, and click Open.

4. Add the following code in the Code window:

```
Option Explicit

Private Function Sum(X As Integer, Y As Integer)
    Sum = X + Y
End Function
```

5. In the Properties window, set the *Name* property to *Math*.

6. In the Project Explorer, double-click Form1.

7. In the properties window for Form1, set the *AutoRedraw* property to *True*.

8. Place in the form a command button with the default name Command1.

9. Double-click on the Command1 command button to open the Code window.

10. Write the following code (shown in bold):

```
Private Sub Command1_Click()
    Dim X As New Math
    Print X.Sum(5, 6)
End Sub
```

11. Run the application.

If you run the sample at this stage, you will get an error telling you that the Sum method doesn't exist. This is because we have made the Sum method private to the Math class module. To correct this, in the Sum Function procedure replace *Private* with *Friend* as follows (shown in bold):

```
Friend Function Sum(X As Integer, Y As Integer)
    Sum = X + Y
End Function
```

Now test the code. Everything should work properly, since the Sum method is now friendly to all other code in the project. However, if you decide later to expose the Math object by means of COM interfaces, a client of the Math object won't be able to call the Sum method. This is because *Friend* procedures do not appear in the type library of their class.

In this chapter, you have learned about the object-oriented programming features of Visual Basic. When applied with care, these features should enable you to develop better designs that are built with cleaner and more reusable code. In the upcoming chapters, we will use these object-oriented techniques to build complex COM components, ActiveX controls, and Active Documents.

Chapter 4

Internet Backgrounder

The Internet, from its relatively humble beginnings in the mid-1970s, has come to serve more than 65 million users worldwide. Currently, about 12 percent of the U.S. population use the Internet, according to some estimates. An early predecessor to the Internet got its start when the Advanced Research Projects Agency (ARPA), a branch of the Defense Department, was awarded its first contract for technology that linked computers. This first network, ARPANET, based its computer-to-computer links on the revolutionary concept of packet switching— a technology devised for, but never used by, the U.S. military. ARPANET functioned for many years as an experimental network to test concepts and technologies in networking. The connected Internet actually began around 1980, when ARPA started converting machines attached through its research networks to the new TCP/IP (Transmission Control Protocol/Internet Protocol) collection of transmission protocols. What we call TCP/IP today isn't limited to these two protocols; instead, the name TCP/IP is used to refer to the entire suite of protocols used on the Internet.

ARPA then encouraged university researchers to adopt the new protocols. Since most university computer science departments at that time were running UNIX, ARPA funded development of its TCP/IP protocols for UNIX. This effort was successful partly because many departments were just then acquiring second or third computers and wanted to connect them together. The departments needed a communication protocol, and nothing besides TCP/IP was generally available. Over time, ARPA's TCP/IP protocols were used to connect computers locally within most university computer science departments. This is hard to believe today because we have come to associate the TCP/IP protocols with worldwide interconnection.

The most popular version of UNIX at the time was the University of California's Berkeley Software Distribution (commonly referred to as BSD UNIX). BSD UNIX became popular in part because it offered services above and beyond the basic TCP/IP protocols. Berkeley provided utilities such as remote file copying and a network-programming interface known as *sockets*. The sockets interface was important because it allowed programmers to relatively easily write software that communicated using TCP/IP protocols, thus encouraging experimentation.

The early success of the Internet based on TCP/IP technology interested other groups. The National Science Foundation took an active role in expanding the TCP/IP Internet to reach as many scientists as possible. Beginning in 1985, the National Science Foundation expanded its efforts to establish networks to connect its supercomputer centers. Later it provided funding to launch many regional networks for connecting scientific research institutions. All these connected networks use the TCP/IP protocols, and all are now part of the Internet. After all, the Internet isn't a new kind of physical network. Instead, it is a global network of interconnections, based on the TCP/IP protocol suite. In fact, the Internet is the ultimate virtual structure—imagined by its designers and implemented entirely in software.

As the popularity of the Internet has increased, so has its size. Most of the early users of the Internet were sophisticated and willing to invest energy in adopting new services as they became available. For increasing numbers of users, electronic mail (e-mail) and file transfer supplanted other forms of communications. The incredible potential of the Internet for sharing and distributing information became apparent as more and more people started using it. The National Science Foundation, which had almost completely funded the Internet in the United States until 1991, lifted its ban of commercial traffic on the Internet and dropped most of its funding. This gave the Internet more widespread exposure and opened the door to many commercial ventures.

Nowadays, corporations and telecommunication giants are busily reinventing themselves to profit from the Internet. New companies with Internet as their middle name attract investors in droves, contributing to the boom in technology stocks on Wall Street. New corporate alliances are being formed to develop standards and security mechanisms that will take the Internet to new heights. Consider, for instance, the capability to receive real-time voice and video so that you can see the person you're talking to, or the capability to order a pizza or to watch a movie using the Internet. The possibilities are limitless. Your ability to leverage the benefits of the Internet for your company or personal use will become increasingly valuable as more and more people across the world are exposed to the Internet.

TCP/IP

Communication networks can generally be divided into two basic types: *circuit-switched* and *packet-switched*. A circuit-switched network operates by providing a dedicated connection (circuit) between two points. The telephone system operates in this way. When you place a phone call, the call is connected directly through the phone company's local switching office, across trunk lines, to a remote switching office, and finally to the phone you are calling. Once established, that connection is reserved solely for your use.

Packet-switching networks are usually used to connect computers. These types of networks divide data traffic into little chunks called packets (sometimes called datagrams) that are multiplexed onto intermachine connections. The chief advantage of packet-switched networks is that a single connection can be used for multiple concurrent communications. The disadvantage, of course, is that as the network activity increases, each individual pair of communicating computers receives less of the network bandwidth.

The IP part of TCP/IP was designed as an intelligent router whose sole purpose is to move packets to and from other connections. The IP router looks at the destination address and decides where to send the packet for the fastest arrival at its destination. This means that when two computers are communicating over the Internet (say a World Wide Web browser is requesting a particular page from a server), the packets sent from the Web server to the browsing computer might not travel directly from server to client. This is because most often there is no direct connection between two arbitrary computers on the Internet.

For example, a typical user gains access to the Internet through a dial-up Internet Service Provider such as the Microsoft Network (MSN). The user then browses a particular Web site, such as *www.ibm.com*. In this case, there is no direct connection between the user's computer and IBM's server. Instead, data is routed by any available path (possibly including intermediary machines) from IBM's server to Microsoft's server and finally to the user's computer.

The ability to determine the path of least resistance is what makes IP extremely efficient and reliable. As in most distributed environments, one must assume that at a given time a large number of network resources can be offline; consequently, software must be written in such a way that it won't assume that certain resources will be available. The network must be able to adapt to the possibility of numerous gateways being shut down by sending data in some alternate manner.

IP Addresses

The TCP/IP routing is based on an address that is set up for each site. This address is called its *Internet address* or *IP address*. Each computer is assigned a unique 32-bit IP address that is used in all communication with that computer. An IP address consists of four 8-bit numbers (for a total of 32 bits) from 0 through 255, separated by dots. A 32-bit IP addressing scheme theoretically yields more than 4 billion (2^{32}) unique addresses. Unfortunately, the designers of TCP/IP weren't too generous with their use of these addresses. They defined three basic classes of networks that are part of the Internet: large (class A) networks, medium-size (class B) networks, and small (class C) networks. This was done by using the different 8-bit sections of an IP address to differentiate between the various classes.

Class A networks have the first 8 bits of their IP address preassigned by the Internet Network Information Center (InterNIC). Because only 8 bits have been defined, 24 bits remain to be set by the company's internal network administrators. This means that companies with class A addresses can have more than 16 million (2^{24}) hosts connected to the Internet. The leftmost 8 bits defined by the InterNIC have values from 0 through 126, allowing for 127 class A networks on the Internet. Companies such as IBM and Hewlett-Packard have class A addresses, and unfortunately all class A addresses have already been handed out.

Class B networks, intended for use by medium-size companies, have the leftmost 16 bits preassigned by the InterNIC, leaving 16 bits for local use. Class B addresses start with values of 128 through 191 in the first byte, and a value of 0 through 255 in the second. There are 16,384 possible class B networks, each of which can have up to 65,536 (2^{16}) hosts. All the class B addresses are already gone, too.

Class C networks have the leftmost 24 bits preassigned by the InterNIC, which leaves them only 8 bits for 256 (2^{8}) possible hosts. This is really quite limiting; even a small company might have more than two hundred computers that need to connect to the Internet. Class C addresses have values from 192 through 223 in the first byte. The second and third bytes of the IP address can be from 0 through 255, which means that there are potentially more than two million class C networks possible. Class C addresses are still available for the time being.

An IP address can also have a user-friendly name. For example, while the IP address of Microsoft's Web server is 207.68.137.60, its name is *www.microsoft.com*. IP addresses and domain names (such as *microsoft.com*) are currently issued by the InterNIC, through which, for a nominal fee, you can apply to register a domain name.

While domain names are certainly user-friendly, they are not very useful for Internet software, which can access computers only by means of IP addresses. Therefore, before any communication can take place, domain names must be converted to IP addresses. There are two primary methods for resolving names into numerical addresses. The older method, still in use, involves listing each name with its associated IP address in a text file called HOSTS. In Microsoft Windows 95 and Microsoft Windows 98, this file lives in the Windows folder; in Microsoft Windows NT, it is in the Winnt40\System32\Drivers\Etc folder. The format of the file is very simple: on each line, an IP address is specified and is followed by at least one space and its friendly name. For example, you might add the following entry to your HOSTS file:

```
207.68.137.60        microsoft.com
```

The other, more advanced, method for resolving names involves the Domain Name System (DNS). DNS is a distributed database, meaning that copies of the database exist on multiple computers on the Internet. DSN contains IP addresses for all registered Internet hosts (all computers connected to the Internet). DNS is what enables you to type *www.microsoft.com* into a Web browser and have the browser locate Microsoft's Web site automatically.

Ports

An IP address identifies a host computer on the Internet, but how do we know what process we want to communicate with on that computer? After all, most computers, especially servers, have many processes running concurrently; we need to have a way to specify exactly which application we want to interact with. To identify a particular process, a port number in addition to the IP address is normally required. Only with these two pieces of information is communication possible.

Standard port numbers have been defined for some common Internet applications. For example, all Web servers are written to use port 80 for communication. This is what makes it possible for Web browsers such as Microsoft Internet Explorer to jump among Web sites in an instant. Wherever the user points it, Internet Explorer always asks for port 80. Whatever answers must be a Web server. There are quite a few reserved ports for standard Internet applications. The following table lists a number of the more popular Internet applications and the ports they use.

Internet Application	Port Number(s) Used
HTTP (WWW)	80
FTP	20 and 21
Gopher	70
SMTP (e-mail)	25
POP3 (e-mail)	110
Telnet	23
Finger	79

Sockets

A *socket* is a network endpoint that is the combination of an IP address and a port number. The word socket is used as a metaphor because the information contained in a socket can be plugged directly into the requested process on the target computer on the Internet. A socket can be created to identify an application running anywhere on the Internet.

Berkeley Sockets (sometimes called BSD Sockets) is the name of a network programming interface widely used in the world of UNIX programming for TCP/IP communications. The BSD Sockets API has also been ported to Windows under the name Windows Sockets, abbreviated as WinSock. Windows 95, Windows 98, and Windows NT now include Microsoft's implementation of WinSock, WinSock.DLL, which contains 44 functions. Sockets represent the lowest level on which it is possible to do Internet programming in Windows-based applications. Perhaps predictably, sockets programming is quite complex.

Protocol Stacks and the OSI Model

In the early 1980s, the International Organization for Standardization (ISO) was engaged in developing a conceptual framework for the design and implementation of computer networks. As a result of this effort, the Open Systems Interconnection (OSI) reference model became a standard explanatory device for network operations. The OSI model describes a stack of seven discrete layers. At the top is your application, at the bottom is the network hardware, and everything in between supports the top and bottom layers. Think of data originating in an application on one computer moving down the layers to the hardware, across the network, and then up the layers on the destination computer. Figure 4-1 illustrates the OSI seven-layer model.

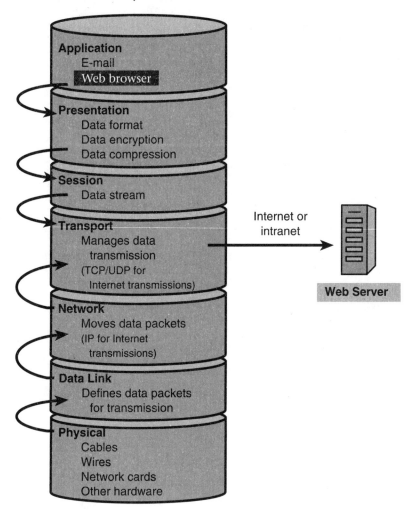

Figure 4-1. *The seven-layer OSI model.*

From top to bottom, these layers are called application, presentation, session, transport, network, data link, and physical. Each layer performs functions to move the data forward in the stack, and each has its own interface to adjacent layers. The idea is to allow different software vendors to provide interchangeable modules that perform the functions of a particular layer without affecting the data flow within the stack.

The application layer is where your application resides. Electronic mail applications, Web browsers, and similar programs all receive data on top of the presentation layer.

The presentation layer determines the format of the data to be transmitted. Data encryption and compression are also handled at this layer.

The session layer provides a data stream to a user during the session. This is the same approach as that normally employed on a Local Area Network (LAN) to ensure that no two users attempt to access the same session at exactly the same time.

The transport layer is concerned with managing data transmission. On the Internet, TCP or User Datagram Protocol (UDP) accomplishes data transmission.

The network layer moves packets of data from point to point. This is handled on the Internet by the IP.

The data link layer defines packets of data for transmission by the physical layer.

At the physical layer are the cables, wires, network cards, and other hardware that actually connect computers together.

While TCP/IP isn't an OSI protocol, it bears some relation to the seven-layer model. Most accepted descriptions of the TCP/IP model include four layers: application, host-to-host, Internet, and network access. At each layer, a special header is tacked onto each packet as it passes down the stack. When data travels up the stack at the receiving application, the header information is stripped off at each layer.

At the bottom of the TCP/IP model is the network access layer. Its job includes mapping IP addresses to physical network addresses and encapsulating IP datagrams (packets) into data that the local network understands.

The Internet layer sits on top of the network access layer and is really the driving engine of TCP/IP. At this level, IP provides the structure for the delivery of data from point to point. IP is connectionless, meaning that no handshaking, acknowledgment, or error handling takes place here—these are taken care of by other protocols, such as TCP.

Above the IP layer is the host-to-host transport layer, which contains the TCP and UDP protocols.

The application layer of the TCP/IP model performs all the functions of the application, presentation, and session layers of the OSI seven-layer model.

User Datagram Protocol

In the TCP/IP protocol suite, UDP is the primary mechanism used to send datagrams to other applications. UDP uses the underlying IP to transport a message from one machine to another. The UDP model provides unreliable, connectionless datagram delivery. This means that UDP messages can be lost, duplicated, delayed, or arrive out of the order in which they were sent. Packets might also arrive faster than the recipient is able to process them. Having packets arrive in the wrong order isn't as uncommon as it might sound, if you remember that IP might route datagrams from the same sender along different routes. Some of the packets might arrive by way of Israel, while the rest make stops in Hong Kong or Australia.

Any application that uses UDP implicitly accepts full responsibility for the potential problems associated with the protocol. This doesn't mean that you should not use UDP. In fact, the main advantage of UDP is its speed. Because it doesn't do any error handling, UDP is significantly faster than TCP. For some types of applications, UDP is inherently the better protocol to use. For example, when you connect to a timeserver on port 37, you receive a string containing the time of day (GMT) over and over. If a particular packet is lost, it doesn't make any difference; your application will get the next one.

Transmission Control Protocol

At the lowest TCP/IP model level—the network access layer—computer networks provide unreliable packet delivery. Packets can be lost or damaged because of transmission errors, hardware failures, or network overload. Protocols such as UDP that route packets dynamically can deliver them out of order (after a substantial delay), deliver duplicates, or not deliver anything at all. At the highest model level—the application layer—applications often need to send large amounts of data from one computer to another. Here reliability and speed are both important. To meet the needs of applications, the TCP/IP protocol suite offers TCP, a reliable stream service.

TCP is a connection-based error-handling protocol. It ensures that data was sent and is received in the proper order. If the sender doesn't receive an acknowledgment message within a predetermined period of time after sending a packet, the sender automatically retransmits the packet. More difficult to detect and respond to are situations in which duplicate packets are received or packets are received out of the order in which they were originally sent. This is solved by assigning each packet a sequence number and requiring the receiver to check which sequence numbers it has received. Checksums can also be used to ensure that the data received is valid.

INTRANETS

In this book, *intranet* refers to any TCP/IP network that isn't connected to the Internet but that uses Internet communication standards and tools to provide information to users on the private network. For example, a company can set up Web servers that can be accessed only by its own employees in order to publish company newsletters, sales figures, and other corporate documents. Employees gain access to the information by using Web browsers. The advantage of intranets is that they allow corporations to reuse for in-house purposes existing technologies on which a wide range of useful software has already been built. The same technology used in your company's public Web site can by employed by the company's intranet.

Most people think, and we concur, that the intranet market will be at least as pervasive as the Internet in the years to come, and it will probably be much more profitable for developers and consultants. Chances are that much of the software you are likely to build with the knowledge you gain from this book will be targeted toward internal corporate intranets. Most of this book uses the term Internet to apply to both the Internet and intranets and excludes intranets only in those rare cases in which we are describing a connection to a public host available on the Internet. We'll explicitly point out these cases.

THE WORLD WIDE WEB

There is a perception in the industry that the World Wide Web is the Internet. Although the Internet has many other applications and uses, the Web has certainly captivated our imagination. Based on a very simple page metaphor, with hypertext and forward/backward buttons with which to navigate, the Web has brought the Internet to millions of computer users. Finding useful content on the Web requires effort, but learning to simply "surf the Net" is extremely intuitive. Libraries, cafés, schools, barbershops, home users, and (let's not forget) multinational corporations are all getting wired. The Web is like an interactive television that puts thousands of channels at your fingertips.

In early 1989, the European Laboratory for Particle Physics (CERN) proposed the Web as an easier way for scientists to exchange data over the Internet. Work proceeded methodically, and in the fall of 1990, the first text-only browsers were implemented, enabling CERN scientists to access hypertext files and information at CERN. Over the next several years, work at CERN proceeded on defining the hypertext language used to create Web documents and the protocol used to transfer these documents across the Internet. Outside of CERN, however, the Web didn't arouse much interest. Truth be told, the Web was boring—it was just a bunch of academic and scientific texts sitting on servers available for browsing. In early 1993, there were still only about 50 Web sites worldwide (not really much of a Web at all). Then a wonderful thing happened. Researchers at the National Center for Supercomputing Applications (NCSA) developed Mosaic, the first graphical Web browser. That's when interest in the Web truly began—first in a trickle but soon in a tidal wave of support for the Internet and the Web. In hindsight, it seems as if the Web sprang to life overnight.

Hypertext Transfer Protocol

The Hypertext Transfer Protocol (HTTP) is the primary protocol used to distribute information on the Web. HTTP is used to transmit Web documents and associated graphics files over the Internet to browsers. Like other Internet protocols, such as FTP (File Transfer Protocol) and Gopher, HTTP is a client/server protocol. This means that the browser (client) running on the user's machine sends a message requesting data to an HTTP server running on another computer on the Internet. The server responds to the request by sending data back to the client. At a conceptual level, HTTP servers behave much like anonymous FTP servers, delivering files as requested by browsers. HTTP servers offer additional features, however, such as the ability to deliver not only files but also data generated by other programs running on the server computer. HTTP servers also have the ability to take data from the browser and pass this information on to other programs on the server for further processing.

HTTP is a connectionless protocol like UDP. When a browser requests a Web document, the browser locates the server, connects, makes a request, gets a response, and disconnects. Because a connection to the server isn't maintained, no system resources are taken after the transaction is completed. This allows Web servers to service thousands of hits in a short period of time with low overhead. The drawback of a connectionless protocol like HTTP, however, is that every time a user requests additional information the browser must reestablish the connection, resulting in a delay. HTTP is also known as a stateless protocol, which means that the server stores no information about a client between transactions. Every time a browser requests data from the server, it is as if the browser and server are starting their relationship anew—even if they just exchanged data seconds earlier.

Uniform Resource Locators

A browser needs three types of information to retrieve a file from a server. The browser must know the address of the server, the directory in which the desired file is stored on that server, and the protocol to use when talking to the server. A Uniform Resource Locator (URL) specifies this information. Standard URLs follow the format *protocol://server_host:port/path_to_file*. Thus, *http://www.microsoft.com:80/default.html* is a URL for a site on the Web. The port number in this example is optional; if omitted, the port number defaults to 80 because this is the standard port number used by HTTP servers. The document requested can also be omitted, in which case the Web server sends the default file—normally a site's home page. Removing the optional information leaves us with a more typical URL of *http://www.microsoft.com*.

Hypertext Markup Language

Hypertext Markup Language (HTML) is the basic document format used on the Web. HTML, a subset of Standard Generalized Markup Language (SGML), is an ASCII-based document format (as opposed to a binary format) that is normally viewed using a Web browser such as Microsoft Internet Explorer. Besides text, an HTML document contains a description of the formatting to be used when displaying the document. In addition to text-formatting options, HTML contains many tags that provide numerous options for creating rich documents—documents containing graphics, multiple fonts, colors, hyperlinks, and tables. If you are familiar with Microsoft's Rich Text Format (RTF) specification, HTML will be somewhat familiar.

There are several ways to create HTML documents for use on the Web. The most basic is to use an ASCII text editor such as the Notepad utility that comes with Windows. You can exercise full control over an HTML document by using an ASCII text editor; however, this is a tedious, time-consuming way to develop HTML documents, and it requires you to be an expert user of HTML tags. Another method is to use a special application designed to help you create HTML documents. The best of these—such as Microsoft FrontPage—provide a WYSIWYG environment in which you see exactly what the end user will see in the Web browser. Finally, it is often desirable to convert existing documents in other formats to HTML for use on the Web. Web conversion utilities such as those included in Microsoft Word, Microsoft Excel, and Microsoft PowerPoint can automatically perform such conversions.

Regardless of how you intend to develop HTML documents, it is helpful to have a basic understanding of what HTML looks like at the ASCII level. The following is a sample HTML document:

```
<HTML>
<HEAD>
<TITLE>Web Page Name</TITLE>
</HEAD>
```

```
<BODY>
<B>This is a basic HTML document.</B>
<IMG SRC=MyPicture.GIF>
<A HREF="http://www.microsoft.com">Click to visit Microsoft</A>
</BODY>

</HTML>
```

The various commands enclosed by angle brackets are called tags. The Web browser doesn't display these tags; instead, they affect how the Web page text is formatted. For example, a <B> tag begins a section of text that will be displayed in a bold font, and the </B> tag signifies the end of that section. To include graphics in a Web page, you insert an image (<IMG>) tag that references the name of the graphic file to be downloaded from the server and displayed. To add hypertext links to a Web page, you use the anchor (<A>) tag. In the preceding sample HTML code, the text "Click to visit Microsoft" will be displayed in a browser with an underline, signifying that the user can click this link to jump to *http://www.microsoft.com*.

Cascading Style Sheets and Dynamic HTML

One of the original intents of HTML was to enable authors to separate content from presentation. Practically, however, this was not possible because HTML documents incorporated tags such as <B> and <FONT> to describe the appearance of content. Cascading Style Sheets (CSS) was defined as an addition to HTML to enable the definition of a document's appearance. Style sheets are an abstraction where the presentation of a document is defined separately and divorced from the actual content of the document.

Dynamic HTML is an object model supported by Internet Explorer 4 that can be used to control all aspects of a document displayed in the browser. Dynamic HTML builds on CSS so that the style and contents of any element on a Web page can be altered dynamically. The browser immediately renders any changes without server-side intervention, making Dynamic HTML and CSS an excellent combination on a low bandwidth, high latency network like the Internet. Note that Dynamic HTML is not a programming language; JavaScript, JScript, VBScript, C++, Java or any other programming language can be used to access the Dynamic HTML object model.

Scriptlets: Building COM Objects in HTML

Continuing in the grand tradition of making COM objects accessible to any language, Microsoft enables scripts that are embedded in an HTML file or in a Developer Studio macro to access COM objects. Even more amazing, however, is the capability to actually create COM objects in script code stored in an HTML file. COM objects defined in this way are called *scriptlets*. Thus, there are now three ways to package a COM object:

- Native code (.DLL and .EXE files)

- Java classes (.class files)

- Scriptlets (HTML files)

In some respects, scriptlets may be the most powerful of the three packaging techniques. Scriptlets enable developers to create COM objects using Dynamic HTML and a scripting language. If the HTML document contains user interface elements, it can be treated as an ActiveX control. Otherwise, you can simply work with it as a standard COM object. For example, the following scriptlet qualifies as a COM object:

```
<HTML>
<SCRIPT LANGUAGE="VBScript">
Function public_Sum(X, Y)
    public_Sum = X + Y
End Function
</SCRIPT>
</HTML>
```

While this scriptlet is written in VBScript, scriptlets do not have to be written in any particular language; any available ActiveX scripting engine will suffice. Also, scriptlet clients can be built in any development environment that supports COM. For example, a scriptlet could be used by another HTML page or from an applet written in Java. For demonstration purposes, let's build a client program in Visual Basic that will call the scriptlet shown above. Here are the steps to follow:

1. Open a new Standard EXE project in Visual Basic.

2. Choose Components from the Project menu. On the Controls tab of the Components dialog box, check the Microsoft Scriptlet Component (MSHTMLWB.DLL) option and choose OK.

   NOTE   The scriptlet component installs with Internet Explorer 4.

3. Place a scriptlet control on the form.

4. Set the control's *Visible* property to *False* and the *URL* property to the name of an HTML file containing the scriptlet shown in the preceding code.

5. In the Code window, enter the following code:

```
Private Sub Form_Click()
    MsgBox "Calling scriplet: 6 + 12 = " & _
        Scriptlet1.Sum(6, 12)
End Sub
```

6. Run the program, and test it by clicking on the form.

Common Gateway Interface

Many Web sites are pushing the envelope of what is possible to do within HTML. These sites attempt to create interactive pages—pages that not only advertise their company or person but also actually allow the user to do something. A great example of this type of interactive Web site of the future is E*Trade (*http://www.etrade.com*). E*Trade is an online brokerage firm that allows you to trade securities on line directly from its Web pages. Amazon.com (*http://www.amazon-.com*) and Barnes & Noble (*http://barnesandnoble.com*) are examples of online booksellers that use server-side technology. Expedia (*http://www.expedia.com*) is an online travel agent. These are but a few of the Web sites pushing the envelope of electronic commerce.

How do you create a Web page that collects data from the user and then goes off and trades stocks on the floor of the New York Stock Exchange? The Common Gateway Interface (CGI) is one way to implement this type of functionality. CGI is an interface between a Web server and other applications running on the server computer. CGI allows users to access data and functionality not specifically provided for within the realm of HTTP servers and HTML documents. The main job of CGI is to provide an interface for transferring data collected from the user to the desired application and then returning the output of that application to the Web server, which in turn presents it to the user. CGI applications, sometimes called scripts, are written in scripting languages that are similar to an MS-DOS batch file. In most UNIX implementations, CGI scripts are typically written in languages such as Perl or TCI. The applications called by a CGI script can be written in any programming language.

Virtual Reality Modeling Language

The Virtual Reality Modeling Language (VRML) is a text-based language for defining three-dimensional worlds for Web sites. As we said previously, the Web started as a simple way to view hypertext documents. Over time, many additional features have been added to the HTML language to enable multimedia features such as graphics and audio. For the most part, however, the Web has remained two-dimensional. The idea of VRML is to enhance Web sites with three-dimensional models through which users can navigate, creating a type of virtual reality. To enter virtual reality worlds (.WRL files) on the World Wide Web, you need a browser that supports VRML. Internet Explorer supports VRML by way of an add-in ActiveX control that can be downloaded free of charge from Microsoft's Web site.

Rather than defining an entirely new graphic modeling language, VRML is based on the Open Inventor ASCII file format developed by Silicon Graphics. Open Inventor in turn is based on the OpenGL (Graphics Language) language also developed by Silicon Graphics and supported by Microsoft in Windows NT. The advantage of using an established standard such as Open Inventor is that many tools already exist for creating virtual worlds in the necessary format for VRML.

For a sense of what a VRML world file looks like, see the following sample code. The code creates a three-dimensional model of the letters "vr", which you can "walk" around, above, or even through in a Web browser.

```
#VRML V1.0 ascii

Separator {
    Material { diffuseColor 0.78 0.43 0.22 }
    Scale { scaleFactor 4 4 4 }
    MatrixTransform      { matrix 1 0 1 1 .32 1 0 0 0 1 0 0 0 0 1 }
    Separator {
        Translation { translation .1 .21 0 }
        Separator {
            Rotation { rotation 0 0 -1 -.42 }
            DEF a Cylinder { radius .06 height .50 }
        }
        Translation { translation .21 .01 .1 }
        Separator {
            Rotation { rotation 0 0 -1 .4 }
            USE a
        }
    }

    Translation { translation .5 0 0 }
    Separator {
        Translation { translation .05 .2 0 }
        Cylinder { radius .06 height .5 }
```

```
        Translation { translation .15 .12 0 }
        Separator {
            Rotation { rotation 0 0 -1 1.62 }
            Cylinder { radius .06 height .26 }
        }
    }

Translation { translation .5 .1 0 }
}
```

OTHER INTERNET PROTOCOLS

The Internet has spawned many protocols based on TCP/IP. While many of these protocols have disappeared, some, such as HTTP, have flourished and become synonymous with the Internet. Several other protocols have maintained a minor presence on the Internet. It seems likely that HTTP will eventually replace most of them. Some protocols, such as Gopher and FTP, still persist because they have dedicated users.

The Gopher Protocol

Gopher is a protocol originally developed at the University of Minnesota in 1991. Minnesota is the Gopher state, hence the name of the protocol. Gopher was developed to standardize the search and retrieval of documents and files on the Internet. Originally, universities used Gopher to publish documents, making them globally available through the Internet. Using a Gopher client program, you can browse the hierarchical menus of files available through Gopher. Gopher lets you download files and associated utilities such as Veronica, which let you search for particular documents on all the Gopher servers available on the Internet. The collection of Gopher Internet servers and their files is called *Gopherspace*. The use of Gopher has been dwindling since it was eclipsed by the advent of the Web. Therefore, this book won't spend more time with Gopher.

Network News Transfer Protocol

Following e-mail and the Web, Usenet news is perhaps the third most popular service on the Internet. Recall that one of the original goals for the Internet in the scientific and academic communities was to enable researchers to share data with one another. Usenet news, which is sort of like a giant distributed bulletin board system, is a very popular way to enable this type of communication. Usenet is a network of news servers on the Internet that propagate messages posted to the discussion groups (called newsgroups). A huge number of newsgroups exist on the Internet, with topics ranging from knitting to vintage cars to the Internet itself. If you are familiar with bulletin board systems (BBSs), you have the basic idea of how Usenet appears to the user. Usenet is quite different architecturally from most standard BBS's, such as those available on CompuServe, America Online, or the Microsoft Network. Those types of BBS's are centralized, meaning that all messages posted to a particular discussion group are stored on the main computer run by the online network. Like most services on the Internet, Usenet news is dispersed on hundreds of thousands of computers throughout the world.

A Usenet message (called an article) is similar to an e-mail message. Unlike e-mail, however, which is directed at specific recipients, a news article can be read by anyone who has access to the Internet. When an article is posted to a newsgroup, that article is then propagated to all the machines on the Internet that have subscribed to that newsgroup. The Network News Transfer Protocol (NNTP) is the usual protocol for delivering and gaining access to Usenet news over the Internet. News servers use NNTP to bounce news from server to server, and news clients use it to read and post articles. Usenet software is generally easily available. Internet Explorer, for example, has a news reader add-on called Internet News.

Electronic Mail (SMTP, POP3)

While many TCP/IP-based networks are initially justified and funded based on a network's projected ability to help users share data, they often end up as electronic mail carriers. E-mail enables network users to send and receive correspondence and is one of the most widely used services on the Internet. The Simple Mail Transport Protocol (SMTP) and Post Office Protocol (POP3) are two popular protocols available on most e-mail servers on the Internet. E-mail clients are generally easy to acquire. Windows ships with an Internet e-mail client called Microsoft Outlook Express.

SMTP is the standard TCP/IP protocol for sending messages and transporting mail from one host to another. As the name suggests, SMTP was designed to be fairly simple. POP3 is the protocol by which e-mail messages are retrieved from an Internet server, enabling e-mail to be read from a remote system. This facility is useful when you prefer to read your mail on a computer that might not be connected to the Internet all the time. In this case, e-mail is collected by a server and then downloaded by POP3 to the computer when you want to read your e-mail.

File Transfer Protocol

The simplest way to access a file on another host across the Internet is to copy that file to a local machine. FTP is a standard for protocols designed to transfer files across the Internet. Prior to 1994, when the Web took over the Internet, FTP was one of the most widely used protocols on the Internet. Using an FTP client, one can connect to an FTP server, navigate through the available directories, and transfer files. To transfer files from an FTP server, the client must normally have an account with that server, giving specific rights to certain files and directories. In addition to such private FTP sites, thousands of public access FTP sites on the Internet allow anyone to connect and transfer files irrespective of whether they have an account with that server. This is called anonymous FTP. Windows 95, Windows 98, and Windows NT come with a client-side FTP utility (FTP.EXE) that can be used to exchange files with other computers on the Internet.

INTERNET EXPLORER COMPONENTS

Internet Explorer is more than a Web browser that displays static pages containing text and graphics—although, as you shall see, it does this very well. Beyond that, Internet Explorer is designed to be a great host to your future Web applications—applications that can explode with live, programmable content.

Microsoft Internet Explorer has a rather interesting architecture. The main executable of Internet Explorer 4 (IEXPLORE.EXE) is 64 KB. Of course, the entire Web browser isn't implemented in 64 KB; instead, IEXPLORE.EXE is a simple process that provides a message pump and a shell window (*IEFrame*) for the actual browser. Contained within the *IEFrame* window class is a *Shell DocObject View* window class, which is an Active document container. The *Shell DocObject View* window class is implemented in the *Shell DocObject* and Control Library (SHDOCVW.DLL). So IEXPLORE.EXE is, in fact, just a glorified Active Documents container.

So where is the Web browser? The real Web browsing takes place in the *HTML_Internet Explorer* window class, which is provided by an Active Documents server called MSHTML.DLL. MSHTML.DLL, which is a more reasonable 2.3 MB, is the HTML parsing and display code. MSHTML.DLL is an in-process COM object that implements the interfaces required of a great Active Document.

As a COM component, Microsoft Internet Explorer has an object model that is exposed to other applications. You can instantiate these objects and call their properties and methods. Specifically, Internet Explorer exposes an automation interface called *InternetExplorer* and an ActiveX control called the *WebBrowser*.

AUTOMATING INTERNET EXPLORER

A neat feature of Internet Explorer is the automation object model that it exposes. This object model is accessible to both inline VBScript code in an HTML document and to any other application that supports automation, including Microsoft Visual Basic and Microsoft Visual C++. For example, running the following code from a Visual Basic form launches Internet Explorer, connects to the Internet, and opens Microsoft's home page.

```
Private Sub Form_Click()
    Dim IE As Object
    Set IE = CreateObject("InternetExplorer.Application")
    IE.Navigate "http://www.microsoft.com"
    IE.Visible = True
End Sub
```

The *InternetExplorer.Application* object allows another program to create and control an instance of the Internet Explorer application.

Exercise 4-1

In this exercise, you build an application to launch Internet Explorer and then take its automation interface through its paces.

1. Open a new Standard EXE project in Visual Basic.

2. For the default form, set the *Caption* property to *To Internet Explorer* and the *BorderStyle* property to *3 – Fixed Dialog.*

3. Place these controls on the form: five command buttons, five check boxes, one label, and one text box. Set their properties as follows:

Object	*Property*	*Value*
Command1	*Caption*	Load
Command2	*Caption*	Navigate
Command3	*Caption*	Quit
Command4	*Caption*	Backward
Command5	*Caption*	Forward
Check1	*Caption*	Visible
Check2	*Caption*	FullScreen
Check3	*Caption*	MenuBar
	Value	*1 – Checked*

Object	Property	Value
Check4	*Caption*	ToolBar
	Value	*1 – Checked*
Check5	*Caption*	StatusBar
	Value	*1 – Checked*
Label1	*Caption*	StatusText
	AutoSize	*True*
Text1	*Text*	(Set the property to blank.)

4. The form layout should look like that shown in Figure 4-2.

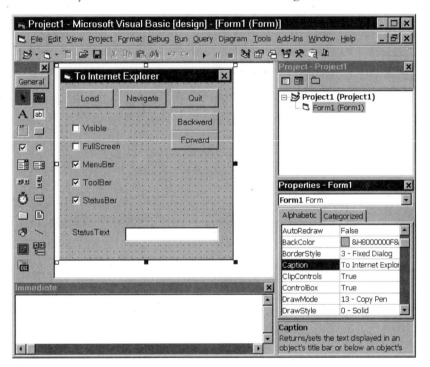

Figure 4-2. *The form layout for Exercise 4-1.*

5. Double-click the form to display the Code window, and add the code (shown in bold) on the following page.

```
Option Explicit
Dim IE As Object

Private Sub Check1_Click()
    On Error Resume Next
    IE.Visible = Check1.Value
End Sub

Private Sub Check2_Click()
    On Error Resume Next
    IE.FullScreen = Check2.Value
End Sub

Private Sub Check3_Click()
    On Error Resume Next
    IE.MenuBar = Check3.Value
End Sub

Private Sub Check4_Click()
    On Error Resume Next
    IE.ToolBar = Check4.Value
End Sub

Private Sub Check5_Click()
    On Error Resume Next
    IE.StatusBar = Check5.Value
End Sub

Private Sub Command1_Click()
    Set IE = CreateObject("InternetExplorer.Application")
End Sub

Private Sub Command2_Click()
    On Error Resume Next
    IE.Navigate InputBox("Where would you like to go?", _
    "Explore")
End Sub

Private Sub Command3_Click()
    On Error Resume Next
    IE.Quit
    End
End Sub

Private Sub Command4_Click()
    On Error Resume Next
    IE.GoBack
End Sub
```

```
Private Sub Command5_Click()
    On Error Resume Next
    IE.GoForward
End Sub

Private Sub Text1_Change()
    On Error Resume Next
    IE.StatusText = Text1.Text
End Sub
```

6. Run the program, and click on the Load button first. Then you can experiment with the other options to fully view the program. Enjoy!

In Exercise 4-1, you used late binding to automate Internet Explorer. To be able to trap any of the events fired by the *InternetExplorer* Automation object, you need to use early binding. This will allow you to use the *WithEvents* keyword in order to intercept the desired events. As we discussed previously, *WithEvents* enables an application to intercept events fired from objects. Chapter 3 discusses in detail *WithEvents* and the ability for objects to raise custom events.

Exercise 4-2

The following steps modify Exercise 4-1 so that the automation is done via early binding and events can be intercepted.

1. Choose References from the Project menu, and in the References dialog box check Microsoft Internet Controls (SHDOCVW.DLL). Choose OK.

2. Double-click the form to display the Code window. Comment the two lines of code as follows, and replace them with the early-bound versions shown in bold.

```
Option Explicit
' Dim IE As Object
Dim WithEvents IE As InternetExplorer

Private Sub Command1_Click()
    ' Set IE = CreateObject("InternetExplorer.Application")
    Set IE = New InternetExplorer
```

3. In the Code window, select *IE* from the Object box. In the Procedure box, notice that all the *InternetExplorer* events are listed. Implement the *BeforeNavigate2*, *DownloadBegin*, *DownloadComplete*, *NavigateComplete2*, and *OnQuit* events by entering the code (shown in bold) on the following page.

```
Private Sub IE_BeforeNavigate2(ByVal pDisp As Object, _
    URL As Variant, Flags As Variant, TargetFrameName As _
    Variant, PostData As Variant, Headers As Variant, _
    Cancel As Boolean)
    MsgBox "BeforeNavigate2: " + URL
End Sub

Private Sub IE_DownloadBegin()
    MsgBox "DownloadBegin"
End Sub

Private Sub IE_DownloadComplete()
    MsgBox "DownloadComplete"
End Sub

Private Sub IE_NavigateComplete2(ByVal pDisp As Object, _
    URL As String)
    MsgBox "NavigateComplete2: " + URL
End Sub

Private Sub IE_OnQuit()
    MsgBox "OnQuit"
    End
End Sub
```

4. Run and test the program. For each message box that appears, the
InternetExplorer object fires the corresponding event.

THE *WEBBROWSER* CONTROL

Using the Internet Explorer automation interface described in the preceding
section, you can build Visual Basic applications that launch and control the Web
browser. For instances where the desired user experience is from within the
context of the browser, the automation interface is ideal. For example, in applications in which the user selects a Web link from a Help menu item, it makes
sense to launch the browser as a separate window on the desktop.

Of course, there will be many times when you will want to give your application the features of a Web browser—for example, an application in which the
user will be moving seamlessly between local content and Web content. In these
situations, actually moving user focus from your application to another application (that is, a separate browser) can significantly affect the user experience.

Installed with Internet Explorer is an ActiveX control that provides everything you need to build browser functionality into your applications. Using the *WebBrowser* control provided by Internet Explorer, you can actually provide all the features of a browser in an embedded format—presented from within your application—in the context you want. Of course, if you take the route of using the *WebBrowser* control, you will need to completely build the user interface. The menu, toolbars, and status bar displayed in Internet Explorer are not part of the *WebBrowser* control. This section demonstrates the use of the ActiveX *WebBrowser* control included with Internet Explorer and illustrates the basics of programming the control and handling event notifications.

The *WebBrowser* control supports a subset of the properties, methods, and events supported by the *InternetExplorer* automation object. Specifically, the *WebBrowser* control doesn't support the *FullName*, *FullScreen*, *HWND*, *Menu-Bar*, *Name*, *Path*, *StatusBar*, *StatusText*, and *ToolBar* properties; the *ClientTo-Window*, *GetProperty*, and *PutProperty* methods; and the *PropertyChange* and *OnQuit* events.

One feature notably missing from the current version of the *WebBrowser* control is printing support; no print method is provided. As a workaround to this limitation, you can use the Visual Basic *SendKeys* statement to send the Ctrl-P key sequence to the *WebBrowser* control, as follows:

```
WebBrowser1.SetFocus
SendKeys "^p"
```

Exercise 4-3

In this exercise, you will build a Visual Basic application that contains an integrated Web browser.

1. Open a new Standard EXE project in Visual Basic.

2. Set the *Caption* property of the default form to *Web Browser*.

3. Choose Components from the Project menu, and on the Controls tab of the Components dialog box check Microsoft Internet Controls (SHDOCVW.DLL). Choose OK.

4. Place a *WebBrowser* control on the form, and set its *Visible* property to *False*.

5. Place one label control and one text box control on the form. Set the *Caption* property of the label control to *URL,* and set *AutoSize* to *True*. Set the *Text* property of the text control to blank.

6. Choose Menu Editor on the Tools menu to add a menu to the form. (You might need to click the background of the form to view the Menu Editor dialog box.) The menu should have the following items:

Caption	Name
File	mnuFile
Refresh	mnuFileRefresh
Stop	mnuFileStop
Print	mnuFilePrint
Go	mnuGo
Back	mnuGoBack
Forward	mnuGoForward
Home	mnuGoHome
Search	mnuGoSearch

7. The form layout should look like the one in Figure 4-3.

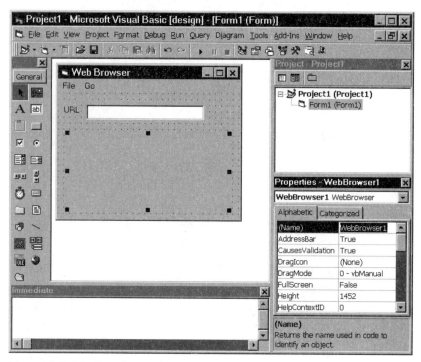

Figure 4-3. *The form layout for Exercise 4-3.*

8. Write the following code (shown in bold):

```
Private Sub mnuGoBack_Click()
    On Error Resume Next
    WebBrowser1.GoBack
End Sub

Private Sub mnuGoForward_Click()
    On Error Resume Next
    WebBrowser1.GoForward
End Sub

Private Sub mnuGoHome_Click()
    WebBrowser1.GoHome
End Sub

Private Sub mnuGoSearch_Click()
    WebBrowser1.GoSearch
End Sub

Private Sub mnuFileRefresh_Click()
    On Error Resume Next
    WebBrowser1.Refresh
End Sub

Private Sub mnuFileStop_Click()
    WebBrowser1.Stop
End Sub

Private Sub mnuFilePrint_Click()
    On Error Resume Next
    WebBrowser1.SetFocus
    SendKeys "^p"
End Sub

Private Sub Form_Resize()
    WebBrowser1.Top = Text1.Top + Text1.Height
    WebBrowser1.Left = 0
    If ScaleHeight - WebBrowser1.Top > 0 Then
        WebBrowser1.Height = ScaleHeight - _
            WebBrowser1.Top
    End If
    WebBrowser1.Width = ScaleWidth
End Sub
```

(continued)

```
Private Sub Text1_KeyPress(KeyAscii As Integer)
    On Error Resume Next
    If KeyAscii = 13 Then
        KeyAscii = 0
        WebBrowser1.Navigate (Text1)
    End If
End Sub

Private Sub WebBrowser1_BeforeNavigate2(ByVal pDisp As _
    Object, URL As Variant, Flags As Variant, _
    TargetFrameName As Variant, PostData As Variant, _
    Headers As Variant, Cancel As Boolean)
    WebBrowser1.Visible = True
    Text1.Text = URL
End Sub
```

9. Run the program, and go to your favorite Web site. Figure 4-4 shows the Web browser displaying a sample site. Try the various menu items to see the effect they have.

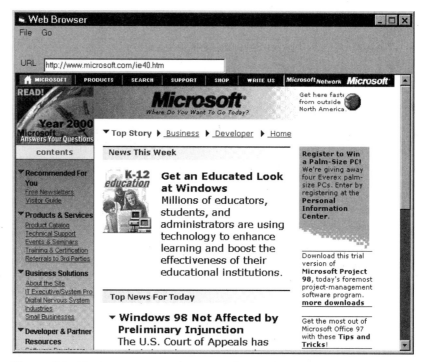

Figure 4-4. *The browser created in Exercise 4-3 displaying the Microsoft Web site.*

Congratulations; you have built a custom Web browser.

Part II

Building Components in Visual Basic

Chapter 5

COM Programming in Visual Basic

The term *component* is used to describe a self-contained block of software providing a particular service. Components can be used by other software or combined to form new applications. Reusing existing code in these ways is called *component software development*, one of the latest buzzwords to infect the software world. The hope in reusing standard, tested, and verified components is that middle managers with little or no technical knowledge will miraculously regain control of their runaway software development projects, and software that actually works and costs less will reign over all.

As we discussed in Part I of this book, a component is a unit of executable code, such as an .EXE, .DLL, or .OCX[1] file, that complies with the COM specification. COM lets you assemble reusable software components into applications. You can buy components that provide generic services (such as numerical analysis) or user interface elements (such as grid controls); or you can create your own components to encapsulate your company's business rules. Components can run on the client or server side of a client/server system, or on any tier of a multi-tier system.

Be careful not to confuse COM-based programming with object-oriented programming. Object-oriented programming is a way of thinking about and designing code in an object-oriented manner, as discussed in Chapter 3. By using object-oriented programming, you can develop object-based software components

---

1. Microsoft ActiveX controls are saved with the .OCX extension but are really DLLs.

such as a spelling checker component. With COM, you can combine existing components regardless of the language with which they were developed. In other words, object-oriented programming is concerned with creating objects; COM is concerned with making objects work together.

To make this distinction specific, imagine that a developer uses an object-oriented development tool such as Microsoft Visual C++ to create some classes. Another C++ developer might later inherit functionality from these basic classes, enhancing them to suit his or her needs. The Microsoft Foundation Class (MFC) library works like this. Microsoft has created a library of classes in C++ that handle the many rudiments of Microsoft Windows programming. Developers using Visual C++ can now inherit functionality from MFC, making it easier to create custom Windows applications. The drawback is that the MFC classes can be used from C++ only. However, if classes are packaged as a COM-based component, they can be used and further extended in any programming environment supporting COM. For example, it is possible to use and extend code written in C++ from Microsoft Visual Basic, as long as the code has been written in accordance with the COM specification.

COMPONENTS

If you're still a little unsure what exactly a component is, perhaps it will help if we let you in on a little secret: a component is simply the new name for what used to be called an OLE server. This terminology change was brought about by the confusion caused by programs that were both OLE clients and OLE servers. Consider, for example, a case in which application A needs to use the services of application B by means of COM. Here we have a clearly distinguishable client and server. What if server B, in order to service the original request of the client, goes on to call application C? Server B is now both a server to application A and a client to application C, as shown in Figure 5-1. This scenario could conceivably be repeated down the line, blurring the distinction between clients and servers even further. Calling all of these servers "components" brings their connection into focus. Now the example is clearer. Application A uses component B, which in turn calls component C.

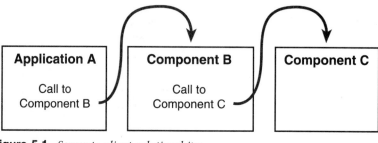

Figure 5-1. *Server-to-client relationships.*

COMPONENTS IN VISUAL BASIC

What types of applications can you create using components? Visual Basic supports three types of components: ActiveX controls, ActiveX Documents, and standard UI-less code components. When you first start Microsoft Visual Basic, it displays a dialog box offering the types of projects you can create in Visual Basic. These are Standard EXE, ActiveX EXE, ActiveX DLL, ActiveX Control, VB Application Wizard, Data Project, IIS Application, Addin, ActiveX Document DLL, ActiveX Document EXE, and DHTML Application. Five of these project types create COM components: ActiveX EXE, ActiveX DLL, ActiveX Control, ActiveX Document DLL, and ActiveX Document EXE.

As you recall from Chapter 2, a COM component contains classes and can be built as either a .DLL file or an .EXE file. In Visual Basic, the ActiveX EXE and ActiveX Document EXE projects correspond to COM EXE components; and the ActiveX DLL, Active Document DLL, and ActiveX Control projects correspond to COM DLL components.

In this chapter, we will concentrate on the Standard EXE, ActiveX EXE, and ActiveX DLL project types. Later chapters will focus on ActiveX Control and ActiveX Document projects.

We'll look at the Standard EXE project type because it is the obvious choice for the typical stand-alone application. This was the only project type available prior to Visual Basic 5. A Standard EXE doesn't expose components for use by other applications because all classes are private to the application; therefore, Standard EXE projects are not COM components. Internally, however, you can still use any object-oriented feature of Visual Basic. This includes implementing an object-oriented design by dividing your project into class modules and using the polymorphic features of the *Implements* keyword, as well as inserting ActiveX controls. In fact, many of the exercises in this and upcoming chapters use the Standard EXE project type and simply insert other modules as necessary. You will find that it is often easier to work initially with a Standard EXE project and then to use the subprojects features of Visual Basic, which allow multiple projects to be open simultaneously.

Code Components

Standard code components with no user interface are libraries of classes that can be used by any application. A client application uses a class in a code component by creating a new instance of the class and then calling its properties and methods. A code component might be used to provide a particular service to your company applications.

For example, you might package in a code component the code that dials in and communicates with an application on the company mainframe. This code component could then be shared by all applications needing this service, ensuring that all applications process data from the mainframe consistently. In addition, every time the mainframe group modified the communication protocol (mainframe people are known for this), only that code component would need to be updated. Then all applications relying on the component would work once again.

By dividing a project into components, you can enable small teams of programmers to work on individual components that can then be assembled into the final application. Each group needs to fully understand and code only one component. The user interface is simply a front end that uses the various components, tying the software together. For project managers, this divide-and-conquer approach has obvious benefits: reusability and a better component-based design result, right? Wrong!

Visual Basic code components come in two flavors: ActiveX EXE and ActiveX DLL. An ActiveX EXE[2] can run in one of three ways: as a stand-alone application, as a local component (sometimes called an out-of-process component), or as a remote component. Local components run on the same computer as the client, but instead of being run in-process, local components are loaded in their own private process address space. This approach requires that all communication between the client and the component go through certain COM interfaces so that data can be exchanged. Consequently, ActiveX EXE projects are somewhat slower as code components than ActiveX DLLs. The advantage of an ActiveX EXE is that in addition to being a COM code component, it can also be a regular stand-alone program. Applications such as Microsoft Word fit this bill. Word can either be used as a straightforward word processor to write a letter, or it can be used as a component by another application. A custom application might send some data to Word for formatting and then instruct Word to print a report, for example.

THE BASIS FOR ASSIGNING COMPONENTS

The managers who define project components often base them on user requests for specific output data. Most often, every screen output becomes a component, and later several groups of programmers find themselves rebuilding from scratch similar routines for seemingly separate "components." To address this problem, software developers need to assign components based on programming objectives after defining user information needs.

---

2. The new name for an ActiveX EXE is a COM EXE.

An ActiveX DLL[3] runs as an in-process code component. This means that it is always loaded into its caller's process address space. For this reason, access to in-process components is very fast. An ActiveX DLL component effectively becomes part of the calling program at run time, even though different developers using different programming languages might have written the calling application and the DLL code component.

A remote code component is an ActiveX EXE running on a remote computer connected by means of a network, possibly over the Internet. ActiveX DLLs can also be run remotely by running them in the system-supplied surrogate process (DLLHOST.EXE) on the remote machine. Remote code components enable you to develop distributed applications in Visual Basic. Distributed applications work by dividing the bulk of processing into smaller segments and then sending those segments to different computers for processing. In this manner, several computers are working on one problem at the same time, enabling a well-designed system (and herein lies the rub) to complete the processing much more quickly.

When you are developing a distributed application from remote code components, keep in mind the overhead associated with network communication. For example, calling a method in a remote object to add the numbers 5 and 3 would certainly not result in an overall performance improvement of the application. In fact, just the opposite would occur since the overhead of calling a remote object would far outweigh the advantage of having two numbers summed by a remote processor. To make remote execution worthwhile, the work processed must be complicated and lengthy enough to outweigh the network overhead inherent in remote access.

Visual Basic provides two ways to access remote code components: remote automation and Distributed COM (DCOM). Remote automation was first introduced with Visual Basic 4, but now is retained only for compatibility with 16-bit components. For new development, DCOM is the recommended way to access remote code components.

Standard modules and class modules

Code components in Visual Basic always consist of one or more class modules. The class module (.CLS file) is the Visual Basic module type that allows you to define a class, enabling object-oriented programming. A class module differs from a standard module (.BAS file) in several respects. Perhaps most importantly, a class module stores data differently than a standard module. There is never more than one copy of a standard module's data. This means that if one part of the program sets the value of a variable in a standard module and another part

---

3. The new name for an ActiveX DLL is a COM DLL.

of the program subsequently reads the variable, it will get the same value. By contrast, class module data exists separately for each instance of the class.

As an example, let's explore the differences when the following code is placed, without any modification, in both a standard module named Module1 and a class module named Class1:

```
Public Total As Integer

Public Function Sum(X As Integer, Y As Integer) As Integer
    Total = X + Y
    Sum = Total
End Function
```

The syntax used to access these two pieces of identical code is somewhat different. Calling the Sum method in the standard module looks like this:

```
Print Module1.Sum(5, 3)
```

Calling the Sum method in the class module requires instancing the class, as shown here:

```
Dim Math As New Class1
Print Math.Sum(5, 3)
```

Beyond this, several additional and subtler differences exist. Consider the following code that uses both the standard and class modules:

```
Print Module1.Sum(0, 0)

Dim FirstMath As New Class1
Print FirstMath.Sum(1, 1)

Dim SecondMath As New Class1
Print SecondMath.Sum(2, 2)

Print Module1.Total       ' 0
Print FirstMath.Total     ' 2
Print SecondMath.Total    ' 4
```

In this case, you see that while only one Module1 object can exist, you can create multiple instances of Class1—each with its own copy of the Total variable. Since each instance of Class1 has its own copy of the Total variable, you might be wondering whether each instance of Class1 also has its own copy of the Sum method. Since code isn't modified at run time, only one copy of the code exists and all instances of Class1 refer to the same code in memory; a new copy of all variables is created for every instance of Class1.

From time to time, you might decide to have a particular variable shared by all instances of a specific class. In object-oriented terminology, this is called *static class data.* While static class data generally violates the idea of encapsulation, that isn't always a bad thing. Suppose for a moment that you want to keep track of the total number of instances of a class. The following code, placed in a class module, takes a stab at this:

```
Public UsageCounter As Integer

Private Sub Class_Initialize()
    UsageCounter = UsageCounter + 1
End Sub
```

The idea is that every time you instantiate the class the *Initialize* event procedure is automatically called, and therefore incrementing a UsageCounter variable should do the trick. However, we know that every time an object is created it gets its own copy of all the class's variables. Thus, the value of UsageCounter for each object will always be one. To actually track the total number of instances of a class requires violating the much-lauded encapsulation and creating a static class variable. In Visual Basic, static class variables are defined in standard modules. Remember that variables declared in a standard module are never instanced—that is, only one copy exists. In a standard module, this statement creates the static class variable:

```
Public GlobalUsageCounter As Integer
```

After creating the variable, the following code in the Class_Initialize event procedure does the trick:

```
Private Sub Class_Initialize()
    GlobalUsageCounter = GlobalUsageCounter + 1
    UsageCounter = GlobalUsageCounter
End Sub
```

Now the UsageCounter variable is being assigned from the static class variable GlobalUsageCounter, providing a true counter of the number of class instances. In general, you should avoid making the code in your classes dependent on global data as shown in the preceding example. When designing a class that uses static data, remember that your class might be providing objects to several client applications simultaneously. All objects created from the class will share that static data, even if they are being used in different applications.

Instancing

Class modules also enable developers to expose interfaces to other applications. This is controlled by means of the *Instancing* property of a class module, which can be set to one of six values: *Private, PublicNotCreatable, SingleUse, GlobalSingleUse, MultiUse,* and *GlobalMultiUse.*

Instancing *Setting*	*Description*
Private	The component is private to the project.
PublicNotCreatable	The component can be used but not created by outside applications.
SingleUse	For every outside application that uses the component, a new copy is launched.
GlobalSingleUse	Like *SingleUse*, but the outside application doesn't have to create the object.
MultiUse	All outside applications using the component share one copy.
GlobalMultiUse	Like *MultiUse*, but the outside application doesn't have to create the object.

When the *Instancing* property of a class module is set to *Private*, that class is private to the application and can't be used in any manner by any outside application or component. With *PublicNotCreatable*, other applications can use objects of this class only if your component creates the objects first. Other applications can't use the *CreateObject* function or the *New* operator to create objects from the class. Objects of class modules with the *Instancing* property set to *PublicNotCreatable* are called dependent objects, which are typically parts of more complex objects. For example, you might have a Car object containing four Door objects. Since doors are of no value without a car, you want the Door object to exist only as part of a Car object. In this case, you would set the Door class's *Instancing* property to *PublicNotCreatable*.

SingleUse allows other applications to create objects from the class, but every object of this class that a client creates will start a new instance of your component. *GlobalSingleUse* is like *SingleUse* except that properties and methods can be invoked as if they were simply global functions. *MultiUse* allows other applications to create objects from the class. Your component can provide any number of objects created in this fashion, regardless of how many applications request them. *GlobalMultiUse* is like *MultiUse* except that properties and methods of the class can be invoked as if they were simply global functions. You don't need to explicitly create an instance of the class because an instance will automatically be created.

Creating Code Components

Code components consist of one or more class modules in an ActiveX EXE or ActiveX DLL project. These class modules can internally use any of the object-oriented programming features available in Visual Basic. The interfaces exposed by class modules can contain properties, property procedures, methods, and events.

User-interface decisions

The user-interface requirements of a code component must be weighed carefully. Although code components can display any type of interface, doing this isn't always recommended. Code components generally fall into one of three user-interface styles: those with no interface whatsoever, those with an interface consisting of dialog boxes that are displayed depending on circumstances, and those with a complete user interface.

The type of user interface that you choose for a code component depends on the component's purpose and implementation. Object hierarchies such as Data Access Objects (DAO) fall into the category of code components with no interface at all. These types of components generally provide some programmatic function and have no need to interact with the end user. Some components fall into the second category and provide functionality to the application. On occasion, they might need to get information from the user. For example, a component designed to query a remote database might display a dialog box asking for the user name and password in order to log on to the remote computer.

Most ActiveX EXE code components fall into the last category, having a complete user interface for those times when they are run as stand-alone applications. Even those components that have a user interface might choose not to display it under certain circumstances. Microsoft Word is an example of this type of component. If you load Word to type a letter to your friend, you get the full user interface treatment. On the other hand, if you control Word via Automation, by default no interface is displayed. The following sample Visual Basic code automates Microsoft Word invisibly:

```
Dim myWord As New Word.Application
myWord.Documents.Add
myWord.Selection.Font.Size = 20
myWord.Selection.Font.ColorIndex = wdBlue
myWord.Selection.Font.Bold = True
myWord.Selection.Font.Animation = wdAnimationSparkleText
myWord.Selection.TypeText "Hello, Word; this is Visual Basic"
myWord.ActiveDocument.SaveAs "C:\MyFile.doc"
myWord.Quit
```

Using this type of code, you might tell the Word component to check the spelling of text in your program. The end user would probably never even realize that Word had been used for this purpose. On the other hand, Word does provide a method to reveal its user interface if you so desire. Adding the *Word.AppShow* statement after the *CreateObject* call to the preceding code would do the trick.

For code components created in Visual Basic, you can implement similar behavior using the *StartMode* property of the *App* object. The *App* object is always available and provides runtime information about the project. The *StartMode* property of the *App* object provides information regarding the way in which the application was started. For example, if the application runs as a stand-alone program, *StartMode* will contain the value *vbSModeStandAlone*. Alternatively, if the program is being used as a component, *StartMode* will have the value *vbSModeAutomation*.[4]

The *StartMode* property is normally used in the Sub Main procedure on startup of an ActiveX EXE. The Sub Main procedure is always called first in a program, giving the code a chance to decide whether to display a user interface. This is in contrast to the way a Standard EXE works by default, where the startup form is automatically displayed. The following example code shows the *StartMode* property being used in a Sub Main procedure:

```
Public Sub Main()
    Form1.Show
    If App.StartMode = vbSModeAutomation Then
    ' Code to start invisibly
    Else    'App.StartMode = vbSModeStandAlone
    ' Code to show main form
    End If
End Sub
```

In the case of a remote component running on another computer connected over a network, the user interface design must be considered even more carefully. Chances are that the end user won't have access to the server on which the component is executing, so displaying a dialog box for the user to interact with will not work. If the user is in an office in New York and a dialog box is displayed on a server in Tokyo, user interaction will not work smoothly. For this reason, if remote components display a user interface at all, it is mostly for monitoring and administration purposes on the server rather than for interactivity with the user.

Designing programming interfaces

Although determining the type of user interface to be displayed is important, designing the programmatic interface is perhaps most crucial of all when developing an ActiveX code component. As you already know, an interface consists of properties, methods, and events. Each class module in a project becomes one interface in the final component. The challenge is not only figuring out what properties, methods, and events your interface will need to expose, but also figuring out the structure in which those interfaces exposed from the component will be available to client applications.

---

4. It is rather pointless to use the *StartMode* property in an ActiveX DLL since these components are never run as stand-alone components, and therefore *StartMode* always equals *vbSModeAutomation*.

First you need to consider the type of code component you are creating. Is this a component, similar to DAO in Visual Basic, that provides an entire hierarchy of objects as shown in Figure 5-2? Object hierarchies help give structure to a complex object-based program. By implicitly defining the relationships between objects, object hierarchies can make programming more logical. However, no rule says that code components must have an object hierarchy. Instead, one could create a single object with a zillion methods. This is part of the object-oriented design and analysis you will have to engage in when developing code components in Visual Basic. These are decisions that no one can make for you. We will, however, provide some global suggestions.

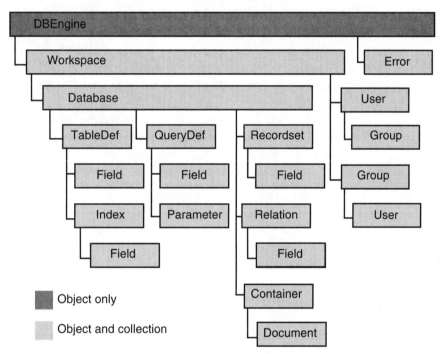

Figure 5-2. *An example of the DAO hierarchy.*

■ Make interfaces as simple as possible, but no simpler.

Designing an object with a zillion methods won't endear you to the users of your component. Instead, try to make each object as logically concise as possible. Have it deal with only one *thing*, and design its properties, methods, and events to support that. Some objects are necessarily complex, but if an object is becoming so unwieldy that you, the developer, are having a hard time understanding all of its features at one time, it might be time to think of dividing it into several smaller objects.

- Don't force objects into hierarchies: leave logically distinct objects alone.

  Don't create an object hierarchy just to impress the users of your component. Some developers feel including one is a badge of honor: if you don't have an object hierarchy, you haven't created a real component. You might, for example, have a personal finance component that has several objects: loan calculator, mortgage planner, savings calculator, retirement planner, and interest estimator. While some relationship among these objects could be devised, it is probably best to simply leave each object as a separate, stand-alone object in the component.

- Organize object hierarchies to show containment, not inheritance.

  Organize object hierarchies to show the relationship of containment (aggregation) rather than inheritance. For example, a Car object and Door objects could be arranged in an object hierarchy since a car contains doors. Don't use an object hierarchy to create a Car object containing a Convertible, Coupe, Sedan, Hatchback, Minivan, and Station Wagon. Although Visual Basic does support the *Implements* keyword, which enables inheritance of interfaces, this is better used for polymorphism than inheritance.

- Complex object hierarchies are a lot of work; use them only when necessary.

  Creating a complex object hierarchy is no small feat. Linking all the objects together, providing methods for creating dependent objects, and maintaining collections of those objects entails a lot of work. Microsoft has created some complex object hierarchies, such as DAO, which you can use as a model. DAO encompasses the functionality of the complete Microsoft Jet database engine. If you are creating a component that has a similar degree of functionality, a complex object hierarchy makes sense. Otherwise, keep it simple.

Designing object hierarchies

When a component becomes very complex, you need a way of organizing its various parts. An object model makes it easy to expose this organization to the user of your component. If you have decided that an object hierarchy is the way to go for your code component, you need to consider some of the issues this section of the chapter will outline.

Be aware that object hierarchies require that you invest more time at the design stage, determining how your objects will interact and how they will be used. Invest adequate time and effort designing your object hierarchy to avoid having to redefine objects or to split one object into two in a future release of your component. Such changes will cause major headaches for the developers using your component and are outlined later in this chapter in the section titled "Version Compatibility."

The design of an object model is affected by the fact that an object can be exposed in two different ways—as an externally creatable object or as a dependent object. This aspect of an object is controlled by the *Instancing* property of a class module, discussed previously. An externally creatable object is one that a client application can create by using the *New* operator or by calling the *CreateObject* function. A dependent object is used when one object is part of another. For example, a cell would be a dependent object of a spreadsheet. For client applications, the difference between a dependent object and an externally creatable object lies in the fact that although dependent objects can manipulate other dependent objects—as can externally creatable objects—they can't create dependent objects using *CreateObject* or *New*. You can design a dependent object by setting the *Instancing* property of the class module that defines it to *PublicNotCreatable*. Also note that a dependent object in your hierarchy might contain dependent objects of its own. For example, the Bicycle object contains two Wheel objects; the Wheel object might in turn contain a Tire object and a collection of Spoke objects.

Finally, you might also have objects that are used internally by classes in your component and that you do not want to expose to developers using your component. For these objects, setting the *Instancing* property of the class module to *Private* will ensure that no client has access. Although there is no limitation on how complex an object hierarchy can become, there might be a natural limit to a client developer's willingness to learn a complex component.[5]

Once you have a solid understanding of the functionality to be provided by your component, you are in a position to complete several important steps toward designing your object hierarchy.

1. Decide what objects are needed.

2. List the properties and methods of each object.

3. Determine the relationships between the objects.

4. Identify the top-level objects that need to be created by client applications.

After you have completed these preliminary design steps, you might still be left wondering how to implement such an object hierarchy in Visual Basic. Although you know how to create the individual objects using class modules

---

5. The distinction between externally creatable objects and dependent objects is made for the sake of client applications using a component. Within a component, all objects are creatable regardless of the value of the *Instancing* property.

and how to control their exposure using the *Instancing* property, you still don't know how to connect the various objects together to form the hierarchy. There are several ways to link objects together in Visual Basic. The method chosen usually depends on the relationship between two objects, as identified in step 3.

Linking by using properties

In cases where a one-to-one relationship is identified, a property is the simplest way to connect the objects. For example, a Bicycle object needs only one Frame object. The following code fragment from the class module of the Bicycle object describes the link to the Frame object:

```
Private mFrame As Frame        ' The internal frame reference

Public Property Get Frame() As Frame
    Set Frame = mFrame
End Property

Private Sub Class_Initialize()
    Set mFrame = New Frame
End Sub
```

Notice that no *Property Let* procedure has been defined, meaning that *Frame* is a read-only property. For this reason, it is important to define such properties using a property procedure rather than a simple public variable, as shown below:

```
Public mFrame As Frame    ' A bad idea
```

When implemented in this fashion, the property isn't read-only, allowing an ignorant or malicious programmer to potentially set the *Frame* property to *Nothing*. I leave to your imagination the effect this would have on the user of the Bicycle object.

Even when an object contains several instances of a dependent object, it might make sense to implement these as properties. For example, a Bicycle object always contains two Wheel objects:

```
Public FrontWheel As New Wheel
Public BackWheel As New Wheel
```

Once again, it would be advisable to implement these as property procedures rather than as public variables.

Using collections

When the relationship between two objects in a hierarchy is such that one object contains an indeterminate number of the other, the easier way to implement this link is with a collection. As an example, consider that a Bank collection contains many Account objects. Account objects are created and manipulated through the Bank collection, and therefore the *Instancing* property of the Account class module is set to *PublicNotCreatable*. The linkage mechanism in the Bank collection is accomplished through the use of methods and property procedures, as shown here:

```
Private mAccounts As New Collection

Public Property Get Accounts(AccountNumber As Integer) As _
  Account
    Set Accounts = mAccounts.Item(AccountNumber)
End Property

Public Function CreateAccount(Name As String, Address As _
  String, Balance As Currency) As Account
    Dim NewAccount As New Account
    NewAccount.Name = Name
    NewAccount.Address = Address
    NewAccount.Balance = Balance
    mAccounts.Add NewAccount
    Set CreateAccount = NewAccount
End Function

Property Get Count() As Integer
    Count = mAccounts.Count
End Property
```

A Code Component Example

In Chapter 3, you learned about the tools that Visual Basic provides for creating object-oriented programs, including property procedures, the *Implements* statement, the *Friend* keyword, and collections. Now let's create and experiment with a sample ActiveX code component—in other words, a COM component—that uses many of these features.

Exercise 5-1

1. Start a new ActiveX EXE project in Visual Basic.

2. Open the Properties window of the default class module and set the *Name* property to *ClassCalc*.

3. In the *Declarations* section of the class module, dimension a Name property as a string variable (property variables must be *Public*):

    ```
    Option Explicit
    Public Name As String
    ```

4. In the Object box, select *Class*.

5. In the Class_Initialize event procedure, write code (shown in bold) to print *ClassCalc: Initialize*.

```
Private Sub Class_Initialize()
    Form1.Print "ClassCalc: Initialize"
End Sub
```

6. In the Class_Terminate event procedure, write code (shown in bold) to print *ClassCalc: Terminate*.

```
Private Sub Class_Terminate()
    Form1.Print "ClassCalc: Terminate"
End Sub
```

Now let's add a method to your new class.

7. Choose Add Procedure from the Tools menu.

8. In the Procedure dialog box, enter *Sum* in the Name box and select a type of Function. Choose OK.

Code the *Sum* function so that it accepts two parameters as integers and returns their sum. It should also print the *Name* property, as follows:

```
Public Function Sum(X As Integer, Y As Integer) _
  As Integer
    Sum = X + Y
    Form1.Print "ClassCalc: Sum method called by " _
      & Name
    Form1.Print Chr(9) & "Received " & X & " and " & _
      Y & " Returning " & Sum
End Function
```

Now let's add a form to test the class module.

10. Choose Add Form from the Project menu. Accept the default *Form* type, and choose Open.

11. Create a command button on the form with the default name Command1.

12. Double-click the form to display the Code window. In the Code window, select the Command1_Click event procedure and write the following code (shown in bold):

```
Private Sub Command1_Click()
    Dim MyVariable As New ClassCalc
    MyVariable.Name = "MyName"
    Print "Form1: " & MyVariable.Sum(5,3)
End Sub
```

13. Choose Properties from the form's shortcut menu.

14. In the Properties window, set the *AutoRedraw* property to *True*. This is so that we won't lose our printed messages if other windows cover them.

15. Choose Add Module from the Project menu. Accept the default module type, and choose Open.

16. Since we are creating an ActiveX EXE, we need a Sub Main startup object. Add a Sub Main procedure that simply displays Form1, as follows:

```
Public Sub Main()
    Form1.Show
    If App.StartMode = vbSModeStandalone Then
        Form1.Print "Running stand-alone"
    Else
        Form1.Print "Running automated"
    End If
End Sub
```

17. Choose Project1 Properties from the Project menu to display the Project Properties dialog box. In the Startup Object box, select Sub Main.

18. Select the Component tab, and in the StartMode area select Stand-alone. Choose OK.

19. Press F8 to step through the code line by line until you reach the end of the Sub Main procedure.

20. Click the command button to activate its *Click* event.

21. Continue pressing F8 to step through your code. What statement in your code caused the Class_Initialize event procedure to be called? What statement in your code caused the Class_Terminate event procedure to be called?

22. View the output on Form1.

23. Choose End from the Run menu.

24. Choose Save Project from the File menu. Use the name SERVER for the form, ClassCalc for the class module, Sub Main for the module, and SERVER for the project. Leave this project running for the next exercise.

Exercise 5-2

In this exercise, you will add to the previous exercise and create two components: a client and a server. COM interfaces will enable one component to call the other.

1. Choose Project1 Properties from the Project menu.

2. On the General tab, set the Project Name to *SERVER* and choose OK.

3. Open the Form1 Form window.

4. Open the Code window for Form1.

5. Cut all the code contained within the Command1_Click event procedure to the Clipboard.

6. Close the Code window.

7. Delete the Command1 button from the form.

8. Open the Properties window for the form, and set the Caption property to *SERVER*.

9. Choose Save Project from the File menu.

10. Choose Start from the Run menu to start the server.

11. Leave the server running, but minimize its window.

12. Minimize Visual Basic.

13. Start a new instance of Visual Basic.

14. Accept the default Standard EXE project type, and choose Open.

15. In the Properties window for the default form, set the *AutoRedraw* property to *True*.

16. Set the form's *Caption* property to *CLIENT*.

17. Add a command button named Command1 to the form.

18. In the Code window for the Command1_Click event procedure, paste the following code from the Clipboard.

```
Private Sub Command1_Click()
    Dim MyVariable As New ClassCalc
    MyVariable.Name = "MyName"
    Print "Form1: " & MyVariable.Sum(5, 3)
End Sub
```

19. Choose References from the Project menu. Check SERVER, and choose OK.

20. Press F8 to step through the code.

CALLING CODE COMPONENTS ACROSS THE NETWORK WITH DCOM

Visual Basic's built-in ability to call components across a network was a Microsoft Visual Basic 4 Enterprise Edition special feature called *Remote Automation*, which extended the existing OLE Automation model so that it supported the separation of the client and server applications by a network. The functionality provided by Remote Automation was a precursor to DCOM. DCOM is an operating-system-level service that is built into Microsoft Windows NT 4 and is available for Microsoft Windows 95. It enables COM objects to communicate across a network. Remote Automation is still available in Visual Basic to support 16-bit client programs, because DCOM is supported only on 32-bit operating systems.

The current idea of client/server architecture is the many-clients-to-one-server model, in which work is separated between the client (the user's desktop computer) and the server (some other computer). Although this is a type of distributed computing—a single task is split among several computers (in this case, two)—it is a very primitive form. That is particularly troublesome to database application developers in the design of the client-side program; the server is often simply Microsoft SQL Server acting as a data repository. The client, however, is the site of all the business logic—the code that actually understands what the data means and how to interact with it. For example, if you have many client applications in your department that query a common database server, it is quite possible that many of these client applications have redundant code designed to handle the complex business logic required by your company's business.

A much more flexible model is *partitioned* applications. A partitioned system is one in which two or more parts work together to provide a service to the user. It isn't even necessary that these parts run on separate computers, although this is common. An approach becoming popular for database applications is the so-called three-tier architecture. This model has a client and a database server, and also introduces a middle layer between the two that acts as the business, or intelligent, application server. Developers can then simplify the client application by moving the business logic of the system to the application server, which might (or might not) reside on the same computer as the database server. This often can speed development and lower distribution costs, not to mention make the code more maintainable. The application server will then make requests of the database server on the clients' behalf. This not only simplifies the development and maintenance of the clients, but it also means that you need to update only one application when the company's business logic changes.

The partitioned approach to application development has become even more popular with the widespread adoption of the Internet as a basis for client/ server computing. A Web browser such as Microsoft Internet Explorer is a lightweight client that can run on almost any machine and requires a minimum effort to install and configure. The Internet server is another off-the-shelf component that becomes a partition. The custom application is often a third partition written as an extension to the Internet server using the Internet Server API or Active Server Pages (discussed in Chapter 12). The custom server application usually accesses data from a SQL server located on the same or another machine by means of ODBC or OLE DB, comprising a fourth partition. Such partitions make for very flexible systems that utilize many off-the-shelf components.

DCOM isn't the only way to build distributed applications. For example, one could simply use the Winsock control to communicate among processes on a network. DCOM is simply a set of system services that make the development of well-designed partitioned applications much easier. In addition, DCOM enables the components you create to interface automatically with other compatible components on a network.

Client applications that want to instantiate objects on a remote machine using DCOM need to specify the name of the target computer on the network. The easiest way is to configure the registry using the DCOM configuration utility DCOMCNFG.EXE. (This utility comes with the Windows 95 DCOM add-on included in this book's accompanying CD and also with Windows 98 and Windows NT 4.) Figure 5-3 shows the DCOM configuration utility being used to specify the machine on which a particular object should be instantiated. Now any call to the *CreateObject* function or the *New* keyword to instantiate the object will be forwarded to the remote machine. While configuring the name of a remote machine in the registry is convenient, it doesn't offer a great degree of flexibility. Imagine that an application wanted to instantiate objects on different machines based on a dynamic load-balancing algorithm. In this case, configuring the registry in advance simply will not do.

As an alternative, the *CreateObject* function offers an optional second parameter that can be used to specify the name of the machine on which you want to instantiate an object. If specified, this machine name will override any registry settings that might have been previously configured. Be aware that DCOM supports remote launching of components on Windows NT only. Client applications can connect to objects of components already running on Windows 95 or Windows 98, but for security reasons these systems won't automatically launch a component in response to a client request. Also note that Visual Basic's *New* keyword can't be used to instantiate remote objects on machines specified at run time.

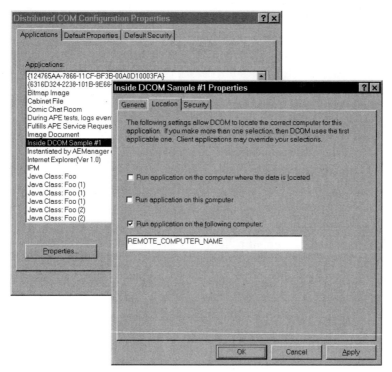

Figure 5-3. *The DCOM configuration utility.*

Exercise 5-3

Setting up an existing application for distributed computing involves several
steps. The following example assumes you want to use DCOM with Microsoft
Word from Visual Basic. The Visual Basic application is a very simple program
that creates an instance of the *Word.Application* object with which to control
Word. If you want to try these features yourself, first test while running the Visual
Basic application and Word on the same computer. Be sure to set a reference to
the Microsoft Word 8.0 Object Library. The code for the Visual Basic application
should look something like this:

```
Dim myWord As Word.Application
Set myWord = CreateObject("Word.Application", "RemoteMachineName")
myWord.Documents.Add
myWord.Selection.Font.Size = 20
myWord.Selection.Font.ColorIndex = wdBlue
myWord.Selection.Font.Bold = True
myWord.Selection.Font.Animation = wdAnimationSparkleText
myWord.Selection.TypeText "Hello Word, this is Visual Basic"
myWord.ActiveDocument.SaveAs "C:\MyFile.doc"
myWord.Quit
```

Once you have tested this code locally and verified that it works, try using this code to remotely activate Microsoft Word.

GENERATING AND HANDLING ERRORS

When you are the creator of a component, the method by which you handle run-time errors becomes a very important responsibility. This task includes handling errors caused by the incorrect use of your component and errors internal to your component. There is no such thing as an error that isn't handled in a component. Any errors not trapped by a component are automatically propagated to the client application using the component.

Two basic types of errors need to be dealt with in a component. The first type of error is caused by the dumb client. Let's say that a client program calls a method of your component to request that it do some work on a particular file. The client passes the name of the file to the method, but it later turns out that the file doesn't exist. What should your component do now? Raising errors or returning error codes to the client is the appropriate response. A well-behaved component doesn't intrude on the end user's peace of mind by displaying message boxes containing error messages, especially since end users may be blissfully unaware that your component is part of the application. Receiving errors from some unknown software isn't likely to help end users or your component solve the problem.

The second type of error is caused by the dumb component. Perhaps your component is using another component internally, and that component has reported an error. Now it is the job of your component to respond to the error. If possible, the error should be handled inside your component rather than being propagated to the client application. Remember that the client application is using your component. Its job is to know how to respond to errors from your component and not some other component that your component might be using.

It is best to consider the issue of error handling early in the design of a new component. While designing a component, you can choose between two basic approaches to error handling: Basic style or Windows API style. Basic-style error handling involves raising errors when necessary and implementing error handlers to trap errors. This is the recommended way to manage errors in Visual Basic. The Windows API style specifies that errors are not raised but instead are delivered as return codes by methods of the component. This is the style of error reporting used by the Windows API and by most programs written in C.

In general, Basic-style error management is recommended over the Windows API style because Visual Basic programmers are more familiar with the former than the latter. When making the choice, consider the convenience of the developer who will use your component. Keep in mind that if you select the Windows API style of error management, the developer using the component must use inline error handling; that is, return codes must always be tested after calling a method. On the other hand, if you use the Basic style of error management, the developer has a choice between inline error handling using the *On Error Resume Next* statement or more centralized error handling using *On Error GoTo.* Overall, perhaps even more important than the method used is choosing one method and sticking with it. Consistency is the hallmark of a well-designed component.

Raising Errors in COM Components

Raising errors from a COM component is no different than raising errors in a standard Visual Basic application. The *Raise* method of the *Err* object is used to raise errors that can be trapped by client applications. Before raising errors in a component, be sure that local error handling isn't enabled. If you are using error handling to trap internal errors, disable it with the *On Error GoTo 0* statement before raising the error. Neglecting to do this will cause the local error handler to respond instead of generating the error in the component's client.

The actual error numbers raised from a component must be chosen with care. Visual Basic specifies that all components should raise errors in the range between *vbObjectError + 512* and *vbObjectError + 65535*. The use of the intrinsic constant *vbObjectError* is required to avoid colliding with predefined Visual Basic error numbers. The following code shows an example of raising an error from a component:

```
Err.Raise vbObjectError + 512, , "MySillyError"
```

This error will be raised regardless of the language in which the client application was written. For example, errors raised from a COM component written in Visual Basic will be trapped by client applications written in Visual Basic, Visual C++, Microsoft Access, or any other environment supporting the COM specifications.

Setting Base Addresses for ActiveX DLLs

As discussed previously, code components built as ActiveX DLLs are loaded into the process space of the calling application and so are often called in-process components. However, the address at which these components are loaded needs to be addressed (pun intended). All DLLs have what is known as a default base address: the address in the client process space where the DLL would prefer to be loaded. Unless you interfere, Visual Basic sets an in-process component's default base address to *&H11000000 (285,212,672).*

32-Bit Addressing

On systems supporting the Win32 Application Programming Interface (Win32 API)—Microsoft Windows 95, Windows 98, and Windows NT—each application is loaded into a private 4-GB address space. This is different from the way 16-bit systems such as Microsoft Windows 3.1 work. In Windows 3.1, each program is loaded at a different address within a single address space. See Figure 5-4 for a comparison of these two systems. The Windows 3.1 approach is considered dangerous because an errant pointer in an application can accidentally corrupt another program or even corrupt the operating system itself. By starting each process in a private address space, a program can't easily access the memory belonging to another process.

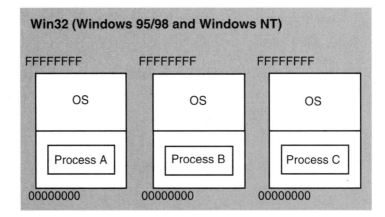

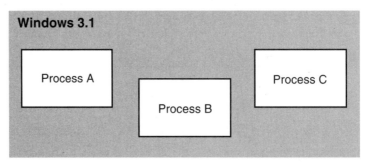

Figure 5-4. *Comparison of Win32 and Windows 3.1 memory models.*

Of course, most computers do not have 4 GB of RAM (at least not yet). So the address space allocated to each process is virtual. In a physical memory system, if a computer has 24 MB of RAM, no more than 24 MB of memory can be allocated by software at one time. In a virtual memory system, such as Windows 95, Windows 98, or Windows NT, the system doles out memory addresses left and right since there are 4 GB (2^{32}) of potential memory. This is called reserving memory; the system simply reserves a range of addresses for a program. As an application actually begins to store data at those addresses, physical memory is allocated and the data is stored. This is called committing memory. Windows also has a swap file to which it can transfer data if it becomes low on memory.

In Windows 95, Windows 98, and Windows NT, the top 2 GB of address space in every process is reserved by the operating system.[6] This means that only the lower 2 GB are actually available for use by the application. In addition, remember that DLLs are loaded into the process space of their callers. So if your application calls any DLLs, these DLLs will also consume space in the lower 2 GB of your address space.

One of the neat things about DLLs is that multiple processes can share them. For example, if you have three applications—A, B, and C—and all of them want to use the DLL D, only one copy of the DLL needs to be loaded, as shown in Figure 5-5. You might be wondering how this is possible, especially in light of the fact that each process is loaded into a private address space. How can a DLL be shared? Well, remember that Windows is a virtual memory system. While each process is loaded into a separate address in virtual memory, all the programs share the same physical memory of the computer. So, while the DLL is mapped into the address space of three separate processes, only one copy of it is loaded into the physical memory of the computer.

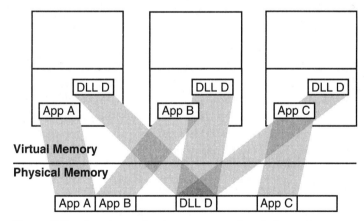

Figure 5-5. *The relationship between virtual and physical memory.*

---

6. Windows NT Server, Enterprise Edition, partitions the address space so that the lower three gigabytes of memory are available to applications and only the top gigabyte is reserved for the system.

Base addresses would not be an issue if it were not for the problems that arise when the default base address of a component is in use. Let's say your program is using a particular component loaded at address *&H11000000*, and then you load another component that wants the same base address. Obviously, two components can't be loaded at the same address, so Windows automatically takes care of this problem by reassigning the second component to another, vacant address. Windows does this by dynamically recalculating the logical memory addresses where code and data are loaded. This is all fine and dandy, except that the process of reassigning base addresses slows the load process and consumes memory.

Assigning different base addresses consumes memory because the Windows loader needs to modify the actual code of the DLL. Since several different programs might share this code, Windows can't permit the code of the shared DLL to be modified. To circumvent this limitation, the Windows loader allocates some memory, makes a copy of certain parts of the DLL that it needs to modify, and then makes changes to the copy of the DLL. Thus, the different programs using the DLL are not sharing all the code in the DLL. Instead, several copies of certain portions of the DLL exist. The moral of this story is to choose a good base address.

To reduce the likelihood of such address space collisions, Visual Basic allows you to change the default base address for ActiveX DLLs, ActiveX Controls, and ActiveX Document DLLs. From the Project menu, choose Project1 Properties and click the Compile tab. In the DLL Base Address box, you can change the default, as shown in Figure 5-6. If you neglect to change this value, your component will conflict with every other component built in Visual Basic that uses this default. So it's best to stay well away from this address. Microsoft recommends that base addresses be chosen in the range of 16 MB (&H1000000) to 2 GB (&H80000000). Base addresses must be expressed in multiples of 64 KB.

Since there is really little way to know what addresses will be in use when your component is loaded, the best practice is simply to choose an address at random from the suggested range and then round to the nearest multiple of 64 KB. If you and your organization produce many in-process COM components, it might be a good idea to select one base address at random and then stagger the base addresses of the other components above the first. In this way, you can guarantee that at least your components won't have base address conflicts among themselves.

VERSION COMPATIBILITY

Since versioning presupposes that you have an existing component, this section might not seem to be of much interest if you are only now learning how to create a component. However, we urge you not to skip this section now if this chapter is to be at all helpful; if you go on to build a component, you will eventually have the problems described here. Being aware of such problems when you are initially designing a component might help you avoid some of the potential pitfalls.

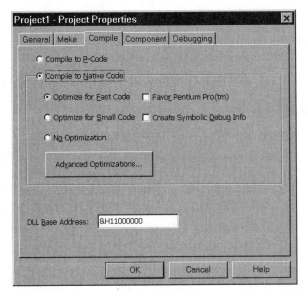

Figure 5-6. *The Compile tab of the Project Properties dialog box.*

To state the problem concisely, versioning raises the issue of what to do once you have created a COM component, released it to customer sites where it is being used by perhaps thousands of applications, and then want to update the component and change its interface. Changing the programmatic interface exposed by a component will cause its existing client applications to fail. The first rule of versioning, therefore, is to not change the programmatic interface.

The desire to modify the interface of an existing component usually has one of two motivations. Either you screwed it up the first time and now want to go back and risk screwing it up again, or your component was such an unqualified success and met with such adulation that it sparked requests for enhancements. Either way, the problems are the same: changing the interface breaks existing clients.

While the first rule of versioning is certainly the best, it isn't very realistic. Any successful software will need to evolve over time—at some point requiring that its interface change. Remember, however, that an interface is a contract between a component and its client application. By changing the interface, you break the contract. To help with the version compatibility problem, Visual Basic defines three levels of version compatibility for the interface of a component.

Version Identical

Once your component has been released and is in use, there are several reasons you might want to change it. One of the most innocuous is a desire to optimize the performance of the component. You might, for example, want to optimize a particular method that turned out to be a bottleneck for users of the component.

If these types of changes are made internally to the component without affecting its programmatic interface, the new version is said to be version identical. The advantage of releasing a new version of a component with a version-identical interface is that existing clients will work without any modifications.

Version Compatible

Sometimes it is possible to enhance a component by adding new features to its interface. If this is done without changing any aspects of the existing interface, the updated component is said to be version compatible. The following types of changes meet the requirement of backward compatibility:

- Adding new public interfaces.

- Adding new public properties, methods, or events to existing interfaces.

A client built for the previous version of the component will still work with the updated component since none of the previously available interface features were modified. Clients that are updated with knowledge of the enhanced component will be able to take advantage of the additional interface features.

Version Incompatible

Sometimes it is impossible for you to change the interface of a component in a backward-compatible fashion. In these cases, the new component is exactly that: a new component. Version-incompatible interfaces are generally not a good idea because existing code won't work with a new component at all. The new component must be given a new name and be treated completely separately from the old version. The following changes will cause version incompatibility:

- Changing the project name.

- Changing the *Name* property of any public class module.

- Removing a public class module.

- Removing a public property or method.

- Changing the data type of a public property.

- Changing the name, data types, number, or order of the parameters of a public method.

If you have identified a necessary change that will cause your component to become incompatible with earlier versions, it is a good idea to reevaluate the the entire interface of your component. Remember the first rule of version compatibility: don't change the interface. Instead, follow the advice in the section below on how to avoid incompatible interfaces. Nevertheless, if you have decided to plunge ahead, now is the time to make all of the needed changes you can foresee to the interface. Concentrating all the changes that you can anticipate into one release will minimize future problems. Creating a version-incompatible component won't endear you to anyone; doing it more than once might cause developers to switch to a component from your competitor. Remember, when you create a version-incompatible interface, you are in fact creating a new component. Treat it that way, and redesign the component from the ground up.

Avoiding Incompatible Interfaces

In most cases, you should be able to avoid making changes that would cause a component to become incompatible with previous versions. This is accomplished by adding new class modules to the component with similar functionality and similar names to the old interfaces. Let's say you have an interface called Math that encapsulated some mathematics-related functionality. Later, you want to modify some attributes of the Math interface that would cause version incompatibility. Instead, it would be better to leave the Math interface alone and create a new interface called Math2 containing the new functionality. You could use the *Implements* keyword to inherit the old interface and then make the changes you want in the Math2 interface.

In this way, you would now have a version-compatible interface; older clients could continue to use the original Math interface and updated clients could call Math2. This method of solving version incompatibilities might also allow a component to share code among the multiple versions of interfaces. For example, although the Math and Math2 interfaces are separate and will be used by different client applications, internally the mathematics engine could be shared by both interfaces.

Visual Basic Version-Compatibility Features

To help you determine the degree of compatibility between two versions of a component, Visual Basic has introduced a new version-compatibility feature. Select Project1 Properties from the Project menu, and then click the Component tab, as shown in Figure 5-7 on the following page. In the Version Compatibility section, you can select No Compatibility, Project Compatibility, or Binary Compatibility. You should use the default setting, Project Compatibility, when first developing a component.

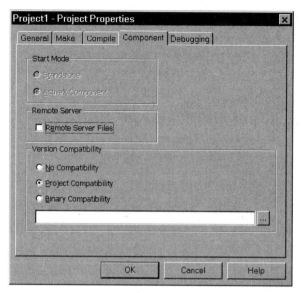

Figure 5-7. *The Component tab of the Project Properties dialog box.*

Once the component has been released and enhancements need to be made, switch to Binary Compatibility and point the file name box (the box with the ellipses button on the right) to the previously released component file. Doing this gives Visual Basic a reference point by which to determine compatibility. From then on, whenever you build the component or even run it in the development environment, Visual Basic will compare the interface you have created with the interface of the previous component. If the changes have resulted in version-identical or version-compatible interfaces, Visual Basic simply updates the type library version number according to the level of compatibility between the interfaces. On the other hand, if the changes made have resulted in a version-incompatible interface, Visual Basic provides the warning shown in Figure 5-8. This warning message provides you with the opportunity to accept the change, resulting in a version-incompatible interface (a new component), or to go back and fix the code if you made the change unintentionally.

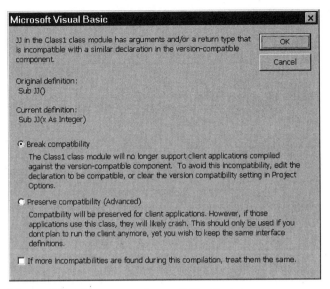

Figure 5-8. *The Version Compatibility Warning.*

Chapter 6

Creating ActiveX Controls

A wide assortment of development tools—including Microsoft Visual C++, Microsoft Visual J++, Microsoft Visual Basic, Microsoft Visual FoxPro, Borland Delphi, PowerBuilder, and Microsoft Access—support ActiveX controls. Until recently, however, the only tool available for creating ActiveX controls was Visual C++. This relegated development of ActiveX controls to the province of those who knew lower-level programming languages such as C and C++. With Visual Basic, Microsoft has given developers another tool for creating ActiveX controls. Using Visual Basic, you can create controls for your own software projects or for distribution and sale to other developers for use in their software. In fact, a developer writing applications in C++ and Java can use the ActiveX controls you create in Visual Basic.

ActiveX controls that you build in Visual Basic (or any language, for that matter) are not only useful in development tools but also in end-user applications. For example, you can embed an ActiveX control created in Visual Basic in an HTML document that will be viewed in a Web browser such as Microsoft Internet Explorer. The application in which an ActiveX control is displayed is referred to as the control's *container*. Visual Basic is the ActiveX control container used for most of the examples in this chapter—however, keep in mind that your control might be activated in containers other than Visual Basic.

ActiveX controls are comparable to applets written in Java. An *applet* is any small program or utility, but of late, the term applet has come to mean a small application embedded in an HTML document that can be displayed by a Web browser. In fact, the Microsoft Java VM (virtual machine) exposes Java Bean components as ActiveX controls. The advantage to this is that applets can be thought of as ActiveX controls, which in turn means that they can be scripted using ActiveX Scripting languages such as VBScript or JScript.

WHAT MAKES ACTIVEX CONTROLS DIFFERENT FROM STANDARD EXE PROJECTS?

Despite all the racket I made in previous pages about true programmers being felled by Visual Basic interlopers, creating an ActiveX control is (fortunately) difficult, even in Visual Basic. Controls are definitely one of the most complex project types to develop—so much so, that even experienced Visual Basic developers might have a hard time grasping the essence of creating ActiveX controls. Part of this complexity stems from the fact that controls are very different creatures from other types of software that you can build with Visual Basic.

For starters, having two personalities is beneficial when you are engaged in creating ActiveX controls in Visual Basic. ActiveX controls (and their developers) basically have two separate personalities. You are a Dr. Jekyll when you are developing a control in Visual Basic, sacrificing yourself on the altar of science. The developer using your component, however, sees you as a Mr. Hyde: a ruthless, self-serving murderer of innocent code. Once you comprehend both facets of working with an ActiveX control, developing an ActiveX control in Visual Basic will be much easier.

Let's leave nineteenth-century literature and return to contemporary software. Think of a Standard EXE project. You develop the program in design mode and then test the program in run mode. Once you have the program working, you create an EXE file that always executes in run mode. Controls, likewise, are developed in design mode and are tested in run mode. However, since controls never run as stand-alone applications, you always need a test container in which to execute the control. The oddity is that once you have developed a control, produced an .OCX file[1], and given it to other developers to use in their software, the control is back to working in Visual Basic's design mode. This is the peculiar fact about the life of a control: even when Visual Basic is in design mode, controls are running.

---

1. ActiveX controls are DLLs saved with an .OCX extension.

WHY CREATE ACTIVEX CONTROLS?

If ActiveX controls are basically dangerous to your health, why should you bother with them? After all, most of us leave strenuous mental pursuits to others. For the few who are ready to tame these intellectually challenging beasts, the advantages of learning how to create controls in Visual Basic outweigh the efforts required. Knowing the process involved in creating controls is good for you. It will make you a better human being, or at least a better user of third-party controls. You will gain a broader understanding of how controls operate. Think of it this way: controls and containers have to work together. Historically, Visual Basic has been a big consumer of controls, and Visual Basic developers have always seen things from the side of the container. In Visual Basic, however, you have a chance to see the world from the side of the control. Understanding the perspective of developers who create controls is a big step toward better and more efficient use of controls in general.

Beyond making better use of existing controls, you might want to extend those controls in new and innovative ways. For example, a particular control might have a basic functionality that you like, but you want it to work just a little differently. Visual Basic allows you to make such changes, but only if you know how to create controls. Imagine the possible benefits if you create a control for use in your project that can then be reused in other software projects at your company. You might decide to take the totally awesome control you created for your own software and market it as a reusable component for use in other people's software. Who would have ever imagined that you could get this far in Visual Basic?

By structuring parts of your application as ActiveX controls, you make your software more maintainable since it is divided into multiple components with distinct interfaces. In addition, you also position your code to allow for one of the main benefits of object-oriented software: code reuse.

TYPES OF ACTIVEX CONTROLS

Visual Basic defines three basic models for control creation. You can:

- Write your own control from scratch.
- Enhance an existing control.
- Assemble a new control from several existing controls.

Writing Your Own Control from Scratch

Writing a control from scratch affords you the greatest flexibility since you are not limited by any existing functionality. This allows you to do anything you want with your control's appearance and interface simply by putting code into the *Paint* event procedure used to draw your control. This is the model to select when creating a new visual widget such as a super-duper button.

Enhancing an Existing Control

Enhancing an existing control means using that control as a starting point and then adding your own properties, methods, and events. You have complete freedom in specifying the programmatic interface for your enhanced control. The constituent control's properties will be exposed only if you decide to expose them.

Modifying the appearance of an existing control is more difficult than creating a control from scratch, however, because the control you are enhancing already contains code to paint itself. Experienced Microsoft Windows programmers can use the *AddressOf* operator to make the constituent control a subclass so that it will notify you of its *Paint* events, but this is not an easy task. Using these hybrid controls is similar to what is done in the object-oriented concept of aggregation. Recall that aggregation occurs when you build a new object by accumulating objects that already exist.

Assembling a New Control from Several Existing Controls

The last control creation model expounded by Visual Basic is assembling a control from several existing controls. This model is similar to the second model in that they both utilize existing controls to build new controls.

THE *USERCONTROL* OBJECT

An ActiveX control created in Visual Basic is always composed in a *UserControl* object, just as a Visual Basic application is always composed in a *Form* object. Like a Visual Basic *Form* object, a *UserControl* object has a code module and a visual designer (the UserControl designer), as shown in Figure 6-1. Note that you can also use class modules inside an ActiveX control project. In addition to a *UserControl* object, an ActiveX control in Visual Basic can have any other controls—called *constituent controls*—that you choose to place on the *User-Control* object. You use constituent controls only if you want to enhance an existing control or create a hybrid control consisting of several existing controls. You place constituent controls on the UserControl designer and set their properties in the same way you do when placing controls on a form.

When saved by Visual Basic, a *UserControl* object is stored in a plain text file with a .CTL extension. The .CTL file contains the source code and property settings for the *UserControl* object and for any constituent controls that might be present. If a *UserControl* object or its constituent controls use graphical elements, such as bitmaps, which can't be stored as plain text, Visual Basic stores those elements in a .CTX file with the same name as the .CTL file.

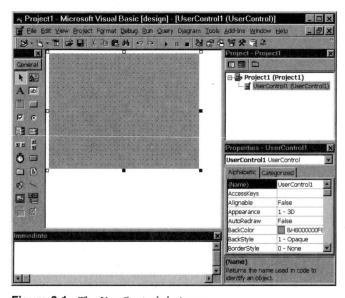

Figure 6-1. *The UserControl designer.*

The *UserControl* Object's Interface

If you have worked with Visual Basic for any length of time, you know that there are three basic members you use with controls: properties, methods, and events. Some items, however, are unique to *UserControl*. These are described in the following tables, which you can peruse to get an idea of the functionality available. We will go into detail on the important items later in this chapter and in successive chapters.

NOTE The following table includes properties that are not shown in the Properties window.

UserControl *Property*	*Property Description*
AccessKeys	String containing all mnemonics (hot keys) for this control.
Alignable	Determines whether the *UserControl* object can be aligned in its container.
Ambient	Returns a *UserControl* object that allows the programmer read-only access at run time to the ambient properties of the container, such as the *BackColor* property.
CanGetFocus	Determines whether the *UserControl* object can have the focus.
ClipBehavior	Indicates how a windowless UserControl's appearance is clipped.
ClipControls	Determines whether graphics methods in *Paint* events repaint an entire object or only newly exposed areas.
ContainedControls	Returns the set of controls contained within the *UserControl* object.
ControlContainer	Determines whether the *UserControl* object can act as a container for other controls at design time.
DataBindingBehavior	Determines whether the *UserControl* object supports data binding.
DataSourceBehavior	Determines whether the *UserControl* object is a data source.
DefaultCancel	Determines whether the *UserControl* object behaves like a standard command button.
EditAtDesignTime	Determines whether the *UserControl* object will have an *Edit* verb on the control's menu that, if set to True, allows the control to become active at design time.
EventsFrozen	Indicates whether the container is ignoring events on the control.
Extender	Returns an object to the control that contains the values for the properties or the methods of the container.
ForwardFocus	Determines which control receives focus when an access key is pressed.

UserControl *Property*	*Property Description*
HasDC	Determines whether a unique display context is allocated for the control.
HitBehavior	Indicates which mode of automatic hit testing a windowless control employs.
Hyperlink	Returns a *Hyperlink* object used for browser-style navigation.
InvisibleAtRuntime	Determines whether the *UserControl* object is invisible at run time.
ParentControls	Returns the set of controls used by the *UserControl* object's container.
PropertyPages	Determines the type, number, and order of property pages for the *UserControl* object.
Public	Determines whether the control is accessible to other clients.
RightToLeft	Determines text display direction and visual appearance on a bidirectional system such as Arabic or Hebrew.
ToolboxBitmap	References a graphic that represents the *UserControl* object in the toolbox.
Windowless	Determines whether the *UserControl* object can be activated as windowless in a container that supports it.

UserControl *Method*	*Method Description*
AsyncRead	Asynchronously reads data from a URL or path.
CancelAsyncRead	Cancels an asynchronous read.
CanPropertyChange	Asks the container of the *UserControl* object whether a control property can be changed.
DataMemberChanged	Notifies clients that a data member of this data source has changed.
PropertyChanged	Signals that a property of the *UserControl* object has changed.

UserControl *Event*	*Event Description*
AccessKeyPress	Occurs when the user of the control presses one of the control's access keys, or when the Enter key is pressed after the developer has set the *Default* property to *True*, or when the Escape key is pressed after the developer has set the *Cancel* property to *True*. The author of the control enables the *Default* property and the *Cancel* property by setting the *DefaultCancel* property to *True*.
AmbientChanged	Occurs when the container of a *UserControl* object changes an ambient value.
AsyncReadComplete	Occurs when all of the data is available as a result of the *AsyncRead* method.
AsyncReadProgress	Occurs when more data is available as a result of the *AsyncReadProgress* method.
EnterFocus, ExitFocus	Occurs when the *UserControl* object is activated (*UIActivate*) or deactivated (*UIDeactivate*)—that is, receives or loses the focus.
GetDataMember	Occurs when a client is asking this data source for one of its data members.
Show, Hide	Occurs when the *UserControl* object is shown or hidden.
HitTest	Occurs in a windowless user control in response to mouse activity.
InitProperties	Occurs the first time a new instance of a *UserControl* object is created.
ReadProperties	Occurs when a *UserControl* object is asked to load an old instance in the persisted state from the *PropertyBag* object.
WriteProperties	Occurs when a *UserControl* object is asked to write an instance of a persistent state to a *PropertyBag* object.

Key Events in the Life of a *UserControl* Object

As we have mentioned before, you might develop an ActiveX control in Visual Basic at design time, and then another programmer might use this control to develop software at design time that in turn executes the control at run time. As a result, an ActiveX control needs to deal with many situations. As we mentioned early in this chapter, ActiveX controls are actually running most of the time that Visual Basic is in design mode. While the UserControl designer is open, an ActiveX control is in design mode. However, as soon as the UserControl designer closes, the control enters run mode automatically. The only indication of this transition to a running state is that the control's icon in the Toolbox becomes enabled.

The life of an ordinary form in a standard Visual Basic application is punctuated by certain key events, such as *Initialize, Load, QueryUnload,* and *Unload.* To create well-behaved software, you need to know at what stage in the form's life these events are fired. The same is true for controls. The key *UserControl* events are *Initialize, InitProperties, ReadProperties, WriteProperties,* and *Terminate.* Notice that ActiveX controls are missing *Load* and *Unload* events. These events are superseded by the *ReadProperties* and *WriteProperties* events. *Load* and *Unload* events don't make sense for controls since controls aren't loaded and unloaded like forms.

WHY THE EXERCISES USE STANDARD EXE PROJECTS

In this chapter, Standard EXE projects are used for the exercises. This may seem odd since the focus of this chapter is ActiveX controls. To make the development of the exercises easier, ActiveX controls are added to Standard EXE projects. The controls work identically to those created in an ActiveX control project, with one exception: they are part of a standard .EXE file instead of being an .OCX file and are therefore private to the project. These controls can't be used by other software projects. This is a very easy problem to overcome. Once you have finished developing the control, simply create a new ActiveX control project and add the saved control (.CTL file) to it. Then you can build your control as an .OCX file. Visual Basic can have multiple projects open concurrently, and with this feature we could have built the controls as ActiveX control projects from the start. I often find, however, that it is easy to get lost and confused with too many projects and files floating around. This is why we use Standard EXE projects instead.

Exercise 6-1

Let's create a test control that simply displays messages in response to the important events in this life of a control.

1. Open Visual Basic, and start a new Standard EXE project.

2. Choose Add User Control from the Project menu. On the New tab of the Add User Control dialog box, select the default User Control and click Open.

3. In the Properties window for the user control, set the *BorderStyle* property to *1 – Fixed Single*.

4. Close the UserControl designer.

5. Now place the new control on Form1.

6. In the Project window, double-click UserControl1 to reopen the UserControl designer.

7. Double-click the UserControl designer to open the Code window.

8. Code the following event procedures. You can use the Procedure box to select the event procedures and then add the message box code (shown in bold).

```
Private Sub UserControl_Initialize()
    MsgBox "Initialize"
End Sub

Private Sub UserControl_InitProperties()
    MsgBox "InitProperties"
End Sub

Private Sub UserControl_ReadProperties(PropBag As _
    PropertyBag)
    MsgBox "ReadProperties"
End Sub

Private Sub UserControl_WriteProperties(PropBag As _
    PropertyBag)
    MsgBox "WriteProperties"
End Sub

Private Sub UserControl_Terminate()
    MsgBox "Terminate"
End Sub

Private Sub UserControl_Resize()
    MsgBox "Resize " & ScaleWidth & ", " & ScaleHeight
End Sub

Private Sub UserControl_Show()
    MsgBox "Show"
End Sub
```

9. Close the Code window, and then close the UserControl designer. Note that the control's icon in the toolbox has become enabled. This indicates that the control has been placed in run mode.

    Note that the message boxes appear in the following order:

```
Initialize
Resize 1524, 1284
ReadProperties
Show
```
(Your resize values will reflect the size of your control.)

10. Choose Save Project from the File menu. Save the files as LIFE.CTL, LIFE.FRM, and LIFE.VBP. Note that you must save a project with a control before you can run the project.

11. Choose Start from the Run menu. Notice the events fired:

```
Terminate
Initialize
Resize 1524, 1284
ReadProperties
Show
```

12. Choose End from the Run menu. Notice the events fired:

```
Initialize
Resize 1524, 1284
ReadProperties
Show
```

13. When the message boxes become too annoying (they probably have already), go back into the UserControl designer's Code window and replace all the *MsgBox* statements with *Debug.Print*, which will direct all output to the Immediate window. Close the UserControl designer when you've finished.

14. Close the Form1 Form window. Notice the event fired in the Immediate window.

```
Terminate
```

15. In the Project window, double-click Form1 to open the Form window again. Notice the event fired in the Immediate window.

```
Initialize
Resize 1764, 1164
ReadProperties
Show
```

16. Right-click on Form1's background (not on UserControl1), and select Update UserControls. Notice the string of events in the Immediate window.

The purpose of this exercise is to observe that ActiveX controls are alive from the moment the UserControl designer is closed. This action implicitly puts controls in the running state necessary to enable a developer to work with them. *UserControl* objects actually run in two modes: in Visual Basic's design mode when software is being developed, and as part of another program at run time. Many Visual Basic programmers (not you, gentle reader) put a control on a form and thereafter erroneously think of the control as a permanent fixture of the form. By observing the *Terminate* and *Initialize* events as they occur in this exercise, you can see that the ActiveX controls are continually being created and destroyed in the Visual Basic environment.

INTRINSIC CONTROLS

Visual Basic comes with a bouquet of built-in controls. These are now called *intrinsic* controls to differentiate them from other types of controls, such as custom-built ones. The intrinsic controls are: *CheckBox, ComboBox, Command-Button, Data, DirListBox, DriveListBox, FileListBox, Frame, HScrollBar, Image, Label, Line, ListBox, OptionButton, PictureBox, Shape, TextBox, Timer,* and *VScrollBar.*

PROPERTIES

Now let's turn our attention to properties. Visual Basic has three basic categories of control properties: ambient, extender, and custom. *Ambient* properties provide your control with information about the state of its container. *Extender* properties are those that seem to be part of your control but that are actually provided at run time by the container. *Custom properties* are ones that you implement entirely on your own.

It might initially seem surprising that there is such a variety in types of properties. Most developers who write applications in Visual Basic think of the properties that appear in the Properties window as belonging to a control. In fact, other properties not displayed in the Properties window exist, and of the properties displayed, some do not belong to the control. Consider the *Top* and *Left* properties of a control. They describe where the control is situated within the container. These types of properties belong to the container rather than the control, even though they appear in the Properties window.

Ambient Properties

The container provides ambient properties, and you can think of these properties as providing your control with information regarding its current environment. In fact, ambient properties are exposed by the client site in which the control is embedded, and they reflect values that the container wants to communicate to the control so that the control will take on the characteristics of the form in which it lives. These are, effectively, hints about how the control can best display itself in the container. Think of a chameleon that camouflages itself by changing color to match its surroundings. The purpose of ambient properties is to help your control camouflage that it is not really a native part of its container.

For example, the ambient property *BackColor* informs a control of the background color of its container. This can then be used to set the control's own background color to blend better with the container. Ambient properties don't need to be obeyed strictly, but it is polite to do so when it makes sense. Visual Basic makes ambient properties available to your control through an *Ambient-Properties* object, a reference to which is available in the *Ambient* property of the *UserControl* object. This leads to this syntax for accessing ambient properties:

```
UserControl.Ambient.AmbientPropertyName
```

Ambient properties are properties of the *UserControl* object and are therefore available to the control only. They neither appear in the finished control's Property window list nor are they available to applications that use the control.

Since the container provides ambient properties, some containers might not implement all the ambient properties. For example, if your ActiveX control is used in an application created in Borland's Delphi, it is possible that all ambient properties won't be available to your control. To circumvent this problem, the *AmbientProperties* object implemented by Visual Basic contains all of the standard ambient properties defined by the ActiveX controls specification, regardless of whether they are actually provided by the container. If a container doesn't implement a particular ambient property, the *AmbientProperties* object simply returns a default value. This is advantageous because you don't have to worry about getting error messages when using an ambient property that is not available.

By the same token, some containers might implement additional ambient properties. These properties will not be visible in the Object Browser because they are not in Visual Basic's type library; nonetheless, the *AmbientProperties* object will expose them. You can learn about such properties in the documentation for a container and then access them as properties of the *AmbientProperties* object. Note that since these additional properties are not in the type library, Visual Basic cannot verify their existence at compile time. Therefore, you should use error handling when working with these properties; it is likely that your control will be used in another container where these properties might not be available.

As a consequence of this lack of type library information, any calls to container-specific ambient properties are late-bound. By contrast, any calls to standard ambient properties are early-bound. Recall that early binding requires type library information to be available at compile time so that all information regarding the object's interface is obtained. Late binding uses the *IDispatch* interface, so no interface information is sought at development time, and thus no error checking can be performed. Instead, all the finding and creating of the object is deferred to run time. In Visual Basic, a call to *CreateObject* always signifies late binding, while setting a reference to an interface by means of the References dialog box indicates early binding.

The standard ambient properties are as follows: *BackColor, DisplayAsDefault, DisplayName, Font, ForeColor, LocaleID, MessageReflect, Palette, RightToLeft, ScaleUnits, ShowGrabHandles, ShowHatching, SupportsMnemonics, TextAlign, UIDead,* and *UserMode*. In Visual Basic, you can safely ignore many of these ambient properties since default functionality in response to these properties is built in. The following are the ambient properties that you should be aware of:

- *DisplayAsDefault* tells you whether your control is the default button for the container. If your control is the default, pressing the Enter key is equivalent to clicking on the control. Controls that are the default (*DisplayAsDefault* = *True*) should draw an extra-heavy border that identifies the default button to the end user.

- *DisplayName* is the name of the particular instance of the control. It should be used when raising errors at design time so that the developer who receives the error can identify the control instance causing the error.

- *ForeColor, BackColor,* and *Font* are hints your control can use to make its appearance match that of the container. For example, in the *InitProperties* event, which is fired whenever an instance of your control is first placed in a container, it is highly recommended to set your control's *ForeColor, BackColor,* and *Font* properties to the values supplied by the ambient properties.

- *TextAlign* tells the control how the client site would like the control to arrange the text it displays. If the value of the property is 0, the control should obey "general" alignment principles: text aligned to the left, numbers to the right. A value of 1 means left alignment, 2 means centered alignment, 3 means right alignment, and 4 means justified alignment.

- *LocaleID* tells the control in which locale (language and country) the control should consider itself to be running.

■ *Palette* provides the current palette of the container.

■ *UserMode* allows an instance of your control to determine whether it is executing at design time (*UserMode = False*) or at run time (*UserMode = True*).

The *AmbientChanged* Event

Assuming that you want to follow the recommendations provided by the ambient properties, what should your control do if one of those ambient properties changes at run time? Let's say you set your control's *BackColor* property based on the ambient *BackColor* property so that your control blends with its container. Eventually, during execution of the application, the background color of the container changes. This causes your control to stick out like a chicken without feathers. To avoid this sort of embarrassing situation, you can write code that responds to the *AmbientChanged* event. The *AmbientChanged* event is fired whenever the value of one of the ambient properties changes, allowing you to respond to this situation gracefully. You declare the *AmbientChanged* event procedure as follows:

```
Private Sub UserControl_AmbientChanged(PropertyName As String)
```

The *PropertyName* argument provides your code with the name of the ambient property whose value changed. This will save you from having to reset all the ambient properties values used in your control.

The Extender Object

Another type of property, known as an *extender property* in Visual Basic, is one that an average user would certainly regard as being associated with the control but that is actually implemented by the container. For example, a control's size and position, its order in the tab sequence, and the *Tag* property fall into the category of extender properties. These properties are associated with something called the *extender object*, which is an object implemented by the container, generally by aggregating with the control. When the container gets or sets a property or invokes a method on the control, the extender object gets access first. If the extender object recognizes the property or method as belonging to it, it performs the actions required; if the extender object doesn't recognize the property or method, it is passed on to the control itself.

A common example of this is the *Enabled* property. The typical visual control will implement this property to reflect the current state of the control. A control, however, knows only its internal state. The control might think it is enabled, but if the control is part of a form that is currently disabled, the control is also disabled.

> **NOTE**   If you are familiar with creating ActiveX controls using Visual C++, you are already familiar with extender properties; in Visual C++ they are called *extended* properties.

The extender object provided by the Visual Basic run time system provides a rich set of properties, methods, and events. The properties it provides are *Cancel, Container, Default, DragIcon, DragMode, Enabled, Height, HelpContextID, Index, Left, Name, Object, Parent, TabIndex, TabStop, Tag, ToolTipText, Top, Visible, WhatsThisHelpID,* and *Width.* The methods it provides are *Drag, Move, SetFocus, ShowWhatsThis,* and *ZOrder.* The events it provides are *DragDrop, DragOver, GotFocus,* and *LostFocus.*

Again, be aware that many containers provide only a limited subset of these properties, methods, and events. The following table shows the extender properties that the ActiveX Controls specification says all containers should provide. All containers should implement these properties, but they aren't required to do so. As a result, when your code refers to extender properties it's a good idea to implement error trapping.

Extender Property	*Data Type*	*Access Attribute*	*Description*
Name	*String*	Read	The name the container assigns to the control instance.
Visible	*Boolean*	Read/Write	Indicates whether the control is visible.
Parent	*Object*	Read	Returns the object that contains the control; for example, a Visual Basic form.
Cancel	*Boolean*	Read	*True* if the control is the cancel command button for the container; *False* if not.
Default	*Boolean*	Read	*True* if the control is the default command button for the container; *False* if not.

Exercise 6-2

Let's create our first test control, which will simply display all the data available in the ambient and extender properties.

1.   Open Visual Basic, and start a new Standard EXE project.

2.   Choose Add User Control from the Project menu. Select the default User Control, and click Open.

3. In the Properties window for the user control, set the following properties:

Property	*Setting*
Name	*MyControl*
AutoRedraw	*True*
BorderStyle	*1 - Fixed Single*
Tag	*MyControl's Internal Tag*

4. Double-click the UserControl designer to open the Code window.

5. In the UserControl_Click event procedure, write the following code (shown in bold):

```
Private Sub UserControl_Click()
    Print "Ambient Properties"
    Print , "LocaleID: " & UserControl.Ambient.LocaleID
    Print , "MessageReflect: " & _
      UserControl.Ambient.MessageReflect
    Print , "TextAlign: " & UserControl.Ambient.TextAlign
    Print , "SupportsMnemonics: " & _
      UserControl.Ambient.SupportsMnemonics
    Print , "BackColor: " & UserControl.Ambient.BackColor
    Print , "DisplayName: " & _
      UserControl.Ambient.DisplayName
    Print , "Font: " & UserControl.Ambient.Font
    Print , "ForeColor: " & UserControl.Ambient.ForeColor
    Print , "ScaleUnits: " & UserControl.Ambient.ScaleUnits
    Print , "TextAlign: " & UserControl.Ambient.TextAlign
    Print , "UserMode: " & UserControl.Ambient.UserMode
    Print , "UIDead: " & UserControl.Ambient.UIDead
    Print , "ShowGrabHandles: " & _
      UserControl.Ambient.ShowGrabHandles
    Print , "ShowHatching: " & _
      UserControl.Ambient.ShowHatching
    Print , "DisplayAsDefault: " & _
      UserControl.Ambient.DisplayAsDefault
    Print , "Palette: " & UserControl.Ambient.Palette

    Print "Extender Properties"
    Print , "Name: " & UserControl.Extender.Name
    Print , "DragIcon: " & UserControl.Extender.DragIcon
    Print , "DragMode: " & UserControl.Extender.DragMode
    Print , "Height: " & UserControl.Extender.Height
```

(continued)

```
            Print , "HelpContextID: " & _
              UserControl.Extender.HelpContextID
            Print , "Left: " & UserControl.Extender.Left
            Print , "TabIndex: " & UserControl.Extender.TabIndex
            Print , "TabStop: " & UserControl.Extender.TabStop
            Print , "Tag: " & UserControl.Extender.Tag
            Print , "Top: " & UserControl.Extender.Top
            Print , "Visible: " & UserControl.Extender.Visible
            Print , "WhatsThisHelpID: " & _
              UserControl.Extender.WhatsThisHelpID
            Print , "Width: " & UserControl.Extender.Width
            Print
            Print "UserControl's Tag:" & UserControl.Tag
        End Sub
```

6. Close the UserControl designer. Find the Form window for Form1.

7. Now double-click the MyControl icon in the lower right corner of the toolbox to add a control to the form.

8. Enlarge the form, and then resize the control so that it fills the form.

9. In the Properties window, set the *Tag* property of the form to *My Form's MyControl Tag*.

10. Choose Save Project from the File menu to save your work.

11. Run the program, and click in the control. The output should look similar to Figure 6-2.

12. Observe which *Tag* property is displayed with which object. *My Form's MyControl Tag* is displayed as part of the extender object. *MyControl's Internal Tag* is displayed as part of the *UserControl* object itself.

Adding Custom Properties

Custom properties are by far the most interesting kind of property to talk about, primarily because it is you who implement them. You can name custom properties anything you want, you can accept any parameters you want, and custom properties will generally do your bidding. Controls rarely become useful until you add some custom properties and methods. The simplest type of property to implement is created from a public variable with a line of code such as this:

```
Public PropName As String
```

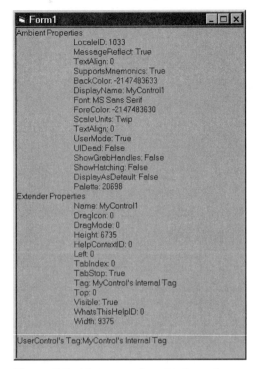

Figure 6-2. *The output from MyControl.*

Property Procedures

Simple properties declared with the statement *Public PropName As Type* are not a good idea for controls. You should always implement control properties with property procedures instead of with public data members; otherwise, your controls might not work correctly in Visual Basic. You might remember the *Let*, *Get*, and *Set* property procedures that we used in a class module in Chapter 3. Property procedures are required because you must notify Visual Basic whenever a property value changes. You do this by invoking the *PropertyChanged* method of the *UserControl* object whenever a property value has been modified, as is shown in the following code fragment:

```
Private m_MyProperty As String

Public Property Get MyProperty() As String
    MyProperty = m_MyProperty
End Property

Public Property Let MyProperty(ByVal NewValue As String)
    m_MyProperty = NewValue
    UserControl.PropertyChanged "MyProperty"
End Property
```

Without calling the *PropertyChanged* method, Visual Basic does not know that the property has been changed and needs to be saved. Since property values can be displayed in more than one place, the development environment must be notified when a property value changes so that it can synchronize the values. For example, if you have the same property in both a property page and the Properties window, both need to have the same value.

Exercise 6-3

Let's create an ActiveX control with a custom property and property procedures to test this feature.

1. Open Visual Basic, and start a new Standard EXE project.

2. Choose Add User Control from the Project menu. Select the default User Control, and click Open.

3. In the Properties window for the user control, set the properties shown in the following table.

Property	*Setting*
AutoRedraw	*True*
BorderStyle	*1 - Fixed Single*
Name	*CustomControl*

4. Double-click the UserControl designer to open the Code window.

5. In the Declarations section, add the following code:

```
Option Explicit
Public MyName As String
Private InternalSecondProperty As String

Public Property Get MySecondProperty() As String
    MySecondProperty = InternalSecondProperty
End Property

Public Property Let MySecondProperty(NewValue As String)
    InternalSecondProperty = NewValue
    UserControl.PropertyChanged "MySecondProperty"
End Property
```

6. In the UserControl_Click event procedure, write the following code (shown in bold):

```
Private Sub UserControl_Click()
    Print "MyName is " & MyName
```

```
        Print "MySecondProperty Procedure = " & _
           InternalSecondProperty
     End Sub
```

7. Close the Code window and the UserControl designer.

8. Find the Form window for Form1. Double-click the CustomControl icon in the toolbox to add the control to the form.

9. Resize the control so that it fills the form.

10. Open the Properties window for CustomControl1. Notice that there is now a MyName property in the property list for CustomControl.

11. Set the MyName property to Hello.

12. Choose Save Project from the file menu, and accept the default names.

13. Run the program, and click the control.

14. Observe that only *MyName is* prints in the control, while *Hello* is missing. Act surprised.

15. Choose End from the Run menu.

16. Return to the Properties window for the *CustomControl1* object, and note that the MyName property is no longer set to Hello. This is because we have not yet implemented property persistence, and property values are not saved. This will be corrected in Exercise 6-4, later in this chapter.

16. Open the Code window for the form Form1, and add the following code (shown in bold) to the Form_Load event procedure:

```
     Private Sub Form_Load()
        CustomControl1.MyName = "HELLO"
        CustomControl1.MySecondProperty = "Hello there"
        MsgBox CustomControl1.MySecondProperty
     End Sub
```

17. Run the program, click the control, and verify that everything works as expected.

18. When you finish experimenting, choose End from the Run menu.

19. It is enlightening to step through this code line by line using the F8 key. Try this now. Then stop the program.

20. Open the Properties window for the CustomControl1 object. You should see the MySecondProperty property.

21. Save your work.

Property Persistence

Property persistence means keeping property values around for longer than the duration of the program that manipulated them. If you create a program that uses an ActiveX control and you set up the properties of that control to be just right for your application, it'll be a little disconcerting when you start the program the next day and find that all the property values you entered have evaporated. In fact, as you saw in the previous exercise, even setting properties by using the Properties window doesn't work. This will be corrected when you make your properties persistent. Here's how.

ActiveX control modules define three events that relate to property persistence: *InitProperties*, *ReadProperties*, and *WriteProperties*. The *InitProperties* event procedure is called when an ActiveX control is first embedded in a form. This gives you a chance to store default values in your custom properties. The *Read-Properties* event is fired whenever Visual Basic needs to retrieve the value of a custom property—when the project is opened and run, for example. When the *UserControl* object receives its *ReadProperties* event, siting has occurred. *Siting* is simply the process of loading a control and placing it in the container. The *Write-Properties* event is fired when a custom property needs to be saved. For example, saving your project always causes the *WriteProperties* event procedure to be called. Here are the declarations for the three property event procedures:

```
Private Sub UserControl_InitProperties()
Private Sub UserControl_ReadProperties(PropBag As _
   PropertyBag)
Private Sub UserControl_WriteProperties(PropBag As _
   PropertyBag)
```

In these event procedures, Visual Basic programs use the *PropertyBag* object to implement property persistence. A *PropertyBag* object is just what its name implies—a "bag" in which property values are saved. You can't see into it, and you have no idea where or how the data is saved. (We'll find out shortly.) All you can do is put values in and take them out. The *PropertyBag* class defines two methods, *ReadProperty* and *WriteProperty*, and one property, *Contents*, as follows:

```
ReadProperty(Name As String[, DefaultValue])
WriteProperty(Name As String, Value[, DefaultValue])
Property Contents As Variant ' Byte array of PropertyBag contents.
```

As you can see, the first argument of the *WriteProperty* method is the name of the property. The *Name* parameter references the property name under which the *Value* argument will be saved. A property value is saved as a *Variant*. Oddly, the third argument is a default value. Why provide a default value when saving a property? Before saving the value, *WriteProperty* compares the default value with the value passed to it for saving. If the *Value* and *DefaultValue* parameters are identical, nothing is saved. The property value doesn't need to be saved because default values will be set automatically when the control is reloaded. If you consider the great number of properties most controls have, it becomes obvious that storing and then reloading the default values for every property is wasteful. It is usually best to define a global constant, such as *PROPDEFAULT_MY-PROPERTYNAME*, to contain the default value for each property. This is because you need to supply it in three different places: the *InitProperties*, *ReadProperties*, and *WriteProperties* event procedures.

The *ReadProperty* method works similarly. *ReadProperty* accepts the name of the property whose value you want to read and returns that value. The optional *DefaultValue* parameter allows you to specify the default value to be returned in case the property you are looking for has not been previously saved. This will always happen the first time the developer using your control puts your control on a form, since the developer will not have set any properties up to that point. It will also happen if the value has never been changed from the default and therefore has never been saved by *WriteProperty*. Consequently, it is a good idea to include error-trapping code in the *ReadProperties* event procedure; this will protect your control from invalid property values that might have been entered directly into the .FRM file by overzealous users armed with text editors.

Exercise 6-4

1. Start Visual Basic, and open the project you created in Exercise 6-3.

2. Open the CustomControl control in the UserControl designer.

3. Choose Code from the View menu.

4. In the code window for *UserControl*, select the *InitProperties* event procedure and enter the following code (shown in bold):

    ```
    Private Sub UserControl_InitProperties()
        MsgBox "InitProperties"
        MyName = "Default"
    End Sub
    ```

5. Select the UserControl_ReadProperties event procedure, and enter the following code (shown in bold):

    ```
    Private Sub UserControl_ReadProperties(PropBag As _
      PropertyBag)
        MsgBox "ReadProperties"
        MyName = PropBag.ReadProperty("MyName", "Default")
    End Sub
    ```

6. Select the UserControl_WriteProperties event procedure, and enter the following code (shown in bold):

```
Private Sub UserControl_WriteProperties(PropBag As _
    PropertyBag)
    MsgBox "WriteProperties"
    PropBag.WriteProperty "MyName", MyName, "Default"
End Sub
```

7. Close the Code window and the UserControl designer for CustomControl. If you get a message box, just choose OK to dismiss it.

8. Open Form1 in the Form window.

9. Open the Code window for the form, and comment out the code in the Form_Load event procedure:

```
Private Sub Form_Load()
    ' COMMENT EVERYTHING OUT
    ' CustomControl1.MyName = "HELLO"
    ' CustomControl1.MySecondProperty = "Hello there"
    ' MsgBox CustomControl1.MySecondProperty
End Sub
```

10. Close the Code window, and open the Properties window for the CustomControl1 object. You should see the MyName property with a *Default* setting caused by the preceding code.

11. Set the MyName property to *Testing*.

12. Run the program. You will get a few message boxes notifying you when properties are being read and written, but everything should work properly.

13. When you are finished experimenting, remove the *MsgBox* statements from the control event procedures and save your work.

What we find really fascinating (and we hope you do too) is that Visual Basic actually executes code in your control even when the test project is not running. This is because even while the test project is in design mode, your control is active and being controlled by Visual Basic. So when Visual Basic needs to read or write property values, it calls the control's event procedures regardless of the current mode. A final thing to look at is the FORM1.FRM file. Open this file in Notepad and you should be able to find the declaration of your CustomControl object and its MyName property value, as shown here:

FORM1.FRM

```
Version 5.00
Begin VB.Form Form1
    Caption         =   "Form1"
... other properties here ...
    Begin Project1.CustomControl CustomControl1
        Height      =   2532
        Left        =   480
        TabIndex    =   0
        Top         =   360
        Width       =   3732
        _ExtentX    =   6583
        _ExtentY    =   4466
        MyName      =   "Testing"
    End
End
Attribute VB_Name = "Form1"
Attribute VB_GlobalNameSpace = False
Attribute VB_Creatable = False
Attribute VB_PredeclaredId = True
Attribute VB_Exposed = False
... procedures begin here ...
```

METHODS

Methods are procedures built into a control that operate on the control. You can implement methods for ActiveX controls by adding *Public Sub* and *Function* procedures to the *Declarations* section of your control. Although you can create any type of method to perform any task, it is also a good idea to implement methods that are commonly found on controls that provide similar functionality to what you want to do. Since other developers will be familiar with standard methods, they will have an easier time learning to work with your control. For example, it would be poor design to add the functionality of a *Print* method to a procedure named *Output*. Since Visual Basic programmers are familiar with the *Print* method, they would be more likely to search for *Print* than *Output*.

Recall that Visual Basic's extender object automatically provides five standard methods for every control: *Drag*, *Move*, *SetFocus*, *ShowWhatsThis*, and *ZOrder*. For a control with a visible interface at run time, it is recommended that you also provide a *Refresh* method. Internally, this method should simply call *UserControl.Refresh*. For developer-drawn controls, this will raise the *Paint* event; for controls built using constituent components, it will force a refresh of the constituent controls. In addition, you might want to selectively implement methods of the *UserControl* object or of its constituent controls.

RAISING EVENTS FROM CONTROLS

You need to distinguish between the events received by your ActiveX control and the events your control raises. Events received by your control are opportunities for you to do something interesting; events your control raises provide opportunities for the developer using your control to do something interesting. You might find it helpful to think of properties and methods as inbound and events as outbound. That is, methods are invoked by developers using your control, while events originate in your control and are propagated outward to the developer. This gives the developer using your control a chance to execute code in response to something that happens inside your control.

Two basic steps are required to raise an event from your control. First, you must declare the event itself, using a statement such as this:

```
Event MyEventName()
```

Second, you use the *RaiseEvent* statement to fire the event at the desired time, using a statement such as this:

```
RaiseEvent MyEventName
```

The *RaiseEvent* statement provides functionality similar to simply calling a procedure. However, when calling a procedure, it is required that the called procedure actually exist. Event procedures, on the other hand, cause no errors if they are not implemented—the event is simply ignored. It is also possible to raise events that provide parameters to the event procedure being called. This is useful with events such as *MouseMove*, where more information describing the event that occurred—in this case, the current mouse coordinates—is required. To implement this type of event, simply declare the event as follows:

```
Event MyEventName(MyParameter As Integer)
```

Then you can raise the event with this code:

```
RaiseEvent MyEventName(100)
```

For the benefit of developers using your control, the control's container can provide additional events beyond those you define. As mentioned earlier, Visual Basic's *Extender* object automatically raises four events on behalf of ActiveX controls: *DragDrop*, *DragOver*, *GotFocus*, and *LostFocus*. It is recommended that most controls raise *Click*, *DblClick*, *KeyDown*, *KeyPress*, *KeyUp*,

MouseDown, MouseMove, and *MouseUp* events. You'll find it beneficial to implement events commonly found on controls that provide functionality similar to what you want.

Exercise 6-5

Let's create an ActiveX control with methods and events.

1. Open Visual Basic, and start a new Standard EXE project.

2. Choose Add User Control from the Project menu. Select the default User Control, and click Open.

3. In the Properties window for UserControl1, set the properties shown in the following table.

Property	Setting
AutoRedraw	*True*
BorderStyle	*1 - Fixed Single*
DrawWidth	*2*
Name	*Scribble*

4. Double-click the user control in the UserControl designer to open the Code window.

5. In the Declarations section, add the following code:

```
Option Explicit
Public DrawColor As Long
Event OutOfBounds(X As Single, Y As Single)
```

6. Add the following event procedure code (shown in bold):

```
Private Sub UserControl_MouseDown _
   (Button As Integer, Shift As Integer, _
   X As Single, Y As Single)
      CurrentX = X
      CurrentY = Y
End Sub

Private Sub UserControl_MouseMove _
   (Button As Integer, Shift As Integer, _
   X As Single, Y As Single)
      If Button = 1 Then
         UserControl.Line _
            (CurrentX, CurrentY)-(X, Y), DrawColor
```

(continued)

```
                          If (X <= 0 Or X >= ScaleWidth Or Y <= 0 Or _
                              Y >= ScaleHeight) Then
                                  RaiseEvent OutOfBounds(X, Y)
                          End If
                      End If
                  End Sub
```

7. Close the Code window and the UserControl designer for the control.

8. Find the Form window for Form1.

9. Add the Scribble control to the form.

10. Add three *OptionButton* controls named Option1, Option2, and Option3 to the form. Set the *Caption* property of the first to *Red*, of the second to *Green*, and of the third to *Blue*.

11. Add the following code (shown in bold) to the *OptionButton* controls' corresponding *Click* event procedures:

```
Private Sub Option1_Click()
    Scribble1.DrawColor = RGB(255, 0, 0)
End Sub

Private Sub Option2_Click()
    Scribble1.DrawColor = RGB(0, 255, 0)
End Sub

Private Sub Option3_Click()
    Scribble1.DrawColor = RGB(0, 0, 255)
End Sub
```

12. Place a *CommandButton* control named Command1 on the form, and set its *Caption* property to *Clear Control*.

13. Add the following code (shown in bold) to the command button's *Click* event procedure:

```
Private Sub Command1_Click()
    Scribble1.Cls
End Sub
```

14. Place a *TextBox* control named Text1 on the form, and clear its *Text* property.

15. Double-click the Scribble control to open the Code window. Add the following code to the Scribble1_OutOfBounds event procedure (shown in bold):

```
Private Sub Scribble1_OutOfBounds(X As Single, Y As Single)
    Text1 = "OutOfBounds " & X & ", " & Y
End Sub
```

16. Choose Save Project from the File menu. Accept the default filenames.

17. Choose Start from the Run menu, and test the program. Notice that the *OutOfBounds* coordinates display in the text box when you drag the mouse from a point within the Scribble control past one of its edges.

HANDLING ERRORS IN CONTROLS

You manage errors in ActiveX controls the same as you do for ActiveX code components, but we have one warning: you should never raise errors within an event procedure since there is nowhere for these errors to be trapped. For example, suppose a *Click* event procedure is fired when the user clicks a control. If the control raises an error in response to this event, the container of the form never has a chance to respond. Visual Basic will simply report the errors and stop the application.

Chapter 7

Designing Advanced ActiveX Controls

While you were creating the Microsoft ActiveX controls in Microsoft Visual Basic described in the exercises in the preceding chapter, you might have had an opportunity to compare your controls with intrinsic Visual Basic controls and notice that your controls aren't as polished and professional looking. There are multitudes of ways you can better integrate your controls with the Visual Basic environment and add advanced functionality. For example, you might add a description line at the bottom of the Properties window that gives the developer using the control information about the purpose of a particular property. This chapter describes and explains many such ways to improve the ActiveX controls you create in Visual Basic.

PROCEDURE ATTRIBUTES

The majority of advanced control features in Visual Basic are available in the deceptively simple Procedure Attributes dialog box, which you access from the Tools menu. However, after you click the Advanced button in the dialog box, you find yourself staring at a long list of settings that you might not understand but that you nonetheless have to make a decision about. The main purpose of the Procedure Attributes dialog box is to allow you to control settings for the various procedures of your control. Remember that properties, methods, and events are all implemented as procedures, so you can use this dialog box for all three of these procedure types. Some of the settings have different effects when applied to different types of procedures, and some areas of this dialog box apply exclusively to either properties or methods.

The Procedure Attributes dialog box, shown in Figure 7-1, is divided into four regions that we'll call Name, Property, Attributes, and Data Binding. The Name region enables you to select and describe each specific procedure of your ActiveX control and to identify any help file and context ID associated with the selected procedure. The Property region enables you to set a property identification number, property page, and property category for the selected procedure. The Attributes region enables you to specify where the property is displayed and allows you to set interface defaults. The Data Binding region enables you to control Visual Basic's data-bound control model.

Name, Description, and Help Context ID

The Name drop-down list box in the Name region enables you to select a procedure to work with in the Procedure Attributes dialog box. All the rest of the settings in the Procedure Attributes dialog box affect the procedure selected in the Name box.

We highly recommend that you provide a concise description for each of your properties, methods, and events. If you click on almost any property in the Properties window, you will notice a description line for that property at the bottom of the Properties window. This same description line appears in the Object Browser for properties, as do description lines for methods and events. The easiest way to create a description for a custom property, method, or event is to type the description in the Description box in the Procedure Attributes dialog box.

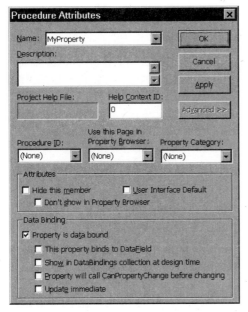

Figure 7-1. *The Procedure Attributes dialog box.*

USING THE OBJECT BROWSER TO CREATE DESCRIPTIONS

A slightly more complicated way to create descriptions involves using the Object Browser itself. This is the only way to create a description of a control or an object. To create a description for a control, follow these steps:

1. Choose Object Browser from the View menu.

2. In the Libraries drop-down list box, select your project.

3. Right-click on the control name in the Classes list, and choose Properties from the shortcut menu.

4. In the Member Options dialog box, type a description in the Description box.

5. Choose OK.

The description now appears at the bottom of the Object Browser window.

The Help Context ID box enables you to specify an identification number for the selected procedure. The Help Context ID entry should match the identification number of the correct topic in the help file. This will allow the Object Browser and the Properties window to display context-sensitive help for that particular item when the end user selects the procedure and presses the F1 key. The Project Help File box will display the name of the help file you've chosen for your project. (To choose a help file, you select *projectname* Properties from the Project menu. On the General tab of the Project Properties dialog box, enter the name of the help file in the Help File Name box.)

Procedure ID

The Procedure ID drop-down list box enables you to select the type of procedure you are creating. Every property, method, and event in your type library has an identification number, called a procedure ID. Some properties, methods, and events are important enough to have standard procedure IDs that are defined by the ActiveX Controls specification.

If a property, method, or event has a standard procedure ID, it's a good idea to use it. For example, if you create a Caption property for your control, it would be advisable to set its Procedure ID to Caption. By assigning a standard procedure ID to a procedure, you inform Visual Basic about the purpose of the procedure in your program. In some cases, this causes Visual Basic to enable special behavior for that property, method, or event.

Every procedure can have only one procedure ID assigned, and no other procedure can have the same procedure ID. If you accept the default procedure ID of *(None)*, it doesn't mean that the procedure won't have a procedure ID. Visual Basic automatically assigns procedure IDs to members marked as *(None)*. Don't confuse *(None)* with the *(Default)* setting; we'll cover *(Default)* a bit later.

> **NOTE** If you are a Microsoft Visual C++ programmer, you will recognize procedure IDs as the Visual Basic equivalent of an *IDispatch* interface identification number, or DISPID.

Property Pages

As you know, simple properties that you create with public variables or property procedures appear in the Properties window automatically, allowing the developer using your control to browse and set these properties. In more complex controls, sometimes several properties relate to one another but the relationship isn't immediately clear to the developer. Property pages are designed to solve this problem. A property page is a tabbed dialog box that is often connected to the (*Custom*) property of a control. When the user double-clicks on the (*Custom*) property, the Property Pages dialog box is displayed, allowing the user to set properties.

Property Categories

The Categorized tab in the Properties window groups the properties by categories that are based on functionality. You can assign each of your control's properties to a particular group using the Property Category box in the Procedure Attributes dialog box. The Property Category drop-down list displays the standard categories: Appearance, Behavior, Data, DDE, Font, List, Misc, Position, Scale, and Text. You can either select from this list or create a new category by typing the new name in the Property Category text box. We highly recommend assigning categories to your properties, since neglecting to do this leaves all your properties in the Misc group. As a general suggestion, look at other controls containing properties similar to those exposed by your control and select your categories similarly. Novices have a tendency to create too many new categories. However, as developers become more experienced, they realize that it is preferable to assign properties to preexisting categories and that most necessary categories already exist.

Attributes

In the Attributes region of the Procedure Attributes dialog box, you can control certain attributes of the procedure in question. The three choices are Hide This Member, User Interface Default, and Don't Show In Property Browser.

When you select the Hide This Member box, the procedure is hidden from view. Your properties do not appear in the Properties window, and neither properties nor methods appear in the Auto List Members list. (The Auto List Members feature of Visual Basic automatically provides a drop-down list of applicable properties, methods, and events in the Code window.) Properties, methods, and events continue to appear in the Object Browser because they are all still part of the control's type library. Developers often select Hide This Member to phase out particular items of a control's interface in successive versions of the software. Programs that rely on these properties, methods, and events will still work, but new software is unlikely to use them since they are not easily available through the drop-down list in the Code window.

When you select the User Interface Default box for a property, this property becomes the default highlighted property in the Properties window. For most controls, the interface default for a property is the *Name* property. When you select the User Interface Default box for an event, this event becomes the default event procedure displayed in the Code window. Selecting the Don't Show In Property Browser box hides a property in the Properties window, effectively making this property available only at run time.

Data Binding

A text box control is an example of a control that can be bound to a data control. You can create an ActiveX control in Visual Basic that can be bound to a Data control in the same manner as the TextBox control. Visual Basic enables you to do this by marking properties of your control as bindable. Another developer can then associate bindable properties with database fields, making it easier to use your control in a database application. To enable data binding, be sure to select the Property Is Data Bound box in the Procedure Attributes dialog box. This automatically provides your code with a *DataBindings* property and a dialog box that enables the developer using your control to associate properties with data fields. After selecting the Property Is Data Bound box, you can choose from among the bindable properties: This Property Binds To Data-Field, Show In DataBindings Collection At Design Time, Property Will Call CanPropertyChange Before Changing, and Update Immediate. These options are discussed in more detail in the section on data binding later in this chapter.

USING THE PROCEDURE ATTRIBUTES DIALOG BOX

Now that you are familiar with the basic layout of the Procedure Attributes dialog box, you are ready to learn what you can do with its features.

Default Control Members

Two types of default characteristics can be set for an ActiveX control in Visual Basic. The first is known as the user interface default, which you set with the User Interface Default box in the Procedure Attributes dialog box, as discussed previously. The second type of default characteristic refers to a control's programmatic interface. By specifying a property as the default, you enable programmers using your control to write code that implicitly references that property. For example, you might have written code such as the following:

```
Text1 = "Hello"
```

For a TextBox control, this code actually means:

```
Text1.Text = "Hello"
```

Since the *Text* property of the TextBox control is the default property, it isn't necessary to explicitly declare this. If your control has a *Value* property, this often will be the default. To make a property the default, simply select *(Default)* in the Procedure ID box of the Procedure Attributes dialog box.

Hidden Members

By default, all properties are available at both design time and run time. There are several reasons why you might want to hide a property, a method, or an event from the developer using your control. Sometimes you might simply have a property that only makes sense at run time, and therefore you do not want the developer to see it in the Properties window at design time. The *ListCount* and *ListIndex* properties of a ListBox control work this way.

Another reason to hide a property from the Properties window is to discourage the developer from using it. For example, a property might have been replaced by another property in a new version of a control, but the control still supports the old property to avoid breaking old code. At the same time, the control's developer wants new software projects to use the new property instead of the old one. In this case, you can hide the old property. This scenario might apply to methods and events in addition to properties.

Sometimes, exactly the opposite will be true. You might have a property you want a developer to set only at design time—such as the *DataSource* property of a data-bound control. Even in these cases, it is considered proper design to allow the property to be read at run time. The following code will satisfactorily address this issue:

```
Private mSecret As Integer

Public Property Get Secret() As Integer
    Secret = mSecret
End Property

Public Property Let Secret(newSecret As Integer)
    If Ambient.UserMode = True Then
        Err.Raise 31013, , _
          "Property is read-only at run time"
        Exit Property
    End If
    mSecret = newSecret
    PropertyChanged "Secret"
End Property
```

This code implements *Get* and *Let* property procedures for the Secret property. When the programmer attempts to set the value of the Secret property, the *Let* property procedure is called. First the procedure uses the *UserMode* property of the *Ambient* object to check whether the control is running in Visual Basic's design mode (*Ambient.UserMode = False*) or in run mode (*Ambient.User-Mode = True*). If the control is currently in run mode, you don't want the programmer to be able to set the property. The code therefore uses the *Err.Raise* statement to generate a run-time error. This effectively creates a property that is read-only at run time. You can also block the programmer from reading the property at run time. In the *Get* procedure for the property, test whether *Ambient.UserMode = True*; if it is, raise an error informing the user that the property isn't available at run time.

Exercise 7-1

This exercise shows you how to better assimilate a control with the Visual Basic development environment.

1.   Open Visual Basic, and start a new Standard EXE project.

2.   Choose Add User Control from the Project menu. Select the default User Control, and click Open.

3.   In the Properties window, set the *Name* property to *MyProperty-Control.*

4.   Double-click the UserControl designer to open the Code window.

5.   Add the following statements to the Declarations section of the Code window:

```
Option Explicit
Public MyDefaultProperty As String
Public MyRunTimeProperty As String
Private mDesignTimeProperty As String
Event MyDefaultEvent()

Public Property Get MyDesignTimeProperty() As String
    MyDesignTimeProperty = mDesignTimeProperty
End Property

Public Property Let MyDesignTimeProperty(newDesign As _
   String)
   If Ambient.UserMode Then
        Err.Raise 31013, , _
          "Property is read-only at run time"
        Exit Property
```

```
            End If
            mDesignTimeProperty = newDesign
        End Property
```

6. Choose Procedure Attributes from the Tools menu.

7. Choose the Advanced button.

8. In the Name box, choose MyDefaultProperty.

9. In the Description box, type *This is my awesome default property* or something to that effect.

10. Set the Procedure ID box to (Default). This makes MyDefaultProperty the default property for coding purposes.

11. In the Property Category box, type *My Properties*. Doing this creates a new category and puts MyDefaultProperty in the My Properties category of the Properties window.

12. Select the User Interface Default box. This makes MyDefaultProperty the default property whenever the Properties window is opened.

13. Choose Apply.

14. In the Name box, choose MyRunTimeProperty.

15. In the Description box, type *This is my awesome run time property* or something to that effect.

16. Select the Don't Show In Property Browser box. This hides MyRun-TimeProperty in the Properties window.

17. Choose Apply.

18. In the Name box, choose MyDesignTimeProperty.

19. In the Description box, type *This is my awesome design time property* or something to that effect.

20. In the Property Category box, type *My Properties*.

21. Choose Apply.

22. In the Name box, choose MyDefaultEvent.

23. In the Description box, type *This is my awesome default event* or something to that effect.

24. Select the User Interface Default box. This makes MyDefaultEvent the default event displayed whenever the Code window is opened.

25. Choose OK.

26. Close the Code window.

27. Close the UserControl designer.

28. Add the new control to Form1.

29. Open the Properties window. You should see MyDefaultProperty and MyDesignTimeProperty. Notice that MyRunTimeProperty is missing. Also check to see the description text at the bottom of the Properties window.

30. Select the Categorized tab in the Properties window, and notice that both properties are in the My Properties group.

31. Double-click on the control to open the Code window. Verify that MyDefaultEvent is the default event displayed.

32. Open the Code window for the form and in the Form_Load event procedure add the following code (shown in bold):

```
Private Sub Form_Load()
    MyPropertyControl1 = "Hello" ' MyDefaultProperty
    MsgBox MyPropertyControl1.MyDefaultProperty

    MyPropertyControl1.MyRunTimeProperty = "Goodbye"
    MsgBox MyPropertyControl1.MyRunTimeProperty

    MsgBox MyPropertyControl1.MyDesignTimeProperty
    MyPropertyControl1.MyDesignTimeProperty = "OhOh"
End Sub
```

33. Choose Save Project from the File menu. Accept the suggested names.

34. Press F8 to step through the program.

35. When you are finished, choose End from the Run menu.

Creating a Caption or Text Property

One of the first things novices notice about Visual Basic is that when they set the *Caption* property of a form, the caption changes as they type. We were quite impressed with this nifty feature. In response to every key we pressed, Visual Basic was calling the Microsoft Windows API function *SendMessage* with the WM_SETTEXT message and our text as arguments. When we created our first ActiveX control, we wondered whether this functionality was also available to developers building controls in Visual Basic. We are happy to report that it is.

To enable this type of functionality, you first need to create a standard Caption or Text property for your control. The property can actually be named anything you want, but we recommend using Caption or Text for a property with this functionality. Then, in the Procedure Attributes dialog box, you set the Procedure ID box to Caption or Text. This tells Visual Basic that this property is acting as the Caption or Text property for this control. From now on, Visual Basic will update the value of your Caption or Text property every time the developer using your control presses a key in the Properties window, instead of only when he or she is finished as with all other properties.

Exercise 7-2

In this exercise, we'll create a Caption property.

1. Open Visual Basic, and start a new Standard EXE project.

2. Choose Add User Control from the Project menu. Select the default User Control, and choose Open.

3. In the Properties window, set the *Name* property to *MyCaption-Control.*

4. Double-click on the UserControl designer to open the Code window.

5. Add the following statement to the Declarations section of the Code window:

    ```
    Option Explicit
    Private m_Caption As String

    Public Property Get MyCaption() As String
        MyCaption = m_Caption
    End Property

    Public Property Let MyCaption(NewString As String)
        m_Caption = NewString
        Cls
        Print m_Caption
        UserControl.PropertyChanged "MyCaption"
    End Property
    ```

6. Choose Procedure Attributes from the Tools menu.

7. Choose the Advanced button.

8. In the Name box, choose MyCaption.

9. Set the Procedure ID box to *Caption.* This enables the special behavior for the MyCaption property.

10. Choose OK.

11. Close the Code window.

12. Close the UserControl designer.

13. Add the new control to Form1.

14. Open the Properties window. You should see the MyCaption property. Set the MyCaption property. Notice that the control is updated as you type.

15. Choose Save Project from the File menu. Accept the suggested names.

Attaching an About Box to an ActiveX Control

Because ActiveX controls are not stand-alone applications and do not normally have a menu, there initially seems to be no place for the authors of the control to display an About box, bestowing upon themselves the credit they surely deserve. Well, where there's a will there's a way. It has become popular to have an About "property," with an ellipsis button, at the top of the Properties window. Clicking the button displays an About box that identifies the control and the software vendor and, in the case of shareware controls, gently prods the developer to do the right thing.

Adding an About box to your ActiveX control in Visual Basic is as easy as adding a standard form to your control project. Once you design a form for the About box to your satisfaction, you create a method that displays the dialog box as part of the control. Then, in the Procedure Attributes dialog box, you select the method in the Name box and select AboutBox in the Procedure ID box. This informs Visual Basic that the specified method will display an About box. Visual Basic will automatically add an About property to your control that, when selected, calls the specified method. This is a bit odd at first, since you are creating a method when you really want a property. Once you see how well it works, however, we are sure you will agree that it is quite neat.

Exercise 7-3

This exercise demonstrates how to add an About box to an ActiveX control.

1. Open Visual Basic, and start a new Standard EXE project.

2. Choose Add User Control from the Project menu. Select the default User Control, and click Open.

3. In the Properties window, set the *Name* property to *MyAboutControl*.

4. Choose Add Form from the Project menu.

5. In the Add Form dialog box, select About Dialog and choose Open. The About Box designer opens, and Visual Basic generates a default About box for you.

6. Adjust the various label controls to reflect your message.

7. Close the About Box designer.

8. Open the UserControl designer.

9. Choose Code from the View menu.

10. In the Declarations section of the Code window, add the following code:

```
Public Sub ShowAboutBox()
    frmAbout.Show vbModal
    Unload frmAbout
    Set frmAbout = Nothing
End Sub
```

11. Choose Procedure Attributes from the Tools menu.

12. In the Name box, choose the ShowAboutBox procedure.

13. Choose the Advanced button.

14. In the Procedure ID box, select AboutBox.

15. Choose OK.

16. Close the Code window and the UserControl designer.

17. Open the Form window.

18. Add the new control to Form1.

19. Open the Properties window for the MyAboutControl1 object.

20. You should see the (About) property. Click on the (About) property, and then click on the ellipsis (...) button.

21. Enjoy your About box.

22. Choose Save Project from the File menu. Accept the suggested names.

Property Lists and Enumerations

Enumerated constants, which were introduced in Visual Basic 5, descended from a similar feature in the C programming language. An enumeration in Visual Basic defines a new type that can have one of several values. Like enumeration in C, values begin at 0, increment by 1, and can be assigned explicitly. Here is a sample enumeration in Visual Basic:

```
Private Enum AccountType
    Existing        ' value 0
    Transfer        ' value 1
    [New Account]   ' names with spaces can be enclosed in [ ]
    Invalid = 255
End Enum
```

This example defines a new data type named AccountType. The new data type can contain one of the enumerated values. According to the rule that enumerated types begin at 0 and increment by 1, *Existing* equals 0, *Transfer* equals 1, *NewAccount* equals 2, and *Invalid* equals 255. All enumerated values become constants, and their values can't be changed at run time.

Although enumerated types are a nice language feature to have and make programming a bit easier, the primary impetus for adding them to Visual Basic was for use in controls. You might have noticed that some properties in the Properties window have drop-down boxes from which you can choose default selections. The *BorderStyle* property of a form has several default selections available in a drop-down list, for example, such as *0 - None*, *1 - Fixed Single*, and *2 - Sizable*. The custom properties of your controls can have exactly the same feature for a drop-down enumeration of possible property values. To do this, you simply specify that the property procedures for the desired property accept and return values of the enumerated type, as shown in the following example:

```
Public Property Get AccountTypeProperty() As AccountType
    AccountTypeProperty = m_Account
End Property

Public Property Let AccountTypeProperty(ByVal NewAccount As _
  AccountType)
    m_Account = NewAccount
    UserControl.PropertyChanged "AccountTypeProperty"
End Property
```

Exercise 7-4

To enable this kind of functionality for custom properties of your control, simply use an *Enum* statement. This exercise shows you how.

1. Open Visual Basic, and start a new Standard EXE project.

2. Choose Add User Control from the Project menu. Select the default User Control, and click Open.

3. In the Properties window, set the *Name* property to *MyEnumControl*.

4. Open the Code window for the user control.

5. In the Declarations section, add the following code:

```
Private m_Account As Integer

Public Enum AccountType
    Existing
    Transfer
    [New Account]
    Invalid = 255
End Enum

Public Property Get AccountTypeProperty() _
  As AccountType
    AccountTypeProperty = m_Account
End Property

Public Property Let AccountTypeProperty(ByVal NewAccount _
  As AccountType)
    m_Account = NewAccount
    UserControl.PropertyChanged "AccountTypeProperty"
End Property
```

6. Close the Code window and the UserControl designer.

7. Open the Form window.

8. Add the new control to Form1.

9. Open the Properties window for the MyEnumControl1 object.

10. The AccountTypeProperty should be visible. Click it, and then click the drop-down arrow to view the possible choices for this property.

11. Choose Save Project from the File menu, and accept the suggested names.

Standard Enumerations

By now, you have the necessary tools to create some sophisticated properties that will make it difficult for anyone to distinguish between the ActiveX controls you create in Visual Basic and the ActiveX controls created in other programming languages. But wait; there's more. Perhaps you've used some of the intrinsic Visual Basic controls and wondered how you could create properties that would allow developers to graphically select a color, a font, or a file. You can do that too! To create a property with this functionality, you create a set of property procedures with *Get* and *Let* values of the appropriate type. For example, to create a Font property, the property procedure should use the *Font* type. For the ability to automatically choose colors, use the *OLE_COLOR* type, as shown here:

```
Public Property Get MyColor() As OLE_COLOR
End Property
Public Property Let MyColor(ByVal vNewValue As OLE_COLOR)
End Property
```

This code will create a MyColor property that, when selected in the Properties window at design time, will look like the one in Figure 7-2.

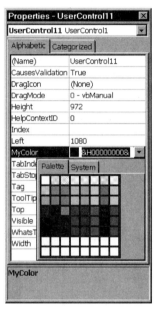

Figure 7-2. *The MyColor property selected in the Properties window with custom properties.*

Exercise 7-5

This exercise creates several properties with colorful default functionality.

1. Open Visual Basic, and start a new Standard EXE project.

2. Choose Add User Control from the Project menu. Select the default User Control, and click Open.

3. In the Properties window, set the *Name* property to *MyCoolControl*.

4. Open the Code window for the user control.

5. In the Declarations section, add the following code:

    ```
    Public Property Get MyFont() As Font
        Set MyFont = Font
    ```

```
            End Property

            Public Property Set MyFont(ByVal vNewValue As Font)
                Set Font = vNewValue
                PropertyChanged "MyFont"
            End Property

            Public Property Get MyPicture() As Picture
                Set MyPicture = Picture
            End Property

            Public Property Set MyPicture(ByVal vNewValue As Picture)
                Set Picture = vNewValue
                PropertyChanged "MyPicture"
            End Property

            Public Property Get MyColor() As OLE_COLOR
                MyColor = BackColor
            End Property

            Public Property Let MyColor(ByVal vNewValue As _
              OLE_COLOR)
                BackColor = vNewValue
                PropertyChanged "MyColor"
            End Property

            Public Property Get MyTristate() As OLE_TRISTATE
            End Property

            Public Property Let MyTristate(ByVal vNewValue As _
              OLE_TRISTATE)
            End Property

            Public Property Get MyExclusive() As OLE_OPTEXCLUSIVE
            End Property

            Public Property Let MyExclusive(ByVal vNewValue As _
              OLE_OPTEXCLUSIVE)
            End Property
```

6. Close the Code window and the UserControl designer.

7. Open the Form window.

8. Add the new control to Form1.

9. Open the Properties window for the MyCoolControl1 object.

10. Find and play with the MyColor, MyFont, MyPicture, MyTristate, and MyExclusive properties.

11. Choose Save Project from the File menu, and accept the suggested names.

Providing a Toolbox Bitmap for Your Control

You can create a custom bitmap for your ActiveX control that's displayed in the Toolbox. The Toolbox control bitmap size is 16 pixels wide by 15 pixels high, as dictated by the ActiveX Controls specification. You can create a bitmap (.BMP file) this size using any bitmap editor and assign it to the *ToolboxBitmap* property of your user control. A bitmap editing tool useful for this purpose is available in the \Common\Tools\VB\Imagedit folder on the Visual Basic CD. It isn't a good idea to assign a standard icon to the *ToolboxBitmap* property because icons are normally 32 by 32 pixels and do not scale well to the Toolbox control bitmap size. Visual Basic automatically uses the class name of your control as the tool tip text when the developer hovers the mouse pointer over your control icon in the Toolbox window. This can't be changed.

Exercise 7-6

This exercise shows how to add a Toolbox bitmap to an ActiveX control.

1. Use the Imagedit tool to create and save a 16-by-15-pixel color bitmap.

2. Open Visual Basic, and start a new Standard EXE project.

3. Choose Add User Control from the Project menu. Select the default User Control, and click Open.

4. In the Properties window, set the *Name* property to *MyIconControl*.

5. Set the *ToolboxBitmap* property to the bitmap you saved in step 1.

6. Close the UserControl designer.

7. Verify that the bitmap appears in the Toolbox and that the tool tip text appears when you position the mouse over the control icon.

8. Choose Save Project from the File menu, and accept the suggested names.

CREATING ACTIVEX
CONTROL PROPERTY PAGES

As you know, the Visual Basic environment always displays standard properties in the Properties window. Sometimes, however, you might want to allow the developer to set property values for your control in a special dialog box of your design. This is called a Property Pages dialog box, because it consists of one or more property pages. A *property page* is a small form containing controls that allow the developer to set the properties of your control.

The Toolbar control that comes with the Microsoft Windows Common Controls 6.0 component (MSCOMCTL.OCX) in Visual Basic has a Property Pages dialog box that allows the user to set many attributes related to the toolbar. Notice in Figure 7-3 that three property pages are displayed in this dialog box, each available through a separate tab.

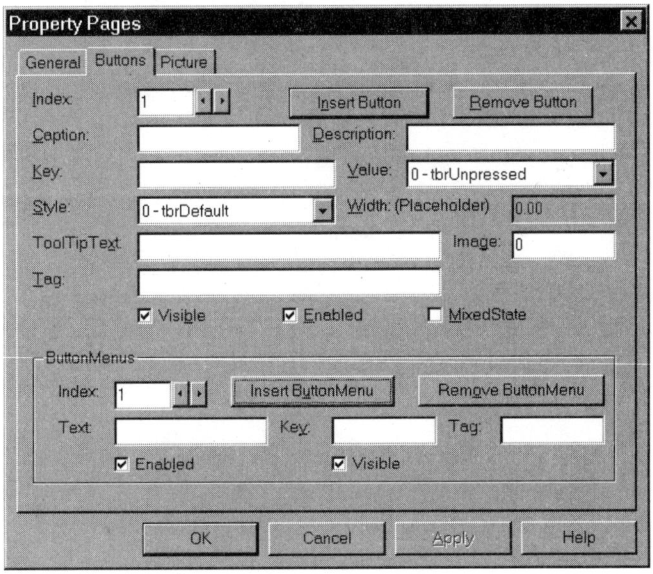

Figure 7-3. *A Property Pages dialog box.*

Instead of using the Properties window, you might consider using property pages as an alternative way of setting properties. This can be advantageous in a variety of situations. In some cases, as in the preceding Toolbar example, property pages provide a way for you to organize properties so that their relationship to one another is obvious. It would be impossible to communicate this type of information in the context of the Properties window alone.

At other times, property pages might allow a developer to set a complex property that you can't represent as a single value. Think of the standard *Font* property on a form. The *Font* property contains information about the selected font's name, style, size, and special effects. It would be quite difficult to set all these attributes with a simple property setting in the Properties window. Instead, when you edit the *Font* property Visual Basic displays a special dialog box, shown in Figure 7-4, to collect this information.

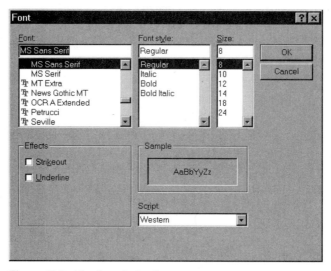

Figure 7-4. *The font dialog box.*

Property pages can also prove useful in development environments that don't have a Properties window. If an ActiveX control that you create in Visual Basic is inserted in an application such as Microsoft Word, how will the developer be able to set the properties of your control? Since Word doesn't have a Properties window that allows you to modify the properties of an ActiveX control, the Word developer won't be able to set any properties unless you provide property pages.

Creating a property page is relatively easy. You choose Add Property Page from the Project menu and then design the property page as you would any standard form in Visual Basic. You can use any controls you want when designing the property page. In the Visual Basic development environment, property pages are saved in .PAG files, and any binary data—such as bitmaps—are saved in a .PGX file with the same name as the .PAG file. Each property page created for a control is displayed as a tab in the Property Pages dialog box. The *Caption* property of a property page specifies the name that is displayed in that page's tab. Visual Basic automatically handles all the details of displaying property pages in the tabbed dialog box format and managing the OK, Cancel, and Apply command buttons.

Once you have created a property page for your control, the next challenge is to connect it with the control so that it is displayed at the appropriate time. Property pages for a control are generally activated by means of the *Custom* property. When a developer using your control selects the *Custom* property in the Properties window and clicks the ellipsis button, your Property Pages dialog box is displayed. Choosing Property Pages from the View menu has the same effect.

The easiest way to connect one or more property pages with a control is to edit the *PropertyPages* property of the control. This will display the Connect Property Pages dialog box that displays the various property pages available, as shown in Figure 7-5. Notice that Visual Basic also provides four prebuilt property pages that you can activate for your control: *StandardFont*, *StandardColor*, *StandardPicture*, and *StandardDataFormat*. In the Connect Property Pages dialog box, check the pages that you want to include in the Property Pages dialog box for your control. You can use the Page Order buttons to change the order in which the pages will appear in your property pages dialog box. After you select the property pages you want, close the Connect Property Pages dialog box. Visual Basic then automatically adds the *Custom* property to the control and displays the selected pages when a developer clicks the *Custom* property ellipsis button. Note that the *Custom* property appears as *(Custom)* in the Properties window.

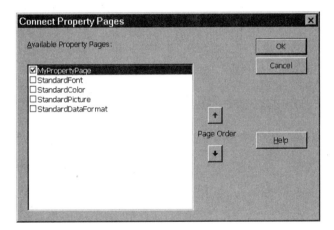

Figure 7-5. *The Connect Property Pages dialog box.*

Another way to activate a property page is to use a custom property of a control. Do not confuse a custom property with the *(Custom)* property. A custom property of a control is any property implemented by the control author—namely you. Clicking on the ellipsis button of a custom property in the Properties window displays the property page.

To enable this functionality for your control, you first need to create a custom property and then link it to a property page by using the Procedure Attributes dialog box. The Use This Page In Property Browser drop-down list box in the Procedure Attributes dialog box contains a list of all the property pages available for the current control. Selecting your custom property tells Visual Basic to display the property page whenever a developer chooses the ellipsis button for your property in the Properties window. Notice the differences between the two methods of displaying property pages. You can use the *(Custom)* property to display multiple property pages. A custom property of the control can display only one property page and is intended to edit one property in particular.

PropertyPage Properties and Events

The *PropertyPage* object in Visual Basic has properties, methods, and events similar to those of a *Form* object. Several of the properties and events, however, are specific to property pages. The properties are: *Changed*, *Selected-Controls*, and *StandardSize*. The events are: *ApplyChanges*, *EditProperty*, and *SelectionChanged*. These are described in the following tables.

Property	*Description*
Changed	Returns or sets whether any changes have been made by the user to the property page values
SelectedControls	Returns the set of controls that the property page should allow to be edited
StandardSize	Sets the page to standard size. Can be set to 0 - Custom, 1 - Small, or 2 - Large

Event	*Description*
ApplyChanges	Occurs when the container of a property page would like the property page to apply its changes to the selected controls
EditProperty	Occurs when the property page container would like a property page to edit a particular property
SelectionChanged	Occurs when the set of selected controls in a property page container changes

When a developer clicks a property that invokes a property page, the *SelectionChanged* event fires first. In response to the *SelectionChanged* event, most programs initialize the settings in the property page. This means the program copies all the required property values of the control to fields in the property page. The *SelectionChanged* event always fires when the property page is first brought up. Thereafter, it fires every time the selection controls in the Form window are changed. For example, if the user selects a different control for editing or selects an additional control, the *SelectionChanged* event fires. If the property page was activated because the user clicked a custom property of the control, the *EditProperty* event fires next. The *EditProperty* event tells the property page to display a particular property for editing. You can use this event to set the focus to the appropriate property for editing.

Next the developer works with the property page displayed. Whenever the developer changes the value of any property, the *Changed* property of the property page must be set to *True*. This has the immediate effect of enabling the Apply command button. Thereafter, whenever the developer clicks the OK or Apply command button, the *ApplyChanges* event fires. In other words, the *ApplyChanges* event fires only when the user modifies a value in the property page. In response to this event, the program normally copies any properties set in the property page to the selected controls. The *SelectedControls* property determines the controls to which the property values are applied.

The *SelectedControls* property references a collection of all the controls selected for editing. Since property page dialog boxes are modeless, the user can select additional controls on a form while the property pages are displayed. Although this can be a wonderful shortcut for the developer using a control, things can get quite tricky for you, the control developer. You can access the various controls that are part of the *SelectedControls* collection with syntax such as *SelectedControls(0)* for the first control, *SelectedControls(1)* for the second, and so on. You can also determine the total number of controls currently selected for editing by means of the *Count* property, with the expression *Selected-Controls.Count*.

The *StandardSize* property

Property pages can be any size you want, although we generally recommend that you use one of the standard sizes offered. By setting the *StandardSize* property to *1 - Small* or *2 - Large*, you ensure that your property pages are the same size as everyone else's. This makes the property pages associated with a variety of ActiveX controls look more uniform. If neither of the standard sizes meets your needs, you can make the property page any size; this causes the *Standard-Size* property value to revert to *0 - Custom*.

Exercise 7-7

This exercise creates a property page for an ActiveX control.

1. Open Visual Basic, and start a new Standard EXE project.

2. Choose Add User Control from the Project menu. Accept the default User Control, and choose Open.

3. In the Properties window, set the *Name* property to *MyPageControl*.

4. Open the Code window for the user control.

5. In the Declarations section, add the following code:

```
Option Explicit
Private mCaption As String

Public Property Get Caption() As String
    Caption = mCaption
End Property

Public Property Let Caption(ByVal vNewValue As String)
    mCaption = vNewValue
    UserControl.PropertyChanged "Caption"
    Cls
    Print mCaption
End Property
```

6. Close the Code window.

7. Choose Add Property Page from the Project menu. Accept the default Property Page, and click Open.

8. In the Properties window, set the *Name* property to *MyPropertyPage*.

9. Set the *Caption* property to My Properties.

10. Place a TextBox control and a Label control on the property page, and arrange them so that they look like the controls in Figure 7-6.

11. Open the Code window for the property page.

12. In the Declarations section, add the following code:

```
Option Explicit

Private Sub PropertyPage_SelectionChanged()
    Text1.Text = SelectedControls(0).Caption
End Sub

Private Sub PropertyPage_ApplyChanges()
    Dim Thingy As Variant
    For Each Thingy In SelectedControls
        Thingy.Caption = Text1.Text
    Next Thingy
End Sub
```

```
Private Sub Text1_Change()
    Changed = True
End Sub
```

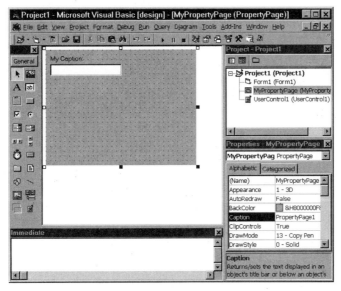

Figure 7-6. *Text box and label controls for Exercise 7-7.*

13. Open the Code window for the MyPageControl user control.

14. Choose Procedure Attributes from the Tools menu.

15. Be sure the Name box contains Caption. Then choose Advanced.

16. Set the Use This Page In Property Browser box to *MyPropertyPage*.

17. Choose OK.

18. Close the Code windows and the PropertyPage designer.

19. Open the user control MyPageControl.

20. In the Properties window, double-click the *PropertyPages* property.

21. In the Connect Property Pages dialog box, check the following property pages: MyPropertyPage, StandardFont, StandardColor, Standard-Picture, and StandardDataFormat.

22. Choose OK.

23. Close the UserControl designer.

24. Open the Form window for Form1.

25. Add the new control to Form1.

26. Open the Properties window for the MyPageControl1 object.

27. The *(Custom)* property should be visible. Double-click it to activate and test the property page. Notice that you can set the *Caption* property value by typing directly into the Properties window or by clicking the ellipsis button and setting it in its property page.

28. Add *MsgBox* statements to the *EditProperty, SelectionChanged*, and *ApplyChanges* events in the Code window of MyPropertyPage (as shown in bold):

```
Private Sub PropertyPage_EditProperty(PropertyName As _
  String)
   MsgBox "EditProperty: " & PropertyName
End Sub

Private Sub PropertyPage_SelectionChanged()
   Text1.Text = SelectedControls(0).Caption
   MsgBox "SelectionChanged"
End Sub

Private Sub PropertyPage_ApplyChanges()
   Dim Thingy As Variant
   MsgBox "ApplyChanges"
   For Each Thingy In SelectedControls
   Thingy.Caption = Text1.Text
   Next Thingy
End Sub
```

29. Retest the property pages, noting when each event is fired.

30. Choose Save Project from the File menu. Accept the suggested names.

Creating Controls That Are Invisible at Run Time

You might want some controls to be invisible at run time. This is useful for controls that provide some functionality to the user, but do not provide any information for, or require any interaction with, the user. The Timer and CommonDialog controls that come with Visual Basic are of this variety. To make a control invisible at run time, you simply set the *InvisibleAtRuntime* property of the *UserControl* object to *True*. The only reason to set the *InvisibleAtRuntime* property for a control is so that developers can take advantage of some feature available only to controls. This provides the convenience of seeing the control in the Visual Basic Toolbox and being able to set its properties at design time by using the Properties window.

Controls that are invisible at run time are generally designed so that they maintain a fixed size at design time and display an icon on the form to herald their existence. You achieve this functionality by setting the *Picture* property of the control to a small bitmap and then responding to the UserControl_Resize event procedure, as shown here:

```
Private Sub UserControl_Resize()
    Size 500, 500    ' In twips
End Sub
```

Before you create an invisible control, consider whether an ActiveX DLL code component would do the job better. ActiveX DLL code components run in-process like an ActiveX control, and they can have properties, methods, and events just like a control. Objects provided by in-process code components require fewer system resources than do controls, even invisible ones. In all other respects, ActiveX DLL code components are basically equivalent to invisible ActiveX controls.

> **NOTE** You shouldn't use the *Visible* property of the *Extender* object to make your control invisible at run time, because the developer using your control can always set the *Visible* property to *True*. User controls with the *InvisibleAtRuntime* property set to *True* are granted only *Name*, *Index*, *Left*, *Tag*, and *Top* extender properties.

Control Containers

Some controls can act as containers for other controls. The *Frame* and *Picture* controls that come with Visual Basic exhibit this capability. To enable your control to be a container of others, simply set the *ControlContainer* property of the *UserControl* object to *True*. Whatever controls are placed on your control are available by means of the *ContainedControls* collection.

Do not confuse the control container capabilities with the ability to put constituent controls on a *UserControl* object. When you build an ActiveX control from constituent controls, you decide which controls to use and how to place them. When you create a control that can act as a container, the developer using your control decides which controls to place on your control.

Be aware that additional overhead is required to allow a developer to place controls on instances of your ActiveX control. For this reason, you should set the *ControlContainer* property to *True* only if it makes sense to do so. For example, it doesn't make much sense for a custom button control built in Visual Basic to be a container for other controls.

Also note that not all ActiveX control containers support this control-nesting feature. To support controls that contain other controls, the container must support the *ISimpleFrame* interface. If an instance of your control is placed on a container that doesn't support *ISimpleFrame*, control nesting is disabled. The control will continue to work correctly in all other respects, but developers will be unable to place other controls on it. In order for the *ContainedControls* collection to be available, the container must also support the *IVBGetControls* interface.

Binding a Control to a Data Source

Many of the intrinsic controls in Visual Basic, such as the PictureBox, Label, Text, CheckBox, ComboBox, ListBox, Image, and OLE controls, support data-bound features through the *DataSource* and *DataField* properties. The *DataSource* property is used to refer to the data control from which the data is to be retrieved; the *DataField* property is used to specify the field in the database to which the control is bound.

More sophisticated data-bound controls, such as the DBList and DBCombo controls, also have a *DataBindings* property that displays the Data Bindings dialog box, shown in Figure 7-7. The Data Bindings dialog box allows the user to associate various properties of a control with a field in a database. In general, controls that have only one property that binds to a data field have *DataSource* and *DataField* properties, while controls that have multiple properties that are bound to a data field have the *DataBindings* property in addition to the *DataSource* and *DataField* properties.

To enable data-binding features for properties of your control, use the Procedure Attributes dialog box. If at least one property in your control has the Property Is Data Bound and the Show In Data Bindings Collection At Design Time boxes selected in the Procedure Attributes dialog box, Visual Basic automatically provides your control with a *DataBindings* property. Double-click the *DataBindings* property in the Properties window to display the Data Bindings dialog box, shown in Figure 7-7. Setting the *DataBindings* property, however, isn't enough to create a data-aware control; the control needs a *DataSource* property.

Recall that the *DataSource* property is used to reference the data control from which the data will be retrieved. In order for Visual Basic to give a control a *DataSource* property, at least one property in the control must have the This Property Binds To DataField option selected in the Procedure Attributes dialog box. If this option is selected, Visual Basic will add *DataSource* and *DataField* properties to your control, in addition to the *DataBindings* property enabled by the Show In DataBindings Collection At Design Time option. Usually, the *Value*, *Text*, or *Caption* property of the control has the This Property Binds To DataField box selected. Only one property of a control should have this attribute.

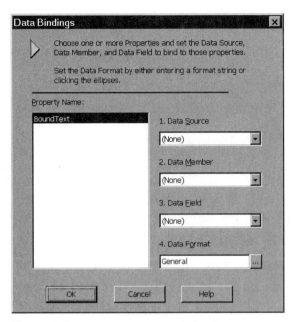

Figure 7-7. *The Data Bindings dialog box.*

The Show In DataBindings Collection At Design Time option specifies that the property will appear in the Data Bindings dialog box and the Properties window at design time. Checking the Property Will Call CanPropertyChange Before Changing box tells Visual Basic that your property will call the *CanPropertyChange* method before changing the value of the specified property. This is to ensure that you do not attempt to update a data field that might be read-only.

The *DataBindings* property is a collection of *DataBinding* objects. Each *DataBinding* object has the properties shown in the following table.

Property	Description
DataChanged	Determines whether the value of a field has changed
DataField	The name of the database field that has been bound to a property of a control
DataSource	The name of the data control to which this property is bound

(continued)

continued

Property	Description
IsBindable	Determines whether this property is bound to a data control
IsDataSource	A Boolean property that determines if the data is source data
PropertyName	The name of the property that might be data bound

Exercise 7-8

This exercise creates a data-bound property for an ActiveX control.

1. Open Visual Basic, and start a new Standard EXE project.

2. Add a Data control to the form.

3. Set the Data control's *DatabaseName* property to *Biblio.mdb*.

4. Set the *RecordSource* property to *Authors*.

5. Add a TextBox control to the form.

6. Set the *DataSource* property of the text box to *Data1*.

7. Set the *DataField* property of the text box to *Au_ID*.

8. Run the program to see that the data appears in the text box, and then end the program.

9. Choose Add User Control from the Project menu. Accept the default User Control, and click Open.

10. In the Properties window, set the *Name* property to *MyDataControl*.

11. Set the *AutoRedraw* property to *True*.

12. Set the *BorderStyle* property to *1 - Fixed Single*.

13. Open the Code window for the user control.

14. In the Declarations section, add the following code:

```
Option Explicit
Private MyData As String

Public Property Get MyDataProperty() As String
    MyDataProperty = MyData
End Property

Public Property Let MyDataProperty(ByVal vNewValue As _
    String)
```

```
        Cls
        MyData = vNewValue
        Print MyData
    End Property
```

15. Choose Procedure Attributes from the Tools menu. Be sure that MyDataProperty is selected in the Name box.

16. Choose Advanced.

17. Select the Property Is Data Bound box.

18. Select the This Property Binds To DataField box.

19. Select the Show In DataBindings Collection At Design Time box.

20. Choose OK.

21. Close the Code window and the UserControl designer.

22. Add the new control to Form1.

23. Open the Properties window for the MyDataControl1 object, and set its *DataSource* property to *Data1*.

24. Set its *DataField* property to *Author*.

25. Double-click the *DataBindings* property, and explore the Data Bindings dialog box. Choose Cancel.

26. Run the program, and verify that it works.

27. Open the Code window for the form.

28. Add the following code:

```
Private Sub Form_Click()
    Dim MyDB As DataBinding
    For Each MyDB In MyDataControl1.DataBindings
        Print "DataChanged: " & MyDB.DataChanged ' False
        Print "DataField: " & MyDB.DataField ' Author
        Print "DataSource: " & MyDB.DataSource ' Data1
        Print "IsBindable: " & MyDB.IsBindable ' True
        Print "IsDataSource: " & MyDB.IsDataSource ' False
        Print "PropertyName: " & _
          MyDB.PropertyName ' MyDataProperty
    Next MyDB
End Sub
```

29. Test the program again. Be sure to click on the form and view the printout.

30. Choose Save Project from the File menu. Accept the default names.

CONSTITUENT CONTROLS

We have talked at length about the two basic styles of ActiveX controls that you can create in Visual Basic: user-drawn controls and constituent controls. Most of this book has so far been concerned with creating user-drawn controls, and none of the controls presented thus far were built from constituent controls.

What about a control as simple as a text box or a command button? Can one of these controls be created in Visual Basic? Think about all the hard work a user-drawn control must do. It must visually show when the control has focus. It must also display its enabled and disabled states. If your control needs to function as a command button, it needs to visually indicate whether it is the default command button on the form.

Let's take the simple example of a text box control. First you need to enable the user to type into the control. Every time you get a *KeyPress* event, you need to display the character in the control. Then, if the user presses the Backspace key, you need to delete the first character to the left. Worse, if the user presses an arrow key to go back through the text and then inserts text in the middle, you have to move the remaining text forward with each key pressed. In a graphical environment such as Microsoft Windows, where every character has a different width, this is a major undertaking. In Visual Basic, it is all but impossible.

The control creation capabilities afforded by Visual Basic will likely be used mainly to prototype controls that will later be rewritten in Visual C++ or to enhance existing controls and combine several existing controls into one. The ability to improve and combine existing controls is the driving force behind ActiveX control creation in Visual Basic.

Exposing the Properties, Methods, and Events of Constituent Controls

Two questions arise. What is so special about building new controls out of existing controls? What do you have to do differently from designing a control from scratch? In truth, it isn't all that different. Controls are still designed on a *UserControl* object. All the same properties, methods, and events of the *User-Control* object are available. The real differences become apparent only as you begin working on them.

To evaluate when it is useful to build controls from existing controls, one has to understand the concept of delegation. In the context of ActiveX controls, delegation means handing responsibility for some task to a constituent control. Normally, the interface of a constituent control is hidden from the user of the control. Let's say that you create an ActiveX control in Visual Basic and place a text box control on it. How is the developer working with your control going to get access to the text box control in order to set its properties, call its methods, and respond to its events? The answer is that the developer will not be able to—unless you provide a mechanism to enable this functionality. Sometimes you might not want the developer to have access to the constituent controls. More often, however, access is desirable. One approach is to provide a property for your control that exposes the entire constituent control, as follows:

```
Property Get TheTextBox As TextBox
    Set TheTextBox = Text1
End Property
```

This solution requires only three lines of code and seems to have the desired effect of exposing the entire constituent control to the user. However, we strongly advise against this method. For starters, this code will not work because TextBox isn't a public data type (although this code would have worked with any nonintrinsic controls). The real reason you should not use this method lies deeper. By permitting developers who use your control direct access to constituent controls, you allow them to bypass a validation code. Developers thus obtain a great deal of freedom: they can decide to destroy the control, move it, resize it, or change the text displayed in the text box. However, this freedom eventually becomes a restriction. In the future, should you want to replace the text box constituent control with another vendor's text control, developers using your control will have to rewrite their code to use it.

So how do you permit users to access constituent controls in a safe manner that will keep you in control? By using delegation, of course. You selectively expose certain properties, methods, and events of constituent controls, and then delegate the implementation of these members to the constituent controls. For example, you might decide to expose the *Text* property of the TextBox constituent control as follows:

```
Public Property Get Text() As String
    Text = Text1.Text
End Property

Public Property Let Text(ByVal vNewValue As String)
    Text1.Text = vNewValue
    PropertyChanged "Text"
End Property
```

Now the developer using your control can access the *Text* property in a safe manner, and your control can perform any special validation before assigning the new data to the constituent control. In the future, if you switch to JoesCoolTextControl, you will need to modify only the *Text* property procedures to set the appropriate property for the control. Developers using your control will remain unaffected.

If you have multiple constituent controls with similar attributes, another possibility presents itself. Say you have a Name control with three text boxes for first, middle, and last names. Rather than exposing three font properties, as in FirstNameFont, MiddleNameFont, and LastNameFont, you might decide that all three text boxes should have the same font. In this case, you can simply expose one Font property that will then set the Font properties of all three text boxes, as in the following example:

```
Public Property Get MyFont() As Font
    Set MyFont = Text1.Font
End Property

Public Property Set MyFont(ByVal vNewValue As Font)
    Set Text1.Font = vNewValue
    Set Text2.Font = vNewValue
    Set Text3.Font = vNewValue
    PropertyChanged "MyFont"
End Property
```

Exposing methods and events works similarly to exposing properties. To enable the developer working with your control to respond to a constituent control event, your control needs to intercept the event and then fire it again, as follows:

```
Private Sub Text1_Change()
    RaiseEvent Change
End Sub
```

Certain events of the *UserControl* object also take on greater importance when constituent controls are involved. The *Paint* event, which is important for user-drawn controls, is often left unused for controls involving constituents, since the constituent controls already paint themselves automatically. The *Resize* event usually takes on greater importance in a control built from constituent controls. If you want to enhance a single control, the control will typically occupy the entire visible surface of the *UserControl* object. You accomplish this by using the *Move* method of the constituent control in the *Resize* event of the user control, as follows:

```
Private Sub UserControl_Resize()
    Text1.Move 0, 0, ScaleWidth, ScaleHeight
End Property
```

More complicated, however, are cases involving multiple constituent controls. In these cases, the code in the *Resize* event procedure can become quite complicated when the size and position of constituent controls are adjusted as the main control's size changes.

A Constituent Controls Example

Microsoft Access users are familiar with a convenient text box control that combines a Visual Basic text box and label control. When designing applications in Visual Basic, we often find ourselves placing both a text box control and a label control on the form and then trying to align them. We thought it would be nice to bring the convenience of this Access feature to the world of Visual Basic. What better way to explore creating ActiveX controls in Visual Basic than by combining and enhancing existing controls?

Exercise 7-9

To see how constituent controls work, let's create an ActiveX control composed of them.

1. Start by creating a Standard EXE project in Visual Basic.

2. Choose Add User Control from the Project menu. Accept the default User Control, and choose Open.

3. In the Properties window, set the *Name* property to *LabelText*.

4. Place a TextBox control and a Label control on the user control as shown in Figure 7-8.

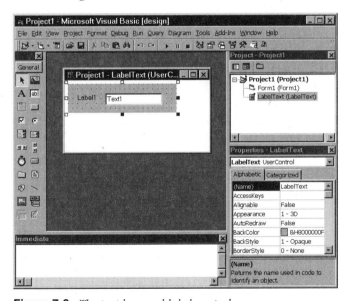

Figure 7-8. *The text box and label controls.*

5. Type the following code into the user control's Code window.

```
Option Explicit
Public Enum AlignmentChoices
    [Left Justify]
    [Right Justify]
    [Center Justify]
End Enum
Event Change()
Private mSeparation As Integer
Private mAlignment As AlignmentChoices

Public Property Get Text() As String
    Text = Text1.Text
End Property

Public Property Let Text(ByVal vNewValue As String)
    Text1.Text = vNewValue
    PropertyChanged "Text"
End Property

Public Property Get Caption() As String
    Caption = Label1.Caption
End Property

Public Property Let Caption(ByVal vNewValue As String)
    Label1.Caption = vNewValue
    PropertyChanged "Caption"
    UserControl_Resize
End Property

Private Sub Text1_Change()
    RaiseEvent Change
End Sub

Private Sub UserControl_Initialize()
    Text1.Top = 0
    Label1.AutoSize = True
End Sub

Private Sub UserControl_InitProperties()
    Text1.Text = Extender.Name
    Label1.Caption = "Caption"
    mSeparation = 200
    mAlignment = AlignmentChoices.[Left Justify]
End Sub
```

```
Private Sub UserControl_ReadProperties(PropBag As _
   PropertyBag)
     Text1.Text = PropBag.ReadProperty("Text", _
       Extender.Name)
     Label1.Caption = PropBag.ReadProperty("Caption", _
       "Caption")
     mSeparation = PropBag.ReadProperty("Separation", _
       200)
     mAlignment = PropBag.ReadProperty("Alignment", _
       AlignmentChoices.[Left Justify])
End Sub

Private Sub UserControl_Resize()
     Text1.Left = Label1.Width + Label1.Left + Separation
     Text1.Width = ScaleWidth - Text1.Left
     Text1.Height = ScaleHeight
     Label1.Top = (ScaleHeight - Label1.Height) / 2
End Sub

Public Property Get Separation() As Integer
     Separation = mSeparation
End Property

Public Property Let Separation(ByVal vNewValue As _
   Integer)
     mSeparation = vNewValue
     PropertyChanged "Separation"
     UserControl_Resize
End Property

Public Property Get Alignment() As AlignmentChoices
     Alignment = mAlignment
End Property

Public Property Let Alignment(ByVal vNewValue As _
   AlignmentChoices)
     mAlignment = vNewValue
     Select Case Alignment
     Case AlignmentChoices.[Center Justify]
         Label1.Left = (Text1.Left - Label1.Width) / 2
     Case AlignmentChoices.[Left Justify]
         Label1.Left = 0
     Case AlignmentChoices.[Right Justify]
         Label1.Left = Text1.Left - Label1.Width
     End Select
```

(continued)

```
                    PropertyChanged "Alignment"
            End Property

            Private Sub UserControl_WriteProperties(PropBag As _
              PropertyBag)
                PropBag.WriteProperty "Text", Text1.Text, _
                  Extender.Name
                PropBag.WriteProperty "Caption", Label1.Caption, _
                  "Caption"
                PropBag.WriteProperty "Separation", mSeparation, 200
                PropBag.WriteProperty "Alignment", mAlignment, _
                  AlignmentChoices.[Left Justify]
            End Sub
```

6. Place an instance of this control on a form, and test it to see that everything works properly.

   This control could also be enhanced to expose font and color properties, which would then set those properties of the constituent controls. Try this on your own.

Creating Lightweight Controls

Standard ActiveX controls can consume a great deal of system resources. Specifically, ActiveX controls always allocate a window handle that is exposed to the control by means of its *hWnd* property. To reduce the system resources used by a control, you can create lightweight ActiveX controls that don't have window handles. Lightweight controls are ideal for Internet applications designed to run in a Web browser or in any other location where system resources are at a premium. The intrinsic Label and Image controls included with Visual Basic are examples of lightweight controls. Although it is very easy to create a lightweight ActiveX control in Visual Basic—you just set its *Windowless* property to *True*—there are several limitations of which you should be aware:

- A lightweight control can contain only other lightweight controls; it can't contain regular constituent controls.

- A lightweight control can't act as a design-time container for other controls, as the *Frame* control does.

- Since a lightweight control doesn't have an *hWnd* property, it can't call any Win32 API calls that require a window handle.

While these restrictions might limit your use of lightweight controls, you should keep this feature in mind whenever designing a new ActiveX control. If your control is not affected by these restrictions, then by all means make it a lightweight control—there is no reason not to. Although not all containers necessarily support lightweight controls, a lightweight control that is activated in a container that doesn't support lightweight controls will automatically run in windowed mode. In other words, Windows will dynamically assign a window handle to the control. This means that it will consume system resources to the same degree as a standard ActiveX control. As of this writing, the containers known to support lightweight controls include Visual Basic, Microsoft Internet Explorer, and Microsoft Office.

The IntelliMouse Control

After discussing the many advanced topics of ActiveX control creation in Visual Basic, let's end the chapter with a genuinely useful ActiveX control. You might have heard of the new Microsoft IntelliMouse, a pointing device with a wheel control (a rotating wheel that is also a middle mouse button). The wheel is normally used by applications for scrolling operations as a hardware alternative to scroll bars. When we first bought the IntelliMouse, we thought it would be neat to add support for the wheel to our Visual Basic applications. Unfortunately, Visual Basic doesn't currently support the wheel. To overcome this limitation, we built an ActiveX control in Visual Basic that enables applications to support all the features of the new mouse.

Performing this feat requires advanced Visual Basic techniques and the Win32 API, but amazingly it doesn't require any C or C++ code. The special features of the IntelliMouse are supported natively in Microsoft Windows NT 4 and Microsoft Windows 98, but they require special drivers that come with the mouse in order to work with Microsoft Windows 95. In the interest of simplifying the sample code, the upcoming exercise supports only Windows 95. A more complete version of this control, which adds support for Windows NT 4 and Windows 98, is on the companion CD for this book.

Whenever the user operates the wheel control of the IntelliMouse, a special message known as *MSH_MOUSEWHEEL* is sent. The Win32 API call *RegisterWindowMessage* is used to obtain the unique identification number of the *MSH_MOUSEWHEEL* message, as follows:

```
rotate_msg = RegisterWindowMessage(MSH_MOUSEWHEEL)
```

To trap this message from a Visual Basic program, a Windows message hook needs to be installed. This is done with the *SetWindowsHookEx* Win32 API call, as follows:

```
hHook = SetWindowsHookEx(WH_GETMESSAGE, AddressOf _
  GetMsgProc, 0, GetCurrentThreadId)
```

SetWindowsHookEx requires the address of a function that Windows will call each time a message is sent to the application. This type of function is known as a callback. You can use the *AddressOf* operator to provide the pointer to a callback function residing in a code module.

```
Public rotate_msg AsLong, hHook As Long
Public MyControl As IntelliMouse

Public Function GetMsgProc(ByVal nCode As Long, ByVal wParam _
   As Long, lParam As MSG) As Long
   If lParam.message = rotate_msg Then
       MyControl.WheelMoved lParam.wParam, 0, lParam.pt.X, _
          lParam.pt.Y
   End If
   GetMsgProc = CallNextHookEx(hHook, nCode, wParam, lParam)
End Function
```

The purpose of the *CallNextHookEx* Win32 API call is to chain the message hook. Since it is possible that some other control installed a message hook prior to this control, it is polite behavior to still allow that control to receive the messages after this code finishes examining them.

```
GetMsgProc = CallNextHookEx(hHook, nCode, wParam, lParam)
```

The callback function's main purpose is to check each incoming message to determine whether it originates from the wheel control. If it does, you want to notify the application using the control that the mouse wheel is being manipulated. The best way to do this is to fire an event in the control. The control defines a WheelRotate event fired whenever the mouse wheel is rotated. The Delta value indicates the degree to which the mouse wheel has been rotated. This value will be some multiple of positive or negative 120. A positive value indicates that the wheel is being rotated toward the screen, and a negative value indicates rotation toward the user.

```
Event WheelRotate(Delta As Long, Shift As Long, X As Long, _
   Y As Long)
```

Events can be fired only from within a user control module; the callback function must be implemented in a code module. For this reason, whenever an *MSH_MOUSEWHEEL* message is intercepted, you call a friend function in the user control module whose sole purpose is to fire the event.

```
Friend Sub WheelMoved(Delta As Long, Shift As Long, _
   X As Long, Y As Long)
    RaiseEvent WheelRotate(Delta, Shift, X, Y)
End Sub
```

Before the control is terminated, you should uninstall the Windows message hook. The Win32 API call, *UnhookWindowsHookEx*, does the trick.

```
UnhookWindowsHookEx hHook
```

> **NOTE** To try this exercise, you will need to have the IntelliMouse connected to your computer and have the drivers properly configured. As a test, make sure that the mouse wheel works in Microsoft Internet Explorer. If the page scrolls as you turn the wheel, you are ready.

Exercise 7-10

In this exercise, you will build an ActiveX control in Visual Basic that supports the IntelliMouse wheel control.

1. Start a new ActiveX control project in Visual Basic.

2. Set the *Name* property of the user control to *IntelliMouse*.

3. Set the *Appearance* property to *0 - Flat*.

4. Set the *BorderStyle* property to *1 - Fixed Single*.

5. Set the *InvisibleAtRuntime* property to *True*.

6. Choose Project1 Properties from the Project menu.

7. Set the Project Name to *IntelliMouseControl*.

8. Set the Project Description to *IntelliMouse Control*. Choose OK.

9. Choose Code from the View menu.

10. Type the following code in the code window.

```
Option Explicit
Event WheelRotate(Delta As Long, Shift As Long, _
  X As Long, Y As Long)

Friend Sub WheelMoved(Delta As Long, Shift As Long, _
  X As Long, Y As Long)
    RaiseEvent WheelRotate(Delta, Shift, X, Y)
End Sub

Private Sub UserControl_ReadProperties(PropBag As _
  PropertyBag)
    Set MyControl = Me
    If UserControl.Ambient.UserMode Then
        rotate_msg = RegisterWindowMessage(MSH_MOUSEWHEEL)
        hHook = SetWindowsHookEx(WH_GETMESSAGE, AddressOf _
        GetMsgProc, 0, GetCurrentThreadId)
```

(continued)

```
        End If
End Sub

Private Sub UserControl_Resize()
    Size 640, 620   ' In twips
End Sub

Private Sub UserControl_Terminate()
    UnhookWindowsHookEx hHook
End Sub
```

11. Choose Add Module from the Project menu. Select the standard Module, and click Open.

12. Set the *Name* property of the module to *Callback*.

13. Write the following code in the Code window for the Callback module.

```
Option Explicit
' Win32API declarations
Declare Function RegisterWindowMessage Lib "user32" _
    Alias "RegisterWindowMessageA" (ByVal lpString As _
    String) As Long
Declare Function SetWindowsHookEx Lib "user32" Alias _
    "SetWindowsHookExA" (ByVal idHook As Long, ByVal lpfn _
    As Long, ByVal hmod As Long, ByVal dwThreadId As Long) _
    As Long
Declare Function UnhookWindowsHookEx Lib "user32" (ByVal _
    hHook As Long) As Long
Declare Function GetCurrentThreadId Lib "kernel32" () As _
    Long
Declare Function CallNextHookEx Lib "user32" (ByVal _
    hHook As Long, ByVal nCode As Long, ByVal wParam As _
    Long, lParam As Any) As Long

Type POINTAPI
    X As Long
    Y As Long
End Type

Type MSG
    hwnd As Long
    message As Long
    wParam As Long
    lParam As Long
    time As Long
    pt As POINTAPI
End Type
```

```
Public Const WH_GETMESSAGE = 3
Public Const MSH_MOUSEWHEEL = "MSWHEEL_ROLLMSG"

Public rotate_msg As Long, hHook As Long
Public MyControl As IntelliMouse

Public Function GetMsgProc(ByVal nCode As Long, _
   ByVal wParam As Long, lParam As MSG) As Long
      If lParam.message = rotate_msg Then
         MyControl.WheelMoved lParam.wParam, 0, _
            lParam.pt.X, lParam.pt.Y
      End If
      GetMsgProc = CallNextHookEx(hHook, nCode, _
         wParam, lParam)
   End Function
```

14. Choose Save Project from the File menu.

15. Accept the default names of the control (IntelliMouse.ctl) and the module (Callback.bas). Name the project IntelliMouse.vbp.

16. Choose Make IntelliMouse.ocx from the File menu.

NOTE In this section of the exercise, you will build a client project to test the control.

17. Choose New Project from the File menu, and accept the Standard EXE type.

18. Choose Components from the Project menu.

19. Check the IntelliMouse Control and the Microsoft Windows Common Controls 6.0. Then choose OK.

20. Place an IntelliMouse control and ProgressBar control on Form1.

21. Choose Code from the View menu.

22. In the Object box, choose IntelliMouse1.

23. Type the following code:

```
Private Sub IntelliMouse1_WheelRotate(Delta As Long, _
   Shift As Long, X As Long, Y As Long)
      Delta = Delta / 100
      If ProgressBar1.Value + Delta _
         >= ProgressBar1.Min And ProgressBar1.Value + _
         Delta <= ProgressBar1.Max Then
            ProgressBar1.Value = ProgressBar1.Value + Delta
      End If
End Sub
```

Run and test the control by operating the mouse wheel.

Chapter 8

Creating ActiveX Controls for the Internet

Up to this point, this book has focused primarily on creating and using COM components—most of them ActiveX controls. We have also introduced the Internet and ActiveX controls designed to take advantage of the Internet. In this chapter, we will focus on creating Microsoft Visual Basic ActiveX controls that are targeted for the Internet—ActiveX controls that run in a Web browser such as Microsoft Internet Explorer.

Putting an ActiveX control on a Visual Basic form requires no excessive effort; you simply choose a control from the toolbox and add it to the form. But how do controls get into a Web browser? Although the process is slightly more difficult than placing a control on a Visual Basic form, displaying a control inside a Web browser is relatively straightforward. You simply add an <OBJECT> tag to the HTML document, and your control will be displayed. For some types of controls, such as buttons and labels, this is sufficient. No special programming is necessary to enable the control for the Internet, as is shown by the following sample HTML code.

```
<OBJECT
    ID="MyControl" WIDTH=100 HEIGHT=50
    CLASSID="CLSID:DABD9872-9DA2-A772-00DBA23466AC"
    CODEBASE="http://www.mycompany.com/control.ocx">
        <PARAM NAME="MyProperty" VALUE="MyValue">
</OBJECT>
```

NOTE Remember to substitute the *CLASSID* used in your Registry for each ActiveX control *CLASSID* used in these programs.

Internet Explorer is a somewhat unusual ActiveX Controls container. In other environments, such as Visual Basic or Microsoft Visual C++, you write a program in advance to display a control at run time. In contrast, Internet Explorer lets you postpone the decision about creating a control until it encounters the <OBJECT> tag in the HTML stream at run time. By inserting the <OBJECT> tag, you provide Internet Explorer with all the information necessary to display the control. Remember that the whole idea behind COM is getting components to work together. Since both Visual Basic and Internet Explorer support the interface necessary to host ActiveX controls, the control you create will work in both environments without any modification. You can think of an HTML document as a program and a Web browser as an ActiveX controls container, although this might require some mental juggling.

Exercise 8-1

Let's create our first test control, which simply displays all the data available in the ambient and extender properties.

1.   Open Visual Basic, and start a new ActiveX control project.

2.   In the Properties window, set the following properties:

Property	*Setting*
AutoRedraw	*True*
BorderStyle	*1 - Fixed Single*
Name	*MyInternetControl*

3.   Double-click the UserControl designer to open the Code window.

4.   In the UserControl_Click event procedure, write the following code (shown in bold):

```
Private Sub UserControl_Click()
        ' In case any properties are not supported
        ' by Internet Explorer
        On Error Resume Next
```

```
        Print "Ambient Properties"
        Print , "LocaleID: " & _
          UserControl.Ambient.LocaleID
        Print , "MessageReflect: " & _
          UserControl.Ambient.MessageReflect
        Print , "TextAlign: " & _
          UserControl.Ambient.TextAlign
        Print , "SupportsMnemonics: " & _
          UserControl.Ambient.SupportsMnemonics
        Print , "BackColor: " & UserControl.Ambient.BackColor
        Print , "DisplayName: " & _
          UserControl.Ambient.DisplayName
        Print , "Font: " & UserControl.Ambient.Font
        Print , "ForeColor: " & UserControl.Ambient.ForeColor
        Print , "ScaleUnits: " & _
          UserControl.Ambient.ScaleUnits
        Print , "TextAlign: " & UserControl.Ambient.TextAlign
        Print , "UserMode: " & UserControl.Ambient.UserMode
        Print , "UIDead: " & UserControl.Ambient.UIDead
        Print , "ShowGrabHandles: " & _
          UserControl.Ambient.ShowGrabHandles
        Print , "ShowHatching: " & _
          UserControl.Ambient.ShowHatching
        Print , "DisplayAsDefault: " & _
          UserControl.Ambient.DisplayAsDefault
        Print , "Palette: " & UserControl.Ambient.Palette
        Print "Extender Properties"
        Print , "Name: " & UserControl.Extender.Name
        Print , "DragIcon: " & UserControl.Extender.DragIcon
        Print , "DragMode: " & UserControl.Extender.DragMode
        Print , "Height: " & UserControl.Extender.Height
        Print , "HelpContextID: " & _
          UserControl.Extender.HelpContextID
        Print , "Left: " & UserControl.Extender.Left
        Print , "TabIndex: " & UserControl.Extender.TabIndex
        Print , "TabStop: " & UserControl.Extender.TabStop
        Print , "Tag: " & UserControl.Extender.Tag
        Print , "Top: " & UserControl.Extender.Top
        Print , "Visible: " & UserControl.Extender.Visible
        Print , "WhatsThisHelpID: " & _
          UserControl.Extender.WhatsThisHelpID
        Print , "Width: " & UserControl.Extender.Width
      End Sub
```

5. Close the Code window.

6. Enlarge the control in the UserControl designer so that it is quite large.

7.   Close the UserControl designer.

8.   Choose Project1 Properties from the Project menu.

9.   In the Project Name box, type *LearnControl*.

10.   Choose OK.

11.   Choose Save Project from the File menu, and save your work.

12.   Choose Make LearnControl.ocx from the File menu.

13.   In the Make Project dialog box, choose OK, and Visual Basic will build the .OCX file.

14.   Using a text editor such as Notepad, create a text file named TEST.HTM.

15.   Type the following HTML code into TEST.HTM, and save the file:

```
<HTML>
<HEAD>
<TITLE>Testing Properties</TITLE>
</HEAD>
<BODY>

<OBJECT
    ID="LearnControl.MyInternetControl"
    CLASSID="CLSID:TYPE CLASS ID HERE"
    WIDTH=300
    HEIGHT=350
</OBJECT>

</BODY>
</HTML>
```

16.   Run Regedit to open the Microsoft Windows Registry Editor, and choose Find from the Edit menu to search for *LearnControl*.

17.   When you find *LearnControl.MyInternetControl*, open the CLSID folder and double-click (Default) in the right pane of the Registry Editor.

18.   Copy the CLSID shown in the Value Data box of the Edit String dialog box, and paste it into TEST.HTM at the specified location. Save and close the file.

19.   Open the HTML document TEST.HTM in Internet Explorer as shown in Figure 8-1. When the control is displayed, click it to activate the test code.

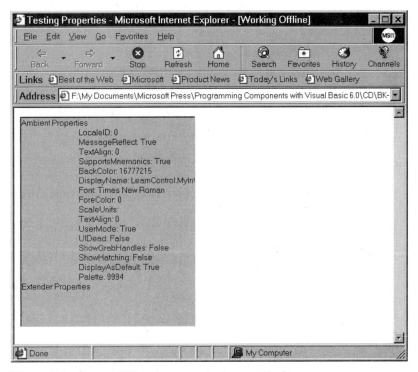

Figure 8-1. *The test HTML document in Internet Explorer.*

ASYNCHRONOUS DOWNLOADING

Designing software for the Internet requires developers to change the way they think about writing programs. As a software platform, the Internet is fundamentally different from the model most programmers are used to—a PC, a hard disk drive, and Microsoft Windows. When you write software for the Internet, your code might be downloaded dynamically. Or, if your code is already on the user's computer, it will probably need to download data. Thus, downloading time becomes a major factor in Internet software design. If there is one thing the Internet is famous for, it is low-speed, high-latency network access.

To avoid stalling the user interface and other components, Internet applications generally try to perform any time-consuming download operations asynchronously. This means that your control starts a particular downloading task, continues processing other work, and is notified when the downloading job is complete—thus the term *asynchronous download*. The Asynchronous Moniker Specification, which is part of the ActiveX Software Development Kit (SDK), was developed to provide this type of functionality. Microsoft has provided this functionality to ActiveX controls written in Visual Basic by means of the *AsyncRead* and *CancelAsyncRead* methods and the *AsyncReadComplete* event of the *UserControl* object.

In general, the asynchronous download feature of Visual Basic is intended to download data into properties of a control. The *AsyncRead* method is used to initiate an asynchronous download of data to a property. This call returns immediately and downloading proceeds in the background, leaving your control free to do any other work. The *AsyncReadComplete* event will be fired at your control when the entire property data has finished downloading. This notifies your program that the data is ready for use. You can use the *CancelAsyncRead* method to cancel the request during the download process.

If your control is running inside a Web browser such as Internet Explorer, a connection to the Internet is probably available for downloading the data. But what happens if your control is being used in the form of a Visual Basic program? In this case, assuming the user has the necessary software installed to connect to the Internet, the Web browser is loaded, the user is probably prompted to log in, and a connection by means of an Internet Service Provider (ISP) is attempted.

The *AsyncRead* Method

The *AsyncRead* method begins the download operation. The declaration for this method is:

```
Sub AsyncRead (Target As String, AsyncType As Long _
   [, PropertyName], [AsyncReadOptions]
```

The *Target* argument is the URL that points to the data being downloaded, such as *http://www.mycompanysite.com/mybitmap.bmp*. The *AsyncType* argument specifies the type of data to be downloaded. It can be one of the three values in the *AsyncTypeConstants* enumeration, as follows:

AsyncType *Constants*	*Description*
vbAsyncTypePicture	*AsyncRead* downloads to a picture object.
vbAsyncTypeFile	*AsyncRead* downloads to a file.
vbAsyncTypeByteArray	*AsyncRead* downloads to a byte array.

The optional *PropertyName* argument defines the name by which this download operation will be known. Normally, this is the property in which you want the downloaded data to be stored. Note, however, that specifying a property name does not cause the data to be automatically assigned to the property.

Instead, this simply allows a control to differentiate between what might be several different asynchronous operations proceeding simultaneously. Whatever name is provided in the *PropertyName* argument is later provided to the control in the *AsyncReadCompleted* event. Here is a sample *AsyncRead* call:

```
AsyncRead "ftp://ftp.mycompany.com/data.dat", _
   vbAsyncTypeFile, "MyData"
```

The *AsyncReadComplete* Event

The *AsyncReadComplete* event notifies your program that a particular asynchronous download has been completed. The declaration for this event is:

```
Sub AsyncReadComplete (AsyncProp As AsyncProperty)
```

AsyncProperty is an object with three properties: *AsyncType*, *PropertyName*, and *Value*. The first two properties are the same values that were passed to the *AsyncRead* method when the download began. This enables a control to determine which download is completed and which type of data was returned. The *Value* property is a *Variant* that contains the downloaded data. It is normally used to assign the downloaded data to a property of the control.

Properties	Type	Description
AsyncProperty.- *AsyncType*	*AsyncTypeConstant*	Type of data from *AsyncType* argument
AsyncProperty.- *PropertyName*	*String*	String passed to *AsyncRead* to tag this *Property* object
AsyncProperty.- *Value*	*Variant*	Default property; returns the downloaded data

The data that ends up in the *Value* parameter obviously will vary with the type of data that is downloaded. Thus, for a picture that was downloaded using the *vbAsyncTypePicture* data type, the *Value* parameter contains an object of the *Picture* type. Conversely, if the *vbAsyncTypeByteArray* was used in the *AsyncRead* call, the data is placed in the *Value* parameter as a byte array; in this case, it is assumed that the control will know how to handle this data. If a particular file was downloaded, the *Value* property will contain a string that indicates the complete path of the file on the local machine. Files are normally downloaded to the C:\Windows\Temp folder and given a temporary file name such as ~DFA034.TMP. Once the file is downloaded, the control can open the file and read its contents by means of normal file-handling features of Visual Basic, such as *Open*, *Input*, *Close*, and so on.

The *CancelAsyncRead* Method

The *CancelAsyncRead* method cancels an asynchronous data download already in progress. The declaration for this method is:

```
Sub CancelAsyncRead ([PropertyName])
```

If a *PropertyName* argument is provided, only the specified download is canceled. All other downloads proceed normally. This method is often called when a user clicks on a Cancel command button to abort a download.

Exercise 8-2

The following exercise creates a control that uses the asynchronous download features of Visual Basic.

1. Open Visual Basic, and start a new Standard EXE project.

2. Choose Add User Control from the Project menu. Select the default User Control, and click Open.

3. In the Properties window of the UserControl designer, set the *Name* property to *InternetControl*.

4. Add a PictureBox control to the UserControl designer.

5. Set the *AutoSize* property of the picture box to *True*.

6. Double-click the UserControl designer to open the Code window.

7. Type the following statements in the Code window:

```
Option Explicit
Private mInternetGraphic As String

Private Sub Picture1_Resize()
    If Picture1.Picture <> 0 Then
        UserControl.Size Picture1.Width, _
            Picture1.Height
    End If
End Sub

Private Sub UserControl_AsyncReadComplete(AsyncProp _
  As AsyncProperty)
    If AsyncProp.PropertyName = "InternetGraphic" _
      Then
        Set Picture1 = AsyncProp.Value
        Debug.Print _
            "AsyncReadComplete: Finished downloading"
    End If
End Sub
```

```
Public Property Get InternetGraphic() As String
    InternetGraphic = mInternetGraphic
End Property

Public Property Let InternetGraphic(ByVal vNewValue _
    As String)
    mInternetGraphic = vNewValue
    If Ambient.UserMode = True And vNewValue <> "" _
        Then
        AsyncRead vNewValue, vbAsyncTypePicture, _
            "InternetGraphic"
    End If
End Property

Private Sub UserControl_Resize()
    Picture1.Move 0, 0, ScaleWidth, ScaleHeight
End Sub
```

8. Close the Code window and the UserControl designer.

9. Add the new control to Form1.

10. In the Code window for Form1, enter the following code:

```
Option Explicit

Private Sub Form_Click()
    ' Next line starts async download
    InternetControl1.InternetGraphic = InputBox( _
        "Enter the URL of the picture file you " & _
        "want to display")
    Debug.Print "Form_Click finished: " & _
        "async download proceeding..."
End Sub
```

11. Run the program, and test it by clicking the form's background.

12. In the dialog box that is displayed, enter the URL to any graphic file. If you have a live Internet connection, you might try *http://www.microsoft.com/library/images/gifs/homepage/h_microsoft.gif*. Otherwise, enter a URL path to a graphic file on your local hard drive (for example, *file://c:/windows/bubbles.bmp*).

13. In the Immediate window, you should see the message *Form_Click finished: async download proceeding...*, followed by the message *AsyncReadComplete: Finished downloading*. You might also try stepping through the code line by line to better see the order in which actions are executed.

In addition to using this asynchronous download technique on the Internet, you can also use it for files on a local machine. One popular use of asynchronous download capabilities is to progressively render bitmaps. Progressive rendering means that the bitmap is displayed as it is downloaded, either bit by bit (don't take that too literally), or in low-detail followed by mid-detail and high-detail renderings. For this to work, the system must provide notification events periodically during the download process, instead of sending the notification only once when the download is complete. You can also use this idea of progressive rendering for types of data other than graphics. An application might simply use the notification events to display a progress bar that indicates to the user what percentage of the download is complete.

ACTIVEX HYPERLINKING

Part of the ActiveX specifications defines an area of functionality called ActiveX hyperlinking. *ActiveX hyperlinking* specifies a model of interaction among applications, documents, and controls that occurs during hyperlink exploration of the World Wide Web. The Web is known for its ease of use. Moving around the Web by means of a browser can be accomplished with URLs, point-and-click hyperlinks, a history list, and a favorites list. ActiveX hyperlinking offers a similar model to your applications.

ActiveX hyperlinking works in hosts that implement the ActiveX hyperlinking specification, such as Microsoft Internet Explorer, Microsoft Visual Basic, and the Microsoft Office 97 applications. For ActiveX controls running within Internet Explorer, hyperlinking offers full integration with the history list and URL-based exploration of the Web. In a container such as a Visual Basic form, the hyperlinking feature launches Internet Explorer to accomplish hyperlink exploration.

Visual Basic exposes the ActiveX hyperlinking capability by means of the *Hyperlink* property of the *UserControl* object, which provides a reference to a *Hyperlink* object. The *Hyperlink* object gives your control access to the ActiveX hyperlinking functionality and supports the following three methods:

Method	Description
GoBack	Go backward in the history list
GoForward	Go forward in the history list
NavigateTo	Go to a URL and, optionally, to a location within the URL target

Using these methods of the *Hyperlink* object, your control can request a hyperlink-aware container, such as Internet Explorer, to jump to a given URL or to move through the history list. If your control isn't running in Internet Explorer, the *Hyperlink* property might be 0. You should always check for this status before using the *Hyperlink* reference. The *Hyperlink* object in Visual Basic calls Internet Explorer via Automation interfaces.

The *Hyperlink* object is perhaps most useful on corporate intranets where it can be used to direct users to specific documents.

CREATING INTERACTIVE CONTENT FOR THE WEB

The Web lies somewhere between the worlds of print and broadcast media. It possesses the up-to-date quality of broadcast media without being quite so transient. When you watch the late evening news on television, you get the latest information available, but you have to tune in at eleven o'clock to get it. If you read a weekly news magazine, you are sacrificing the up-to-the-minute aspect of broadcast media for the convenience of being able to read the magazine at any time.

On the Web, you do not need to make these kinds of sacrifices. A Web site is always waiting for you—you just type in the URL for the site, and you're there. The Web site can also be updated as often as its author wants. In fact, some Web sites receive continuous data streams from news wire services or the stock market. A Web site can offer the best of both worlds: it can be as up-to-date as the evening news, and it's always available.

Until recently, attractions on the Web have been somewhat dull and two-dimensional. Static text and graphics on a Web page look nice, but what can they *do*? A big part of the impetus for the ActiveX specifications came from Microsoft's desire to help make content on the Internet more dynamic. This means making sites more interactive and adding animation, multimedia, and virtual reality.

How do you transform a bunch of static, boring, HTML documents into something more alive, more interactive? There are two techniques you can use: HTML tags and code. Some of the newer HTML tags make Web pages more exciting. You can add blinking text or text that scrolls across the screen. You can format Web pages into tables or separate frames of data that users can scroll independently. You can use tables, forms, fields, frames, and other features of advanced HTML. However, if you want even more dynamic pages, at some point you will want more than HTML has to offer and you will have to consider code. An HTML document is a simple ASCII text file that describes formatting options for text, but code lets you harness all the capabilities of a computer to make a Web experience memorable. In reality, most interactive Web sites use a combination of advanced HTML tags and code. In a well-designed Web site, the viewer should not be able to tell where HTML tags end and code begins.

Server-Side Code

There are several ways to include code in a Web site. One popular way is to write scripts in a scripting language using the Common Gateway Interface (CGI) and to put them on a Web server, where they can be called by a Web browser. In this way, an HTML document can collect data from users—say, names and addresses using an HTML form—and then send the data to the Web server. The Web server then launches a script (on the server) to accept the data and then possibly save it in a database. The script can also generate an HTML page for the Web browser to display in response. One problem with putting your code on the server has been speed. Since a new CGI process has to be launched for each client, the Web server can quickly get bogged down if too many clients request services at the same time.

Client-Side Code

Another way to add code to a Web site is to write it so that it will execute on the client computer. However, code targeted for the client computer has special problems that code running on a server does not have. How does the code get to the client computer in the first place? You need to provide some mechanism to download the code as data and then execute it.

The second issue, perhaps even more crucial than the first, is security. Although you might know that the code you placed on the Internet is safe, think about the situation from the user's perspective. Browsing the Web used to be relatively safe if you were only passively viewing published documents. Today the demand for more interactive Web content has led to browsers that are no longer simply viewers; rather, they are more like application hosts, with Web sites acting as the applications. Code is now commonly downloaded to the end-user's computer, creating the real possibility of a user accidentally downloading malicious code, such as a computer virus. Even if the code was benign when placed on the Internet by its author, a malevolent person might have tampered with it since then. As a result, we urgently need some way to ensure the safety of code that is downloaded and executed on the client computer.

Although these drawbacks are important and need to be addressed, there are many advantages to having code execute on the client side. The first advantage is speed. Code that executes on the client computer does not drag down the Web server, enabling the server to handle many more users simultaneously. The second advantage is the range of capability. Since the code is executing on the client side it can easily interact with the user and the user's data. Thus, you can write code that displays fancy animation or graphics, such as virtual reality, or code that reads data from files on the user's computer. The possibilities are nearly limitless. In the coming pages, we'll explore two basic types of code that can be downloaded and executed on the user's computer: scripts and binary code.

ActiveX Scripting

The idea of using a scripting language to create interactive Web content began at Netscape. Developers at Netscape decided that although HTML was neat, it would be neater still if some simple programming constructs were added. So, in conjunction with Sun Microsystems, Inc., Netscape added support for a scripting language named JavaScript to its Navigator browser. A Web scripting language allows developers to insert snippets of code directly into an HTML document, as in the following example.

```
<HTML>
<HEAD>
<TITLE>A JavaScript Sample</TITLE>
</HEAD>

<SCRIPT LANGUAGE="JavaScript">
function push_me()
    {
    alert("Hello, World!")
    }
</SCRIPT>

<BODY>
<CENTER>
<FORM>
<INPUT TYPE="BUTTON" VALUE="Push Me"
NAME = "Command1" OnClick="push_me()">
</FORM>
</CENTER>
</BODY>
</HTML>
```

When Microsoft developers considered adding scripting support to Internet Explorer, they realized that although JavaScript was nice and popular, it was not a good idea to lock developers into only one scripting language for the Internet. This was the impetus behind the design of the ActiveX Scripting specification, wherein Microsoft has defined a COM-based interface within which

ActiveX Scripting engines and ActiveX Scripting hosts interact. ActiveX Scripting engines are implemented as in-process component DLLs, although it isn't currently possible to create a scripting engine in Visual Basic.

An ActiveX Scripting engine is the language interpreter. It defines the syntax, format, execution model, and all other details of the programming language. An ActiveX Scripting host is an application that supports scripting engines. Microsoft Internet Explorer, for example, is an ActiveX Scripting host; it supports any scripting language implemented as an ActiveX Scripting engine. Microsoft currently supplies two ActiveX Scripting engines with Internet Explorer: VBScript (VBSCRIPT.DLL) and JavaScript (JSCRIPT.DLL).

A major benefit of the ActiveX Scripting interfaces is that they relieve the developer of a Web browser from having to implement special code for each script language he or she might want to support. Whenever Internet Explorer encounters a script in the HTML document, it loads the appropriate ActiveX Scripting engine and sends it the script code to execute. By supporting the ActiveX Scripting specifications, the browser will integrate with any scripting engine. The script specifications also enable many different scripting languages to be developed separately from the Web browser and to be used by hosts other than Web browsers.

VBScript

Microsoft Visual Basic Scripting Edition, colloquially known as VBScript, is a lightweight subset of Visual Basic implemented as an ActiveX Scripting engine. VBScript can be used to add scripting capabilities to Web pages viewed by Microsoft Internet Explorer and any other browser supporting ActiveX Scripting interfaces.

By now, you are probably beginning to wonder how VBScript looks in an HTML document. I'll keep you in suspense no longer; here's a sample.

```
<HTML>
<HEAD>
<TITLE>VBScript Web Page</TITLE>
</HEAD>

<SCRIPT LANGUAGE="VBScript">
<!--
    MsgBox "Hello World!"
-->
</SCRIPT>

<BODY>
<B>This is a basic HTML document.</B>
```

```
</BODY>
```

```
</HTML>
```

Notice several things about this simple example. First, the VBScript code is mixed directly into the HTML document. Nothing separates the VBScript tags and code from the other HTML tags. Second, the VBScript code will be down-loaded as part of the HTML document ASCII text. This means that users will be able to view the script source code just as they can view standard HTML documents. Finally, realize that VBScript (like JavaScript) is purely an interpreted language. At run time, the Web browser loads the correct ActiveX Scripting engine specified by the <SCRIPT> tag and then passes the code to the scripting engine to execute.

VBScript is a somewhat limited version of Visual Basic and, as such, does not support several leading features of Visual Basic. Most important, VBScript does not provide a design-time environment. In fact, VBScript does not have any support for user interface features. All VBScript code is written directly into HTML documents. The standard parts of the HTML document define what the user sees in the browser. VBScript can be used only to activate existing parts of the Web page. File-handling features of Visual Basic are also not supported by VBScript. Finally, although calls such as *CreateObject* that access ActiveX code components are part of the VBScript language specification, they are not available in the browser for security reasons. Chapter 12 discusses using VBScript on the server, where such features are enabled.

The <SCRIPT> Tag

The <SCRIPT> tag, shown in the previous code example, extends standard HTML to support client-side scripting of HTML documents and objects embedded within HTML documents. The World Wide Web Consortium (W3C) is currently in the process of adopting the <SCRIPT> tag as part of the HTML standard.

Notice that in the following example, the VBScript code is contained within HTML comment tags (<!-- and -->). This is for the benefit of browsers that do not yet support the <SCRIPT> tag and prevents them from mistakenly display-ing the VBScript code as text on the Web page. Browsers supporting the <SCRIPT> tag will ignore all HTML comment tags contained within a <SCRIPT> tag. To comment VBScript code, use the Basic REM statement or an apostrophe (').

```
<SCRIPT LANGUAGE="VBScript"><!--
    ' This is a comment.
    REM This is a comment too.
    MsgBox "Hello, world"
--></SCRIPT>
```

As mentioned earlier, any code that is downloaded and executed on the client machine presents a potential security risk. This risk extends far beyond the apparent simplicity of the code that can be seen in the HTML. There are two basic ways to address the issue of security: either you don't allow the code to do anything potentially dangerous, or you somehow verify that the code is safe. Microsoft Internet Explorer takes the first approach with script code, a process sometimes known as running code "in the sandbox." The problem with the sandbox approach is that by restricting the script code from doing anything dangerous, you consequently restrict it from doing many interesting and useful things. For example, VBScript does not support any file-handling features. This stops a malicious script from destroying the user's data, but it also prevents a benign script from saving or retrieving data on the local hard disk.

Binary Code

In addition to incorporating scripts in HTML documents, you can embed precompiled components in HTML documents to make the documents more interactive. These components include ActiveX controls and Java applets. Since these components are precompiled, you do not represent them inside an HTML document by ASCII text. Instead, you reference these components in HTML with the <OBJECT> tag.

Because ActiveX controls are not stored in the HTML document, they must be downloaded separately. This, in itself, isn't such a big deal—after all, graphic images are routinely downloaded in conjunction with a Web page. However, .GIF files don't contain executable code as do controls and applets, and therefore they can't be used to destroy data on the end user's computer.

The <OBJECT> Tag

The <OBJECT> tag supports the insertion of a Java applet, an ActiveX control, an ActiveX document, or any of a wide range of other plug-ins. The <OBJECT> tag was designed to be as general as possible in order to support a variety of uses. The following sample <OBJECT> tag inserts an ActiveX control into a Web page:

```
<OBJECT
    ID="SuperButton" WIDTH=120 HEIGHT=40
    CLASSID="CLSID:D7053B42-CE69-11CD-A777-00DD01143C57"
    CODEBASE="http://www.mycompany.com/superbtn.ocx">
        <PARAM NAME="Caption" VALUE="MyButton">
        <PARAM NAME="Size" VALUE="2540;846">
        <PARAM NAME="FontCharSet" VALUE="0">
        <PARAM NAME="FontPitchAndFamily" VALUE="2"
</OBJECT>
```

The ID attribute names the control—*SuperButton*, in this case. You can think of this as a Name property that identifies the control within the HTML document. This is similar to the *Name* property that identifies a command button within a Visual Basic form. The CLASSID attribute specifies the COM class identifier number for the component. Visual Basic assigns class identifier numbers automatically; the easiest way to locate the class identifier for a component is to open the Windows Registry Editor and search for the component's name. The CODEBASE optional attribute specifies a URL where the component is located. If the component is already installed on the user's computer, the CODEBASE attribute is ignored. Otherwise, this URL is used to download the component.

A <PARAM> tag allows a property of a control to be initialized. The name of the property is specified with the NAME attribute. The value assigned to the specified property is defined by the VALUE attribute. You assign property values with the <PARAM> tag after the control is running. Thus, an HTML page can contain only properties that can be set at run time; design-time properties are never available. In addition, a control in a Web browser never receives *ReadProperties* or *WriteProperties* events; since there isn't anywhere to save property values, there are no saved properties to retrieve. The control will get an *InitProperties* event, which sets property defaults.

Internet Component Download

Since ActiveX components referenced with the <OBJECT> tag will often need to be downloaded and installed on the user's computer, Microsoft developed the Internet Component Download specification. Internet Component Download is a mechanism by which ActiveX components can be packaged, downloaded, verified, and finally installed on a client computer.

Surprisingly, the Internet Component Download service consists of a single COM function: *CoGetClassObjectFromURL*. Internet Explorer calls this amazing little function whenever it encounters the <OBJECT> tag in an HTML document. It basically takes a URL and returns an instance of the specified object. Internally, it downloads the component, verifies it, and then installs it, all before instancing the object.

The steps performed by the Internet Component Download service are as follows:

1. Checks to see whether the necessary components are installed. If so, skips to step 6.

2. Downloads the necessary file or files to temporary files using URL Monikers.

3. Calls *WinVerifyTrust* to ensure that all downloaded files are safe to install.

4. Registers ActiveX components. This involves running .EXE files with the /RegServer flag and calling the *DLLRegisterServer* function for .DLL and .OCX files.

5. Adds registry entries to keep track of downloaded code.

6. Calls *CoGetClassObject* for the object.

The Internet Component Download service uses URL Monikers to actually download the code and then calls the *WinVerifyTrust* function to verify the code. *WinVerifyTrust* is the main function of the Authenticode module, which is described later in this chapter.

The Internet Component Download service installs most code in the C:\Windows\OCCache folder. Currently this is implemented as a permanent storage place, meaning that installed components are never removed. In the future, a more sophisticated algorithm might be implemented, whereby code installed but not used for a certain length of time would be removed automatically, thus freeing up disk space.

Packaging ActiveX Controls for Download

The Internet Component Download service is currently able to download .OCX, .DLL, .CAB, and .INF files. An .OCX file is obviously an ActiveX control, and a .DLL file is probably an ActiveX code component. Downloading a component is simplest when the component is an .OCX or a .DLL, but in these cases the Internet Component Download service can download only one file at a time and can't use file compression.

A .CAB (cabinet) file contains one or more files that the Internet Component Download service downloads together in a compressed format. The cabinet file format is a good choice when you want to download several files together and take advantage of compression to speed up the download time. Windows has cabinet file decompression software built in, so the Internet Component Download service has no trouble installing files packaged in this manner.

An .INF (information) file is an ASCII setup script that specifies the various files that need to be downloaded and set up for the component. Using an .INF file is a good idea for a complicated component that might need many files from many places. Information files are often used when an attempt is being made at platform independence. For example, you might develop several versions of an ActiveX control for different process architectures, such as Intel, Motorola, DEC, or MIPS (all running Windows, of course). Depending on the type of processor in the client computer, a different version of the control could be downloaded. You can accomplish this only by using an information file for setup directives.

ActiveX components created in Visual Basic require the MSVBVM60.DLL file to be installed on the client computer in order to run. This is true regardless of whether a component is compiled to p-code or native code. Obviously, you want to be sure that your component will run correctly on the user's computer even if it is downloaded over the Internet. You wouldn't want to require downloading a 1.3-MB DLL that most users probably already have. To solve this problem, the Package and Deployment Wizard creates a setup script that checks to see whether the necessary Visual Basic support files are present on the user's computer. If not, the browser is directed automatically to download these files from Microsoft's Internet servers. This relieves you of the burdens of checking for this yourself and providing the Visual Basic support files on your servers.

Code Security Issues

The security mechanisms for ActiveX controls and Java applets are more complicated than those employed for scripting. Recall that safe scripting is ensured by limiting what scripts can do. This method isn't used for ActiveX components because Microsoft felt that this would be too restrictive and would stifle the market for these types of components. If no restrictions are placed on ActiveX components, how then can the user be protected from dangerous programs?

A major problem with including code in a Web site is the security risk. Since code can really do anything, users need to be protected from rogue code, especially in as egalitarian an environment as the Internet. The problems with executing code over the Internet are well expressed by questions that a sophisticated user might pose, such as the following:

- How do I know the code won't damage data on my computer?

- How do I know who wrote the code?

- How do I know the code hasn't been tampered with?

- Where does the code execute?

As with many good questions, a good answer is provided by another question. When people walk into a software store and see a bunch of nice, clean, sealed boxes of software on the shelf, they get a nice, warm, fuzzy feeling. Why? Because, they figure, if those boxes are in a nice store and have a nice logo on the well-sealed box from the nice company that created it, the software must be safe.

Now let's bring this model to the Internet. When most technically savvy people visit Microsoft's Web site, they feel pretty safe about downloading code that Microsoft has posted. Why? Because they reason that if this code is on Microsoft's server, it must be safe. If any program downloaded from Microsoft's Internet servers ever had a virus in it, the news would be all over the front page of the morning paper. However, any person who has ever been plagued by a computer virus might justifiably have qualms about downloading a cool program from Jerry's or Beverly's home page.

The problem is that even the code you download from Microsoft's Internet servers isn't 100 percent safe; it is theoretically possible that someone could intercept the code on its way from Microsoft's computers to yours and modify the code in some malicious fashion. For this reason, we need more than just the domain name of a big company to feel safe on the Internet.

Authenticode

It is currently unrealistic to scan most types of code[1] to determine whether they are malicious. Microsoft has therefore devised a code-signing specification called Authenticode, which is part of the Microsoft Internet Security Framework. Rather than attempting to determine whether the code itself is dangerous, Authenticode informs users about the component they are downloading—specifically, the name and the author of the component, as well as the name of the company that certified the component author. This gives end users a chance to consider whether they want to have this component installed on their machines. Without this information, users might not even realize that a component is part of the Web site. In addition, Authenticode verifies that the code has not been tampered with since its release.

In summary, Authenticode ensures authenticity and integrity. By "authenticity," we mean that Authenticode verifies that the code is actually what it claims to be. This protects the user from code that tries to impersonate another developer. For example, a hacker might try to represent his or her code as having been created by a major corporation. Authenticode ensures this can't succeed. By "integrity," we mean that Authenticode verifies that the code has not been tampered with since its release. Thus, you can think of Authenticode as shrink-wrap for Internet components.

---

1. You can scan viruses, most of which carry a specific signature for their own identification purposes.

Digital Signatures

Authenticode works by requiring component developers to digitally sign their software. A digital signature contains the following information:

- Information about the component

- Information about the developer

- A public key[2]

- An encrypted digest of the file's contents

Internet Explorer enables the user to control the safety level of the browser by choosing Internet Options from the View menu and setting the security level on the Security tab, as shown in Figure 8-2.

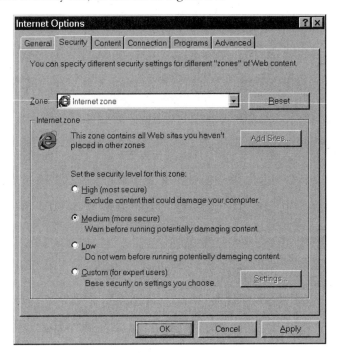

Figure 8-2. *The Security tab of the Internet Options dialog box.*

---

2. A Public Key Certificate Standard #7 (PKCS#7) object is a signed data object containing information used to sign a file. It contains the signer's certificate, public key, and the root certificate.

By default, safety for sites on the Internet is set to High. This means that unsigned code is avoided, and you are notified of this with a warning message. If you want to be able to use unsigned components, you must change the security setting to Medium or Low. Assuming it is set to Medium and the user visits a Web site that tries to install an unsigned component on the user's computer, another warning message is displayed. If the user so chooses, he or she can ignore the warning. Setting the security level to Low provides no warning when unsigned components are installed.

Assuming that the file was digitally signed, after the Internet Component Download service has finished downloading the component, the *WinVerifyTrust* function is called to verify that the digital signature is genuine. Here is the set of steps that Authenticode goes through to verify a digital signature:

1. A one-way hash of the file is produced.

2. The encrypted digest of the component stored in the digital signature is decrypted using the public key.

3. If the digest's procedure in steps 1 and 2 verifies that the code is what it claims to be, it is deemed to be safe. Otherwise, it is deemed to be questionable.

If the digests do not match, then the user is warned of the possibility that this code was tampered with. Of course, it is also possible that the code was signed incorrectly or corrupted on download. Again, the user has the opportunity to override the warning and proceed with the installation of the erroneously signed component.

Assuming that the digital signature checks out, a dialog box something like the one in Figure 8-3 is normally presented to the user, displaying the credentials of the component in question. The name of the component and its developer are displayed. Both might be hyperlinks, which allow the user to connect easily to the developer's Web site for more information about this component and its author. Also displayed is the name of the Certificate Authority (CA) who granted the certificate to the component developer for code-signing purposes. Certificate Authorities publish criteria for granting a certificate and then grant certificates to those meeting the specified criteria.

In this dialog box, the user has two major options: he or she can either accept the installation of this component by choosing Yes or reject it by choosing No. If the user chooses Yes, the component is installed permanently on the user's computer in the C:\Windows\OCCache folder. Any future attempts to use this component will not require downloading or security checks. The object will simply be instantiated from the file on the local computer.

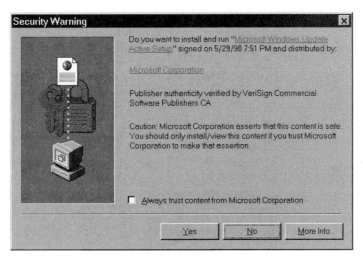

Figure 8-3. *A sample security certificate.*

At the bottom of the security certificate, the user has the option of specifying the component developer as trustworthy. If this is done, future components
signed by that developer will be downloaded and installed with no warnings
whatsoever. For example, the user might decide that code signed by Microsoft
is trustworthy and therefore he or she does not want to be bothered with notification messages regarding Microsoft components. Keep in mind that a component written by Microsoft could be used in someone else's Web page and
downloaded from his or her site. This does not make it any less safe, however,
since Authenticode checks to ensure that the code has not been modified.
However, there is one potential problem with unsafe scripting. Even code that
is safe and that is signed can become a weapon in the hands of a malicious script.

The Safety Settings step of the Package and Deployment Wizard, shown
in Figure 8-4 on the following page, lets you mark your control as safe for initialization or safe for scripting. When you select these options, you are giving
your guarantee that your component will not harm the user's system, even if it
is initialized with corrupt data or controlled by a malicious script. The first kind
of security breach—initialization with corrupt data—arises when someone pur-
posely passes corrupt initialization data to a control by means of the PARAM attributes of the <OBJECT> tag in the HTML. You should designate your control
as safe for initialization only if initialization data can't cause your control to change
system settings or create, modify, or delete files on the user's computer. The
source of the second potential security hazard is malicious script code written
in VBScript or JavaScript. Designate your control as safe for scripting only if you
are certain that your control can't be manipulated into doing harm by script code
with malevolent intentions.

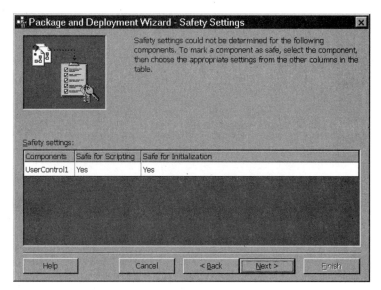

Figure 8-4. *The Safety Settings dialog box of the Package and Deployment Wizard.*

Code Signing

Digitally signing ActiveX components built in Visual Basic is no different from signing components built in any other development environment. First you have to produce the code, normally by creating an .OCX file. If your component has many files that need to be downloaded, consider creating a .CAB file using the Cabinet Development Kit (CABDevKt.EXE), which comes with the Platform SDK. The Platform SDK comes with all the tools needed to sign code. These programs are listed below, and you can find them in your C:\INetSDK\Bin folder.

File	*Purpose*
Cert2SPC.Exe	Creates a PKCS#7 Software Publishing Certificate (SPC) from an X.509 certificate
CertMgr.Exe	Displays and manages certificate information
ChkTrust.Exe	Calls *WinVerifyTrust* to simulate the behavior of Internet Explorer on encountering the file
MakeCert.Exe	Creates a test X.509 certificate
PeSigMgr.Exe	Checks to see that the file was signed
Root.cer	A root certificate for testing purposes only
SignCode.Exe	Digitally signs a component using an SPC

The X.509 Certificate

An X.509 certificate is a cryptographic certificate that contains the vendor's unique name and public key. The X.509 protocols include a structure for public key certificates. A Certificate Authority (CA) assigns a unique name to each user and issues a signed certificate containing this name and the user's public key. Following are the definitions for each field:

Field	Meaning
Version	Identifies the certificate format.
Serial Number	Identifies the certificate, which is unique to the CA.
Algorithm Identifier	Identifies the algorithm used to sign the certificate, together with any necessary parameters.
Issuer	The name of the CA.
Period of Validity	A pair of dates. The certificate is valid during the time period between the two.
Subject	The name of the user.
Subject's Public Key	Contains the public key algorithm name, any necessary parameters, and the public key.
Signature	The CA's signature.

Code-Signing Steps

Let's say that you have built an ActiveX control in Visual Basic and compiled it to an .OCX file. Since you intend to distribute this control from your Web site on the Internet, you want to digitally sign it so that users will feel comfortable downloading your code. To sign an ActiveX control named SILLY.OCX, you execute the following statements at the command line. You can use the Windows Run command on the Start menu or use the MS-DOS prompt.

```
makecert -u:GuyEddon -k:guyeddon.pvk -n:CN=GuyEddon →
  -d:"Guy Eddon" guyeddon.cer
cert2spc c:\inetsdk\bin\root.cer guyeddon.cer guyeddon.spc
signcode -prog silly.ocx -spc guyeddon.spc →
  -pvk guyeddon.pvk -name Silly -info →
  http://www.mycompany.com -individual
regedit wvtston.reg
pesigmgr -l silly.ocx
chktrust silly.ocx
```

The MakeCert program generates a certificate (.CER) and a private key (.PVK) test file. This utility is used for testing purposes only, and you should not use it once you obtain a valid X.509 certificate from a CA.

Next, the Cert2SPC program wraps the X.509 certificate and a root certificate into a PKCS#7 signed-data object (.SPC file). The ROOT.CER file is a test certificate supplied with the ActiveX SDK. You'll find it, along with the rest of these programs, in the C:\INetSDK\Bin folder. Let us say again that this program is for test purposes only, and you should not use it once you obtain a valid Software Publishing Certificate (SPC) from a CA.

The SignCode program does the real work. If you simply type *SignCode* with no command-line parameters, a wizard-style interface guides you through the various options. The SignCode program signs the specified ActiveX component by using a valid .SPC file. Using SignCode is the only step necessary if you have obtained a valid SPC from a CA. In our case, however, since we are using the test SPC generated with Cert2SPC, we need to set a registry setting so that Internet Explorer will recognize the test SPC. The ActiveX SDK comes with a registry file named WVTSTON.REG that enables this. The PeSigMgr program displays the information about the certificates contained in our signed component.

```
Certificate    0 Revision 256 Type    PKCS7
```

Note that signing the SILLY.OCX file added about 1 KB to its total size. Now we are ready to see our signed code certificate in all its glory using the ChkTrust program.

The HTML code to insert the Silly control into a Web page might look as follows:

```
<HTML>
<HEAD>
<TITLE>VBScript Web Page</TITLE>
</HEAD>

<BODY>
<B>This is a basic HTML document.</B>

<OBJECT
    ID="SuperWidget" WIDTH=300 HEIGHT=200
    CLASSID="CLSID:6C72B8A3-0AF4-11D0-A879-10005A758DE1"
    CODEBASE="c:\silly.ocx">
    <PARAM NAME="SillyQuotient" VALUE="100">
</OBJECT>
</BODY>
</HTML>
```

Scripting ActiveX Controls

You have learned how to create an ActiveX control for the Internet, compile it to an .OCX file, digitally sign it, and then use the <OBJECT> tag to embed the control in an HTML document. What's next? Well, when you place a control on a form in Visual Basic, that form will normally set the properties of the control, call its methods, and respond to its events. Now that Internet Explorer is the container for your ActiveX control, how can code be written to do all this? In Internet Explorer, you write VBScript code, such as the following:

```
<SCRIPT LANGUAGE = "VBScript">
<!--
<OBJECT
    ID="SuperWidget"
    CLASSID="CLSID:6C72B8A3-0AF4-11D0-A879-10005A758DE1"
    WIDTH=300
    HEIGHT=200
    CODEBASE="c:\silly.ocx">
    <PARAM NAME="SillyQuotient" VALUE="100">
</OBJECT>
-->
</SCRIPT>
```

In our look at the <OBJECT> tag, we have already discussed how to set properties of the control using <PARAM NAME>. This is somewhat analogous to setting properties in the Visual Basic Properties window. Beyond that, however, you might want to set properties as the user works with the Web page, and we still need to address the issue of methods and events.

The following HTML snippet displays a message box on startup and then creates a command button on a Web page using the <OBJECT> tag. Clicking the command button calls the CommandButton1_Click event procedure. The code displays a message box notifying the user that the command button was clicked and then changes the *Caption* property of the command button to *Bye-bye*. From this example, you can see that working with an ActiveX control in VBScript code isn't at all difficult.

```
<SCRIPT LANGUAGE="VBScript">
<!--

MsgBox "Testing VBScript"

Sub CommandButton1_Click()
    MsgBox "Button Clicked"
    CommandButton1.Caption = "Bye-bye"
End Sub
```

(continued)

```
-->
</SCRIPT>
<OBJECT
    ID="CommandButton1"
    CLASSID="CLSID:D7053240-CE69-11CD-A777-00DD01143C57">
    WIDTH=120
    HEIGHT=40
    <PARAM NAME="Caption" VALUE="Hi There">
    <PARAM NAME="Size" VALUE="2540;846">
    <PARAM NAME="FontCharSet" VALUE="0">
    <PARAM NAME="ParagraphAlign" VALUE="3">
</OBJECT>
```

Microsoft Internet Explorer Scripting Object Model

Internet Explorer exposes an object model that scripting languages such as VBScript and JavaScript can use. This object model allows script code to use the properties, methods, and events of the various objects available. There are 11 objects in the HTML object model.[3]

Object	Description
Window	Represents the Internet Explorer window and its methods and properties.
Frame	Each frame is a window that has its own properties, including a document.
History	Accesses the history list from the browser.
Navigator	Contains information about the browser application.
Location	Provides information about the location of the window's URL.
Script	Identifies any scripting function defined using the SCRIPT element in the window scope.
Document	Identifies the document in the current window.
Link	A link object is constructed for every link <A HREF> that appears in the HTML document.
Anchor	An anchor object is constructed for every anchor <A> tag found in the HTML document.
Form	Represents a <FORM> in the HTML document.
Element	Elements are intrinsic HTML controls or ActiveX controls inserted in HTML by means of the <OBJECT> tag.

3. Note the similarity to the properties and methods of the *InternetExplorer* object automated from Visual Basic, as described in Chapter 4.

Chapter 9

Creating Active Documents

In addition to the COM code components and Microsoft ActiveX controls we've covered so far, you can create one other type of COM component in Microsoft Visual Basic: an Active document[1]. Active documents began life as a proprietary technology in the Microsoft Office suite. The Microsoft Office Binder, an Active document container included with Microsoft Office, works as a sort of electronic paper clip to bind documents together, helping users to work on several related documents.

In a way, Office Binder does for Office documents what the project capability does for Visual Basic programs. A Visual Basic project file (.VBP file) groups references to all the files contained in the entire project. When a developer wants to work on a particular form, normally he or she simply opens the project and all the files are automatically loaded. In Office, someone might use Microsoft Word to create a business proposal, Microsoft PowerPoint to create a presentation, and Microsoft Excel to back up the proposal with figures and graphs. Rather than a user having to launch each application separately and remember what each file was named, Office Binder lets a user open a collection of documents within the Office Binder interface. As the various Office applications are needed, Office Binder automatically loads and displays them, as shown in Figure 9-1 on the following page.

---

1. An Active document is also known as an ActiveX document.

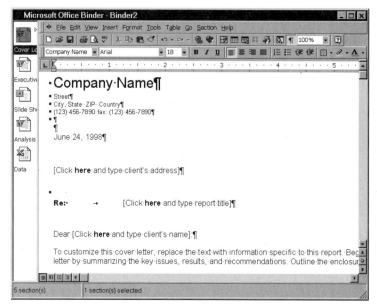

Figure 9-1. *Microsoft Office applications open in Office Binder.*

Notice in Figure 9-1 that although the title bar says "Microsoft Office Binder," it appears as if Microsoft Word is running. That is because Office Binder is displaying an open Word document. The column of icons on the left lists the Active documents in the open binder. You can see the icons for Word, Excel, and PowerPoint files. Whenever the user selects one of the files for editing, Office Binder automatically loads and displays the necessary application. The menus and toolbars that Office Binder displays belong to the application that created the Active document.

You might be thinking, "OK, so what's the big deal? I could have done that before with in-place activation." Think again. Using in-place activation, you can embed and then activate only a little bit of content in an application. For example, you can embed an Excel worksheet in a Word document and then in-place activate the worksheet. That causes Excel to load and enables you to edit the worksheet from within Word. However, it doesn't enable you to activate an entire document with another application. Think of it this way: in-place activation is concerned with activating snippets of data, while Active document technology is concerned with activating documents.

Of course, there are similarities between in-place activation and Active documents. In fact, Active documents are basically a superset of the services offered as part of in-place activation. The extensions consist of additional interfaces—*IOleDocumentSite*, *IContinueCallback*, and *IOleCommandTarget*.

These interfaces expand the functionality of embedded in-place activation so that, instead of simply activating a single piece of content, an Active document can represent an entire document.

When Microsoft first introduced Office Binder, the interfaces necessary to support Active documents were essentially undocumented. Only Office Binder and the rest of the Office applications could work with them. However, Microsoft later published the Active document specifications, enabling anyone to write an Active document container or component. An Active document container is a program, such as Office Binder, that supports the interfaces necessary to display Active documents within its user interface. An Active document component is a program, such as Word or Excel, that can open documents within an Active document container.

Microsoft made the Active document specifications publicly available once they realized how important this functionality is to many different types of applications. The idea of document-centric computing has long been considered a goal of a user-friendly system. Instead of requiring users to know which application to launch in order to edit a certain type of data, that kind of system can automatically open the necessary program, permitting the user to concentrate on the work to be accomplished instead of how to work with the computer.

Microsoft Internet Explorer supports Active document interfaces. With Internet Explorer, as with Office Binder, you can open any Active document. Word, PowerPoint, and Excel all qualify as Active documents. Currently, Internet Explorer, Binder, and Microsoft Developer Studio are the only Active document containers in widespread use; that type of functionality is required by only a few specialized applications. Many applications, however, can benefit from becoming Active document components. Applications that do so enable users to browse application documents from within containers such as Internet Explorer and Office Binder.

In Figure 9-2 on the following page, you can see how a Microsoft Word document looks when it is opened inside Internet Explorer using Active document interfaces. That type of functionality is of special interest to developers at corporations who want to publish documents on a corporate intranet. Instead of having to be converted to HTML, the data can remain in its native format and still be viewed on the intranet so long as the applications are enabled for Active documents. If you want to try this out for yourself, create a test Word document named WORD.DOC, a test Excel document named EXCEL.XLS, and a test PowerPoint document named POWER.PPT. Then open the following HTML document in Internet Explorer:

```
<HTML>
<HEAD>
<TITLE>Active documents</TITLE>
```

(continued)

```
</HEAD>
<BODY>
Active documents demonstration. <BR><BR>
<a href="word.doc">Click here to open WORD.DOC</a><BR>
<a href="excel.xls">Click here to open EXCEL.XLS</a><BR>
<a href="power.ppt">Click here to open POWER.PPT</a><BR>
</BODY>

</HTML>
```

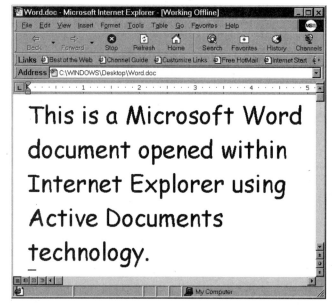

Figure 9-2. *A Word document in Internet Explorer using Active document interfaces.*

ACTIVE DOCUMENTS: THE FUTURE OF FORMS

As you might already know, an Active document differs from an ActiveX control in this way: an ActiveX control is a COM component used to build other applications, whereas an Active document is the application. You don't, for example, put a bunch of Active documents on a form, as you do with ActiveX controls. Instead, an Active document is the form, and you put ActiveX controls on it. Active documents can have properties, but those properties don't show up in the Properties window.

So you see, an Active document is really more like a sophisticated *Form* object. Perhaps in the future, all forms will be Active documents. The idea is to move away from stand-alone, monolithic applications and toward COM components that are loaded on an as-needed basis.

Most developers do not write word processor or spreadsheet applications and resist using Active documents, thinking this stuff is for document-based applications. That isn't the case. The Microsoft Foundation Classes in Microsoft Visual C++, which are built around a document-view architecture, face similar resistance from developers. All of us sometimes face situations where clinging to preconceived notions prevents us from moving ahead and applying novel solutions to the problem at hand. Just because you are not writing a word processor application doesn't mean that your application can't benefit from Active document interfaces. You can think of the data you are working with as your document.

If you are writing an arcade-style game, for example, your document might consist of the current number and location of monsters. Admittedly, games probably do not stand to gain much from Active document interfaces. The point is, whatever data your program works with constitutes your document, and whatever user interface it has can be displayed as an Active document, as shown in Figure 9-3.

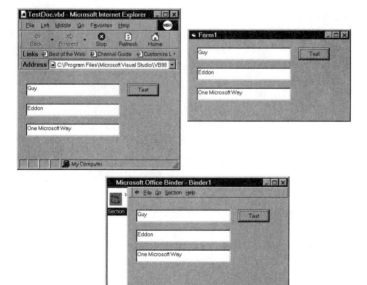

Figure 9-3. *An Active document opened in different applications.*

THE *USERDOCUMENT* OBJECT

The Active document technology is supported in Visual Basic by a special *UserDocument* object, just as ActiveX controls are supported by the *UserControl* object. The *UserDocument* object has a visual designer that looks identical to that of the ActiveX controls designer. You design and organize your document using any controls you want, in the same way you would design a standard Visual Basic form. You also set properties, call methods, and respond to events in standard Visual Basic fashion. Visual Basic saves a *UserDocument* object in a .DOB file.

The *UserDocument* object has several interesting properties, methods, and events. Like ActiveX controls, Active documents support hyperlinking, asynchronous downloads, and persistent properties by means of the various properties, methods, and events described in Chapter 6. In addition, the *UserDocument* object has some unique properties, methods, and events intended specifically for Active documents that are not supported by ordinary forms.

Item	*Type*	*Description*
Scroll	*Event*	Occurs when you reposition the scroll box on a control
SetViewport	*Method*	Sets the viewport coordinates
ContinuousScroll	*Property*	Returns or sets a value indicating whether scrolling is continuous or redraw takes place on scroll thumb release
HScrollSmallChange, VScrollSmallChange	*Property*	Returns or sets the scroll distance for the *UserDocument* object
MinHeight, MinWidth	*Property*	The minimum width and height of the document viewport before scroll bars are added
ScrollBars	*Property*	Returns or sets a value indicating whether an object has vertical or horizontal scroll bars
ViewportHeight, ViewportLeft, ViewportTop, ViewportWidth	*Property*	The current height, left, top, and width values of the viewport. The viewport is the current size of the Active document in a container

VIEWING ACTIVE DOCUMENT COMPONENTS CREATED IN VISUAL BASIC

Once you have created an Active document component in Visual Basic, how do you run it? Standard applications are executed by being run, and ActiveX controls are executed in a container, such as a Visual Basic form; but what about Active document components? In addition to the .EXE or .DLL file produced when an Active document component is compiled, Visual Basic creates a special document .VBD file. That document file, in some ways analogous to a Word .DOC file, is the file that must be opened in an Active document container such as Internet Explorer or the Office Binder[2]. The .DLL or .EXE file, which actually contains the code implementing your document, is loaded automatically whenever the document is opened in a container.

ACTIVE DOCUMENT .DLL AND .EXE FILES

We have already discussed the differences between in-process components (DLLs) and out-of-process components (.EXE files) in Chapter 2, so we won't bore you with that again. There are, however, several interesting issues relating specifically to Active documents. Some applications, such as Microsoft Word, can run either as a stand-alone application or as an Active document in a container such as Internet Explorer or Office Binder. Such applications must be implemented as Active document .EXE files. Other applications, which provide only a document interface, can be implemented as Active document DLLs.

The interesting thing about Word and other similar applications is that when running as stand-alone applications, they sport a Multiple Documents Interface (MDI). When running as a component within an Active document container, however, they simply provide a single document at a time to a container that might or might not be implemented as an MDI application. Currently, neither Internet Explorer nor Office Binder is an MDI application.

One last point to note is that Active document DLLs can display only modal forms. To display a modeless form, you must create an Active document .EXE file.

---

2. Visual Basic can't be used to run Active documents because it doesn't support the necessary interfaces to qualify as an Active document container.

VIEWPORT, *MINWIDTH*, AND *MINHEIGHT* PROPERTIES

Like ActiveX controls, Active document components always require a container in which they can be displayed. Unlike ActiveX controls, however, Active documents currently have two major containers available: Office Binder and Internet Explorer. When an Active document component is displayed in one of these containers, a mechanism exists for the container to control the amount of screen real estate allocated to your document. The display area for a document is called its *viewport*. The *UserDocument* object has four properties that enable you to discover the current coordinates of your document's viewport: *ViewportHeight*, *ViewportLeft*, *ViewportTop*, and *ViewportWidth*. Keep in mind that these properties change often because the viewport size changes every time the user resizes the container.

Since the area where your document is displayed isn't under your control, Visual Basic provides the *MinWidth* and *MinHeight* properties. These properties define the minimum space your document needs before scroll bars are required. Anytime the viewport dips below these minimums, scroll bars are added automatically.

KEY EVENTS IN THE LIFE OF A *USERDOCUMENT* OBJECT

Although Active document components look and in some respects act like standard Visual Basic forms, by now you probably realize that they are much more than standard forms—one could almost call them superforms. The events received by an Active document component are quite similar to those received by forms and ActiveX controls. In fact, only the *Scroll* event is specific to Active documents, and even that event is supported by some controls such as scroll bars.

Since Active document components are hosted by other applications, standard events are received in the order fired by the container. The key events in the life of a *UserDocument* object are *Initialize*, *InitProperties*, *Show*, *Hide*, and *Terminate*. The order in which these events are received, whether they are received at all, and what effect they have are determined in large part at the discretion of the container. For that reason, we can't speak of any particular event and say it does this or that because the discussion might be accurate for one container but not another. Luckily, at the moment there are only two major Active documents containers, Internet Explorer and Binder—so that limits the possibilities.

The best way to understand when these events are fired is to get in and play, which we will do in Exercise 9-1. Before we start, however, a few interesting characteristics of these events are worth noting. In both Internet Explorer and Office Binder, the *Initialize* event is raised when the Active document component is first loaded into the container. The *Initialize* event is followed by *InitProperties* and finally the *Show* event. Here the similarities between the two containers end, however.

When the user proceeds to another Web page in Internet Explorer, the browser fires the *Hide* event, informing the document that it is no longer displayed. If the user returns to the document in short order, Internet Explorer raises the *Show* event. If the user browses a bunch of other documents, the container grows tired of waiting and fires a *Terminate* event at the document. The *Terminate* event informs the document that it is being destroyed and is no longer in the browser History list. Should the user later find his or her way back to the document, the document will be re-created from scratch, with all the startup events firing properly.

In Office Binder, the *Show* and *Hide* events are not fired. Instead, only the *EnterFocus* and *ExitFocus* events are fired as the user switches among documents in the current binder. A *Terminate* event isn't fired until the user either closes Office Binder or removes the document from the current binder.

Exercise 9-1

In this exercise, we'll experiment with the *UserDocument* object.

1. Open Visual Basic, and start a new ActiveX document DLL project.

2. In the Project window, double-click the *UserDocument1* object to open the document designer.

3. In the Properties window, set the *Name* property to *TestDoc*.

4. Set the *HScrollSmallChange* property to *16*.

5. Place three *TextBox* controls and one *CommandButton* control on the TestDoc designer.

6. Clear the *Text* properties of the three *TextBox* controls. Set the *Caption* property of the *CommandButton* to *Test*. So far, your document should look like the one in Figure 9-4 on the following page.

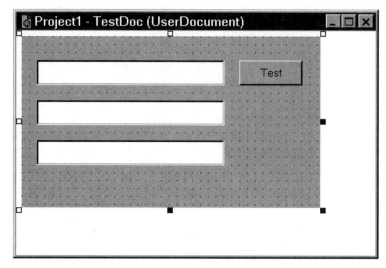

Figure 9-4. *The sample document in Exercise 9-1, step 6.*

7. Choose Code from the View menu to open the Code window, and write the following code:

```
Option Explicit

Private Sub Command1_Click()
    Stop
    MsgBox Text1 + Text2 + Text3
End Sub

Private Sub UserDocument_Resize()
    Debug.Print "Resize"
End Sub

Private Sub UserDocument_Scroll()
    Debug.Print "Scroll"
End Sub

Private Sub UserDocument_Show()
    Debug.Print "Show"
End Sub

Private Sub UserDocument_Hide()
    Debug.Print "Hide"
End Sub

Private Sub UserDocument_Initialize()
    Debug.Print "Initialize"
End Sub
```

```
Private Sub UserDocument_Terminate()
    Debug.Print "Terminate"
End Sub

Private Sub UserDocument_InitProperties()
    Debug.Print "InitProperties"
End Sub
```

8. Choose Step Into from the Debug menu to begin running the Active document.

9. The Project Properties dialog box will appear. Choose OK to accept the default settings.

10. Repeatedly press the F8 key to step through your code in Visual Basic. You step through the event procedure, printing the following messages to the Immediate window:

```
Initialize
Resize
InitProperties
Resize
Show
```

11. When you tire of stepping through the code, simply press F5 to run the program. Visual Basic will stop you no more.

12. Now return to the Internet Explorer window, where your document should be visible, as shown in Figure 9-5.

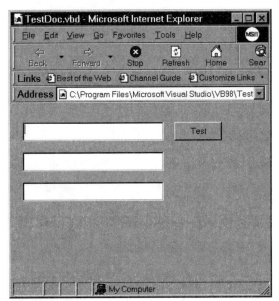

Figure 9-5. *The document in Exercise 9-1, step 12, shown in Internet Explorer.*

13. Type some text into the three text boxes in the document. Then choose the Test command button.

Notice how control again shifts to Visual Basic, this time at the Command1_Click event procedure. That is because of the *Stop* statement, which basically inserts a breakpoint.

14. Press F8 to step through the code. When the message box appears, verify that it contains the correct data and then choose OK.

15. Press F8 again, and then return to the Internet Explorer window.

16. In the Address box, type the path of any HTML document on your machine and press Enter.

17. When Visual Basic appears, press F8 to step through the UserDocument_Hide event procedure. *Hide* will be displayed in the Immediate window.

18. Return to the Internet Explorer window.

19. Click the Back button on the Internet Explorer toolbar.

20. When Visual Basic appears, press F8 to step through the UserDocument_Show event procedure. *Show* will be displayed in the Immediate window.

21. Return to the Internet Explorer window.

22. Now resize Internet Explorer so that both scroll bars are visible, and attempt to scroll. Notice that immediately Visual Basic appears in the UserDocument_Scroll event procedure.

23. Since it will be very difficult to scroll with Visual Basic popping up all the time, choose Continue from the Run menu in Visual Basic to run the document.

Focus now returns to Internet Explorer, where you can experiment with resizing the window. Notice that as you do that, resize messages are continually displayed in Visual Basic's Immediate window. Also pay attention to what size the Internet Explorer window is when the scroll bars are automatically added; it should be exactly the size of your *UserDocument* object in Visual Basic.

24. Test the scroll bars again. Notice that as you scroll around, scroll messages are continuously displayed in Visual Basic's Immediate window.

The horizontal scroll bar should work differently from the vertical scroll bar when you click the arrow buttons. That is because we set the *HScrollSmallChange* property to 16 and we left the *VScrollSmallChange* property at the default 228.

25. Close Internet Explorer, and return to Visual Basic.

26. Scroll to the end of the Immediate window, and check the last event procedures called when Internet Explorer shut down. You should see the following:

```
Hide
Terminate
```

Note that this exercise also works with Office Binder.

27. Without closing Visual Basic or stopping the Active document from running, open Microsoft Office Binder.

28. Choose Add from the Section menu.

29. Select Project1.TestDoc, and select OK.
That's all there is to it.

30. Test your Active document, shown in Figure 9-6, in Microsoft Office Binder.

31. When you are finished, close Office Binder.

32. Be sure to save your work because later exercises will build on this one.

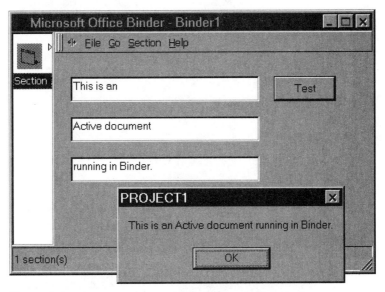

Figure 9-6. *The Active document running in Office Binder.*

PROPERTY PERSISTENCE
IN *USERDOCUMENT* OBJECTS

Saving data from an Active document is an important but difficult proposition. Currently, Visual Basic provides only the *ReadProperties* and *WriteProperties* events for this purpose. For the sake of Active documents, *ReadProperties* and *WriteProperties* events are fired in Internet Explorer, but only if the *PropertyChanged* method was called previously. Recall that the *PropertyChanged* method is supposed to be called by a component every time a property value is changed. Active documents opened in Office Binder will automatically receive the *ReadProperties* and *WriteProperties* events.

When users exit Office Binder or Internet Explorer, they will be asked to save any data entered. If the user chooses the Yes command button, the *PropertyBag* object will store any saved properties into a stream in the specified file. When the document file is reopened, the *ReadProperties* event is fired instead of *InitProperties* event, and the stored property values are read from the file.

Exercise 9-2

In this exercise, we'll experiment further with the *ReadProperties* and *WriteProperties* events.

1. Open the project saved in Exercise 9-1.

2. Open the TestDoc designer.

3. Open the Code window for TestDoc, and add the following code:

```
Private Sub UserDocument_ReadProperties(PropBag As _
   PropertyBag)
    Debug.Print "ReadProperties"
    Text1.Text = PropBag.ReadProperty("MyString1", "")
    Text2.Text = PropBag.ReadProperty("MyString2", "")
    Text3.Text = PropBag.ReadProperty _
      ("MyString3", "")
End Sub

Private Sub UserDocument_WriteProperties(PropBag As _
   PropertyBag)
    Debug.Print "WriteProperties"
    PropBag.WriteProperty "MyString1", Text1.Text, ""
    PropBag.WriteProperty "MyString2", Text2.Text, ""
    PropBag.WriteProperty "MyString3", Text3.Text, ""
End Sub

Private Sub Text1_Change()
    PropertyChanged
End Sub
```

```
Private Sub Text2_Change()
    PropertyChanged
End Sub

Private Sub Text3_Change()
    PropertyChanged
End Sub
```

4. Choose Run from the Start menu, and leave Visual Basic in the running state.

    Now test the Active document component in both Internet Explorer and Office Binder as follows.

5. In Internet Explorer, enter some data into the text boxes and then go to some other Web page. Notice how Internet Explorer asks you if you want to save the data, as shown in Figure 9-7.

Figure 9-7. *The Active documents save dialog box.*

6. Choose the Yes command button.

7. Click Back on the Internet Explorer toolbar to return to the Active document. Notice that the data is saved.

8. Switch back to Visual Basic, and notice which events were generated. On startup, the first three events listed below were generated. The last three are a result of saving the document (*WriteProperties*), switching to another document (*Hide*), and finally returning to the Active document (*Show*) as shown in the following code in the Immediate window:

    ```
    Initialize
    InitProperties
    Show
    WriteProperties
    Hide
    Show
    ```

9. Return to Internet Explorer, go to some other Web page, and then go to three more HTML documents.

10. Switch back to Visual Basic, and make sure that the *Terminate* event was executed. If so, the document was destroyed. Close Internet Explorer.

11. Now open the Active document in Internet Explorer again. Notice that your data is still there.

12. Exit Internet Explorer, and open Office Binder.

13. Open the document as you did earlier in steps 28 and 29 of Exercise 9-1, and add some data.

14. Switch back to Visual Basic and notice that the *InitProperties* event was generated (along with the rest of the standard events).

15. Close Office Binder, and save a Binder document (.OBD) file. Then run Office Binder again and reopen the previously saved Office Binder document. Notice that your persistent data is still there.

16. Switch back to Visual Basic, and notice that no *InitProperties* event was generated this time. Instead, only the *ReadProperties* event procedure was called (along with the rest of the standard events).

17. Close Office Binder.

18. Switch back to Visual Basic, and choose End from the Run menu.

19. Choose Save Project from the File menu to save your work.

MENU DESIGN FOR ACTIVE DOCUMENTS

Menu design is a delicate topic for Active documents. Since a document is always displayed in a container, it relies on the container to display its menu. The container, however, more than likely already has a menu of its own. That is a problem. The container wants to be a good host to your document, but both your document and the container are competing for space on a single menu bar. The menus of the container and the document somehow need to be merged into a single menu. Since the menu bar rightfully belongs to the container, the container gets to decide how the menu of an Active document component is displayed. When defining the menu for an Active document component in Visual Basic, you can provide some suggestions as to how you would like your document's menu displayed.

You can add menus to your Active document component using the Menu Editor. In Visual Basic, menus for Active document components are defined in the same way that menus for regular forms are defined. You choose Menu Editor from the Tools menu to display the Menu Editor dialog box. The only special area of this dialog box to note for creating an Active document component is the *NegotiatePosition* property. In this drop-down list box, you can select *1 - Left*, *2 - Middle*, *3 - Right*, or *0 - None* as the preferred position of a menu in its container. The *NegotiatePosition* property is the only way an Active document can provide information to its container about how it would like its menu displayed. Since both the Active document and the container share the same menu bar, you must consider menu negotiation when adding a menu to an Active document component.

A menu that has the *NegotiatePosition* property set to *0 - None* isn't displayed in the container[3]. The *1 - Left* setting specifies that you would like this menu to appear leftmost on the menu bar of the Active document container. Keep in mind that this option allows you only to suggest the preferred menu positioning and that different containers might respond differently to this request. Currently, the Active document specification states that the leftmost menu of an Active document component will never be the leftmost menu of the container, because the leftmost position is normally occupied by the container's File menu. At best, the leftmost menu of an Active document will be to the right of the File menu, in the position normally used for the Edit menu. The idea behind that requirement is that the container should have control over opening, saving, and printing files; exiting; and other similar application-wide responsibilities.

Setting the *NegotiatePosition* property of a menu to *2 - Middle* means that the menu will be to the right of any menus requesting leftmost status. Setting the *NegotiatePosition* property of a menu to *3 - Right* gives that menu special behavior. In a standard Windows-based application, the Help menu appears as the rightmost menu on the menu bar. Once again, the container has the privilege of reserving the rightmost menu for itself. Your Active document, however, is entitled to some space on that menu. What if the user wants help on working with your Active document? Besides, you need some place to display a beautiful About box. Thus, assigning *3 - Right* to a menu's *NegotiatePosition* property causes the container to merge the Active document's menu with the container's rightmost menu. The result is that the Active document's Help menu appears as a submenu on the container's Help menu.

As a general suggestion, an Active document should not implement a File menu because the container will provide one. An Active document can otherwise implement any other menus it wants, until it gets to the Window and Help

---

3. This option is sometimes used for context menus that are not displayed on the menu bar.

menus. Window menus are normally used by MDI applications for switching between various open documents. Even if your application uses MDI when running standalone, the Active document always runs as a single document in someone else's application and therefore shouldn't implement a Window menu. It is left for the container to decide how the document-switching functionality should be implemented. Internet Explorer provides that functionality under the File menu; Office Binder has an icon-based navigation bar down the left side of its window that lists all the open documents. As we've already discussed, an Active document's Help menu is merged with, or perhaps submerged in, the container's Help menu.

Exercise 9-3

In this exercise, we'll create three menus using the Menu Editor.

1. Open the project saved in Exercise 9-2.

2. Open the TestDoc designer.

3. Choose Menu Editor from the Tools menu.

4. In the Caption box, type *&Help*.

    NOTE Don't forget the ampersand that indicates the menu's access key.

5. In the Name box, type *mnuHelp*.

6. In the NegotiatePosition drop-down list box, select *3 - Right*.

7. Select the Next command button.

8. In the Caption box, type *&About TestDoc....*

9. In the Name box, type *mnuHelpAbout*.

10. Choose the right arrow button to indent the menu item.

11. Add Left and Middle menus, each with an Item menu command, as shown in Figure 9-8. Assign any names you want to these menu items; they are for testing purposes only.

12. Be sure to set the Left menu's *NegotiatePosition* property to *1 - Left* and the Middle menu's *NegotiatePosition* property to *2 - Middle*.

13. When you are finished, select OK.

Figure 9-8. *The Menu Editor showing the menu items created in Exercise 9-3.*

14. Choose Add Form from the Project menu.

15. Select About Dialog, and select Open.

16. Close the About form.

17. Open the Code window for TestDoc.

18. In the mnuHelpAbout_Click event procedure, add the following code (shown in bold):

```
Private Sub mnuHelpAbout_Click()
    frmAbout.Show vbModal
End Sub
```

19. Run the program in Visual Basic by pressing F5. Then open the TestDoc.vbd file in Internet Explorer or Office Binder for testing purposes.

You should see how your menus blended with the container's menus, as shown in Figure 9-9 on the following page.

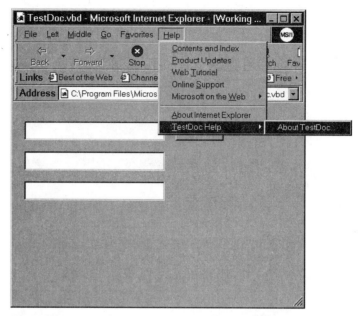

Figure 9-9. *TestDoc with menus open in Internet Explorer.*

Part III

Using Database and Web Technologies

Chapter 10

Universal Data Access

In this chapter, we'll explore the data access features of Microsoft Visual Basic from their humble beginnings through today's plethora of choices. Specifically, we'll examine the data access characteristics of the following components and how to use them from Microsoft Visual Basic: Data Access Objects (DAO), Open Database Connectivity (ODBC), Remote Data Objects (RDO), OLE DB, and ActiveX Data Objects (ADO). While different groups within Microsoft developed each of these data access technologies at different times with dissimilar goals, they are tied together by the fact that each is a COM-based component.

THE MICROSOFT JET DATABASE ENGINE

Visual Basic 3 arrived on the market in 1993 with a built-in data control. We'll call this data control the Jet Data control to differentiate it from the RemoteData control that we'll discuss later in this chapter. In addition, Visual Basic 3 provided data-aware controls that a developer could bind to a Jet Data control, and an object-oriented programming interface to the Jet 1.1 database engine called Data Access Objects. Utilizing the Jet engine, Visual Basic–based applications can access three types of data sources: Microsoft Access .MDB files; files created by third-party desktop database programs, including dBASE, Paradox, and Microsoft Visual FoxPro; and ODBC data sources.

The Jet engine's native database file format is the Microsoft Access .MDB file format, but this shouldn't come as a surprise since Access uses the Jet engine. A variety of external desktop database files are supported by the Jet engine as well. The Jet engine can import the external data, or it can work with the data in the external format. The Jet engine also supports ODBC data sources, which usually consist of a back-end SQL server (such as Microsoft SQL Server, Sybase System 11, or Oracle 7 Server) or any other data store for which an ODBC driver is available. Not only can the Jet engine retrieve and update data located in any of these types of data sources, it can also connect to different types concurrently. Using the Jet engine, developers quite commonly write programs that fetch and join heterogeneous data from one or more ODBC data sources and desktop database files.

A Visual Basic database system usually has three parts, as shown in Figures 10-1 and 10-2. The first part is your Visual Basic application, which consists of forms, controls, and associated code. The application interacts with the second part, the Jet database engine. The Jet engine in turn performs the requested operations on the third part—the data store—and returns the results to the application. The data store consists of the file or files that contain the actual data.

Figure 10-1 shows the architecture of a single-user, personal Visual Basic database application. Figure 10-2 shows the configuration of a multiuser Visual Basic database system with a remote data store. In the second case, the clients run your application, which calls the Jet engine. This is a multiuser system, but it's still a far cry from a true client/server configuration. Every client has its own copy of the Jet engine, and the server is used for nothing more than shared disk space.

What if you want a true client/server system? Luckily, the Jet engine can provide access to a full-featured database server, such as Microsoft SQL Server, via ODBC, as shown in Figure 10-3 on page 266. With this configuration, the Jet engine does not update the physical data store directly. Instead, it connects to the ODBC data source, optimizes queries, and acts as a general conduit of data between your application and the real database engine—for example, Microsoft SQL Server. This allows one remote database engine to control access to the data, as opposed to having each client's local Jet engine attempt to cooperate with other clients' Jet engines.

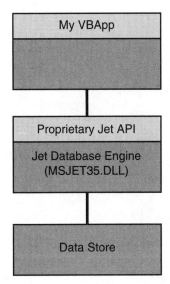

Figure 10-1. *A single-user database application.*

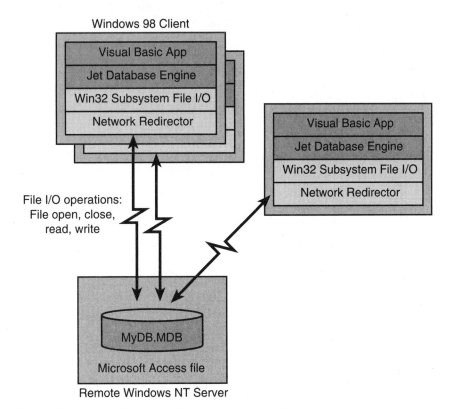

Figure 10-2. *A multiuser database application with a remote data store.*

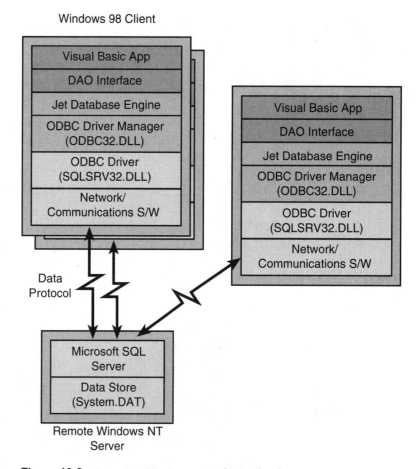

Windows 98 Client

Remote Windows NT
Server

Figure 10-3. *Accessing SQL Server via the Jet database engine.*

The simplest way to access data from Visual Basic is by means of the Jet Data control. With applications that use the Jet Data control, users can view and update records from any of the supported data sources without your having to write a single line of code. You achieve this functionality by using the Jet Data control in combination with data-bound controls. You can determine whether a control is data-aware (whether it can be bound to a Jet Data control) by checking to see if it has the *DataSource* and *DataField* properties. By setting the *DataSource* property to the data control's *Name* property, and setting the *Data-Field* property to the field in the data control's *RecordSource* property, you can bind that control to the specified field in a table. As the user moves through the records in the table, the control—for example, a text box—will display data from the specified field of the current record. The control will also update the record to reflect any changes to the data.[1] Although these are powerful features, they lack some functionality—for example, methods to delete records, process transactions, and create new tables.

DATA ACCESS OBJECTS

To meet the needs of a somewhat more sophisticated database application, the Jet engine exposes DAO, an object-oriented programming interface for the Jet engine. DAO provides full access to the features of the Jet database engine, unlike the limited capabilities of the Jet Data control.

As you can see in Figure 10-4 on the following page, DAO closely models the structure and hierarchy of database components—including the database and the tables, fields, indexes, and relationships contained within it. The beauty of DAO is that you are working with objects that refer to components of a virtual database. Your actions on these objects cause the Jet engine to manipulate the physical data store. For example, the physical database can be an .MDB file stored on your local machine or an Oracle server running on a VAX; in both cases, the code you write is identical.

> **NOTE**   To use DAO from Visual Basic, you need to set a reference to the DAO component. Choose References from the Project menu, and check the Microsoft DAO 3.51 Object Library.

The features of DAO can be split into two broad categories: those designed to define the schema for a database and those designed to work with data in an existing database. The first category is sometimes called the Data Definition Language (DDL), and the second is called the Data Manipulation Language (DML). These are not different languages, just different operations that DAO supports.

In Visual Basic, the *DBEngine* object represents the Jet database engine. *DBEngine* contains within it a collection of workspaces. Visual Basic automatically creates the first workspace, *Workspaces(0)*. A *Workspace* object is a session in which you can create and open a database object. The following example uses the DDL features of DAO to create an .MDB database file:

```
Dim MyDB As Database, MyWs As Workspace, MyTable As TableDef
Dim MyField As Field
Set MyWs = DBEngine.Workspaces(0)
```

(continued)

---

1. Data controls use the concept of a current record. At any given time, bound controls are displaying data referenced by the current record of the Jet Data control.

```
Dim MyDB As Database, MyWs As Workspace, MyTable As TableDef
Dim MyField As Field
Set MyWs = DBEngine.Workspaces(0)
Set MyDB = MyWs.CreateDatabase("MYDBNAME.MDB", _
  dbLangGeneral)
Set MyTable = MyDB.CreateTableDef("MyTableName")
Set MyField = MyTable.CreateField("MyFieldName", dbText)
MyField.Size = 100
MyTable.Fields.Append MyField
MyDB.TableDefs.Append MyTable
MyDB.Close
```

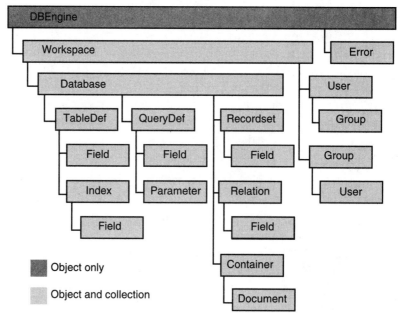

Figure 10-4. *The DAO hierarchy.*

You will find the sample program Createdb.vbp on the companion disc to this book in the \BK-SAMP\Chap10\Createdb folder.

Writing code that uses DAO isn't the only way to create an .MDB database. You can, for example, use Microsoft Access or Visual Data Manager[2] to create the database interactively. Once a database is defined, it can be opened and manipulated by using the DML features of DAO. The following example uses the *Open-Database* method. Notice that the objects defined within the database—tables, fields, and so on—are immediately available once the database is opened.

---

2. Visual Data Manager is a database management and definition tool that comes with Visual Basic.

```
Dim MyDB As Database, MyWs As Workspace, MyTable As TableDef
Dim MyField As Field
Set MyWs = DBEngine.Workspaces(0)
Set MyDB = MyWs.OpenDatabase _
  ("C:\Program Files\DevStudio\VB\BIBLIO.MDB")
Set MyTable = MyDB.TableDefs("Authors")
Set MyField = MyTable.Fields("Author")
```

When you are working with the database "objects," such as *Database*, *Workspace*, and *Recordset* objects, you are actually working with variables that refer to the underlying objects—in other words, references. This is why Visual Basic requires the *Set* keyword; it says, "Set this variable to refer to that object."

Once a database table has been opened, you can open a *Recordset* and display the records as follows:

```
Dim MyRs As Recordset
Dim Count As Integer

Set MyRs = MyTable.OpenRecordset

For Count = 1 To 10
    Print MyRs.Fields(0), MyRs.Fields(1), _
      MyRs.Fields(2)
    MyRs.MoveNext
Next Count
MyDB.Close
```

You will find the sample Opendb.vbp program on the companion disc to this book in the \BK-SAMP\Chap10\Opendb folder.

You can add or delete records as follows:

```
MyRs.AddNew
MyRs![Author] = "Data in my record!"
MyRs.Update
```

You can also use DAO to query ODBC data sources, as shown here:

```
Set MyDB = MyWs.OpenDatabase("", dbDriverNoPrompt, _
  False, "ODBC;DSN=MyDSN;UID=MyUserID;PWD=MyPassword;")
Set MyRs = MyDB.OpenRecordset("Select * From Authors")

Do Until MyRs.EOF
    Print MyRs.Fields(0), MyRs.Fields(1), MyRs.Fields(2)
    MyRs.MoveNext
Loop
```

DAO and the Jet Data control are not mutually exclusive interfaces. In fact, they are often used together. Although DAO is a powerful programming interface, it provides no facilities for binding a control to the fields of a database table. In contrast, the Jet Data control combines sparse programming features with a powerful data-bound control model. DAO and the Jet Data control complement each other well. The *Database* property of the Jet Data control exposes the underlying *Database* object being used. By using this and other properties of the Jet Data control, you can manipulate the database using DAO. Using the Jet Data control in conjunction with DAO can be quite handy, particularly when you are accessing data from an .MDB file or another supported desktop database file. You get the programmability of DAO with the high-level features of the Jet Data control.

DAO and the Jet engine, however, have their limitations. There's a price to be paid for a high-level interface that masks the difference between a local database file and a connection to a remote SQL server. When you are using a remote database server connected to an ODBC data source, the price is diminished performance due to the extra Jet engine layer. Since most client/server applications written in Visual Basic end up using an ODBC connection to a remote database server, this sluggish performance of ODBC data sources that are accessed by the Jet engine is a big concern. Many developers have resorted to learning how to use the ODBC API directly from Visual Basic to improve performance. By using this approach, developers bypass the Jet engine and the Jet engine data control entirely.

The *ODBCDirect* Mode

To address some of the performance issues, Microsoft added support for the *ODBCDirect* mode to DAO. *ODBCDirect* is an alternative mode of DAO that allows you to access ODBC data sources directly. By using *ODBCDirect*, you can bypass the Jet engine and take full advantage of the remote data source's processing capabilities. *ODBCDirect* is targeted at developers who use DAO against an ODBC data source and want to improve the performance of their applications. It isn't intended as a replacement for enterprise development components such as RDO, which are discussed later in this chapter. Internally, *ODBCDirect* is actually implemented using the ODBC API.

To specify *ODBCDirect*, you set the *DBEngine.DefaultType* property to *dbUseODBC*. Subsequent queries executed within the workspace do not incur the overhead of the Jet engine.

```
Dim MyDB As Database, MyWs As Workspace, MyRs As Recordset
DBEngine.DefaultType = dbUseODBC
Set MyWs = DBEngine.Workspaces(0)

Set MyDB = MyWs.OpenDatabase("", dbDriverNoPrompt, _
  False, "ODBC;DSN=MyDSN;UID=MyUserID; _
  PWD=MyPassword;")
```

```
Set MyRs = MyDB.OpenRecordset("Select * From Authors")

Do Until MyRs.EOF
    Print MyRs.Fields(0), MyRs.Fields(1), MyRs.Fields(2)
    MyRs.MoveNext
Loop
```

UNDERSTANDING ODBC

The ODBC API is a set of functions that define an interface for querying database servers using SQL, and it was designed to be used with C or C++. Most SQL servers provide an API with which you can connect to the server and pass SQL statements for processing, but this process restricts you to using that vendor's database server. (Incidentally, the database vendors don't seem to mind.) The beauty of ODBC is that, rather than having to learn a database vendor's proprietary API, you can use the ODBC API to access any data source for which an ODBC driver is available. One of the major design goals of ODBC is to provide performance that is equivalent to that of the database management system's (DBMS) native API. This means that if on Monday morning your boss decides to switch an entire department's data repository from Oracle to Microsoft SQL Server, applications that use the ODBC API will require virtually no modification. However, to use ODBC, you must know SQL and the ODBC API.

The ODBC architecture is broken into four components: the application, the driver manager, the drivers, and the data sources. In this model, the application is your Visual Basic program. Based on the user's actions, it makes requests of the driver manager by means of the ODBC API. The driver manager (ODBC32.DLL) is the middleman between your application and the ODBC driver. The purpose of the ODBC driver manager is threefold: it enables the user to create a Data Source Name (DSN); it loads and unloads the ODBC drivers; and it reflects ODBC API calls into the appropriate ODBC drivers.

DSNs are the primary connection vehicles in ODBC. A DSN is actually an alias to an ODBC data source. The idea is that users should not have to know the database name and location to connect to an ODBC data source. Instead, all this information should be collected and stored in one place (the Microsoft Windows Registry) and then simply referred to later by means of a user-given name—the DSN. The user or administrator can create DSNs by way of the ODBC icon in the Windows Control Panel.

Without the driver manager, your application would have to load and unload the appropriate drivers, collect the connection information, and so on. In addition to handling these tasks, the driver manager can load several ODBC drivers at once. For example, several applications on your machine can simultaneously access different data sources that require different drivers, or you can query data from two servers that require different drivers. This is one of the major reasons for using the driver manager: the driver manager can manage multiple, concurrent connections to multiple ODBC drivers. An ODBC driver is responsible for:

- Implementing the ODBC API functions.

- Establishing a connection and submitting requests to the data source.

- Returning results to the application.

- Translating errors into standard error codes.

- Declaring and manipulating cursors.

- Managing transactions.

The goal is to insulate an application from a database vendor's proprietary API. As mentioned earlier, the application communicates through the ODBC API, the driver manager interprets these calls and loads the necessary ODBC driver, and the driver interacts with the actual data source. Your application can access any data source with a single API.

Although ODBC was designed to fit into a client/server environment, it is flexible enough to handle a DBMS that isn't client/server. For example, ODBC drivers are available for interacting with .MDB files, other desktop database files, text files, and even Microsoft Excel (.XLS) files. To deal with both client/server and non–client/server data sources, ODBC defines two different kinds of drivers: one-tier drivers and two-tier drivers.

DSN TYPES

There are three types of DSNs: user, system, and file. User DSNs, the standard type, are available only to the user who created them and only on that user's computer. System DSNs are available to anyone using the computer, including Microsoft Windows NT services. Because Microsoft Internet Information Server (IIS) is implemented as a set of Windows NT services, data sources for use with IIS need to be of the system type. Normally, information for a DSN is stored in the Windows Registry. File DSNs store DSN information in a file on the disk. File DSNs enable users on other machines to share the data sources over the network, assuming that they have the necessary ODBC drivers installed.

A one-tier ODBC driver accesses a desktop database file such as an .MDB or a flat text file. The usual configuration of such a system has the database located on the same machine—or tier—as the driver. One-tier drivers usually have relatively large memory footprints, since they are a driver and DBMS rolled into one. For example, the .MDB ODBC driver contains a special version of the Jet engine. Since the Jet engine already provides access to most standard PC desktop database formats, one-tier drivers aren't all that useful from Visual Basic. More common is the two-tier driver, which fits into the classic client/server mold. The driver (client) sends SQL requests to, and receives results from, the DBMS (server), usually across a network.

The ODBC standard defines three levels of driver conformance: core, level 1, and level 2. The core functions correspond to the functions in the X/Open and SQL Access Group (SAG) specification on which ODBC is based. Levels 1 and 2 are two sets of extended functionality defined by Microsoft. These provide features such as scrollable cursors and asynchronous processing. Each ODBC API function is categorized in one of these three levels. The following table lists the core ODBC functions and their uses.

THE CORE ODBC FUNCTIONS

Task	*Function Name*	*Purpose*
Connection to a data source.	SQLAllocEnv	Obtains an environment handle. One environment handle is used for one or more connections.
	SQLAllocConnect	Obtains a connection handle.
	SQLConnect	Connects to specific driver by data source name, user identification, and password.
	SQLDriverConnect	Connects to specific driver using more connection information, additional dialog boxes, or even partial connection information.
Preparing SQL requests.	SQLAllocStmt	Allocates a statement handle.
	SQLPrepare	Prepares an SQL statement for later execution.

(continued)

THE CORE ODBC FUNCTIONS *continued*

Task	Function Name	Purpose
	SQLGetCursorName	Returns the name associated with a statement handle.
	SQLSetCursorName	Specifies a cursor name.
Submitting requests.	SQLExecute	Executes a prepared statement.
	SQLExecDirect	Executes a statement.
Retrieving results and information about results.	SQLRowCount	Returns the number of rows affected by an insert, update, or delete request.
	SQLNumResultCols	Returns the number of columns in the result set.
	SQLDescribeCol	Describes a column in the result set.
	SQLColAttributes	Describes the attributes of a column in the result set.
	SQLBindCol	Assigns storage for a result column and specifies the data type.
	SQLFetch	Returns multiple result rows.
Terminating a statement.	SQLFreeStmt	Ends statement processing.
	SQLCancel	Cancels an SQL statement.
	SQLTransact	Commits or rolls back a transaction.
Terminating a connection.	SQLDisconnect	Closes the transaction.
	SQLFreeConnect	Releases the connection handle.
	SQLFreeEnv	Releases the environment handle.

USING THE ODBC API

In this section, we'll look at how a Visual Basic application can directly call the ODBC API. This isn't as trivial as it might sound. As we mentioned previously, the ODBC API was designed for use primarily by applications written in C or

C++. Because of differences in the way languages pass arguments to procedures and store data types (such as strings) in memory, calling the ODBC API from Visual Basic is difficult. In C, for example, procedure arguments are passed by value, as expected by the ODBC API; in Visual Basic, they are passed by reference. Although you can handle this by placing the Visual Basic *ByVal* keyword in front of parameters when calling a procedure, you might find it tricky to determine when this is necessary. As with any other DLL procedures you intend to call from Visual Basic, you must first declare them. Visual Basic 4.0 shipped with a file—ODBC32.TXT—that contained all the declarations for the ODBC API. This file is provided on the companion CD for this book. You can either add this file to your project, or copy and paste the parts you need into your application.

Like most of the Microsoft Windows API, the ODBC API is handle-based; handles are used to reference the objects you work with. ODBC applications work with three handle types: environment, connection, and statement.

Every application that uses ODBC begins by using *SQLAllocEnv* to allocate one environment handle and ends by using *SQLFreeEnv* to free that environment handle. The environment handle is the parent handle; it is associated with all other ODBC resources allocated for the application.

```
Dim rc As Integer       ' Return code for ODBC functions.
Dim henv As Long        ' Environment handle
rc = SQLAllocEnv(henv)  ' Allocate the environment handle.
```

Next an application uses *SQLAllocConnect* to allocate the connection handle. The connection handle manages all information about a connection to an ODBC data source. As you can see, the *SQLAllocConnect* function takes the environment handle as the first argument so that it can associate the newly-created connection handle with the environment handle.

```
Dim hdbc As Long        ' Connection handle
' Allocate a connection handle.
rc = SQLAllocConnect(ByVal henv, hdbc)
```

No ODBC driver has been loaded at this point. We have been interacting with the driver manager only. Once the connection handle has been allocated, you can use it to make a connection to a target data source. You do this by using the *SQLConnect* function, which takes the DSN, the user's ID, and the user's password as arguments. The driver manager then looks up the information associated with the DSN in the Registry and retrieves information that includes the name of the required ODBC driver, the name of the server, and the name of the database.

In the following code, we ask ODBC to look up the DSN and to log in. At this stage, the driver manager loads the driver referenced by the DSN. It then calls the *SQLAllocEnv* and *SQLAllocConnect* functions in the driver automatically. (Remember that the driver wasn't loaded when we called these functions in the driver manager.) Finally the driver manager calls the *SQLConnect* function in the loaded ODBC driver.

```
Dim DSN As String, UID As String, PWD As String
DSN = "MyDSN"              ' The data source name
UID = "MyUserID"           ' The user's identification
PWD = "MyPassword"         ' The user's password
rc = SQLConnect(hdbc, DSN, Len(DSN), UID, Len(UID), PWD, _
  Len(PWD))
```

The next step depends on the ODBC driver. If the loaded ODBC driver is one-tier, not much happens at this stage because the driver has only to open a database file and there's no network connection to make. However, if we're referencing a remote database server, processing the *SQLConnect* call involves using the network interface installed on the client machine to make a connection to the physical server specified by the DSN that's stored in the Registry. The remote server then validates the user ID and password. If all goes well, the application now has a valid connection to the server.

The next step is to use *SQLAllocStmt* to obtain a statement handle that enables your application to query the remote server. The statement handle is the workhorse of any ODBC application.

```
Dim hStmt As Long                  ' Statement handle
rc = SQLAllocStmt(hdbc, hstmt) ' Allocate a statement handle.
```

Finally we want to pass an SQL query to the ODBC data source. *SQLExecDirect* takes the statement handle and SQL string as arguments. The SQL server then receives and executes the requested SQL statement—in this example, a command to select the LastName field from the Employees table:

```
Dim SQLIn As String
SQLIn = "Select LastName from Employees"
' Execute the SQL string.
rc = SQLExecDirect(hStmt, SQLIn, Len(SQLIn))
```

When the *SQLExecDirect* function returns, your application can receive the results of the query. The *SQLFetch* function begins this process by returning a row of data from the result set. Then the *SQLGetData* function actually gets the data from the row returned by *SQLFetch* and stores it in a string variable (called field_value, in our example). This continues in a loop until no more rows are available in the result set and the return code of *SQLFetch* no longer equals *SQL_SUCCESS*.

```
Dim field_value As String * 255
Dim LenRead As Long
field_value = String(255, 0)
Do While SQLFetch(hStmt) = SQL_SUCCESS
rc = SQLGetData(hStmt, 1, SQL_C_CHAR, field_value, 254, _
  LenRead)
MsgBox field_value
Loop
```

An ODBC API application ends by closing the connection to the ODBC data source and freeing the handles.

```
rc = SQLFreeStmt(hStmt, SQL_DROP)' Frees the statement handle
rc = SQLDisconnect(ByVal hdbc)   ' Closes the connection
rc = SQLFreeConnect(ByVal hdbc)  ' Frees the connection handle
rc = SQLFreeEnv(ByVal henv)      ' Frees the environment handle
```

Using *SQLBindCol* with 32-bit Visual Basic

If you are an experienced ODBC API programmer, you are probably familiar with the intricacies of using advanced ODBC functions such as *SQLBindCol* and *SQLExtendedFetch*. If this sounds like you, Visual Basic has an interesting "gotcha" that can cause you trouble. In 16-bit versions of Visual Basic, everything worked as you would expect:

```
Dim ReturnString As String
rc = SQLBindCol(hStmt, 1, SQL_C_CHAR, ReturnString, 100, _
  cbRetStr)
rc = SQLExtendedFetch(ByVal hStmt, SQL_FETCH_NEXT,1, cbrow, _
  RowStatus)
```

SQLBindCol binds data from the first column in the result set to the Return-String variable. The next call—*SQLExtendedFetch*—fetches one row from the result set and stores it in the variable referenced in the *SQLBindCol* call (ReturnString).

Here's the catch: when you are using *SQLBindCol* from 32-bit Visual Basic applications, you must take special care when handling string data types. Because of the manner in which Visual Basic converts strings passed from DLLs into Unicode, you can't directly bind result-set columns to string or variant variables. Instead, you must bind string-type result-set columns to byte arrays that are not subject to Unicode conversions.

```
Dim ReturnBuffer(100) As Byte
rc = SQLBindCol(hStmt, 1, SQL_C_CHAR, ReturnBuffer(0), _
  100, cbRetStr)
rc = SQLExtendedFetch(ByVal hStmt, SQL_FETCH_NEXT, 1, _
  cbrow, RowStatus)
```

Although this code correctly retrieves data into the ReturnBuffer byte array, the question now is what to do with it. You can't display a byte array using *MsgBox* or assign it to the *Text* property of a text box because all these options require a normal string. Based on an example in older Visual Basic documentation, we have written a procedure called BytesToString that performs the desired conversion.

```
Public Function BytesToString(byte_array() As Byte) As _
  String
    Dim Data As String, StrLen As String
    Data = StrConv(byte_array(), vbUnicode)
    StrLen = InStr(Data, Chr(0)) - 1 ' Find first
                                  ' terminating null.
    BytesToString = Left(Data, StrLen)
End Function
```

This function accepts an array of bytes and converts it to a string. Once we have the data in a string, we can work with it in any way we like. The only difference between this version and the one in the Visual Basic documentation is that in our example, we want only the portion of the byte array that contains our data (up to the null terminator). The original version converts the entire byte array into a same-length character string.

Now the only problem is how to put the data back in the database. Let's say you read a LastName field from a table and display it in a text box. When the user changes the name, you want to update the table to reflect the change. You now have the data as a string, but to update the database you will need to convert the string back to a byte array. The following procedure—StringToBytes—automates this task for you.

```
Public Sub StringToBytes(Data As String, ByteLen As _
  Integer, return_buffer() As Byte)
    Dim StrLen As Integer, Count As Integer
    For Count = 0 To Len(Data) - 1
        return_buffer(Count) = Asc(Mid(Data, Count + 1, 1))
    Next Count
    For Count = Len(Data) To ByteLen
        return_buffer(Count) = 0
    Next Count
End Sub
```

You can now call *SQLSetPos* with the *SQL_UPDATE* flag to save the data back to the database, as follows:

```
rc = SQLSetPos(ByVal hStmt, 1, SQL_UPDATE, SQL_LOCK_NO_CHANGE)
```

REMOTE DATA OBJECTS

As Visual Basic evolved, Microsoft realized that DAO and the Jet database engine were too limited for most production client/server systems. The Jet engine is a feature-rich and powerful technology. However, as we mentioned earlier in this chapter, the Jet engine tries to abstract database programming to the point that it masks the differences between desktop database files and remote SQL servers, and this imposes too big a performance penalty. Microsoft also realized that the ODBC API is simply too cumbersome and difficult for most Visual Basic developers. So Microsoft developed Remote Data Objects.

Like the DAO part of the Jet engine, RDO is an object-oriented database programming interface. Unlike the Jet engine, RDO isn't a database engine but rather a thin layer of code implemented on top of ODBC. In other words, RDO is Visual Basic's interface to the ODBC API, and, like the ODBC API, it uses SQL statements to access and query ODBC data sources. Although RDO can access any ODBC data source—including desktop database files and back-end SQL servers—it has been optimized to take advantage of sophisticated query engines in products such as Microsoft SQL Server and Oracle. There are five main advantages to using RDO when compared with the ODBC API:

- You don't need to learn how to use the ODBC API from Visual Basic.

- Performance approximates that of the ODBC API.

- RDO is a native Visual Basic programming interface.

- Remote data control and data-bound control models are available.

- The ODBC API can be used in conjunction with RDO.

Figure 10-5 on the following page shows the RDO object model and reveals the close relationship between RDO and the ODBC API. The three handle types of the ODBC API (environment, connection, and statement) have corresponding object types in RDO: *rdoEnvironment*, *rdoConnection*, and *rdoResultset*. Although it's an oversimplification, you could say that RDO is to the ODBC API what the Microsoft Foundation Class library (MFC) is to the Windows API.[3]

> **NOTE** To use RDO from Visual Basic, you need to set a reference to the RDO component. Choose the References command from the Project menu, and check Microsoft Remote Data Object 2.0.

---

3. Note that RDO and ODBC database terminology is somewhat different from that of the Jet engine; in RDO, a field is called a column and a record is called a row.

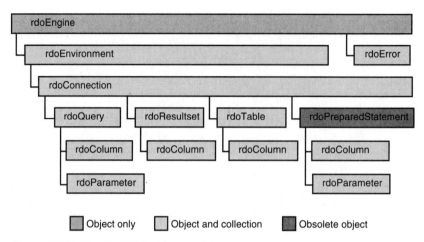

Figure 10-5. *The RDO 2.0 object model.*

NOTE   The *rdoPreparedStatement* object is obsolete and is supported for backward compatibility purposes only. You should switch to using the new *rdoQuery* object, which supports a superset of the *rdoPreparedStatement* object's functionality.

Let's digress for a moment and discuss the concepts of containers and collections. The *rdoEngine* object sits at the top of the object hierarchy chart in Figure 10-5. It is a container object and contains the *rdoEnvironment* and *rdoError* objects. A container's objects are referenced with the usual dot notation:

```
rdoEngine.rdoEnvironment
```

The *rdoEngine* object actually contains a collection of *rdoEnvironment* objects, called *rdoEnvironments*. A collection is a named group of related components—basically, an array of objects of the same type. A member of a collection is referenced with the normal array notation:

```
rdoEngine.rdoEnvironments(n)
```

There is no need to create the *rdoEngine* object—it is predefined, and only one can exist in an application. You can use the *rdoEngine* object to create environment objects with the *rdoCreateEnvironment* method, or to register an ODBC data source with *rdoRegisterDataSource*. One initial environment is created by the *rdoEngine* object automatically, and it can be referenced as the *rdoEnvironments(0)* object contained by *rdoEngine* as follows:

```
Dim myEnv As rdoEnvironment
Set myEnv = rdoEngine.rdoEnvironments(0)
```

You can create additional *rdoEnvironment* objects with the *rdoCreate-Environment* method of the *rdoEngine* object. These new *rdoEnvironment* objects then become part of the *rdoEnvironments* collection.

```
Dim myEnv As rdoEnvironment
Set myEnv = rdoEngine.rdoCreateEnvironment _
  ("MyEnvName", "MyUserID", "MyPassword")
```

Environments can also determine transaction scope. You use the *Begin-Trans, CommitTrans,* and *RollbackTrans* methods of an *rdoEnvironment* object to control transactions within that environment. All open *rdoConnection* databases in the environment are affected. Once you have a valid *rdoEnvironment* object, the next step is to open a connection with an ODBC data source by using the *OpenConnection* method; this establishes a physical link to the data source. The *OpenConnection* method accepts the parameters shown in the following table.

THE *OPENCONNECTION* METHOD PARAMETERS

Parameter	Meaning
DsName	The name of a registered ODBC data source.
Prompt	A flag that specifies whether the ODBC driver manager should display a dialog box prompting the user for connection information.
Readonly	A Boolean flag that specifies whether you want to update data through this connection. (A false setting indicates that you do.)
Connect	A string that supplies arguments to the ODBC driver manager for the connection. (Different ODBC data sources require different parameters.)

The following code creates an *rdoConnection* object and calls its *Establish-Connection* method to connect to the server. Then the code executes an SQL query by using the *OpenResultset* method and displays the records returned.

```
Dim myCon As New rdoConnection
Dim myRes As rdoResultset
myCon.Connect = "DSN=MyDSN;UID=MyUserID;PWD=MyPassword;"
myCon.EstablishConnection rdDriverNoPrompt, False
Set myRes = _
  myCon.OpenResultset("Select au_lname from Authors")
```

(continued)

```
Do Until myRes.EOF
    Print myRes.rdoColumns(0)
    myRes.MoveNext
Loop
```

To query and retrieve rows from the data source, you need an *rdoResultset* object created by calling the *OpenResultset* method, as shown in the previous code. Three RDO objects that support the *OpenResultset* method are *rdoConnection*, *rdoQuery*, and *rdoTable*. Using the *rdoConnection* object is a good idea if you want a one-time, ad hoc query that you do not intend to execute again—for example, a query entered by the user. Using an *rdoQuery* object is recommended when you are creating a query that you intend to run multiple times. The *rdoQuery* object even lets you create queries with parameters that are substituted in the query before being run, as shown in the following code. (We will talk more about this shortly.)

```
Dim myCon As New rdoConnection
Dim myQry As rdoQuery
Dim myRes As rdoResultset

myCon.Connect = "DSN=MyDSN;UID=MyUserID;PWD=MyPassword;"
myCon.EstablishConnection rdDriverNoPrompt, False

Set myQry = myCon.CreateQuery("MyFirstQuery", _
  "Select au_lname, au_fname From Authors")
Set myRes = myQry.OpenResultset

Do Until myRes.EOF
    Print myRes.rdoColumns(0), myRes.rdoColumns(1)
    myRes.MoveNext
Loop
```

Defining RDO Cursors

A cursor is a logical set of records managed by the data source or ODBC driver manager on the client machine. The type of *rdoResultset* cursor created by the previous code example is the forward-only type, which is the default. The other types of cursors available (depending on the capabilities of the ODBC driver) are static, keyset, and dynamic. Forward-only result sets retrieve data quickly and with the least overhead. A couple of limitations of this type of result set are that it exposes a single record at a time and you can only move forward in the result set. One other drawback is that rows in the result set are not refreshed as they change in the data source. Nevertheless, it might be more efficient for your code to rebuild a forward-only result set than to use one of the other types.

A static cursor is similar to the Jet engine Snapshot-type *Recordset* object. The main difference between a forward-only result set and a static cursor is that with a static cursor you can move both forward and backward in the result set.

A keyset cursor is similar to a Jet engine Dynaset-type *Recordset* object. A keyset result set is scrollable, and rows reflect changes made after the result set was created. A keyset is established when the cursor retrieves only the unique keys for the records from the data source, instead of the data itself. These record identifiers are called keys, and a table of keys is called the keyset. When a specific record is requested, the cursor uses the key for that record to get the full contents of the record.

A dynamic cursor is identical to the keyset type, except that membership isn't frozen; this means that RDO constantly checks to see whether new or updated records in the data source meet the restrictions of the query. Due to this checking, this type of cursor carries the largest overhead.

The following table summarizes the four types of *rdoResultset* cursors.

RDORESULTSET CURSOR ATTRIBUTES

Cursor Type	Updatable?	Membership	Visibility	Move current row	Result of a join?
Forward-only	No*	Fixed	One row	Forward	Yes
Static	Yes	Fixed	Cursor	Anywhere	Yes
Keyset	Yes	Fixed	Cursor	Anywhere	Yes
Dynamic	Yes	Dynamic	Cursor	Anywhere	Yes

* Yes, when using server-side cursors on Microsoft SQL Server 6.0 or later.

Some data sources—for example, Microsoft SQL Server—support server-side cursors. When that is the case, the remote database engine builds keyset cursors on the server. Server-side cursors reduce the memory and disk space required on client machines but shift those requirements to the server. You can set the *rdoEnvironment* object's *CursorDriver* property to control whether cursors are created and maintained on the client or server machine, using the options listed in the table on the following page.

CONTROLLING CURSOR CREATION
WITH THE *CURSORDRIVER* PROPERTY

Property Option	Description
rdUseClientBatch	RDO uses the client batch cursor library.
rdUseIfNeeded	(Default.) The ODBC driver automatically chooses the appropriate style. Server-side cursors are used, if available.
rdUseNone	RDO creates a result set without cursors.
rdUseODBC	RDO uses the ODBC cursor library, which builds the cursor on the client computer. This option gives better performance for small result sets, but performance degrades quickly for larger result sets.
rdUseServer	Server-side cursors are always used, if available. This option usually gives better performance but can cause more network traffic.

Traversing and Editing Rows with RDO

At any time, a cursor exposes only one row for data retrieval or modification: the row referenced by the current row pointer. You can change the current row by using Visual Basic methods such as *Move, MoveNext, MovePrevious, MoveFirst,* or *MoveLast,* or by setting the *AbsolutePosition* or *PercentPosition* properties of an *rdoResultset* object. You can modify data in the current row using the *Edit* method, assuming the *Updatable* property of the *rdoResultset* is set to *True.* You set the column values and use the *Update* method to save the row back to the data source, as shown in the following code. If you change your mind, you can use the *CancelUpdate* method to abandon the edits. You might also add and delete rows by using the *AddNew* and *Delete* methods.

```
Do Until myRes.EOF
    If myRes.Columns("au_lname").Value = "White" Then
        MyRes.Edit
        myRes.rdoColumns("au_lname").Value = "Eddon"
        myRes.Update
    End If
    myRes.MoveNext
Loop
```

Instead of using the *Edit, AddNew, Delete,* and *Update* methods, you can use the *Execute* method to carry out an SQL query that contains one or more *UPDATE, INSERT,* or *DELETE* statements. For example, the preceding code could be written more efficiently as an SQL update query, as follows:

```
myCon.Execute "Update Authors Set au_lname = 'Eddon' " & _
  "Where au_lname = 'White'"
```

The *Execute* method is designed to execute action queries that do not return rows.

You can control how an *rdoResultset* object created by the *OpenResultset* method manages concurrency by setting the *LockType* argument to one of the flags shown in the following table.

LOCKTYPE ARGUMENT FLAG

LockType *Flags*	*Description*
rdConcurBatch	The client batch cursor library is being used, and you want to defer all updates until you use the *BatchUpdate* method.
rdConcurLock	Pessimistic locking. The row or rows being updated are locked as soon as the *Edit* or *AddNew* methods are executed, and the lock is held until the *Update* method is called and has updated the data source.
rdConcurReadOnly	The cursor is read-only. This is the default.
rdConcurRowver	Optimistic locking. The rows are locked only for the actual update, based on row identifier. A time stamp value is compared to determine whether the row has changed since it was last retrieved.
rdConcurValues	Optimistic locking. The rows are locked only for the actual update, based on row values. The data in each column of the row is compared to determine whether it has changed.

Processing Multiple Result Sets

Using RDO, you can create queries that will return multiple result sets. When you are developing client/server systems that run over a wide area network or over the Internet, sending a query is much more costly than, for example, calling a server in the next building. In such cases, submitting multiple SQL queries at one time can be a much more efficient way to interact with the server, especially when the cost of network requests is high. Packing the requests into a single statement or stored procedure and allowing the server to send back multiple results at one time also eliminates the need for the client to handle multiple sessions with the server.

The following example is made up of three parts: two *SELECT* clauses, which return columns from tables, and one *UPDATE* statement, which does not return any rows.

```
Dim myCon As New rdoConnection
Dim myQry As rdoQuery
Dim myRes As rdoResultset

myCon.Connect = "DSN=MyDSN;UID=MyUserID;PWD=MyPassword;"
myCon.EstablishConnection rdDriverNoPrompt, False

Set myQry = myCon.CreateQuery("MySecondQuery", _
   "Select au_lname from Authors;" & _
   "Select hire_date from Employee;" & _
   "Update Authors Set state='NJ' Where state='CA'")

myQry.RowsetSize = 1
Set myRes = myQry.OpenResultset
```

The preceding code creates the query and then executes it by calling the *OpenResultset* method. This opens the first result set, corresponding to the first *Select* statement, which returns the au_lname column of all rows in the Authors table. The following code executes a loop that displays the first column (column 0) of the result set in a message box.

```
Do Until myRes.EOF
    Print myRes.rdoColumns(0)
    myRes.MoveNext
Loop
```

When you finish working with data from the first result set, you can activate the next one by running the *MoreResults* method (after which the first result set will no longer be available). The following code selects the next result set and then loops through and displays all rows.

```
If MyRes.MoreResults Then
    Do Until myRes.EOF
        Print myRes.rdoColumns(0)
        myRes.MoveNext
    Loop
End If
```

You are now ready to process the last result set of the query, which was generated from an *Update* statement that does not return rows. Nevertheless, the result set must be processed. The only potentially useful information returned in this result set is available by means of the *RowsAffected* property of the *rdoResultset* object, which is set to the number of rows that were affected by the query.

```
If MyRes.MoreResults Then
    MsgBox myQry.RowsAffected & " rows updated."
End If
```

You will find the sample Morers.vbp program on the companion disc to this book in the \BK-SAMP\Chap10\Morers folder.

Creating Parameter Queries

Sometimes you might want to execute the same query several times but with different parameters each time. For example, you might have a query in your application that returns the last names of people making $30,000 a year or more, such as *Select LastName from Employees Where Salary >= 30,000*. Depending on user input, you might want to change the monetary criteria and have this, in turn, determine what rows are included in the result set. One possibility is to create and execute a new query for each given amount. However, this is slow and inefficient because the SQL server needs to recompile the query every time it is executed. It is much more efficient to create a query specifying the salary criterion as an unknown value—for example *Select LastName from Employees Where Salary >= ?*. (The question mark is the symbol for an unknown.) For every *?* in the SQL string, an *rdoParameter* object is created automatically and added to the *rdoParameters* collection. This enables you to assign values to the parameters, by referencing the object in the collection using the *rdoParameters(n)* notation.

The first parameter in an SQL string is *rdoParameters(0)*, the second parameter is *rdoParameters(1)*, and so on. The missing values must be assigned before executing the query with the *OpenResultset* method, as shown in bold in the following example:

```
Dim myCon As New rdoConnection
Dim myQry As rdoQuery
Dim myRes As rdoResultset

myCon.Connect = "DSN=MyDSN;UID=MyUserID;PWD=MyPassword;"
myCon.EstablishConnection rdDriverNoPrompt, False

Set myQry = myCon.CreateQuery("MyThirdQuery", _
    "Select au_lname, au_fname, state from Authors " & _
    "Where state=?")
myQry.rdoParameters(0).Value = "CA"
Set myRes = myQry.OpenResultset

Do Until myRes.EOF
    Print myRes.rdoColumns(0), myRes.rdoColumns(1)
    myRes.MoveNext
Loop
```

To execute the query again with a different parameter value, you can simply change the value of the *rdoParameter* object and use the *Requery* method, as shown in bold in the following example:

```
myQry.rdoParameters(0).Value = "UT"
myRes.Requery

Do Until myRes.EOF
    Print myRes.rdoColumns(0), myRes.rdoColumns(1)
    myRes.MoveNext
Loop
```

Although the use of *rdoParameter* objects is relatively straightforward, RDO supports a shortcut that makes using parameters even easier. Once you have defined a query by using the *CreateQuery* method, the name of that query (in this example, *MyThirdQuery*) automatically appears as a new method of the *rdoConnection* object in which it was created. You can pass arguments to the new method to set parameter values, as shown in bold in the following code:

```
MyCon.MyThirdQuery "MI"
Set myRes = myCon.LastQueryResults

Do Until myRes.EOF
    Print myRes.rdoColumns(0), myRes.rdoColumns(1)
    myRes.MoveNext
Loop
```

Since the *OpenResultset* method isn't called when you use this shortcut, you can use the *rdoConnection.LastQueryResults* property to retrieve a reference to the *rdoResultset* returned by the query. You will find the sample Rdoparam.vbp program on the companion disc to this book in the \BK-SAMP\Chap10\Rdoparam folder.

Running Stored Procedures

A stored procedure is a set of Transact-SQL statements that is stored in a database on the SQL server. You can think of a stored procedure as a piece of code that is stored, maintained, and executed under the auspices of SQL Server. The primary reason to use stored procedures is to move application code off a client workstation and onto the database server. In a typical client/server environment, each SQL request must be sent across the network from the client to the server to be executed. The results of each statement must also be sent from the server to the client. With stored procedures, overhead is minimized because the client can invoke a single stored procedure that invokes multiple SQL statements. In particular, this minimizes network traffic and enhances the overall performance of the application.

Stored procedures can further enhance performance because they are stored in a parsed format. This eliminates the parser overhead each SQL statement requires before it can be executed. In addition, once compiled and optimized, stored procedures remain in a cache on the server.

To call a stored procedure from Visual Basic using RDO, create a query with the special syntax *{call procedurename(param1, param2,...)}*. When executing a query that calls a stored procedure on the server, you might want to receive a return value from the procedure. To do this, you set the *rdoParameter* object's *Direction* property. In the following code, we call a stored procedure, *sp_add*, which takes two parameters and returns their sum:

```
Dim myCon As New rdoConnection
Dim myQry As rdoQuery
Dim myRes As rdoResultset
myCon.Connect = "DSN=MyDSN;UID=MyUserID;PWD=MyPassword;"
myCon.EstablishConnection rdDriverNoPrompt, False

Set myQry = myCon.CreateQuery("MyFourthQuery", _
  "{ ? = call sp_add (?, ?) }")

myQry.rdoParameters(0).Direction = rdParamReturnValue
myQry.rdoParameters(1).Value = "5"
myQry.rdoParameters(2).Value = "3"

myQry.Execute       ' Execute the stored procedure query.

MsgBox "5 + 3 = " & myQry.rdoParameters(0).Value
```

In this code, you can see that we have created a query with three parameters. We set the value of the first parameter's *Direction* property to *rdParamReturnValue*, which indicates a return value. The *Direction* property of the second and third parameters isn't set in this example because *rdParamInput* is the default. (Actually, even the *rdParamReturnValue* value doesn't need to be set; RDO can usually figure out what you are doing.) Next we use the *Execute* method to run this query, instead of using the *OpenResultset* method used in previous examples, because this action query does not return a set of rows (a result set). After the *sp_add* stored procedure runs, the first parameter's *Value* property contains the value returned by the procedure—in this case, 8. Note that SQL Server creates temporary stored procedures for *rdoQuery* statements. SQL Server automatically cleans up these temporary stored procedures if your application's connection to the server is broken abnormally.

An implementation of the *sp_add* stored procedure in the Transact-SQL language used by Microsoft SQL Server looks like the following:

```
create proc sp_add @x int = 0, @y int = 0 as →
return @x + @y
```

An impressive feature of Visual Basic's Enterprise Edition is the ability to remotely debug Transact-SQL stored procedures. This is accomplished with a Visual Basic add-in called the Visual Basic T-SQL Debugger. After installing the server-side debugger components according to the Visual Basic documentation, you choose Add-In Manager from the Add-Ins menu and check the VB T-SQL Debugger. Then choose T-SQL Debugger from the Add-Ins menu. The dialog box shown in Figure 10-6 appears.

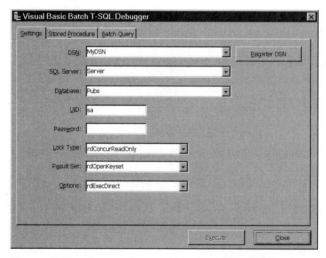

Figure 10-6. *The Visual Basic T-SQL Debugger dialog box.*

In the dialog box, enter the DSN of the server you want to connect to for debugging purposes. You'll find additional debugger options by choosing T-SQL Debugging Options from the Tools menu. Now, using the Visual Basic debugger, step through the code. When you step into the statement that calls the *rdo-Query.Execute* method, the T-SQL Debugger will pop up, connect to the server, download the stored procedure, and allow you to debug. Using the add-in, you can remotely step through code running on Microsoft SQL Server, watch variables, and set breakpoints. Using the Stored Procedure tab of the T-SQL Debugger dialog box, you can also interactively debug any available stored procedure of your choosing, as shown in Figure 10-7.

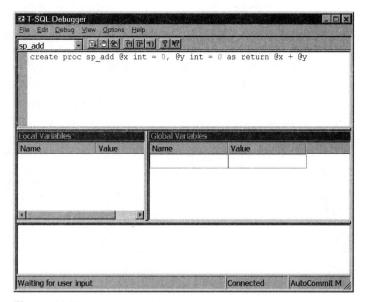

Figure 10-7. *The interactive debugger: T-SQL Debugger.*

Handling Asynchronous Queries

Normally, when you call the *OpenResultset* method of an *rdoQuery* object, your application's execution is suspended until the query is completed. This is wasteful since most of the processing is taking place on the server. RDO makes it possible to run the query asynchronously, which means that execution focus will be returned to your application immediately, even though the server has not yet fulfilled the query. To turn on asynchronous operation, pass the *rdAsync-Enable* flag to the *OpenResultset* method as shown in bold in the following code:

```
Dim WithEvents myCon As rdoConnection
Dim myRes As rdoResultset

Private Sub Command1_Click()
    Set myCon = New rdoConnection
    Dim myQry As rdoQuery
    myCon.Connect = "DSN=MyDSN;UID=MyUserID;PWD=MyPassword;"
    myCon.EstablishConnection rdDriverNoPrompt, False
    Set myQry = myCon.CreateQuery("MyFifthQuery", & _
      "Select au_lname, state from Authors " & _
      "Where state='KS'")
    Set myRes = myQry.OpenResultset(, , rdAsyncEnable)
End Sub
```

You can't yet begin to use the new *rdoResultset* object because it has not been created. There are two options for determining when the query has completed and the *rdoResultset* is ready for use. The first is to test the *StillExecuting* property of the *rdoResultset*. This option has the disadvantage of requiring you to continuously poll the *StillExecuting* property. The second, and more sophisticated, way is to respond to the *rdoConnection_QueryComplete* event, which is fired when the query has finished executing. By using this method, your application can submit a query, go off and do something else, and then be asynchronously notified when the query has completed by means of the *QueryComplete* event, as shown in the following code:

```
Private Sub myCon_QueryComplete(ByVal Query As _
  RDO.rdoQuery, ByVal ErrorOccurred As Boolean)
    Do Until myRes.EOF
        Print myRes.rdoColumns(0), myRes.rdoColumns(1)
        myRes.MoveNext
    Loop
End Sub
```

Recall that the *WithEvents* keyword we used in a previous code example is needed to intercept events fired by components such as RDO. After submitting the query, you can abort the operation by using the *Cancel* method.

Using the ODBC API with RDO

One of the features that makes RDO very extensible is that its objects expose the underlying ODBC handles, similar to the way in which Visual Basic form objects have an *hWnd* property that exposes the window handle. The following table lists the ODBC handles that are available through RDO.

Handle-type	RDO Object.Property	Handle created by the ODBC API
environment	*rdoEnvironment.hEnv*	*SQLAllocEnv*
connection	*rdoConnection.hDbc*	*SQLAllocHandle* and *SQLDriverConnect*
statement	*rdoResultset.hStmt, rdoQuery.hStmt*	*SQLAllocStmt*

You can use these handles to make direct calls to the ODBC API from Visual Basic, creating a type of hybrid program that uses both RDO and the ODBC API. Be aware that incorrect use of the ODBC API on RDO handles (for example, closing a connection handle using the ODBC API and then trying to use the *rdoConnection* object) can cause unpredictable behavior.

The RemoteData Control

Although RDO is powerful and efficient, it can't use data-bound controls. To support the Visual Basic data-bound control model, you need the RemoteData control. You can bind standard data-aware controls to the RemoteData control. The data-bound controls can't tell the difference between the Jet Data control and the RemoteData control, which looks and behaves like the Jet Data control. But there is a big difference between them: the Jet Data control is obviously implemented using the Jet database engine, while the RemoteData control is implemented by calls to the ODBC API, giving you a powerful data-bound control model without the Jet engine. In addition, just as you can combine the Jet Data control with DAO, the RemoteData control can be combined with RDO code.

OLE DB

Although ODBC provides access to data stored in a variety of database management systems, it has a couple of limitations. First, it is based on a call-level interface designed for programs written in C. Second, ODBC does not provide access to all data types. The OLE DB specification is a new standard intended to address the limitations of ODBC. OLE DB is made up of a set of COM-based interfaces that provide applications with uniform access to data stored in diverse information sources.

To understand the need for a new data access specification, you need to recognize that a vast amount of critical information necessary to conduct day-to-day business is found outside traditional, corporate production databases. Instead, this information is found in flat files, in personal databases such as those created by Microsoft Access, and in productivity tools such as spreadsheets, word-processing documents, project-management planners, and electronic mail. To take advantage of database technology such as SQL queries, transaction processing, and security, businesses must first move the data from its original location into a DBMS. This process is expensive and redundant.

With OLE DB, the traditional database becomes a component called an *OLE DB data provider*. In addition to databases, other sources of data, such as spreadsheets, documents, and electronic mail, can expose the interfaces necessary to be classified as OLE DB data providers. Application programs that access data by means of OLE DB interfaces are called *OLE DB data consumers*. These programs can access data from any OLE DB data provider.

For example, consider a sales representative who wants to find all e-mail messages that were received within the last week from customers in a particular geographic region to which no one has yet replied. This query involves searching the mailbox containing the sales representative's e-mail, as well as searching a database of customers stored in a corporate database. OLE DB makes it possible to formulate an SQL query that would retrieve this type of information.

Using OLE DB, a DBMS becomes a conglomerate of cooperating components that consume and produce data through a uniform set of interfaces. By defining a uniform set of interfaces to access data, OLE DB components contribute not only uniform data access among diverse information sources, they also help to reduce the applications' footprints by enabling them to use only the DBMS functionality they need. The OLE DB functional areas include: data access and updates (rowsets), query processing, catalog information, notifications, transactions, security, and remote data access.

ODBC technology has matured to the point where ODBC is an ideal technology for accessing SQL databases. As a result, an integral part of OLE DB is a new OLE DB driver manager that enables OLE DB consumers to talk to ODBC providers. This enables OLE DB data consumer tools and products to have full access to all ODBC drivers and ODBC-based data. Microsoft is providing this support by supplanting the ODBC driver manager with an OLE DB provider to ODBC data. In this manner, no new layers are added. The only material difference is that OLE DB consumers communicate with OLE DB interfaces rather than with the ODBC APIs. The following table compares technical aspects of ODBC and OLE DB.

	ODBC	*OLE DB*
Programming interface	C-level API	COM-based interfaces
Data format	SQL-based data	All tabular data
Query method	SQL-based standard	COM-based standard
Providers	Native providers	Component architecture

ActiveX Data Objects

OLE DB interfaces are primarily designed for use by C++ programmers. To make the advantages of OLE DB available to higher-level development environments, Microsoft has implemented an Automation-based object model called ActiveX Data Objects. Just as RDO is implemented using the ODBC API, ADO is implemented using OLE DB interfaces. At first, it might seem confusing to have three separate object models for accessing data from Visual Basic: DAO, RDO, and ADO. But ADO is an evolution of the earlier object models. Over time, things will probably standardize on ADO and OLE DB.

ADO enables you to write a client application to access and manipulate data in a database through a provider. ADO's primary benefits are ease of use, high speed, low memory overhead, and a small disk footprint. The following table compares the size of the different data access components discussed in this chapter.

Data Access Component	Main DLL	Size
DAO	DAO350.DLL	568 KB
RDO	MSRDO20.DLL	372 KB
ADO	MSADO15.DLL	322 KB

The ADO object model is shown in Figure 10-8.

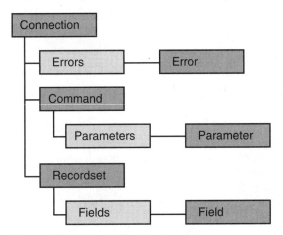

Figure 10-8. *The ADO object model.*

In ADO, the *Connection*, *Command*, and *Recordset* objects are the main interfaces to data. These objects also have a *Properties* collection, as shown in Figure 10-9.

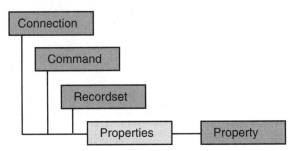

Figure 10-9. *The* Properties *collection of the* Connection, Command, *and* Recordset *objects.*

In ADO, the object hierarchy is de-emphasized. Unlike with DAO or RDO, you no longer have to navigate through a hierarchy to create objects because most ADO objects can be independently created. This allows you to create and track only the objects you need. This model also results in fewer ADO objects and thus a smaller working set. ADO supports features for building client/server and Web-based applications, including the following:

- Independently-created objects.

- Batch updating.

- Stored procedures with in/out parameters and return values.

- Different cursor types, including the potential for support of back-end–specific cursors.

- Advanced recordset cache management.

- Limits on number of returned rows and other query goals.

- Multiple recordsets returned from stored procedures or batch statements.

- Free-threaded objects for efficient Web server applications.

When you use ADO from Visual Basic, you can implement late binding by using the *CreateObject* function, or early binding by using the References dialog box. The following code, which uses the second approach because of its better performance, uses ADO to execute an SQL query and display the results against an ODBC data source. To set the reference to ADO, choose References from the Project menu and check the Microsoft ActiveX Data Objects 2.0 Library.

```
Dim adoRs As New ADODB.Recordset
adoRs.ActiveConnection = _
  "DSN=MyDSN;UID=MyUserID;PWD=MyPassword"
adoRs.Open "Select au_lname, au_fname from Authors"

Do Until adoRs.EOF
    Print adoRs.Fields(0), adoRs.Fields(1)
    adoRs.MoveNext
Loop

adoRs.Close
```

To update records using ADO, the recordset's *LockType* property must be set to *adLockOptimistic* or *adLockBatchOptimistic*, as shown in bold in the following example:

```
Dim adoRs As New ADODB.Recordset
Dim NewLastName As String
adoRs.ActiveConnection = _
  "DSN=MyDSN;UID=MyUserID;PWD=MyPassword"
adoRs.LockType = adLockOptimistic
adoRs.Open "Select au_lname from Authors"

Do Until adoRs.EOF
    NewLastName = InputBox("Last name is " & _
      adoRs.Fields(0) & _
      ". What do you want to change it to?")
    If NewLastName = "" Then Exit Do
    adoRs.Fields(0) = NewLastName
    adoRs.MoveNext
Loop

adoRs.Close
```

In the preceding code fragments, the connection is made automatically by using the ODBC DSN passed to the *Open* method of the *Recordset* object. Although this is acceptable for sample code, applications that want to have greater control over the connection process can explicitly create a *Connection* object, as shown in bold in the following example:

```
Dim adoCon As New ADODB.Connection
Dim adoRs As New ADODB.Recordset

adoCon.Open "MyDSN", "MyUserID", "MyPassword"
adoRs.ActiveConnection = adoCon
adoRs.Open "Select au_lname, au_fname from Authors"

Do Until adoRs.EOF
    Print adoRs.Fields!au_lname, adoRs.Fields!au_fname
    adoRs.MoveNext
Loop

adoRs.Close
```

This example calls the *Open* method of the *Connection* object. Then it sets the *ActiveConnection* property of the *Recordset* object to the *Connection* object. A *Command* object can be used to exercise greater control over the database commands, as shown in bold in the following example:

```
Dim adoCmd As New ADODB.Command
Dim adoRs As ADODB.Recordset
```

(continued)

```
adoCmd.ActiveConnection = _
   "DSN=MyDSN;UID=MyUserID;PWD=MyPassword"
adoCmd.CommandText = "Select au_lname from Authors"
Set adoRs = adoCmd.Execute
Do Until adoRs.EOF
    Print adoRs.Fields!au_lname
    adoRs.MoveNext
Loop

adoRs.Close
```

The preceding code fragment calls the *Execute* method of the *Command* object to execute an SQL query. Notice that the *Execute* method returns a *Recordset* object that is stored in an object variable.

THE VBDB TIMING APPLICATION

The VBDB timing application, which you'll find on the companion CD for this book, compares four of the major data access methods of Visual Basic we discussed in this chapter: DAO, ODBC, RDO, and ADO. All four methods are used sequentially to query an ODBC data source that you specify by referencing its DSN. The application also asks you for the user ID and password necessary to connect. (You can leave these blank if they are not required by your data source.) The VBDB timing application is shown in Figure 10-10.

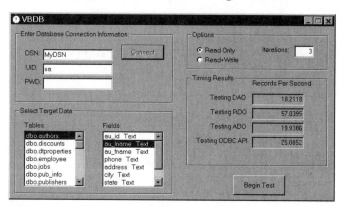

Figure 10-10. *The VBDB timing application.*

VBDB connects and queries the database by means of DAO to determine which tables and fields are available on that data source. Choose a single field from the table on which you will run the tests. You can decide whether you want to test reading records on the server only or to test both reading and writing records on the server. If you tell VBDB to test both reading and writing records, it first reads a record and then reverses the data and writes it back. If you display the data on the server at this point, you will find that it has been reversed. If you then run the program again, it will reverse the data back to its original form. We do not recommend running this test against important data; you might want to create a sample database for the test.

The tests begin by using DAO, continue with RDO and ADO, and then finish with the ODBC API. When the test is finished, the results allow you to compare the access speed of each method. The following table shows sample timing results received when running this application under Microsoft Windows 98 on a 200-MHz Pentium Pro connected over a network to Microsoft SQL Server 6.5 running Microsoft Windows NT 4.0 on a 200-MHz Pentium. The tests were run on the au_lname field of the Authors table of the Pubs database that comes with Microsoft SQL Server.

Data access method	*Number of records read and written per second*
DAO	5
RDO	13
ADO	13
ODBC API	20

You can see that both RDO and the ODBC API left DAO in the dust. The unexpected result is that RDO sometimes outperforms the ODBC API by a small margin when reading records only. The explanation for this discrepancy lies in the way VBDB reads records using the ODBC *SQLExtendedFetch* function. VBDB calls *SQLExtendedFetch* to read one record at a time so as to mimic the way records are read using DAO and RDO. It would be more efficient to read a batch of records with each call to *SQLExtendedFetch*. RDO is doing this type of intelligent caching automatically and thereby improving the speed of RDO. This logic is congruent with the fact that the ODBC API is the fastest access method when both reading and writing records. This type of read-ahead caching can't be done when writing data back to the server since RDO has no idea what we intend to write.

You might want to look at the ReadWrite module of the VBDB project. It contains the timing code for DAO, RDO, ADO, and the ODBC API. You can find the VBDB sample code on the companion disc in the \BK-SAMP\Chap10\VBDB folder.

Chapter 11

Microsoft
Transaction Server

In recent years, there has been much talk about migrating enterprise-wide systems from the two-tier client/server model to the three-tier client/server architecture. The surging popularity of the Internet, the advent of the Java programming language, and the development of the network computer have all spurred interest in the concept of three-tiered client/server architecture.

THREE-TIERED
CLIENT/SERVER ARCHITECTURE

Many new enterprise information systems are developed to run on Microsoft Windows NT. However, few existing systems are ported from mainframes to Windows NT. That is because in many two-tier client/server systems, the user interface and the business logic running on the client are specifically designed to run with the database server on the mainframe. The goal of the three-tier architecture is to separate the business logic from the user interface by moving it to a middle tier that runs on Windows NT. The resulting three-tier architecture consists of the client (the user interface), the business rules component, and the database server. The ultimate goal is to migrate the database servers to Microsoft Windows NT Server as well. When that time comes, your company will unplug the mainframes and build indoor tennis courts in their place.

The Client Tier

The client side of a two-tier client/server system typically encompasses the functionality of both the user interface and the business logic that drives the system, leaving only the database on the server side. This design leads to heavyweight client-side applications that tend to be tied to a particular operating system and can be difficult to deploy and support. In a three-tier client/server architecture, the client tier is designed to be as lightweight as possible, normally handling only the user interface. Such a client might consist of forms designed in Microsoft Visual Basic or of HTML pages designed to run in a Web browser such as Microsoft Internet Explorer.

Client-side applications composed solely of HTML pages are very attractive to many corporations because they are platform-independent and easy to distribute. If you are writing an application that requires a user interface richer than using HTML alone can provide, you might consider including Microsoft ActiveX controls or Java applets in your Web pages. Java applets are platform-independent like HTML, and both Java applets and ActiveX controls offer automated distribution.

The Business Rules Tier

While the two-tier client/server architecture usually deploys the client and the server components on different computers, the business rules component of a three-tier design offers more flexible solutions. For example, the business rules component might be implemented as an in-process COM component designed to run either in the process of the client application or in the process of a Web server. Alternatively, the business rules component might run on a third machine that is separate from both the client and the database server. The particular configuration you choose for a system depends heavily on the network bandwidth available to connect the various machines, as well as the administration and support issues involved in deploying a large distributed system to many client machines.

The Database Server Tier

Where do Distributed COM (DCOM) and Microsoft Transaction Server (MTS) fit into this picture? Suppose you deploy a business-rules component as a COM EXE component. In this scenario, client-tier applications written in C++, Visual Basic, or Java can use DCOM to connect to the business-rules component, which in turn can use ODBC or even OLE DB to connect to a database server, as shown in Figure 11-1.

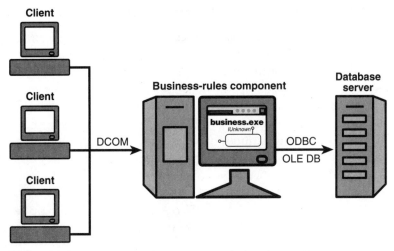

Figure 11-1. *A business-rules component deployed as a COM EXE component.*

If you want an even lighter-weight client—one that doesn't require any client-side installation and configuration—the Web browser might serve as the client portion, making HTTP the protocol of choice. The Web server can then host MTS components that use ODBC or OLE DB to communicate with a database server, as shown in Figure 11-2.

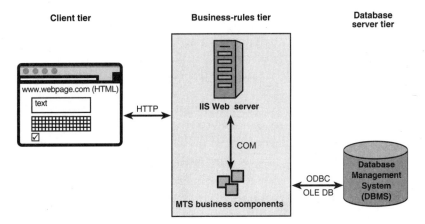

Figure 11-2. *Using a Web browser as the client.*

Problems with a Three-Tiered Architecture

Although Figure 11-2 depicts a successful implementation of a three-tier system, a lot of development effort will be required for you to build the business-rules component. Even if the goals of the business-rules component are relatively modest, you will need to expend a tremendous amount of effort to develop a robust and secure EXE housing for the component. Potential problems abound, some of which are presented here.

First, with many different clients connecting to the business-rules component simultaneously, you will need to ensure that only clients with the proper authorization are able to perform privileged operations by means of the component.

Second, threading will be of concern as you strive to make the component scalable to a large number of clients. You should anticipate times when too many clients attempt to access a component simultaneously. One solution to this problem is to implement a load-balancing feature to direct some of the clients to an instance of the business-rules component that is running on another computer.

Third, you should anticipate possible client failures in the midst of complex operations involving the database server. The client might have been storing data locally, and then be in the process of updating data on the database server based on some of the locally stored information. If the client fails in the middle of this type of operation, you can't be sure of the integrity of the database without implementing some sort of transaction protocol.

Finally, if the internal data structures of the business-rules component become corrupted, you need to detect this before the integrity of the database becomes compromised.

From this list of potential issues, you can see that a major problem with the three-tier client/server model is that developers have to implement an enormous amount of functionality in the second tier—functionality that has little to do with the goals of the system. Enter Microsoft Transaction Server.

AN OVERVIEW OF MICROSOFT TRANSACTION SERVER

Microsoft Transaction Server is a powerful run-time environment designed to host COM components. MTS makes it easier to develop and deploy Internet and intranet enterprise applications that are high performance, scalable, and robust.

MTS defines a set of COM interfaces for developing distributed components and an infrastructure for implementing and administering three-tier solutions. Microsoft Transaction Server is perhaps one of the more misnamed products to come out of Redmond in recent years. The name leads you to think MTS handles only transactions, but MTS encompasses much more than that.

DLL surrogates are processes that load DLL-based components into the surrogates' address space. MTS is the ultimate DLL surrogate; it loads components into the MTS surrogate (MTX.EXE) process along with the MTS Executive (MTXEX.DLL), as shown in Figure 11-3.

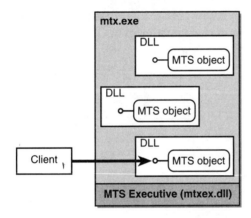

Figure 11-3. *A client calling components that are running under the supervision of MTS.*

Microsoft's continuing research into component development has produced a realization among developers that writing robust server-side systems requires intensive work. Threading, concurrency, security, administration, and robustness are all crucial features of any distributed system, and developing software that has these features seamlessly integrated requires tremendous effort. Further, these features are completely unrelated to the actual processing done by the system. Microsoft SQL Server, for example, is a database server that deals with these issues in addition to its bread and butter work of processing SQL queries.

Microsoft created MTS to help developers build sophisticated three-tier business systems. In some respects, MTS is a server's server. It is a robust runtime environment that deals with most of the issues facing developers of server-side systems, and it enables developers to plug in a COM in-process component containing the business-related functionality.

Designing Components for MTS

Although any COM in-process component qualifies as an MTS component, an in-process component that isn't designed specifically for the MTS environment can't take full advantage of the services offered by MTS. We therefore recommend that you update components that might benefit from running in the MTS environment. Typically, you would update components that do not display a user interface or otherwise interact with the user.

MTS doesn't support EXE components because they can't be loaded into the address space of MTS and therefore can't take advantage of its features. COM components designed to operate within the context of MTS can be written in any language that supports COM. For an in-process DLL component to be hosted by the MTS environment, MTS requires the following features:

■ The component must have a standard class object that implements the *IClassFactory* interface.

■ The *IClassFactory::CreateInstance* method of the class object must return a new instance of the object every time it is called. Singletons[1] are against the MTS way.

■ The component must expose its class object by exporting the standard *DllGetClassObject* function.

■ The component must employ standard COM reference counting.

■ A component running in the MTS process space can't aggregate with components not running in MTS. Aggregation is a feature of in-process COM components, but it isn't supported for objects running in the context of MTS.

■ The component must export the standard *DllRegisterServer* function that registers the program identifier (ProgID), class identifier (CLSID), interface, and TypeLib in the HKEY_CLASSES_ROOT section of the Windows Registry.

■ The component's interfaces and COM classes must be described in a type library.

■ The component must use standard or type-library marshaling; MTS doesn't support custom marshaling.[2] In cases where a component

---

1. A singleton is a COM class that can be instantiated only once. All further attempts to instantiate a singleton return a reference to the same object.

2. Custom marshaling is a basic mechanism for managing marshaling based on the *IMarshal* interface. Components written in Visual Basic can't implement this interface directly.

supports both standard and type-library marshaling, MTS uses standard marshaling.

While these rules might seem daunting at first, they actually mandate what has become standard COM practice. The more standard your component is, the more likely it is that it meets these requirements. For example, components built in Visual Basic and Java automatically meet all these requirements. Although MTS makes certain demands of your components, it offers a lot of functionality in return. MTS offers to handle the concurrency, resource pooling, security, context management, and transaction requirements of your components.

Threading

We recommend that components designed for execution in the MTS environment support the single-threaded apartment (STA) or multithreaded apartment (MTA) model. Components supporting the STA model should have their *ThreadingModel* registry value set to *Apartment*, and MTS objects that support the MTA and STA models should have their *ThreadingModel* registry value set to *Both*. Since components built in Visual Basic 6 do not support the MTA model, always be sure to set a component's threading model to *Apartment*. Legacy single-threaded components do not work well in the MTS environment because all objects in the component must execute in the thread of the main STA. Because such components are not reentrant, execution must be serialized across all objects in the component; this limits their scalability and makes them susceptible to deadlock.

Just-In-Time Activation and Deactivation

From an in-process component's point of view, MTS is a surrogate process with some unique functionality. A client that calls *CoGetClassObject* for a component that is registered with MTS receives a reference to a class object implemented by MTS, rather than a reference to the component's class object. When the client later calls the *IClassFactory::CreateInstance* method, the class object implemented by MTS doesn't actually instantiate the object. Only when the client makes a method call into the component does MTS finally instantiate the object by calling the component's *IClassFactory::CreateInstance* method.

In addition to the late instantiation of components, MTS extends the COM model to allow early deactivation of an object. That permits MTS to deactivate a component while client programs maintain valid references to that component. MTS does this by calling the *IUnknown::Release* method to release all references to the object. That, in turn, causes properly-built COM objects to be destroyed when their internal reference count reaches zero. Should the client request services from an object that has been deactivated by MTS, that object will be transparently reactivated by means of the component's *IClassFactory::CreateInstance* method. While it might appear to a client process that it is using a single COM object from the time it creates the object until the time it releases the object, the client might, in fact, be working with many different instances of the same COM class. Objects, unlike cats, really do have nine lives.

That lazy instantiation of COM objects by MTS is referred to as *just-in-time activation*. Just-in-time activation is a powerful resource-sharing concept because it enables MTS to share the resources of the server more equably than otherwise among the active components. Suppose that a client process spends 10 percent of its time requesting services from a particular object. With the automated deactivation of objects running in MTS, the object will be instantiated only 10 percent of the time instead of 100 percent. Just-in-time activation can make a particular server machine far more scalable than would be possible if all objects remained active for the entire time their client programs are running.

While the code running the object remains unchanged from instance to instance of a COM class, the data stored by an object needs to be protected. MTS terminology refers to this data as the *state* or the *context* of the object. Each object running in the MTS environment is shadowed by a *context object* that maintains information about the object. The context object implements the *IObject-Context* interface described later in this chapter; in addition, it stores the identity of the client that instantiated the MTS object, as well as the transactional requirements and security properties of the object. As shown in Figure 11-4, when MTS deactivates an object, the context object remains. When the client permanently releases the object, the context object associated with that object is also destroyed.

The *IObjectControl* interface

You might want your application to execute code before an object is deactivated and again before it is reactivated. To do that, you can implement the *IObjectControl* interface. The *IObjectControl* interface has three methods: *Activate*, *Deactivate*, and *CanBePooled*. The *IObjectControl* interface is shown in the following Interface Definition Language (IDL) notation:

```
interface IObjectControl : IUnknown
{
    HRESULT Activate(void);
    void Deactivate(void);
    BOOL CanBePooled(void);
}
```

When a client first instantiates an object, MTS queries the object for the *IObjectControl* interface. If MTS finds the interface, MTS will call the *Activate* method immediately before the object is activated and the *Deactivate* method before it is deactivated, enabling the object to execute code at those specific times in the object's lifecycle. After executing the *Deactivate* method, MTS calls the *IObjectControl::CanBePooled* method to determine whether the object is environmentally aware. Such an object returns *True* from the *CanBePooled* method, thereby informing MTS that this object can be recycled. MTS pools objects that support recycling so that, instead of being destroyed, they can be used later by the same client or another client. When a client attempts to access an object of the COM class, MTS will obtain an object from the pool if one is available. Only when the pool of recyclable objects is empty will MTS use the object's class factory to instantiate an object again.

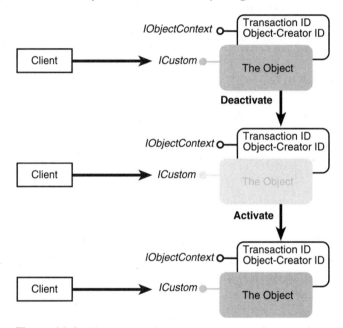

Figure 11-4. *The context object remains even when an object is deactivated.*

Giving MTS permission to recycle an object means that the object must implement the *IObjectControl::Deactivate* method. This method enables MTS to restore the state of the object so it is the same as when it was newly manufactured by the class factory. Your decision whether to support the recycling of an object should be based on evaluating the expense of creating new objects versus the cost of holding the resources of that object while it is being stored in the object pool. An object that takes a long time to create but that holds many resources when deactivated is a good candidate for recycling.

Imagine an object that creates a complex memory structure on startup. If this type of object supports pooling, it could reinitialize the memory structure in the *Deactivate* event method and thereby increase performance at run time;

the object would not need to re-create the memory structure each time it is activated. For other objects, recycling might not be advantageous. For example, an object that is cheap to create and stores a lot of state for each client isn't reusable by other clients and therefore recycling it doesn't offer any benefits.

The following table summarizes the steps taken by MTS when the client calls a method of a deactivated object, when *IObjectControl* isn't implemented, and when it is implemented:

MTS steps	**IObjectControl** *not implemented*	**IObjectControl** *implemented*
1. Activate the object.	Call *IClassFactory:: CreateInstance* to instantiate the object.	Obtain an object from the pool. If the pool does not contain this type of object, call *IClassFactory::Create- Instance* to instantiate the object. Finally, call the *Activate* method.
2. Execute the method.	Call the method.	Call the method.
3. Deactivate the object.	Release all references to the object.	Call the *Deactivate* method. Then call the *CanBePooled* method to de- termine if pooling is supported. If so, add the object to the pool. Other- wise, release all references to the object.

To implement the *IObjectControl* interface in a Visual Basic component, you must set a reference to the Microsoft Transaction Server Type Library (MTXAS.DLL). Note that returning *True* from the *IObjectControl::CanBePooled* method doesn't guarantee that the object will be recycled, but simply indicates to MTS that the object supports this feature. However, returning *False* from *CanBePooled* does ensure that MTS will never recycle the object. Currently, MTS does not recycle objects, regardless of the value returned from the *CanBePooled* method.[3]

State

Object-oriented languages have made developers aware of the class and object concepts for the first time. Subsequently, COM brought the interface and imple- mentation concepts into the limelight. Now MTS advances the concepts of state and behavior. In the MTS world, components are seen as code libraries exposing certain objects. Since the behavior of an object remains consistent throughout

---

3. Object pooling will be implemented in a future release of MTS.

its lifetime, MTS can create, destroy, and pool objects at will. Object-oriented fundamentals dictate that an object encapsulates code (behavior) and data (state). The state of an object is volatile, which can limit the ability of MTS to create and destroy an object while clients maintain valid references to the object. To overcome this problem, MTS recommends that developers build stateless objects. However, since this isn't a realistic solution for many components, MTS defines four specific places where state can be kept in a controlled manner: the client, the object, the database, and the Shared Property Manager. By defining specific places where state can be kept, and the semantics of its storage and usage in those places, MTS effectively champions the state and behavior concepts.

Client state storage

Storing the state of an object in the client application simplifies the implementation of that object because it can basically behave like a stateless object. In this type of system design, the client must pass the object's state with every method of the object. In between method calls, the object itself doesn't retain this state. While this type of design simplifies the implementation of the component, it can complicate the implementation of the client process. Lack of network bandwidth can be a major bottleneck when passing an object's entire state at every method call. Therefore, a client state solution is useful only when there is little state that needs to be transmitted, or when the client and component are connected by means of a high-bandwidth network.

Object state storage

Storing state in the object is the typical approach developers take for objects that are not designed especially for MTS. Objects running in the context of MTS must be careful in their use of object state storage, because each time MTS deactivates an object, that state is lost. Any object that keeps its own state won't be able to take advantage of the resource-sharing, just-in-time activation features of MTS. These types of objects also do not scale well to support a large number of clients. We therefore recommend that when you are rewriting objects to take advantage of the MTS environment, you do not use object state storage.

Database state storage

Most business components are designed to store their durable state in a database. Typically, the business component uses ODBC API or OLE DB to communicate with a back-end database server such as Microsoft SQL Server. It is usually necessary to store the object's durable state in a database. However, the database server is likely to have many clients in contention for its services, and so it is important not to overload it with requests to store temporary data. Additionally, because storing temporary data isn't something most SQL servers are designed to do, a component that attempts to store temporary data in a back-end server will likely suffer a serious performance penalty.

The Shared Property Manager

The Shared Property Manager is an MTS resource dispenser that you can use to store and share state among multiple objects within a server process. The Shared Property Manager is a three-level hierarchy of objects that eliminates naming conflicts by providing shared property groups that contain shared properties. The Shared Property Manager has built-in synchronization that prevents two objects from accessing a shared property simultaneously. This is important, because if two threads attempt to access a shared property concurrently, the value of the property can be left in an unpredictable state. The three-level hierarchy of the Shared Property Manager is depicted in Figure11-5.

Figure 11-5. *The object hierarchy exposed by the Shared Property Manager.*

To access the Shared Property Manager from a component written in Visual Basic, you need to set a reference to the Shared Property Manager Type Library (MTXSPM.DLL). You instantiate the *SharedPropertyGroupManager* object by using the *New* keyword, and then call the *ISharedPropertyGroupManager::CreatePropertyGroup* method to instantiate a property group. Because there is no method of the *ISharedPropertyGroupManager* interface that is designed to open an existing property group, the *CreatePropertyGroup* method provides an outbound Boolean parameter that specifies whether the property group existed before the *CreatePropertyGroup* method was called. The existence of a property group is determined based on the string name of the property group passed as the first parameter of the *CreatePropertyGroup* method.

The second parameter of the *CreatePropertyGroup* method specifies the lock setting that will be employed by the property group object being created. The lock setting can be either *LockSetGet* or *LockMethod*. The *LockSetGet* flag creates a property group that protects the individual properties belonging to the property group during every operation that gets or sets the value of a property. The *LockMethod* flag locks all the properties of the property group while the method of an object that has access to the property group is running. That leads to a higher degree of safety but less concurrency for objects with access to the property group.

Typically, if a method will perform several operations on a shared property, it is best to copy the value of that property to a local variable and then do the operations on the local variable. Only when the operations are completed should you update the value of the shared property. That type of code makes the *LockSetGet* locking flag sufficient and leads to more efficient execution in the MTS environment. In comparison, when a set of operations are performed directly on a shared property, each individual operation is atomic because of the implicit synchronization provided by the Shared Property Manager, but the entire set of operations isn't atomic. That means that other objects might be operating on the same properties, leading to corrupted data. When performing a set of operations directly on a shared property, it is imperative that you employ the *LockMethod* flag.

The third parameter of the *CreatePropertyGroup* method specifies the release mode of the property group. The valid settings are either *Standard*, which indicates that the property group is to be destroyed after all the references to the object have been released, or *Process*, which indicates that the property group isn't to be released until the process in which it was created has terminated. Note that MTS ignores the values of the lock mode and release settings, provided in the second and third parameters of the *CreatePropertyGroup* method, if MTS determines that the property group already exists. In that case, MTS instead proceeds to open the existing property group. When the *CreatePropertyGroup* method opens an existing property group, the second and third parameters return the current settings for those values. Although you can pass the constants *LockSetGet*, *LockMethod*, *Standard*, and *Process* directly to the *CreatePropertyGroup* method, this approach will disable the retrieval of the current settings when the method returns. To retrieve these values, it is better to create variables that are passed to the *CreatePropertyGroup* method by reference. The following Visual Basic code fragment creates a property group named GuyProperties that contains a property named Hair with the value *Brown*:

```
Dim spg As SharedPropertyGroup
Dim sp As SharedProperty
Dim fAlreadyExists As Boolean

Dim isolationMode As Long
isolationMode = LockSetGet

Dim releaseMode As Long
releaseMode = Process
```

(continued)

313

```
Dim spgm As New SharedPropertyGroupManager

Set spg = spgm.CreatePropertyGroup("GuyProperties", isolationMode, _
    releaseMode, fAlreadyExists)

Set sp = spg.CreateProperty("Hair", fAlreadyExists)

sp.Value = "Brown"
```

The *IObjectContext* Interface

The idea that MTS will deactivate a component while clients hold valid references to that component is almost heretical in the world of COM, where *IUnknown* and reference counting rule supreme. However, MTS is designed to deactivate objects only at certain controlled junctures in the object's lifetime. MTS offers the business component developer a great deal of control over the behavior of MTS by means of the *IObjectContext* interface, which is implemented by the context object associated with each object running in the MTS environment. The *IObjectContext* interface is described in the following IDL notation:

```
interface IObjectContext : public IUnknown
{
    HRESULT CreateInstance(
        [in] REFCLSID rclsid,
        [in] REFIID riid,
        [out, retval, iid_is(riid)] void** ppv);
    HRESULT SetComplete(void);
    HRESULT SetAbort(void);
    HRESULT EnableCommit(void);
    HRESULT DisableCommit(void);
    BOOL IsInTransaction(void);
    BOOL IsSecurityEnabled(void);
    HRESULT IsCallerInRole(
        [in] BSTR bstrRole,
        [out, retval] BOOL* pfIsInRole);
};
```

Although the context object created by MTS implements the *IObjectContext* interface and the interface is automatically associated with every MTS object, there is no need for the component to instantiate an object that implements this interface. Instead, MTS offers the *GetObjectContext* function that returns a pointer to the *IObjectContext* interface the context object implements. A component written in Visual Basic obtains access to the context object by using the following code:

```
Dim oc As ObjectContext
Set oc = GetObjectContext()
```

The *CreateInstance* method

Having obtained a pointer to the context object, you can invoke any methods of the *IObjectContext* interface. The *IObjectContext::CreateInstance* method is designed to enable one MTS object to instantiate another MTS object. While you can call the standard *CoCreateInstance* function for the purpose of instantiating an object, this technique has its limitations. Instead, we recommend that you use the *IObjectContext::CreateInstance* method for this purpose, as shown in the following code. The advantage of the *CreateInstance* method is that the newly created object will inherit the activity, transaction, and security identities from the creator's context object. For example, assuming that the object's creator is running in a transaction, if the object being created requires a transaction in order to execute, it will run within the scope of the existing transaction. If the new object doesn't support transactions or require its own transaction, MTS will accommodate that as well.

```
Dim oc As ObjectContext
Set oc = GetObjectContext()

Dim GuysAccount As Bank.Account
Set GuysAccount = oc.CreateInstance("Bank.Account")
```

The *SetComplete, SetAbort, EnableCommit,* and *DisableCommit* methods

You can use the *IObjectContext* interface to control when MTS will deactivate an object by calling the *IObjectContext::SetComplete* method. This method indicates to MTS that the object has successfully completed its work and that its internal representation doesn't need to be retained for future client calls. If the method is executing within the scope of a transaction, the *SetComplete* method also indicates that the object's transactional updates can be committed. When an object that is the root of a transaction calls *SetComplete*, MTS attempts to commit the transaction on return from the current method.

Similarly to the *SetComplete* method, the *IObjectContext::SetAbort* method tells MTS that the object can be deactivated. However, the *SetAbort* method indicates that an unrecoverable error has occurred, making the object's transactional updates inconsistent and therefore mandating that the transaction be aborted. MTS will also deactivate an object whenever a transaction involving that object is committed or aborted, even if the object did not issue the commit or abort operation. These are the only times MTS will transparently deactivate an object. Of course, when the client releases all references to the object, MTS will permanently destroy the object in accordance with COM's reference counting rules. Remember that objects lose state on transaction boundaries. You can use the Shared Property Manager to hold state across transactions or to store the state in a database.

The *EnableCommit* and *DisableCommit* methods of the *IObjectContext* interface are analogues to the *SetComplete* and *SetAbort* methods. The *Enable-Commit* method tells MTS that it is safe to commit the transaction in which the object is participating, but that the object has not yet finished its work and therefore its internal state must be maintained until the object calls *SetComplete* or *SetAbort*, or until the transaction completes. In the meantime, MTS won't deactivate the object. *EnableCommit* is the default state when an object is first activated. For this reason, you should always call *SetComplete* or *SetAbort* before a method returns, unless you specifically want the object's internal state to be maintained for future client method calls.

The *DisableCommit* method is similar to the *EnableCommit* method in that it forces MTS to maintain the object's internal state until the object calls either the *SetComplete* or *SetAbort* method. However, the *DisableCommit* method also informs MTS that the work being performed by the object is currently in an incomplete stage and can't be committed at the present time. In that way, the *DisableCommit* method is useful in preventing a transaction from committing prematurely between method calls to a stateful[4] object. In this respect, the *DisableCommit* method differs from the *EnableCommit* method, which declares that although the object's work isn't necessarily complete, it is safe to commit the object's transactional updates in their present form.

Internally, the *SetComplete*, *SetAbort*, *EnableCommit*, and *DisableCommit* methods set the *Done* and *Consistent* flags in the context object associated with an MTS object. The *Done* flag specifies whether the object has completed its work so that its state no longer needs to be maintained by MTS. The *Consistent* flag indicates whether the transaction can be committed in its current state. These flags, and hence the methods that set them, have no effect until a method finishes executing and returns to its caller. Thus, you can call any combination of the above methods from within a method, but MTS will only act on the last call that is made before the method returns.

The following table shows the effect these four methods have on the internal *Done* and *Consistent* flags maintained by MTS in the context object:

Method	**Done** *Flag*	**Consistent** *Flag*
SetComplete	*True*	*True*
SetAbort	*True*	*False*
EnableCommit	*False*	*True*
DisableCommit	*False*	*False*

---

4. A stateful object is an object that maintains state across transactions.

Transactions

As you probably realize by now, Microsoft Transaction Server is a great DLL surrogate with a myriad of features that can help you to develop robust three-tier systems. Transaction processing is one of MTS's more important features, and MTS enlists the help of the Microsoft Distributed Transaction Coordinator (DTC) to perform the transaction management. Microsoft originally designed the OLE Transactions interfaces (*ITransaction, ITransactionDispenser, ITransactionOptions,* and *ITransactionOutcomeEvents*), an object-oriented, two-phase commit protocol based on COM, and then implemented those four interfaces in DTC, a transaction manager originally bundled with Microsoft SQL Server 6.5. However, Microsoft did not design the transaction management services provided by DTC solely for use by Microsoft SQL Server; DTC is also bundled with MTS.

In addition to the OLE Transactions specification,[5] MTS also supports the X/Open DTP XA standard. XA is the two-phase commit protocol defined by the X/Open DTP group. XA is natively supported by many Unix databases, including Informix, Oracle, and DB2. For MTS to work with XA-compliant resource managers, the Microsoft Transaction Server SDK provides a special component that maps OLE transactions to the XA standard. That makes it relatively straightforward for XA-compliant resource managers to provide resource dispensers that accept OLE transactions from MTS and then execute the transaction with XA.

An application typically initiates a transaction when the application is going to perform some critical operation. To initiate a transaction, the application first notifies a transaction manager such as DTC. The application then enlists the help of various resource managers in performing the work. A *resource manager* is any service supporting the OLE Transactions specification, such as Microsoft SQL Server. Resource managers work in cooperation with DTC so that when the client application calls various resource dispensers, it carries with it information identifying the current transaction.

Transaction processing is most often applied to database access because of the crucial nature of the information stored in databases. However, transaction processing isn't limited to the database management system (DBMS) domain. MTS, for example, provides two resource dispensers: the ODBC Driver Manager and the Shared Property Manager. A resource dispenser manages nondurable shared state on behalf of MTS objects. Resource dispensers are similar to resource managers but without the guarantee of durability. The ODBC Driver Manager is a resource dispenser that manages pools of database connections for MTS components. The Shared Property Manager was discussed earlier in this chapter. In addition, you can develop add-on resource dispensers with the MTS SDK.

---

5. The OLE Transactions specification defines the COM interfaces that must be implemented by a component in order to work with DTC.

A resource manager enlisted to perform work on behalf of a client application registers itself with the transaction manager. The transaction manager then keeps track of that resource manager throughout the remainder of the transaction. A transaction ends when the client application either commits or aborts the transaction. An abort operation causes the transaction manager to notify all resource managers involved in the transaction to roll back any operations performed as part of that transaction. A rollback can be likened to a giant undo operation. If the client application should fail before committing or aborting the transaction, DTC automatically aborts the transaction.

If everything goes well, and the client application requests that the transaction be committed, DTC executes a two-phase commit protocol to commit the operations performed during the transaction. A two-phase commit protocol ensures that transactions that apply to more than one server are completed on all servers or on none at all. The two-phase commit protocol involves coordination between DTC and supported resource managers. First, DTC queries each resource manager enlisted in the transaction to determine whether every resource manager agrees to the commit operation. If any one resource manager fails to respond, or votes to abort the transaction, DTC notifies all the resource managers that the transaction is aborted and their operations must be rolled back. Only if all resource managers agree in that first phase of the protocol will DTC broadcast a second commit message, thereby completing the transaction successfully. The two-phase commit process is shown in Figure 11-6.

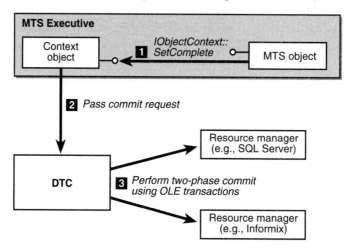

Figure 11-6. *The DTC communicating with the resource managers to control a two-phase commit.*

The ACID properties

A client application using transactions must be guaranteed that concurrent transactions are atomic, consistent, have proper isolation, and are durable once they are committed. These are sometimes referred to as the ACID (atomic, consistent, isolated, and durable) properties of transactions.

Atomic

A transaction is atomic if all the operations that make up that transaction either succeed or fail as a single unit. Being atomic guarantees that a transaction will never be a partial success when some part of the transaction has failed. If a transaction aborts, all of its effects are undone, which, in turn, guarantees the consistency of the data.

Consistent

A transaction guarantees that the data being operated on by one or more resource managers will remain consistent regardless of the outcome of that transaction. For example, if an SQL query updates two related tables in a database, a transaction can ensure that the data in one table will always refer to a valid item in the other table.

Isolated

Isolation protects concurrent transactions from seeing each other's partial and uncommitted results. That isolation, in turn, prevents the application from basing another operation on these temporary results. Transactions that concurrently examine the data operated on by code running in another transaction will see the data either in its pre-transaction or post-transaction state; transactions will never see the data in an intermediate state.

Durable

Durability ensures that all updates, once they are committed, will persist even in the event of a system failure. Transactional logging even allows you to recover the durable state after disk media failures. If a system failure should occur during a transaction, the transaction aborts and the changes are rolled back, thereby ensuring consistency.

Configuring the transaction support in MTS

Each object running in the context of MTS (hereafter called an MTS object) can be set to one of four levels of transaction support. A component can declare that it requires a transaction, requires a new transaction, supports transactions, or doesn't support transactions. The context objects of components that do not support transactions are created without a transaction, regardless of whether their client is running in the scope of a transaction. Unless the component developer or system administrator specifies otherwise, this setting is the default. Components that do not support transactions can't take advantage of many features of MTS, including just-in-time activation. Such components are never deactivated while clients hold valid references because MTS doesn't have enough information about their current state. Thus, we do not recommend using the default value; it is primarily intended to support components not originally designed for use with MTS.

A client declares most MTS objects as either requiring a transaction or supporting transactions. MTS objects that support transactions can participate in the outcome of the transaction if their client is running in the scope of a transaction. If the caller isn't executing within a transaction, no transaction will be available for the MTS object. MTS objects declaring that they require a transaction will either inherit the transaction of the caller, or, if the caller's transaction is unavailable, have MTS automatically initiate a transaction on their behalf. MTS objects that require a new transaction never inherit the client's transaction; MTS automatically initiates a fresh transaction regardless of whether the caller has one. The system administrator can set the level of transaction support, using the Transaction Server Explorer configuration utility, otherwise known as the MTS Explorer, shown in Figure 11-7.

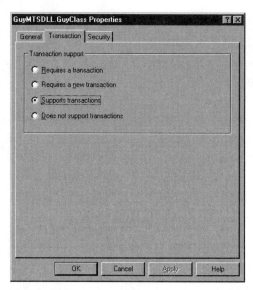

Figure 11-7. *The level of transaction is specified in the Properties dialog box of the Transaction Server Explorer.*

For components that support but do not require a transaction, it might be useful to determine whether the object is currently executing within a transaction scope. An MTS object can call the *IObjectContext::IsInTransaction* method to obtain this information. Components that either require or do not support transactions have no use for the *IsInTransaction* method, since MTS guarantees their transaction status.

Automatic transactions and client-controlled transactions

MTS automatically initiates transactions at certain specific times, as outlined by the two items below. Activation is a general term used to refer to the first instantiation of an object or its just-in-time activation.

■   MTS initiates a new transaction when a base client, or another MTS object that doesn't support transactions, activates a component marked as requiring a transaction.

■   MTS initiates a new transaction when a component marked as requiring a new transaction is activated, regardless of whether the client has a transaction.

Those are the only times and the only ways a transaction can be initiated in the MTS environment. The MTS object ends the transaction by calling either the *IObjectContext::SetComplete* or *IObjectContext::SetAbort* method. The typical base client process instantiates MTS objects using the *CoCreateInstance* function. This technique, however, doesn't afford the client application control over the transaction status of an MTS object. While there is nothing wrong with this approach per se, it limits the client's ability to combine operations that involve multiple objects in one transaction.

One way to enable the client to exercise greater control over the transactional process is to build a special MTS object declared as requiring a new transaction. This object might allow the client to create other MTS objects, which would then inherit the automatic transaction initiated by MTS for the first object. The client could control the outcome of the transaction by calling methods exposed by the first object that call *SetComplete* or *SetAbort* to end the automatic transaction. You don't have to build this type of object, since MTS offers a built-in object that implements the *ITransactionContext* interface to provide the aforementioned functionality.

Since the *TransactionContext* object is declared as requiring a new transaction, MTS is forced to initiate a transaction for it. This enables the base client to instantiate a *TransactionContext* object, call its *CreateInstance* method to instantiate other MTS objects, call various methods on those objects, and finally call *Commit* or *Abort* in the *TransactionContext* object. The operations performed on the MTS objects instantiated using the *TransactionContext* object inherit the automatic transaction initiated by MTS for the *TransactionContext* object. That type of control is only available to components that support or require transactions. MTS objects that either do not support transactions or require a new transaction for every operation can't be grouped into a transaction involving other objects.

The *ITransactionContext* interface

To access the *TransactionContext* object from Visual Basic, you must set a reference to the Transaction Context Type Library (TXCTX.DLL). The *ITransactionContext* interface is defined in IDL notation as follows:

```
interface ITransactionContextEx : IUnknown
{
    HRESULT CreateInstance(
        [in] REFCLSID clsid,
        [in] REFIID riid,
        [out, retval, iid_is(riid)] void** pObject);

    HRESULT Commit(void);

    HRESULT Abort(void);
};
```

A client calls the *ITransactionContext::CreateInstance* method, instead of the *CoCreateInstance* function, to instantiate an MTS object. In turn, the *ITransactionContext::CreateInstance* method instantiates an MTS object by calling the *IObjectContext::CreateInstance* method. The client can then call the *ITransactionContext::CreateInstance* method again to create additional MTS objects, all of which become parts of the single transaction initiated for the *TransactionContext* object. At some point, the client might decide to end the entire transaction by calling the *ITransactionContext::Commit* or *ITransactionContext::Abort* method. That will have the effect of either committing or aborting the operations performed by every MTS object involved in the transaction.

Security

As we discussed at the beginning of this chapter, MTS was designed to relieve developers of the need to code a robust server-side process for every component that runs in the middle tier of a three-tier architecture. To this end, components running in the context of MTS automatically receive help from MTS in managing threading, concurrency, scalability, transactions, and security. The MTS security model leverages the security models of DCOM and Windows NT. To simplify security issues for components running in MTS, two types of security—declarative and programmatic—are available. You can utilize both declarative and programmatic security when designing an MTS object. The MTS security isn't supported for middle-tier components running on Microsoft Windows 95 or Microsoft Windows 98.

The key to understanding the MTS security model is to understand the simple but powerful concept of roles. Roles are central to the flexible, declarative security model employed by most MTS objects. A *role* is a symbolic name that abstracts and identifies a logical group of users, similar to the idea of a user group in Windows NT. During development of an MTS object, you can define roles and use them to perform declarative authorization, as well as to program specific security logic that either grants or denies certain permissions. When an MTS object is deployed, the administrator can bind the roles defined in the component to specific users and user groups. For example, an MTS-based accounting package might define roles and permissions for accountants and attorneys. During deployment, the administrator could assign users Fred and Jane to the role of accountants and the entire legal department to the role of attorneys.

To enable the MTS object to control declarative security, MTS offers the *IObjectContext::IsSecurityEnabled* and *IObjectContext::IsCallerInRole* methods. The *IsCallerInRole* method interrogates the caller to determine whether the user making the call was assigned to a specific role. For example, the accounting package described previously might allow certain operations to be performed only by users in the role of accountants. The following code fragment shows how this could be enforced inside the MTS object:

```
Public Function MethodForUseByAccountantsOnly() As Boolean
Dim oc As ObjectContext
Set oc = GetObjectContext()

If oc.IsCallerInRole("Accountants") = True Then
    ' Code here to proceed with operation and return success.
    MethodForUseByAccountantsOnly = True
Else
    ' Code here to deny access and return failure.
    MethodForUseByAccountantsOnly = False
End If
End Function
```

MTS doesn't support declarative security when running an MTS object in the same process as the base client, and thus we don't recommend this configuration. In such cases, the *IsCallerInRole* method always returns *True*, which can lead the component to grant permissions to ineligible users. To overcome this problem, the client can call the *IObjectContext::IsSecurityEnabled* method to determine whether role-based security is currently being enforced by MTS. The method shown previously might be rewritten as follows to call the *IsSecurity-Enabled* function:

```
Public Function MethodForUseByAccountantsOnly() As Boolean
Dim oc As ObjectContext
Set oc = GetObjectContext()

If oc.IsSecurityEnabled = False Then
    ' Security is not currently available.
    MethodForUseByAccountantsOnly = False
    Exit Sub
End If

If oc.IsCallerInRole("Accountants") = True Then
    ' Code here to proceed with operation and return success.
    MethodForUseByAccountantsOnly = True
Else
    ' Code here to deny access and return failure.
    MethodForUseByAccountantsOnly = False
End If
End Function
```

The *ISecurityProperty* Interface

For those components requiring greater control over the security model than offered by the *IsSecurityEnabled* and *IsCallerInRole* methods of the *IObjectContext* interface, the context object also implements the *ISecurityProperty* interface. An MTS object can use the methods of the *ISecurityProperty* interface to obtain precise information about the identity of its caller stored in the context object. The *ISecurityProperty* interface is defined in the following IDL:

```
interface ISecurityProperty : IUnknown
{
    HRESULT GetDirectCreatorSID(PSID* pSID);
    HRESULT GetOriginalCreatorSID(PSID* pSID);
    HRESULT GetDirectCallerSID(PSID* pSID);
    HRESULT GetOriginalCallerSID(PSID* pSID);
    HRESULT ReleaseSID(PSID pSID);
};
```

Notice that all the methods of the *ISecurityProperty* interface work with a Windows NT security identifier (SID), which is a unique value that identifies a specific user or user group. However, because a SID specifically identifies a unique user, SIDs do not have the flexibility of the role-based security promoted by MTS. After a SID is obtained from a method of the *ISecurityProperty* interface, the MTS object can use that value when calling the security functions of the Win32 API. In this way, the richness and complexity of the Windows NT security model are available to components running in the context of MTS. Note that components written in Visual Basic do not have much use for SIDs and are instead provided with the user name identified by the SID.

Figure 11-8 can aid you in understanding the *ISecurityProperty* interface. As you can see, a base client (Client 1 running as User A) instantiates an MTS object (Object X running as User C). The pointer to Object X is then passed to another base client process (Client 2 running as User B). Client 2 later calls a method on Object X which results in Object X instantiating yet another MTS object (Object Y running as User D). Finally, Object X calls a method of Object Y.

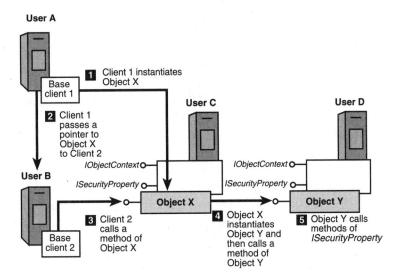

Figure 11-8. *A process demonstrating the use of the* ISecurityProperty *interface.*

If the method in Object Y now calls the methods of the *ISecurityProperty* interface implemented by its context object, the results are as follows:

- *ISecurityProperty::GetDirectCallerSID* returns User C.

- *ISecurityProperty::GetDirectCreatorSID* returns User C.

- *ISecurityProperty::GetOriginalCallerSID* returns User B.

- *ISecurityProperty::GetOriginalCreatorSID* returns User A.

Note that MTS doesn't support an impersonation model, whereby Object X can impersonate User B's security credential when accessing Object Y. Instead, security is simplified by the role-based security model. A role can be defined that allows Object X to access the services of Object Y.

Error Handling

In an ideal world, servers would never fail—or if they did, they would fail in a big way. Believe it or not, it is often better to have a big, dramatic, and immediate system failure instead of having a smaller failure go undetected for some time. Undetected failures usually bring the system down eventually and might also leave a trail of corrupted data spanning hours or days before the failure brought down the system or was otherwise detected. To combat this problem, MTS does extensive internal integrity and consistency checking to ensure that all components are working properly.

If an error in an internal MTS structure is detected, MTS immediately terminates that process. That technique facilitates fault containment and reduces the likelihood that an error will go undetected, leading to a more reliable and robust system. As part of its error-handling mechanism, MTS objects are not permitted to propagate exceptions outside of the object. Unhandled exceptions are trapped by MTS, and the process is terminated. This is done because MTS assumes that an unhandled exception has left the object in an indeterminate and possibly unsafe state.

MTS doesn't typically modify the *HRESULT* value a method of an MTS object returns. One exception to this rule is when the method returns either the *S_OK* or *S_FALSE* value to the caller. In such a case, MTS might change the value returned to the client into an MTS error code. For example, suppose a method of an object calls *SetComplete* to commit a transaction, but for some reason DTC can't commit the transaction and must abort it. MTS will convert the *HRESULT* of the method to *CONTEXT_E_ABORTED* and set all of the method's outbound parameters to *Null*.

Registering Components with MTS

To register a component for execution with MTS, you launch the MTS Explorer and create a new package. An MTS package defines a group of components, identified by a globally unique identifier (GUID), that will be launched in a single server process. The MTS Explorer will prompt you for the name of the package and the Windows NT security account under which it will execute. You can specify the interactive user or a particular user account under which the package should always execute. You can also specify whether the package of components will run in a server process (called a server package), which is the default, or in a client process (called a library package). We don't recommend MTS components that run directly in the client process because they lose the component tracking, role-based security, and process isolation features of MTS.

Once you have created a package, you can add in-process components. The MTS Explorer allows the administrator to choose from components already listed in the Windows Registry, or from components that are present in the directory structure. When you select an unregistered component, the MTS Explorer loads it and then calls its *DllRegisterServer* function to invoke its self-registration routine. At this stage, you can set the transactional attribute of the component. When a component is registered within the MTS environment, MTS clears the component's InprocServer32 registry key and creates a LocalServer32 key. The LocalServer32 registry key points to the MTS surrogate and passes the package identifier as a command-line parameter; for example:

```
C:\WINNT\SYSTEM32\mtx.exe /p:{C300DE46-56AD-11D1-A6FC-0000C0CC7BE1}
```

New roles are also defined within an MTS package. A role can be mapped to one or more users, user groups, or both, and then that role added to a component within the package. This enforces the declarative security model of MTS. A Visual Basic or VBScript program can automate the configuration of all these settings through the Automation interface MTS exposes.

Chapter 12

Internet Information Server

Microsoft Internet Information Server (IIS) is a full-featured Internet server that comes with Microsoft Windows NT Server. You can use it to serve as a local intranet server or, when it is connected to the Internet, as a true Internet host. IIS is easily scalable from a single-server site to large multiple-server installations. For example, Microsoft's Web site (*http://www.microsoft.com*), one of the busiest Web sites on the Internet today, uses multiple servers running Internet Information Server.

IIS supports two popular Internet protocols: HTTP (Hypertext Transfer Protocol) and FTP (File Transfer Protocol). Support for each protocol is implemented by IIS as a separate Microsoft Windows NT service.[1] The Microsoft Internet Service Manager (shown in Figure 12-1 on the following page) is the main utility you use to administer IIS, although you can also administer it remotely over the Internet.

Although FTP is a useful and important protocol, there are not many interesting aspects of this service to discuss. Most FTP clients simply connect to the appropriate server, upload or download files, and then disconnect. The HTTP protocol, on the other hand, drives the World Wide Web. You can think of the Web as another type of client/server technology that uses the Internet as its

---

1. A Windows NT service is a type of background process that doesn't display a user interface.

medium. A Web browser (the client) connects to a Web server to exchange data. A typical exchange on the Web consists of the browser asking the server for a particular HTML file, the server providing it, and then the browser rendering the HTML data on the user's computer.

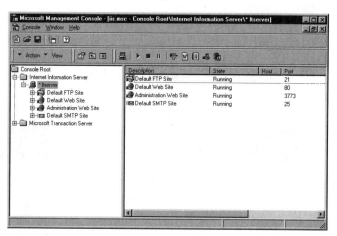

Figure 12-1. *The Microsoft Internet Service Manager.*

HTTP makes Web publishing easy, and it is perhaps one of the reasons the Web has become so popular. To publish a Web page, you simply create some data files in HTML format and then add them to the appropriate home directory on a server. To publish files using IIS, you place the files in the wwwroot folder; the server will automatically provide the files to any Web browser when requested by a URL such as *http://example.microsoft.com/home.htm*.

THE EVOLUTION OF WEB CONTENT

Historically (in Web terms, this means within the last two years), the job of Web servers was to offer up HTML files as requested by Web browsers. Most of the processing power of a server was devoted to responding to the relatively simple HTTP protocol by sending HTML data when requested. Under this model, because each client used very little of the server's processing power, a single Web server could support thousands of clients. However, this model restricted Web servers to a drab existence as large, read-only, shared file systems.

This situation was acceptable so long as most of the content on the Web consisted of boring, static HTML files with a few graphics thrown in for good measure. As the Web has increased in popularity, and Web sites have had to compete for users' affections, developers have been searching for ways to make content more compelling, engaging, dynamic, and interactive than is possible with plain vanilla HTML.

The aspiration to develop Web applications has led developers in many different directions. Sun Microsystems has decided that its Java programming language—originally developed for programming VCRs and toasters—would be perfect for the Web. Netscape has developed JavaScript as a simple, interpreted scripting language that can be embedded directly in HTML documents. Microsoft (not a company that likes to be left out) has decided that what the Web really needs is ActiveX controls, Active documents, Authenticode, VBScript, and the Java Just-In-Time (JIT) compiler that is built into Microsoft Internet Explorer. All of these technologies are much less divergent than they might seem initially. In fact, they all share one crucial attribute: the code you write executes on the client, usually within a Web browser. The Web server isn't involved with your code in any way, other than perhaps in downloading the code to the client.

Why do Java applets, JavaScript, ActiveX controls, Active documents, and VBScript code all execute on the user's computer? After all, to run code on the user's computer your code must be able to be downloaded to the user's computer, which is a major headache considering the slow telephone lines that most people use to access the Internet. In addition, downloading code brings with it the inherent risk of dangerous code roaming free in the user's computer. Added to these problems is the fact that the Web browser might be running on the Microsoft Windows, Solaris, Macintosh, MS-DOS, or OS/2 operating system. If the user's Web browser doesn't support ActiveX controls, Java applets, VBScript, or some other technology, code that depends on these technologies won't work.

Various initiatives have been taken to address some of these issues. For example, to reduce download speeds Microsoft is attempting to make ActiveX controls as small as possible (p-code is starting to look pretty good) and is packaging controls in compressed cabinet files. To allay security fears, Microsoft has developed the Authenticode code-signing technology we examined in Chapter 8. On the cross-platform front, Java code is intended to be platform independent, meaning that a Java applet will run in a Java-enabled browser regardless of the user's hardware and software platform. For its part, Microsoft has yielded control of COM and ActiveX to an industry consortium called The Open Group to encourage the widespread adoption of COM and ActiveX on many platforms. But none of these Band-Aids changes the basic fact that the code is downloaded and runs on the user's computer.

To understand why most interactive Web development efforts have focused on the Web client, you have to go back to the roots of the Web. The Web was originally based on HTML; Web servers would simply send the documents to the browser to be displayed appropriately. To make the Web more interesting, features that incorporate graphics and audio have been added. Most of these improvements have by default focused on the client-side browser. The client side has been where the most compelling interactive media programming can be done.

To be sure, executing code on the client has several major advantages: it doesn't require much server processing power; code executing on the user's computer doesn't have to wait aeons for a response from the server; and the less work the server needs to do for each client, the more clients it can serve. ActiveX controls, for example, provide a high degree of interactivity on the client side without requiring any work of the server. However, having an intelligent, programmable Web server would open entirely new vistas on the Internet. This technology is now available, and with it, Web sites can achieve an unprecedented level of dynamic, interactive content, and enable you to develop true custom Web applications.

ACTIVATING THE SERVER

Our goal is to use code to activate the Web server. Let's consider the advantages to be gained by executing code on the server. First, code executing on the server doesn't suffer from many of the problems that plague code running on the client. Download times, for example, are no longer a factor since the code never travels to the client. Second, executing code on the server has the pleasant side effect of removing security concerns. Because the code is put on the server by an administrator and never travels to the browser, it can do the user no harm. Third, browser compatibility is less of a concern because much of the work is now being done on the server. Fourth, you can normally exercise a great deal more control over the server platform than over the clients' platforms. (However, if you are developing a custom intranet application, you probably have control over, or at least have knowledge of, the clients' platforms as well.)

Now let's consider the disadvantages to executing code on the server. First, code that executes on the server requires a lot of the server's processing power. For example, in the past most server-side code was implemented as executable processes using Common Gateway Interface (CGI) script on UNIX machines. This was problematic because each time a client connected to the server, the server had to launch another copy of the CGI process. As more users connected, the server quickly slowed to a crawl. Second, server-side code is not very good at providing immediate responses to the client. It's hard to imagine implementing a scribble-style applet using code on the server. Client-side interactivity of that sort generally requires that code run on the client. In the final analysis, most sophisticated Web sites use a combination of client-side code and server-side code.

You might find it helpful to compare a Web server with an SQL server. Most people think of an SQL server as a back-end database server; few people would think to use an SQL server without a custom front-end application. You can think of a Web server as the base upon which you can build and publish highly interactive Internet or intranet applications. Part of the application can be the front-end interface that users see in a Web browser, and the other part can be the back end that runs on the Web server. Figure 12-2 shows conceptually what we would like to achieve. In this figure, Web browsers connect to the server, where custom application code resides and executes.

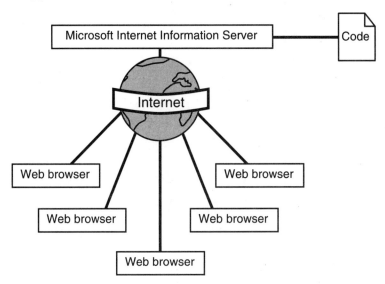

Figure 12-2. *A Web server system with browsers connected.*

What Can Code on the Server Do?

Quite simply, code on the server can do anything you want it to, with one exception: code on the server can't display a visual user interface, because the user may be halfway around the world. As a result, the only thing left for the server-side code to do is to work with data. Server-side code typically falls into one of two categories: database or computation. The code can read and write data to a database, or it can number-crunch the data.

For example, you might use server-side code to keep data on a Web site current. If your Web site consists of static HTML files, those files will be only as up to date as you can keep them by updating them manually. In contrast, if the data displayed in your Web site comes from a database server, the data always remains current. That type of functionality is nearly impossible to implement using the client-side technologies we've discussed previously.

How Do I Put Code on the Server and How Do Clients Interact with the Code?

The code you put on the server can be in several formats. You can package compiled code in an .EXE or .DLL file; or you can create interpreted scripts using languages such as PERL (Practical Extraction and Report Language), VBScript,

JavaScript, or even simple DOS batch files (.BAT or .CMD files). It is up to the administrator of each Web server to decide what type of code the server supports, if any. If your server-side code doesn't require data from the user, the simplest way to execute code on the server is to create an anchor in the HTML file that links to your code. When the user clicks on that anchor, the code on the server executes. An HTML anchor that links to an application that doesn't require input from the user might look like the following example, in which *Scripts* is the virtual directory for interactive applications:

```
<A HREF="http://example.microsoft.com/scripts/test.exe"><IMG
SRC="/gifs/run_me.gif" WIDTH=103 HEIGHT=21 ALT="Run Me"BORDER=0></A>
```

If your server-side code does require input from the user, you can use a form to collect the data from the user. A Web browser collects information by presenting a Web page that contains a form. The form consists of items such as text boxes, menus, and check boxes that the user fills in or selects. When the user clicks a command button to submit the form, the data from the form can be e-mailed to a particular address or sent to the Web server for processing. When the data goes to a server, the server can pass the data to a script or application to be processed.

You can build data entry forms quite easily using HTML. HTML forms are collections of input fields that enable the user to enter data into a Web page. Figure 12-3 shows how an HTML form looks when displayed by Internet Explorer. The form was created using this HTML code:

```
<HTML>
<HEAD><TITLE>Questionnaire</TITLE></HEAD>
<BODY>
<H2>Sample Questionnaire</H2><P>
Please fill out the following questionnaire:
<FORM METHOD="POST" ACTION="scripts/quest.idc"><P>
First Name: <INPUT NAME="fname"><P>
Last Name: <INPUT NAME="lname"><P>
Gender: <INPUT NAME="gender" TYPE=RADIO VALUE="male">Male
        <INPUT NAME="gender" TYPE=RADIO VALUE="female">Female
<P>Thank you for responding to this questionnaire.<P>
<INPUT TYPE=SUBMIT>
</FORM>
</BODY>
</HTML>
```

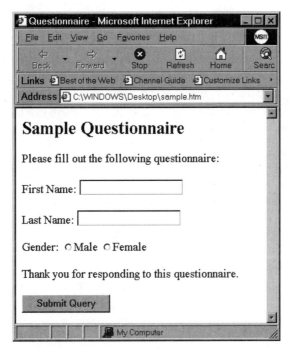

Figure 12-3. *An HTML form in Internet Explorer.*

How Do Clients Get Results
Back from Code on the Server?

If you create a server-side application that needs to return data to the user, your options are limited. Your application must return data in a format the user's browser will understand, which, generally speaking, means HTML. Thus, most server-side applications that need to return data to the user must dynamically generate HTML documents and return them to the user. Creating dynamic HTML documents in response to a user request can be quite arduous.

PUTTING INTERACTIVE CODE
ON INTERNET INFORMATION SERVER

Now that you are aware of the possibilities offered by running code on a Web server, and you have some background knowledge of IIS, you might be wondering whether IIS supports server-side code. Internet Information Server supports two interfaces for creating server-side applications: the Common Gateway Interface and the Internet Server Application Programming Interface (ISAPI).

Common Gateway Interface

CGI is a specification for passing information between a Web browser, a Web server, and a CGI-compliant application. CGI is not a language; it's a standard for how a Web server interacts with server-side applications. Although many CGI-compliant applications are written in PERL, a predominant scripting language on UNIX systems, you can write programs in other languages, such as C or C++, as well. IIS supports most 32-bit applications that run on Windows NT and conform to the CGI specification.

A Web browser interacts with an application created for a CGI environment in a fashion that is typical for a Web application. First, the Web browser displays an HTML form that enables the user to enter data. The browser posts this data to the Web server with a request to call a particular server application. The Web server then calls the specified program, using environment variables to make the user's data available. At this point, the application runs, acquiring the user's data from the environment variables provided by the Web server. When the application is finished processing data, it can generate a dynamic HTML page to provide results. The Web server will then return this HTML file to the user's browser. Figure 12-4 illustrates how a browser, a server, and an application written for a CGI environment exchange information using CGI.

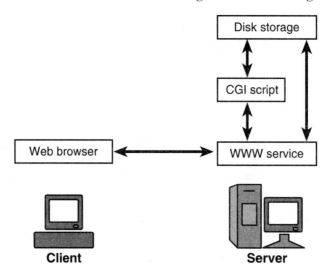

Figure 12-4. *Information exchange between a browser, a server, and an application utilizing CGI.*

Programs written for CGI environments always run in a separate process on the server. The overhead inherent in running such programs is quite high because a separate process address space must be created for each client. That limits the number of concurrent client connections that the server can support. For example, if 50 clients log in to execute the same program, the Web server must launch 50 separate processes. Because of some of those limitations, Microsoft decided that CGI was not a good long-term solution for calling server-side code. As a replacement, Microsoft developed ISAPI.

Internet Server Application Programming Interface

IIS includes ISAPI, which is both an applications programming interface (API) and an interface to IIS. Applications that use ISAPI are compiled as DLLs and loaded by the Web service at service startup. Compared to scripts written for CGI, ISAPI-compliant applications perform much better and require less overhead. Since ISAPI DLLs run in-process with IIS, each user request does not spawn a separate process.

There are two models for ISAPI applications: *filters* and *extensions*. ISAPI filters allow the server to preprocess client requests and post-process responses by using disk storage, as shown in Figure 12-5. This permits Web site–specific handling of HTTP requests and responses.

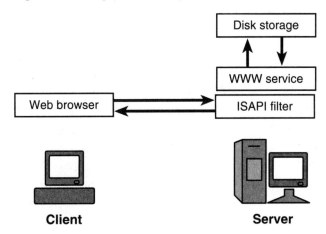

Figure 12-5. *An ISAPI filter model.*

ISAPI extensions are more interesting because you can use them to write custom applications that users activate by clicking a link in an HTML page on your Web site. After a user has filled out your HTML form and clicked the link, the ISAPI extension can take the user-supplied information and do almost anything with it that a program can do, as shown in Figure 12-6 on the following page. The server returns the program results to the client in the form of a dynamically generated HTML document. You can also create complex programs that act as both ISAPI filters and extensions.

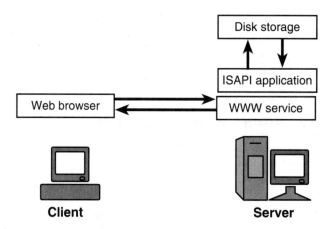

Figure 12-6. *An ISAPI extension model.*

ISAPI extensions can be written only in C and C++ because they require you to export functions directly from the DLL, which is a capability not available in Microsoft Visual Basic. Visual Basic is able to create DLLs, but the DLLs produced by Visual Basic are in-process COM components and can't directly export functions. Visual Basic developers can achieve this functionality by using Active Server Pages (ASP), which are built on top of ISAPI. ASP is discussed later in this chapter.

Internet Database Connector

It is generally best to use client-side code to display graphics and employ interactive features. Developers most often use server-side code to connect to a database. To assist Web developers in creating sites with database access, Microsoft built an ISAPI extension called the Internet Database Connector (IDC), which ships with IIS. IDC (HTTPODBC.DLL) uses the Open Database Connectivity (ODBC) standard to access databases. Conceptually, IDC performs database access as shown in Figure 12-7.

In that model, the application is your Web site. Based on the user's actions, your application makes requests of the Web server, which in turn calls IDC. IDC then calls the ODBC API. IDC simply acts as the go-between for IIS and ODBC. Figure 12-8 on page 340 shows the components for connecting to databases from IIS using IDC.

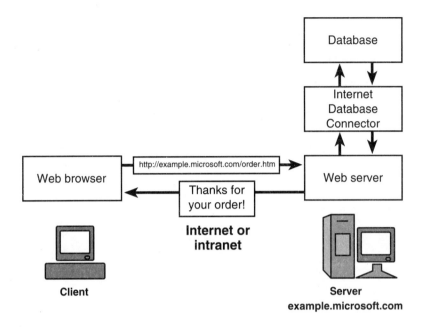

Figure 12-7. *Database flow on a server accessed by a Web browser.*

Using IDC, you can do the following from your Web site:

- Create Web pages with information contained in a database.

- Insert, update, and delete information in the database, based on user input from a Web page.

- Perform other Structured Query Language (SQL) commands.

You can access all of this functionality without having to do any real programming. IDC uses .IDC files to control how ODBC accesses the database and HTML extension (.HTX) files to control how IDC constructs the output Web page. An .IDC file contains the information necessary for the ODBC driver manager to connect to the appropriate ODBC data source and execute the SQL code. An .IDC file also contains the name and location of the .HTX file. The .HTX file is the template for the HTML document that the server returns to the Web browser after the IDC has merged the database information into the .HTX file.

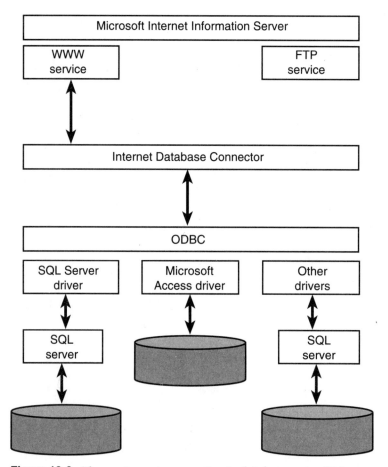

Figure 12-8. *The components connecting to databases using IDC.*

Exercise 12-1

In this exercise, you will create an HTML document that contains a form. Users can enter the names of people they want to search for, and the data is then passed to an .IDC file that executes an SQL query using ODBC. The data returned from the query is then merged into an .HTX file to be returned to the user's Web browser.

> **NOTE** This exercise assumes you have Windows NT Server, Internet Information Server, and Microsoft SQL Server installed on the same computer. If your software or configuration differs, you might need to adjust the steps to match your environment.

1. On the server, use the ODBC icon in the Control Panel to create a data source name (DSN) of Web SQL. The DSN setup dialog box should look like Figure 12-9.

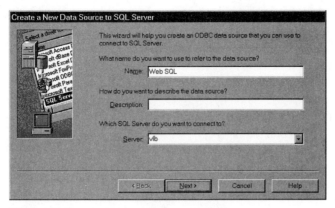

Figure 12-9. *The SQL server setup dialog box.*

2.   Create a file named FINDME.HTM in the C:\InetPub\wwwroot folder.
     Enter the following HTML code into FINDME.HTM:

```
<HTML>
<HEAD><TITLE>Find Me</TITLE></HEAD>
<BODY>
<H2>Find Me</H2><P>
Please enter a name to search for:
<FORM METHOD="POST" ACTION="scripts/findme.idc"><P>
First Name: <INPUT NAME="fname"><P>
Last Name: <INPUT NAME="lname"><P>
<INPUT TYPE=SUBMIT>
</FORM>
</BODY>
</HTML>
```

3.   In the C:\InetPub\scripts folder, create a file named FINDME.IDC
     that contains the following commands. The *%fname%* and *%lname%*
     entries in the SQL query reference the data fields in the preceding
     HTML form. IDC recognizes the two percent signs (%%) following
     the *fname* and *lname* fields as escape codes that it interprets as a
     single percent sign, which is the SQL wildcard character.

     NOTE   Place the .IDC and .HTX files in the C:\InetPub\scripts directory
     or in some other directory that has execute permission.

```
Datasource: Web SQL
Username: sa
Template: findme.htx
SQLStatement:
+SELECT *
+ from pubs.dbo.authors
+ where au_fname like '%fname%%%' and
+ au_lname like '%lname%%%'
```

4. IDC will merge the results of the SQL query in the .IDC file with the following .HTX file. In the C:\InetPub\scripts folder, create a file named FINDME.HTX that contains the following data:

```
<HTML>
<HEAD><TITLE>Find Me Results</TITLE></HEAD>
<BODY>
Query results:<P>
<%begindetail%>
<%au_fname%>, <%au_lname%>, <%phone%>, <%address%>,↵
  <%city%>, <%state%>, <%zip%><BR>
<%enddetail%>
</BODY>
</HTML>
```

5. Using a Web browser, open the FINDME.HTM document using the HTTP protocol, as in *http://myserver/findme.htm*. Enter the name of the person you want to search for, and then press the Submit button. Since the SQL query in the .IDC file uses the SQL wildcard character (%), simply entering a first or last name initial should turn up all people with that initial in the database. Leaving both fields blank and clicking the Submit button will return all the records in the database table.

Hopefully, this exercise has given you a feel for IDC. For more information on IDC, consult the IIS documentation. IDC is still supported, but it has been superseded by the far more powerful and easier-to-use ASP.

The Problems with ISAPI and IDC

When you use CGI or ISAPI, the Web browser can send an HTTP request to execute an application on the server rather than requesting a static HTML file. The server responds by running the program, which can receive user input from environment variables and input values—values that have been entered by the user into an HTML form, for example. When the server-side program is finished running, it normally generates output HTML that is then sent back to the client. In this fashion, you can add a measure of interactivity to your Web pages.

Both CGI and ISAPI have disadvantages, however. As discussed earlier in this chapter, programs that run in a CGI environment use an address space separate from the Web server, slowing things down considerably. ISAPI DLLs, on the other hand, need to be written in C or C++. Consequently, ISAPI DLLs are difficult to write and maintain, and the person or group in your organization responsible for creating HTML pages is probably not the same person or group that develops C or C++ code. This means that an organization using CGI or ISAPI often has two separate and substantially unrelated groups working to develop an interactive Web site. It also means that every time the group creating the HTML pages wants to change the interactive portion of the site, the server-side code needs to be modified too.

ACTIVE SERVER PAGES ARRIVES

ASP is a technology available in IIS that enables you to quickly and easily build interactive Web pages. This feat is accomplished by allowing the group developing the Web pages to include executable scripts directly in the HTML content. Including scripting code isn't a new idea; both VBScript and JavaScript have provided this capability for some time. The new feature that ASP provides is the ability to run the script on the Web server before the HTML is sent to the browser.

With ASP, HTML content creation and server-side code development become the same process, enabling you to focus directly on the look and feel of your Web pages and weave dynamic elements into your pages as appropriate. ASP also is easily extensible with COM components built in Microsoft Visual Basic, Microsoft Visual C++, Microsoft Visual J++, or any other language supporting the ActiveX standards. Figure 12-10 compares the ease of Web development for each platform—plain vanilla HTML, CGI, ISAPI DLLs, and ASP—with the level of interactivity that you can achieve for each platform.

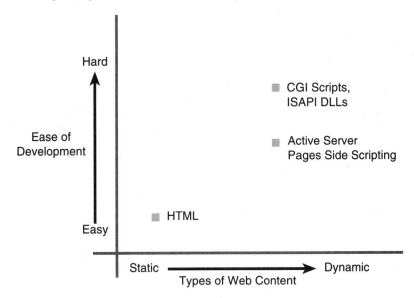

Figure 12-10. *Ease of development vs. richness of content in Web applications.*

A big advantage to using ASP to develop your Web applications is that it will work with any standard Web browser the client might be running. Since the code executes on the Web server, it generates and returns to the client only generic HTML. Thus, you don't need to worry whether a browser can process your pages. ASP is internally implemented as a combination ISAPI filter and ISAPI extension named ASP.DLL. It therefore provides all the advantages of in-process, server-side code execution, along with a quicker development cycle and easier code maintainability.

To execute an ASP page, the browser needs only to request an ASP page that is published on IIS. IIS then calls the ASP DLL, which reads through the file from top to bottom, executing commands as specified in your code, and then sends HTML content back to the browser. Figure 12-11 shows the ASP model.

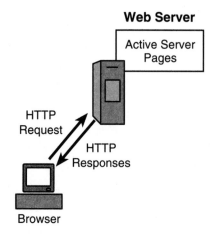

Figure 12-11. *Active Server Pages model.*

An .ASP file is the basic unit of an ASP application. An ASP-based application is defined as all the .ASP files in a virtual directory and its subdirectories. ASP files consist of ASCII text and contain standard HTML tags plus script commands. Thus, to create an .ASP file, you simply rename any HTML file by replacing the existing .HTM or .HTML filename extension with .ASP. IIS uses the .ASP extension to identify Active Server Pages. Anytime a browser requests a file from IIS that ends with the .ASP extension, IIS first passes the file to the ASP module for processing. In the case of a standard HTML file simply renamed as an .ASP file— the simplest type of .ASP file—the ASP module does no work since no special script commands are included. To begin developing interactive Web sites, you need to add scripts to your HTML file.

ASP is not a scripting language. Rather, ASP provides an environment in which you can run script code from your HTML pages. Script code can be written in any language for which an ActiveX Scripting engine is available. Currently

ASP ships with ActiveX Scripting engines for VBScript and JavaScript, both of which you can use to develop code that runs on the server. In Chapter 8, we used VBScript and JavaScript code in HTML pages similar to the following one:

```
<HTML>
<HEAD><TITLE>VBScript Web Page</TITLE></HEAD>

<SCRIPT LANGUAGE=VBScript>
    Document.Write "Hello World!"
</SCRIPT>

<BODY>
<BR><B>This is a basic HTML document.</B>
</BODY>
</HTML>
```

By default, the user's machine will execute the script code within Microsoft Internet Explorer. Using ASP, we can supply the RUNAT attribute with the <SCRIPT> tag to specify that we want the script to execute on the Web server before the HTML is sent to the client:

```
<SCRIPT LANGUAGE=VBScript RUNAT=Server>
    MsgBox "Hello World!"
</SCRIPT>
```

This code explicitly states that we want the code to execute on the server. As a shortcut, ASP defines the special delimiters <% and %> to be equivalent to the *SCRIPT LANGUAGE=VBScript RUNAT=Server* statement. For example, the following code is identical to the slightly more verbose code shown previously:

```
<% MsgBox "Hello World!" %>
```

But what if you want to use JavaScript? It is possible to change the default scripting language for the delimiters <% and %> by using a special command at the beginning of an .ASP file. The syntax for setting the default scripting language to JavaScript, for example, is *<%@ LANGUAGE=JavaScript %>*. The *<%@ LANGUAGE=JavaScript %>* command must be the very first statement in the .ASP file, as follows:

```
<%@ LANGUAGE=JavaScript %>
<HTML>
<% // Server-side JavaScript code here %>
</HTML>
```

There is one little problem with all the preceding code. Since this code will execute on the server, the *MsgBox* statement should appear on the server. Of course, this wouldn't be very informative to a user who might well be several thousand miles away. For this reason, server-side code isn't permitted to display user interface elements on the server; therefore, ASP doesn't support statements such as VBScript's *MsgBox*. The following sample code is recognized as server-side VBScript. Pay particular attention to the way the server-side script code is interwoven with standard HTML.

```
<% If Time >= #12:00:00 AM# And Time < #12:00:00 PM# Then %>
    Good Morning
<% Else %>
    Hello
<% End If %>
```

In this example, the Web server sends the HTML text "Good Morning" or "Hello," depending on whether the time is before noon or after noon. The code uses the VBScript run-time function *Time* to retrieve the current time. The preceding sample code has a little defect that might not be immediately apparent: since the code executes on the server, the server's time is used. Therefore, if the server is in Los Angeles and the user in London, the user will be greeted with "Good Morning" until 8 p.m. London time.

This type of code would perhaps be better written as a client-side script so that it would use the user's time. Remember that using a server-side script in a Web page doesn't preclude using client-side script in the same page. You can still declare code using the <SCRIPT> tag, omitting the *RUNAT=Server* attribute so that the code will be sent to the client's Web browser for execution as part of the HTML page.

Exercise 12-2

One really interesting feature of ASP is that, since the script code executes on the server, the script code is stripped out of the HTML before the page is sent to the client. In the following exercise, you will build a simple .ASP file that displays that behavior.

> **NOTE** If you will be using Notepad to create .ASP files, here's a tip: in the Save As dialog box, be sure to set the Save As Type box to All Files (*.*). If you leave the default setting of Text Documents, the file extension .TXT is added to whatever name is given. So, if you type *Myfile.asp* in the File Name box, the saved file is actually named Myfile.asp.txt.

1. Using a text editor such as Notepad, create a file named HELLO.HTM that contains the following code:

   ```
   <HTML>
   <FONT SIZE=7>Hello World!<BR></FONT>
   </HTML>
   ```

2. Publish HELLO.HTM on your Web server. If you are using IIS or Peer Web Services, this will be in the directory C:\InetPub\wwwroot. If you are using Personal Web Server, this will be in the directory C:\WebShare\wwwroot.

3. Using Internet Explorer, open HELLO.HTM using a URL such as *http://myserver/hello.htm*. The text *Hello World!* should be displayed.

4. In Internet Explorer, choose Source from the View menu and verify that you see the HTML text as you entered it. Close the HTML code.

5. Now, let's modify HELLO.HTM so that it includes some server-side script code. On the server, modify the code so that it looks like the following and then save it with the name HELLO.ASP. (The boldface text indicates the changes.)

```
<HTML>
<% For Count = 1 To 7 %>
<FONT SIZE = <% = Count %> >
Hello World!<BR>
</FONT>
<% Next %>
</HTML>
```

You now need to ensure that the Web server you are using has execute permission set for the directory where the .ASP file is located.

6. If you are using IIS or Peer Web Services, run the Internet Service Manager on the server. Select Default Web Site, and then choose the Properties button. Now select the Home Directory tab and set the Execute permission. Choose OK, and close the Internet Service Manager.

   OR

   If you are using Personal Web Server, open the Personal Web Manager and click the Advanced icon. Select <Home>, and then choose the Edit Properties button. Check the Execute item, and choose OK. Finally, close the Personal Web Manager.

7. On the client, use Internet Explorer to activate *http://myserver/hello.asp*. It should look like Figure 12-12 on the following page.

Figure 12-12. *The HELLO.ASP page in Internet Explorer.*

8. In Internet Explorer, choose Source from the View menu. You might be surprised to see that your ASP page has metamorphosed into the following HTML code. No scripting code is anywhere to be seen.

```
<HTML>

<FONT SIZE=1>
Hello World!<BR>
</FONT>

<FONT SIZE=2>
Hello World!<BR>
</FONT>

<FONT SIZE=3>
Hello World!<BR>
</FONT>

<FONT SIZE=4>
Hello World!<BR>
</FONT>

<FONT SIZE=5>
Hello World!<BR>
</FONT>

<FONT SIZE=6>
Hello World!<BR>
</FONT>
```

```
<FONT SIZE=7>
Hello World!<BR>
</FONT>

</HTML>
```

In this exercise, you have seen how basic ASP works. You run the .ASP file on the server, and the resulting HTML is returned to the Web browser. The browser itself never sees the server-side code that was executed. In this way, your source code is protected because only the results of your program can be seen on the client.

THE BUILT-IN OBJECTS

You have seen the basics of creating a simple .ASP file, but you might be wondering how you can use this to create sophisticated Web applications that interact with the user. To help you create really dynamic and exciting Web content, the ASP framework provides five built-in objects: *Application, Request, Response, Server,* and *Session.* These objects are sometimes called the intrinsic objects because they are always available to scripting code in an .ASP file; you do not need to create them before you can use them.

The *Application* Object

You can use the *Application* object to share information among all users of a given application. To store information in the *Application* object, you simply assign values to variable names, as follows:

```
<%
Application("Greeting") = "Welcome to my Web page"
Application("Number") = 5
%>
```

This script code declares the variables Greeting and Number, which will now be available throughout the application in which they are declared and can be modified at any time. Because the *Application* object can be shared by more than one user, the *Lock* and *Unlock* methods are provided to ensure that multiple users do not try to alter a property simultaneously.

Exercise 12-3

This exercise implements a site counter that displays the total number of times a particular page has been visited by all users.

1. Modify the HELLO.ASP file from Exercise 12-2, adding the code shown in bold on the following page.

```
<HTML>
<% For Count = 1 To 7 %>
<FONT SIZE = <% = Count %> >
Hello World!<BR>
</FONT>
<% Next %>
<%
Application.Lock
Application("NumberOfHits") = ⌐
  Application("NumberOfHits") + 1
Application.Unlock
%>
This site has been visited
<% = Application("NumberOfHits") %>
times!
</HTML>
```

2. On the client, point Internet Explorer to *http://myserver/hello.asp*. Click the Refresh button in Internet Explorer to reload the page and increment the site counter.

    This example uses the application variable NumberOfHits to store the number of times that the page has been accessed. The *Lock* method is called to ensure that only the current client can access or alter *NumberOfHits*. Calling the *Unlock* method then enables other users to access the *Application* object.

The *Request* Object

You can use the *Request* object to retrieve the values that the client browser passed to the server during an HTTP request. This is probably the object you will become most familiar with as you begin to work with ASP. The *Request* object enables access to client data by means of one of its five collections: *Form*, *QueryString*, *Cookies*, *ClientCertificate*, or *ServerVariables*. These collections are described in the following table.

Collection	Description
Form	The values of form elements in the HTTP request body
QueryString	The values of variables in the HTTP query string
Cookies	The values of fields stored in the HTTP request
ClientCertificate	The values of fields stored in the client certificate that is sent in the HTTP request
ServerVariables	The values of predetermined environment variables

One of the most common uses of the *Request* object is to retrieve data a user has entered into an HTML form. The *Request* object exposes HTML form fields as properties of the *Form* collection. For example, the following HTML form provides a name field for the user to enter his or her name:

```
<FORM METHOD=POST Action=name.asp>
Name: <INPUT NAME=MyName SIZE=30>
</FORM>
```

This information can then be retrieved in an .ASP file on the server using the *Request* object as follows:

```
<% = Request.Form("MyName") %>
```

Notice that the name (MyName) coincides with the NAME attribute used in the HTML <INPUT> tag. As a shortcut, the *Request* object also allows you to skip the collection name, as follows:

```
<% = Request("MyName") %>
```

The *Response* Object

You can use the *Response* object to send output to the client, usually to store cookies on the user's machine using the *Cookies* collection. Since HTTP was designed to be a stateless protocol, it is difficult to keep track of users. As you might know, cookies are packets of data that the Web server passes to the browser. The browser stores this information on the user's machine, often in a file, and makes it available to servers on request. Internet Explorer stores cookies in the C:\Windows\Cookies folder. If you want to see cookies as they are received, choose Internet Options from the View menu in Internet Explorer and then choose the Advanced tab. In the Security section, select the *Prompt before accepting cookies* option, and choose OK. Now go to any Web site that dispenses cookies, such as *http://www.microsoft.com*. If you haven't received these cookies before, you will see a warning that looks like the one shown in Figure 12-13.

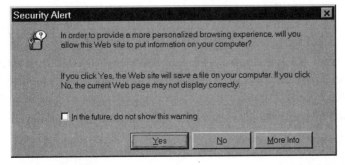

Figure 12-13. *The warning that you're about to receive a cookie.*

Cookies are often used to customize a page according to user preferences. For example, some news services keep track of the type of news a user prefers (international, regional, business, and so on) in a cookie. Whenever you visit such a site, the server asks for the cookie and immediately knows a little bit about you. The following script creates a cookie:

```
<% Response.Cookies("FavoriteNews") = "Sports" %>
```

When executing this command, the server will generate a special HTTP header that it will send to the client Web browser:

```
Set-Cookie:FavoriteNews=Sports
```

The *Cookies* collection of the *Request* object can later be used to retrieve a cookie from the client, as follows:

```
Your favorite type of news is:
<% = Request.Cookies("FavoriteNews") %>
```

The *Server* Object

The *Server* object provides access to methods and properties on the server, most of which serve as utility functions. *CreateObject*, undoubtedly the most useful method of the *Server* object, works the same way the *CreateObject* function does in Visual Basic: it enables a program to instantiate a COM component. Since ASP executes on the server, the *CreateObject* method instantiates COM components on the server computer. The following code creates an instance of the ActiveX Data Objects (ADO) component's *Connection* object:

```
<% Set dbConnection = Server.CreateObject("ADODB.Connection")
```

The *Session* Object

You can use the *Session* object to store information needed for a particular user session. Variables stored in the *Session* object are not discarded when the user jumps between pages in the application; instead, *Session* object variables persist for the entire user session. The server automatically creates a *Session* object when a user who doesn't already have a session requests a Web page from the application. The server destroys the *Session* object when the session expires or is abandoned. One common use for the *Session* object is to store user preferences set on a previous visit to the Web application, such as graphics resolution (high, medium, or low). Note that the session state is maintained only for browsers that support cookies.

```
<%
Application("Name") = "Anna"
Application("Age") = 21
%>
```

Exercise 12-4

Many sophisticated Web sites need to collect information from visitors, either to fulfill an order or to keep demographic information for future marketing efforts. This exercise shows you how to use ASP to retrieve information from a user.

1.   Create a file named ORDER.HTM that contains the following HTML, and publish it on your Web server.

```
<HTML>
<HEAD><TITLE>Order Form</TITLE></HEAD>
<BODY>
Please give us some information, then click Submit.
<FORM METHOD=POST Action=response.asp>
First Name: <INPUT NAME=fname SIZE=25><P>
Last Name: <INPUT NAME=lname SIZE=25><P>
Title: <INPUT NAME=title TYPE=RADIO VALUE=mr>Mr.
<INPUT NAME=title TYPE=RADIO VALUE=ms>Ms.
<HR><INPUT TYPE=SUBMIT><INPUT TYPE=RESET>
</FORM>
</BODY>
</HTML>
```

2.   Create a file named RESPONSE.ASP containing the following HTML, and publish it in the same directory as ORDER.HTM on your Web server.

```
<HTML>
<HEAD><TITLE>Response Form</TITLE></HEAD>
<BODY>
<% Title = Request.Form("title")
LastName = Request.Form("lname")
If LastName = "" Then %>
    Invalid Data Entry!
<% Else %>
    Thanks for placing an order,
    <% If Title = "mr" Then %>
        Mr. <% = LastName %>.
    <% ElseIf Title = "ms" Then %>
        Ms. <% = LastName %>.
    <% Else %>
        <% = Request.Form("fname") & " " & LastName %>.
    <% End If
End If %>
</BODY>
</HTML>
```

3.   Using Internet Explorer, activate *http://myserver/order.htm*, enter some data, and then click the Submit button. Figure 12-14 on the following page shows the sample order form.

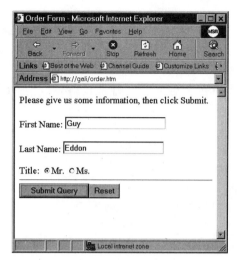

Figure 12-14. *A sample order form in Internet Explorer.*

The result will look like Figure 12-15.

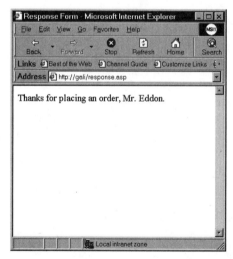

Figure 12-15. *The result of a submittal in Exercise 12-4.*

4. In Internet Explorer, choose Source from the View menu. You should see something like this:

```
<HTML>
<HEAD><TITLE>Response Form</TITLE></HEAD>
<BODY>
```

```
Thanks for placing an order,

    Mr. Eddon.

</BODY>
</HTML>
```

5. Compare the code entered in step 2 with the HTML the server returns after the processing is complete.

ADD-ON COMPONENTS

In addition to the five intrinsic objects we have already discussed, ASP ships with five add-on components. These components are not built into the ASP module itself; instead, they are provided as add-on DLLs with additional, higher-level functionality. The components provided are Ad Rotator, Browser Capabilities, Database Access, Content Linking, and File Access. These components enable you to create dynamic, interactive Web pages using these prebuilt server components in your scripts. These components support base functionality for common Web applications. This leaves plenty of room for third-party innovation (that's you). The opportunity for third-party developers who market COM components for use with ASP may be huge, perhaps as big as that for ActiveX controls.

The Ad Rotator Component

The Ad Rotator component (ADROT.DLL) automates the rotation of advertisement images on a Web page. Each time a user opens or reloads the Web page, the Ad Rotator component displays a new advertisement based on the information you specify in a schedule file. Ad Rotator also enables you to record how many users click each advertisement in an IIS activity log. The following .ASP file uses the Ad Rotator component to display a different advertisement each time a user views the page, based on information in the myads.txt file:

```
<% Set ad = Server.CreateObject("MSWC.AdRotator") %>
<% = ad.GetAdvertisement("myads.txt") %>
```

The *GetAdvertisement* method retrieves a different ad from the ad rotation file specified. The ad rotation file contains the URLs of the different advertisements to be displayed, along with information about how often the various ads should be shown. For the exact format of the ad rotation file, refer to the ASP documentation. A simple ad rotation file, myads.txt, used in the previous code snippet might look like the code on the following page.

```
*
http://MyServer/bed.gif
Francesco's Bed and Breakfast
75
http://MyServer/shrink.gif
Aya's Psychiatric Practice
95
```

The Browser Capabilities Component

Not all browsers support the rapidly expanding array of features available in the hypermedia world. Frames, tables, sounds, Java applets, and ActiveX controls are examples of features that some browsers support and others do not. To present content in a format appropriate for the capabilities of specific browsers, you first need to know what browser the user has and what its capabilities are. The Browser Capabilities component (BROWSCAP.DLL) provides your scripts with the name of the client's Web browser and a description of its capabilities.

When a browser connects to the Web server, it automatically sends an HTTP header. This header is an ASCII string that identifies the browser and its version number. The Browser Capabilities component compares this header to entries in the BROWSCAP.INI file, a text file provided by the Browser Capabilities component that contains entries for each known browser type and its capabilities. For example, the basic entry for Internet Explorer looks like the following:

```
[IE 4.0]
browser=IE
Version=4.0
majorver=4
minorver=0
frames=TRUE
tables=TRUE
cookies=TRUE
backgroundsounds=TRUE
vbscript=TRUE
javascript=TRUE
javaapplets=TRUE
ActiveXControls=TRUE
Win16=False
beta=False
AK=False
SK=False
AOL=False
crawler=False
cdf=True
```

There is even an entry in the BROWSCAP.INI file for the Microsoft Windows CE platform's Pocket Internet Explorer. You can add information about new browsers simply by updating the BROWSCAP.INI file. Microsoft also periodically releases updates to this file as new browsers become available.

Exercise 12-5

In this exercise, you will create an .ASP file that uses the Browser Capabilities component to display a page showing some of the capabilities of the current browser.

1. Create a file named BROWSECAPS.ASP that contains the following HTML, and publish it on your Web server.

```
<HTML>
<% Set bc = Server.CreateObject("MSWC.BrowserType") %>
Browser <% = bc.Browser %><BR>
Version <% = bc.Version %><BR>
Supports frames?
<% If bc.Frames = True Then %>
Yes <% Else %> No <% End If %><BR>
Supports tables?
<% If bc.Tables = True Then %>
Yes <% Else %> No <% End If %><BR>
Supports background sounds?
<% If bc.BackgroundSounds = True Then %>
Yes <% Else %> No <% End If %><BR>
Supports VBScript?
<% If bc.VBScript = True Then %>
Yes <% Else %> No <% End If %><BR>
Supports JavaScript?
<% If bc.JavaScript = True Then %>
Yes <% Else %> No <% End If %><BR>
</HTML>
```

2. Using Internet Explorer, activate *http://myserver/browsecaps.asp*.

DATABASE ACCESS

Since many dynamic Web pages need access to corporate databases, Microsoft has provided a database access component for use with ASP—none other than ActiveX Data Objects, which was discussed in Chapter 10. Using the ADO component in an .ASP file is relatively straightforward. One limitation of ASP is the use of components' built-in constants. Constants such as *adLockOptimistic*, for example, which are immediately available to early-bound components in Visual Basic, can't be used in the late-bound script of an ASP page. To overcome this limitation for the ADO component, Microsoft has provided two include files that declare these constants for use with ASP: Adovbs.inc for use with VBScript ASP pages, and adojavas.inc for use with JavaScript ASP pages. These files are installed with ASP, and you will find them in the C:\InetPub\ASPSamp\Samples directory or the C:\WebShare\ASPSamp\Samples directory.

To use the ADO constants in your ASP files, you need to include the appropriate file by using a feature of IIS called Server-Side Includes (SSI), which you can use to insert information into a file prior to processing. ASP implements only the *#INCLUDE* preprocessing directive of this mechanism. You can use this directive to insert the content of another file into an .ASP file before ASP processes the .ASP file. Use the following syntax:

```
<!-- #INCLUDE VIRTUAL|FILE="filename" -->
```

In Exercise 12-6, we will use the ADO component from VBScript code and will therefore use an *include* statement like this:

```
<!-- #include virtual="/ASPSAMP/SAMPLES/ADOVBS.INC" -->
```

The Content Linking Component

The Content Linking component (NEXTLINK.DLL) manages a list of URLs so that you can treat the pages in your Web site like the pages in a book. You can use the Content Linking component to generate and automatically update navigational links to previous and subsequent Web pages. This is ideal for applications such as online newspapers and forum message listings. This component uses a special Content Linking List file that contains the list of linked Web pages. This list is stored on the Web server. The following .ASP file uses the Content Linking component to dynamically add next-page and previous-page buttons to an HTML file:

```
<% Set nl = Server.CreateObject("MSWC.NextLink") %>
<% If nl.GetListIndex("nextlink.txt") > -1 Then %>
<A HREF=" <% = nl.GetPreviousURL("nextlink.txt") %> " >
Previous Page</A><BR>
<% End If %>
<A HREF=" <% = nl.GetNextURL("nextlink.txt") %> " >
Next Page</A>
```

The Content Linking List file contains one line of text for each URL in the list. Each line ends in a carriage return, and a tab character separates each item on a line. The following sample Content Linking List file, named NEXTLINK.TXT, is for use with the preceding code. (Note that you must use a tab character to separate the page name from the description.)

```
CorpBack.htm       Corporate background information
Invest.htm         Shareholder relations page
Products.htm       Listing of current products
HotLinks.htm       Links to related sites
```

The File Access Component

Using VBScript's *FileSystemObject* and *Textstream* objects enables ASP to retrieve and modify information stored in files on the server. Since these objects are not strictly ASP components, they are not covered in this chapter. Consult the VBScript documentation for more information about the use of these objects.

Exercise 12-6

In this exercise, you will use the ADO component, discussed in Chapter 10, to build an interactive Web site that connects to a database.

1. Create a file named LISTALL.ASP that contains the following HTML, and publish it on your Web server.

```
<HTML>
<% Set dbConnection = ⇁
  Server.CreateObject("ADODB.Connection")
dbConnection.Open "DSN=MyDSN;UID=sa;PWD=;"
SQLQuery = "Select * From authors"
Set rs = dbConnection.Execute(SQLQuery)
Do Until rs.EOF %>
<% = rs.Fields("au_id") %>
<A HREF=moreinfo.asp?ssn=<% = rs.Fields("au_id") %> >
<% = rs.Fields("au_lname") & ", " & ⇁
  rs.Fields("au_fname") %>
</A><BR>
<% rs.MoveNext
Loop %>
</HTML>
```

2. Create a file named MOREINFO.ASP that contains the following HTML, and publish it on your Web server.

```
<HTML>
<% Set dbConnection = ⇁
  Server.CreateObject("ADODB.Connection")
dbConnection.Open "DSN=MyDSN;UID=sa;PWD=;" %>
<% SQLQuery = "Select * From authors where au_id = ⇁
  '" & Request.QueryString("ssn") & "'"
Set rs = dbConnection.Execute(SQLQuery) %>
Author
<% = rs.Fields("au_fname") & " " & ⇁
  rs.Fields("au_lname") %>, of<BR>
<% = rs.Fields("address") %><BR>
<% = rs.Fields("city") & ", " & rs.Fields("state") ⇁
  & " " & rs.Fields("zip") %><BR>
is currently
<% If rs.Fields("contract") = True Then %>
between books.
```

(continued)

```
<% Else %>
   employed.
<% End If %><P>
<% = rs.Fields("au_fname") %>
is the author of the following books:<BR>
<% SQLQuery = "Select au_id, title, ⤸
   titleauthor.title_id, ytd_sales, price from ⤸
   titleauthor, titles Where au_id = '" & ⤸
   Request.QueryString("ssn") & "' And titles.title_id ⤸
   = titleauthor.title_id"
Set rs = dbConnection.Execute(SQLQuery) %>
<% Do Until rs.EOF %>
   <I><% = rs.Fields("title") %></I>
   which has sold
   <% = rs.Fields("ytd_sales") %>
   copies this year for
   $<% = rs.Fields("price") %>
   each.<BR>
   <% rs.MoveNext %>
<% Loop %>
</HTML>
```

You will now set up a DSN to connect to your database.

3. Assuming you are using Internet Information Server or Peer Web Services, open the Control Panel.

4. Double-click the ODBC icon, and select the System DSN tab.

   Since Internet Information Server is implemented as a set of Windows NT services, data sources that you use with IIS need to be System DSNs.

5. Choose Add, select SQL Server, and then choose Finish.

6. Define a System DSN with the same name as that given for the data source in the .ASP file (MyDSN), referencing the Pubs database on your SQL Server. Choose OK twice, and then close the Control Panel.

7. Activate *http://myserver/listall.asp* in Internet Explorer. This gives you the ability to see the authors in the database and then learn more about them.

   NOTE   In the next part of this exercise, you will expand the application by adding a home page and by providing the ability to add new authors to the Pubs database by using the Web.

8. Create a file named PUBS.HTM that contains the following HTML, and publish it on your Web server.

```
<HTML>
<H2>Welcome to the Pubs database, accessible over →
    the Web</H2>
<BR>Click here to view all the records in the
<A HREF=listall.asp>authors</A> table <BR>
To add a new author, <A HREF=newauth.htm>click →
    here.</A><HR>
<!-- Later we will add searching here. -->
</HTML>
```

9. Create a file named NEWAUTH.HTM that contains the following HTML, and publish it on your Web server.

```
<HTML>
Fill out the form below.<P>
<FORM METHOD=POST Action=addauth.asp>
Social Security #: <INPUT NAME=ssn SIZE=20><BR>
Last Name: <INPUT NAME=lname SIZE=25>
First Name: <INPUT NAME=fname SIZE=25><BR>
Address: <INPUT NAME=address SIZE=50><BR>
City: <INPUT NAME=city SIZE=20>
State: <INPUT NAME=state SIZE=2>
Zip: <INPUT NAME=zip SIZE=9><BR>
<INPUT NAME=contract TYPE=CHECKBOX VALUE=ON>Contract<P>
<INPUT TYPE=SUBMIT><INPUT TYPE=RESET>
</FORM>
</HTML>
```

10. Create a file named ADDAUTH.ASP that contains the following HTML, and publish it on your Web server. Notice the use of the *include* statement and the *adLockOptimistic* constant, shown in boldface.

```
<!-- #include virtual="/ASPSAMP/SAMPLES/ADOVBS.INC" -->

<HTML>
<% Set rs = Server.CreateObject("ADODB.Recordset")
rs.ActiveConnection = "DSN=MyDSN;UID=sa;PWD=;"
rs.LockType = adLockOptimistic
rs.Open("Select * from authors")
rs.AddNew
rs.Fields("au_id") = Request.Form("ssn")
rs.Fields("au_lname") = Request.Form("lname")
rs.Fields("au_fname") = Request.Form("fname")
rs.Fields("address") = Request.Form("address")
rs.Fields("city") = Request.Form("city")
rs.Fields("state") = Request.Form("state")
rs.Fields("zip") = Request.Form("zip")
If Request.Form("contract") = "ON" Then
    rs.Fields("contract") = True
```

(continued)

```
Else
    rs.Fields("contract") = False
End If
rs.Update %>
<H3>The author
<% = Request.Form("lname") & ", " & _
   Request.Form("fname") & " " & _
   Request.Form("ssn") %>
has been added to the database.</H3>
</HTML>
```

11. Activate *http://myserver/pubs.htm*. You can now view and add authors. When adding authors to the database, you must fill out the ssn and zip fields properly due to table validation rules for the Pubs database.

    NOTE In the next part of this exercise, you will expand the application so that users can search for a particular author.

12. Modify the PUBS.HTM file by replacing the *<!-- Later we will add searching here. -->* comment with the HTML code below.

```
To search for an author, enter any information available
and click Submit.
<FORM METHOD=POST Action=findauth.asp>
Social Security #: <INPUT NAME=ssn SIZE=20><BR>
Last Name: <INPUT NAME=lname SIZE=25>
First Name: <INPUT NAME=fname SIZE=25><BR>
Address: <INPUT NAME=address SIZE=50><BR>
City: <INPUT NAME=city SIZE=20>
State: <INPUT NAME=state SIZE=2>
Zip: <INPUT NAME=zip SIZE=9><BR>
<INPUT NAME=contract TYPE=CHECKBOX VALUE=ON>Contract<P>
<INPUT TYPE=SUBMIT><INPUT TYPE=RESET>
</FORM>
```

13. Create a file named FINDAUTH.ASP that contains the following HTML, and publish it on your Web server.

```
<HTML>
Found the following authors matching your criteria:<P>
<% Set dbConnection = ⟶
   Server.CreateObject("ADODB.Connection")
dbConnection.Open "DSN=MyDSN;UID=sa;PWD=;"
SQLQuery = "Select * From authors Where au_id Like '" _
   & Request.Form("ssn") & _
   "%' And au_lname Like '" & Request.Form("lname") & _
   "%' And au_fname Like '" & Request.Form("fname") & _
   "%' And address Like '" & Request.Form("address") & _
   "%' And city Like '" & Request.Form("city") & _
   "%' And state Like '" & Request.Form("state") & _
```

```
    "%' And zip Like '" & Request.Form("zip") & _
    "%' And contract = "
If Request.Form("contract") = "ON" Then
    SQLQuery = SQLQuery + "0"
Else
    SQLQuery = SQLQuery + "1"
End If
Set rs = dbConnection.Execute(SQLQuery)
Do Until rs.EOF %>
<% = rs.Fields("au_id") %>
<% If rs.Fields("contract") = True Then %>
    Between books...
<% Else %>
    Employed.
<% End If %><BR>
<% = rs.Fields("au_lname") & ", " & _
    rs.Fields("au_fname") %>
<BR><% = rs.Fields("address") %><BR>
<% = rs.Fields("city") & ", " & rs.Fields("state") _
    & " " & rs.Fields("zip") %><P>
<% rs.MoveNext
Loop %>
</HTML>
```

14. Activate *http://myserver/pubs.htm*. You should see something like what is shown in Figure 12-16.

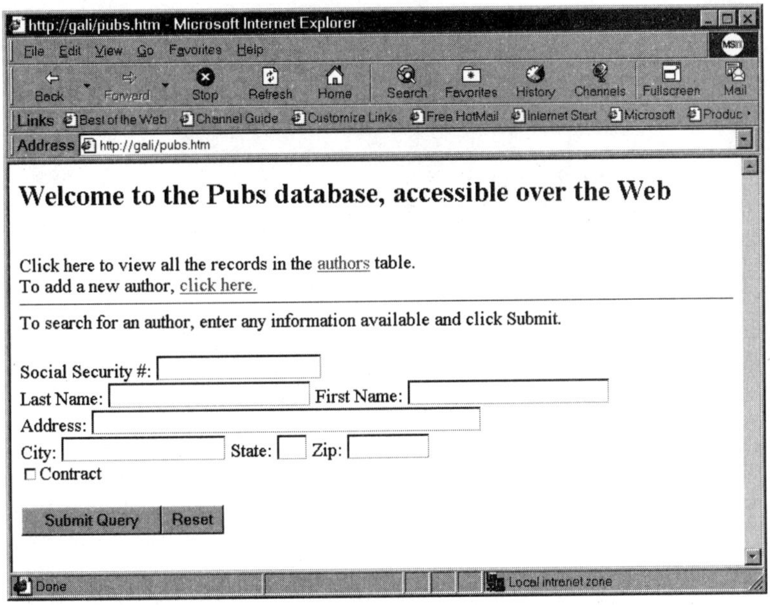

Figure 12-16. *The result of Exercise 12-6.*

UTILIZING COM COMPONENTS

Although ASP is a powerful technology for building interactive Web sites, there are times when you will need special functionality not provided by any of the intrinsic or add-on components. When such cases arise, you can build a custom COM component for use from an ASP page. Figure 12-17 shows a component used from an ASP page.

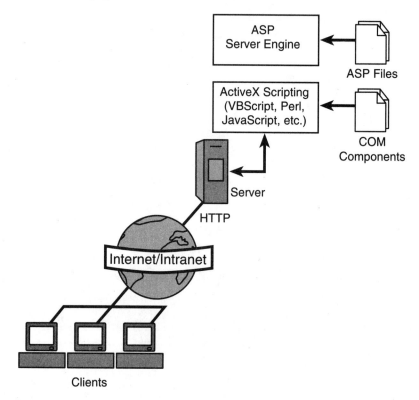

Figure 12-17. *COM components with ASP pages.*

COM components that execute on the server are identical in form to components that execute on the client side. Since they execute on the server, however, there are a few functional differences you should be aware of. First, since they run on the server, such components typically do not display a user interface. Second, we recommend that you package your server-side component as a DLL, because that provides superior performance. By default, calling out-of-process components on the server is disabled.

Although you can develop COM components in any environment that supports COM standards, including Visual C++ and Visual J++, we will focus on building COM components in Visual Basic. Since user interface elements are not permitted to execute on the server, COM components such as controls and documents are not applicable. Only COM code components, discussed in depth in Chapter 5, can be used from ASP pages. When creating a COM component in Visual Basic, you create an ActiveX DLL project. Choose Project1 Properties from the Project menu, and check the Unattended Execution box. Visual Basic will now enforce the ban on any user interface elements. For example, you won't be able to add forms or documents to your project. Visual Basic will also mark your component as supporting the apartment threading model.

By default, in-process components built in Visual Basic support the apartment threading model. Single-threaded components run in exactly one thread, and calls to the component from other threads are marshaled to the main thread. Only one thread at a time can enter a component marked as single-threaded, and it must be the same thread each time. This is a serious limitation for COM components running on the server because there are likely to be many clients that want to use a component's services simultaneously. Components that support the apartment threading model are more flexible. Although each object in the component can be entered by only one thread, recall that a single COM component can expose multiple objects. Components that support the apartment threading model can be entered simultaneously by different threads. This model is recommended for COM server components. The threading model supported by an in-process component can be found in the Registry entry for that component, under the InprocServer32 key.

Exercise 12-7

In this exercise, you will build an in-process COM code component in Visual Basic that computes prime numbers. Then you will develop an ASP page that uses this component.

1. Open Visual Basic, select the ActiveX DLL project type, and then select OK.

2. Set the *Name* property of the class module to *Prime*.

3. Write the following function:

```
Public Function IsPrime(TestNumber As Long) As Boolean
Dim Count As Long, HalfNumber As Long
    HalfNumber = TestNumber / 2 + 1
    For Count = 2 To HalfNumber
        If TestNumber Mod Count = 0 Then
            IsPrime = False
            Exit Function
        End If
    Next Count
    IsPrime = True
End Function
```

4. Choose Project1 Properties from the Project menu.

5. Set the Project Name to *Compute*, and check the Unattended Execution box. Select OK.

6. Choose Make Compute.dll from the File menu.

7. Choose Save Project from the File menu. Accept the default filenames.

8. If you were building the COM code component on the same computer on which you are running your Web server, the component was automatically registered by Visual Basic. If you built the component on another computer, you need to copy the Compute.dll file to the server. If you are running Internet Information Server or Peer Web Services, you should store components used by ASP files in the C:\WINNT\system32\inetsrv\ASP\Cmpnts directory, as recommended. If you are running Personal Web Server, you should store components used by ASP files in the C:\Program Files\websvr\system\ASP\Cmpnts directory, as recommended. Finally, register the COM Server component using the RegSvr32.exe utility, as shown in the following command line:

   ```
   regsvr32 compute.dll
   ```

   To be sure that you are using the correct version of RegSvr32, use the version found in the \ASP\Cmpnts directory.

9. Create a file named NUMBER.HTM containing the following HTML code, and publish it on your Web server.

   ```
   <HTML>
   <HEAD><TITLE>Prime Number Tester</TITLE></HEAD>
   <BODY>
   Please provide a number, and we will tell you
   whether it is a prime number.
   <FORM METHOD=POST Action=isprime.asp>
   Your number: <INPUT NAME=number SIZE=25><P>
   <HR><INPUT TYPE=SUBMIT><INPUT TYPE=RESET><P>
   Thanks for playing.
   </FORM>
   </BODY>
   </HTML>
   ```

10. Create a file named ISPRIME.ISP containing the following HTML code, and publish it on your Web server.

```
<HTML>
<HEAD><TITLE>Prime Number Tester</TITLE></HEAD>
<BODY>
<% TestNumber = Request("number") %>
<H2>The number <% = TestNumber %> is
<% If IsNumeric(TestNumber) Then
    Set MyCompute = Server.CreateObject("Compute.Prime")
    If MyCompute.IsPrime(CLng(TestNumber)) = True Then %>
        prime.
    <% Else %>
        not prime.<P>
    <% End If
Else %>
    invalid!
<% End If %>
</H2>
</BODY>
</HTML>
```

11. Using Internet Explorer, activate *http://myserver/number.htm*, enter a number (in this example, *23*), and choose the Submit button. Figure 12-18 shows the Prime Number Tester.

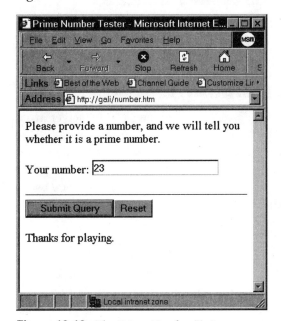

Figure 12-18. *The Prime Number Tester.*

The result will look like what is shown in Figure 12-19.

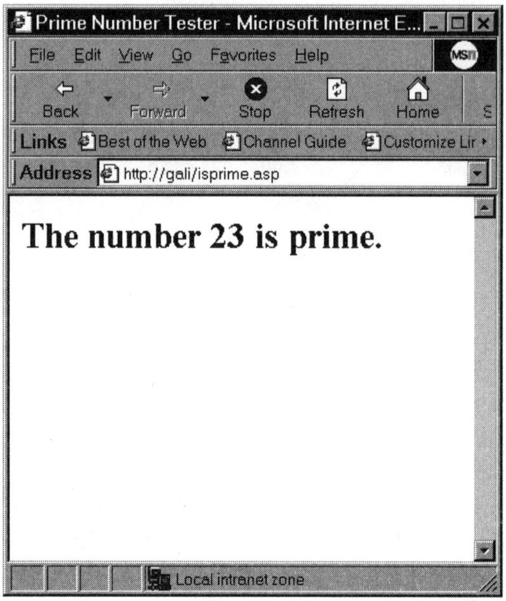

Figure 12-19. *The result of Exercise 12-7.*

MICROSOFT ACTIVE SERVER PAGES OBJECT LIBRARY

As you have seen, creating COM components for the server in Visual Basic is straightforward. Almost any component that doesn't display a user interface can be called from an ASP page. Sometimes, however, you might want to create a more sophisticated component specially designed for use with ASP. In such cases, you can access the five built-in ASP objects (*Application*, *Request*, *Response*, *Server*, and *Session*) from within a component. To use these objects from Visual Basic, set a reference to the Microsoft Active Server Pages Object Library (ASP.DLL) from the Project References command. There are two ways to pass the built-in ASP objects to a component. The simplest is to pass these objects as parameters to methods of your component. This method, however, forces the ASP page writer using your component to continually pass these objects to your component. A better way to do this is to implement the *OnStartPage* method in your component.

You can implement two page-level event methods—*OnStartPage* and *OnEndPage*—in your component. These methods are optional; ASP pages will work with any component, regardless of whether these methods are implemented. When the server creates a component instance, it checks to see if the component has implemented the *OnStartPage* and *OnEndPage* methods. If the component has implemented these two methods, the server will automatically call the *OnStartPage* method during script processing before the component is used, and it will call the *OnEndPage* method when all scripts on the ASP page have been processed. The *OnStartPage* method receives one parameter from the ASP module: a *ScriptingContext*. This object contains references to the other five built-in ASP objects:

```
Dim rp As Response
Dim rq As Request
Dim ap As Application
Dim sr As Server
Dim sn As Session

Public Sub OnStartPage(mySC As ScriptingContext)
Set rp = mySC.Response
Set rq = mySC.Request
Set ap = mySC.Application
Set sr = mySC.Server
Set sn = mySC.Session
End Sub
```

You can use the *OnStartPage* method to access the *ScriptingContext* interface to retrieve pointers to the built-in object interfaces. Your component can then use the built-in object's interface to access that object's collections, methods, and properties. Using *OnStartPage* and *ScriptingContext* to retrieve and use built-in object interfaces and their methods, instead of passing built-in objects as parameters, makes your component easier to use in ASP scripts.

Exercise 12-8
In this exercise, we will modify Exercise 12-7 so that the built-in objects will be used from within the component.

1. Open the Compute.vbp Visual Basic project you created in Exercise 12-7.

2. Choose References from the Project menu, and select the Microsoft Active Server Pages 1.0 Object Library item. Select OK.

3. Modify the code, as shown in boldface in the following:

```
Dim rp As Response
Dim rq As Request
Public Sub OnStartPage(mySC As ScriptingContext)
Set rp = mySC.Response
Set rq = mySC.Request
rp.Write "<I>OnStartPage</I><P>"
End Sub
```

(continued)

```
Public Sub OnEndPage()
rp.Write "<P><I>OnEndPage</I>"
Set rp = Nothing
Set rq = Nothing
End Sub

Public Sub IsPrime()
Dim Count As Long HalfNumber As Long, TestNumber ⇥
  As Long
TestNumber = rq.Form("number")
rp.Write "<H3>Hey there user, this is Visual Basic ⇥
  here.<BR></H3>"
rp.Write "<H3>Thanks for submitting the number " & ⇥
  TestNumber & "<P></H3>"
rp.Write "<H3>Guess what?<T>"
If Not IsNumeric(TestNumber) Or TestNumber < 1 Then
    rp.Write "The number you entered is ⇥
      invalid!</H3>"
    Exit Sub
End If
HalfNumber = TestNumber / 2 + 1
For Count = 2 To HalfNumber
    If TestNumber Mod Count = 0 Then
        rp.Write "The number " & TestNumber & ⇥
          " is not prime.</H3>"
        Exit Sub
    End If
Next Count
rp.Write "The number " & TestNumber & ⇥
  " is prime.</H3>"
End Sub
```

4. Choose Make Compute.dll from the File menu.

5. Choose Save Project from the File menu.

6. Copy Compute.dll to the ASP\Cmpnts directory.

   If you receive an access-denied message, note that before you
   can overwrite the old copy of Compute.dll with the new one you
   will need to stop your Web server. If you are running Internet
   Information Server or Peer Web Services, load the Internet Service
   Manager and stop the WWW service. If you are running Personal Web
   Server, go to the Personal Web Server icon in Control Panel, select
   the Startup tab, and click Stop. Now attempt to copy the file again.

7. After copying the Compute.dll file, run the RegSvr32 utility to register
   the component:

   ```
   regsvr32 compute.dll
   ```

8. Restart the Web server on your computer.

9. Modify the isprime.asp file as shown in the following boldface code. Notice that the prime number entered by the user isn't explicitly passed as a parameter to the Compute.IsPrime method, nor are results displayed to the user in this .ASP file.

```
<HTML>
<HEAD><TITLE>Prime Number Tester</TITLE></HEAD>
<BODY>
<%
Set MyCompute = Server.CreateObject("Compute.Prime")
MyCompute.IsPrime
%>
</BODY>
</HTML>
```

10. Using Internet Explorer, activate *http://myserver/number.htm* and test the application.

In this chapter, we have used ASP to create sample interactive Web sites. In the exercises, we used Notepad as the primary development tool for coding ASP files. Although this is a great way to learn and understand how ASP works, it is obviously not an ideal way to develop applications. To fill this need, Microsoft developed Microsoft Visual InterDev, an integrated development tool for developing Web applications in general and ASP pages in particular. Visual InterDev contains a number of wizards and ActiveX design-time controls that assist in the creation of active Web content. Visual InterDev also works with Microsoft FrontPage, which provides a WYSIWYG editor for HTML pages.

Bibliography

Born, Günter. *Inside the Microsoft Windows 98 Registry*. Redmond, WA: Microsoft Press, 1998.

Box, Don. *Essential COM*. Reading, MA: Addison-Wesley, 1998.

Brockschmidt, Kraig. *Inside OLE*. 2nd ed. Redmond, WA: Microsoft Press, 1995.

Chappell, David. *Understanding ActiveX and OLE*. Redmond, WA: Microsoft Press, 1996.

Craig, John Clark, and Jeff Webb. *Microsoft Visual Basic 6.0 Developer's Workshop*. 5th ed. Redmond, WA: Microsoft Press, 1998.

Denning, Adam. *ActiveX Controls Inside Out*. 2nd ed. Redmond, WA: Microsoft Press, 1997.

Eddon, Guy. *RPC for NT*. Lawrence, KS: R&D Publications, 1994.

Eddon, Guy, and Henry Eddon. *Active Visual Basic 5.0*. Redmond, WA: Microsoft Press, 1997.

Eddon, Guy, and Henry Eddon. *Inside Distributed COM*. Redmond, WA: Microsoft Press, 1998.

Gamma, Erich, et al. *Design Patterns*. Reading, MA: Addison-Wesley, 1995.

Hillier, Scot. *Inside Microsoft Visual Basic Scripting Edition*. Redmond, WA: Microsoft Press, 1996.

McKinney, Bruce. *Hardcore Visual Basic*. 2nd ed. Redmond, WA: Microsoft Press, 1997.

Microsoft Corporation. *Automation Programmer's Reference*. Redmond, WA: Microsoft Press, 1997.

Microsoft Corporation. *Component Object Model Specification*. Version 0.9, October 1995. http://www.microsoft.com/oledev/olecom/title.htm.

Microsoft Corporation. *Microsoft Office 97 Visual Basic Programmer's Guide.* Redmond, WA: Microsoft Press, 1997.

Rogerson, Dale. *Inside COM.* Redmond, WA: Microsoft Press, 1997.

Soukup, Ron. *Inside Microsoft SQL Server 6.5.* Redmond, WA: Microsoft Press, 1997.

Stroustrup, Bjarne. *The Design and Evolution of C++.* Reading, MA: Addison-Wesley, 1994.

Vaughn, William R. *Hitchhiker's Guide to Visual Basic & SQL Server.* 5th ed. Redmond, WA: Microsoft Press, 1997.

Index

Page numbers in italics refer to figures or tables.

Index

Index

Guy Eddon

Although he maintains his original ambition to become a world-famous cello player, Guy has taken a sabbatical to learn about the wonderful world of software development. His first real project was a game, Danny's Rooms, written for the autistic son of his cello teacher. In 1992, Danny's Rooms won an award from the Johns Hopkins National Search for Computing to Assist Persons with Disabilities and was featured on a segment of the National Public Radio program *All Things Considered*. Guy's first article, about OS/2, was published in *Windows Developer's Journal*. He has also written for *Microsoft Systems Journal, Microsoft Interactive Developer,* and *IEEE Proceedings. RPC for NT,* his first book, was published in 1994 by R&D Publications. Since then, Henry and Guy have co-authored *Active Visual Basic 5.0* (1997) and *Inside Distributed COM* (1998), both published by Microsoft Press. At different times, Guy has flown small airplanes, fermented grapes into wine, gone scuba diving, and traded securities. Guy also teaches Visual Basic, Java, and Win32 programming courses for Learning Tree International.

Henry Eddon

Henry's involvement with computers dates back to the IBM 1132 series at Haifa University. There he created the first computerized student admissions record written in Fortran IV. He later graduated from Columbia University with a degree in Mathematics and moved from the Commodore SuperPET to a HERO 1 robot, and later to an original IBM PC. In 1984, Henry and an ophthalmologist friend started AMOS. AMOS was an insurance billing and patient appointment–scheduling program that attained processing speed by bypassing MS-DOS to access video memory directly. Henry has achieved a Master Mechanic license from the National Institute for Automotive Service Excellence, written a 6800 Motorola assembler to enable programming the HERO 1 robot in assembly language instead of machine code, and earned Certified Computing Professional (CCP) status from the Institute for Certification of Computing Professionals (ICCP). He is employed in the information services division of the United Parcel Service and enjoys Dilbert cartoons.

The manuscript for this book was prepared using Microsoft Word 97. Pages were composed by Microsoft Press using Adobe PageMaker 6.52 for Windows, with text in Garamond and display type in Helvetica Black. Composed pages were delivered to the printer as electronic prepress files.

Cover Graphic Designer
Tim Girvin Design, Inc.

Cover Illustrator
Glenn Mitsui

Interior Graphic Artist
Joel Panchot

Principal Compositor
Steven Hopster

Principal Proofreader/Copy Editor
Roger LeBlanc

Indexer
Julie Kawabata

Microsoft Press has titles to help everyone—from new users to seasoned developers—

Step by Step Series
Self-paced tutorials for classroom instruction or individualized study

Starts Here™ Series
Interactive instruction on CD-ROM that helps students learn by doing

Field Guide Series
Concise, task-oriented A–Z references for quick, easy answers— anywhere

Official Series
Timely books on a wide variety of Internet topics geared for advanced users

All User Training   All User Reference

Quick Course® Series
Fast, to-the-point instruction for new users

Running Series
A comprehensive curriculum alternative to standard documentation books

At a Glance Series
Quick visual guides for task-oriented instruction

mspress.microsoft.com

Microsoft Press Online is your road map to the best available print and multimedia materials—resources that will help you maximize the effectiveness of Microsoft® software products. Our goal is making it easy and convenient for you to find exactly the Microsoft Press® book or interactive product you need, as well as bringing you the latest in training and certification materials from Microsoft Press.

Where do you want to go today?®

MICROSOFT LICENSE AGREEMENT
(Programming Components with Microsoft Visual Basic 6.0 - Book Companion CD)

IMPORTANT—READ CAREFULLY: This Microsoft End-User License Agreement ("EULA") is a legal agreement between you (either an individual or an entity) and Microsoft Corporation for the Microsoft product identified above, which includes computer software and may include associated media, printed materials, and "on-line" or electronic documentation ("SOFTWARE PRODUCT"). Any component included within the SOFTWARE PRODUCT that is accompanied by a separate End-User License Agreement shall be governed by such agreement and not the terms set forth below. By installing, copying, or otherwise using the SOFTWARE PRODUCT, you agree to be bound by the terms of this EULA. If you do not agree to the terms of this EULA, you are not authorized to install, copy, or otherwise use the SOFTWARE PRODUCT; you may, however, return the SOFTWARE PRODUCT, along with all printed materials and other items that form a part of the Microsoft product that includes the SOFTWARE PRODUCT, to the place you obtained them for a full refund.

SOFTWARE PRODUCT LICENSE

The SOFTWARE PRODUCT is protected by United States copyright laws and international copyright treaties, as well as other intellectual property laws and treaties. The SOFTWARE PRODUCT is licensed, not sold.

1. GRANT OF LICENSE. This EULA grants you the following rights:
- **a.** **Software Product.** You may install and use one copy of the SOFTWARE PRODUCT on a single computer. The primary user of the computer on which the SOFTWARE PRODUCT is installed may make a second copy for his or her exclusive use on a portable computer.
- **b.** **Storage/Network Use.** You may also store or install a copy of the SOFTWARE PRODUCT on a storage device, such as a network server, used only to install or run the SOFTWARE PRODUCT on your other computers over an internal network; however, you must acquire and dedicate a license for each separate computer on which the SOFTWARE PRODUCT is installed or run from the storage device. A license for the SOFTWARE PRODUCT may not be shared or used concurrently on different computers.
- **c.** **License Pak.** If you have acquired this EULA in a Microsoft License Pak, you may make the number of additional copies of the computer software portion of the SOFTWARE PRODUCT authorized on the printed copy of this EULA, and you may use each copy in the manner specified above. You are also entitled to make a corresponding number of secondary copies for portable computer use as specified above.
- **d.** **Sample Code.** Solely with respect to portions, if any, of the SOFTWARE PRODUCT that are identified within the SOFTWARE PRODUCT as sample code (the "SAMPLE CODE"):
  - **i.** **Use and Modification.** Microsoft grants you the right to use and modify the source code version of the SAMPLE CODE, *provided* you comply with subsection (d)(iii) below. You may not distribute the SAMPLE CODE, or any modified version of the SAMPLE CODE, in source code form.
  - **ii.** **Redistributable Files.** Provided you comply with subsection (d)(iii) below, Microsoft grants you a nonexclusive, royalty-free right to reproduce and distribute the object code version of the SAMPLE CODE and of any modified SAMPLE CODE, other than SAMPLE CODE (or any modified version thereof) designated as not redistributable in the Readme file that forms a part of the SOFTWARE PRODUCT (the "Non-Redistributable Sample Code"). All SAMPLE CODE other than the Non-Redistributable Sample Code is collectively referred to as the "REDISTRIBUTABLES."
  - **iii.** **Redistribution Requirements.** If you redistribute the REDISTRIBUTABLES, you agree to: (i) distribute the REDISTRIBUTABLES in object code form only in conjunction with and as a part of your software application product; (ii) not use Microsoft's name, logo, or trademarks to market your software application product; (iii) include a valid copyright notice on your software application product; (iv) indemnify, hold harmless, and defend Microsoft from and against any claims or lawsuits, including attorney's fees, that arise or result from the use or distribution of your software application product; and (v) not permit further distribution of the REDISTRIBUTABLES by your end user. Contact Microsoft for the applicable royalties due and other licensing terms for all other uses and/or distribution of the REDISTRIBUTABLES.

2. DESCRIPTION OF OTHER RIGHTS AND LIMITATIONS.
- **Limitations on Reverse Engineering, Decompilation, and Disassembly.** You may not reverse engineer, decompile, or disassemble the SOFTWARE PRODUCT, except and only to the extent that such activity is expressly permitted by applicable law notwithstanding this limitation.
- **Separation of Components.** The SOFTWARE PRODUCT is licensed as a single product. Its component parts may not be separated for use on more than one computer.
- **Rental.** You may not rent, lease, or lend the SOFTWARE PRODUCT.
- **Support Services.** Microsoft may, but is not obligated to, provide you with support services related to the SOFTWARE PRODUCT ("Support Services"). Use of Support Services is governed by the Microsoft policies and programs described in the user manual, in "on-line" documentation, and/or in other Microsoft-provided materials. Any supplemental software code provided to you as part of the Support Services shall be considered part of the SOFTWARE PRODUCT and subject to the terms and conditions of this EULA. With respect to technical information you provide to Microsoft as part of the Support Services, Microsoft may use such information for its business purposes, including for product support and development. Microsoft will not utilize such technical information in a form that personally identifies you.

- **Software Transfer.** You may permanently transfer all of your rights under this EULA, provided you retain no copies, you transfer all of the SOFTWARE PRODUCT (including all component parts, the media and printed materials, any upgrades, this EULA, and, if applicable, the Certificate of Authenticity), **and** the recipient agrees to the terms of this EULA.
- **Termination.** Without prejudice to any other rights, Microsoft may terminate this EULA if you fail to comply with the terms and conditions of this EULA. In such event, you must destroy all copies of the SOFTWARE PRODUCT and all of its component parts.

3. **COPYRIGHT.** All title and copyrights in and to the SOFTWARE PRODUCT (including but not limited to any images, photographs, animations, video, audio, music, text, SAMPLE CODE, REDISTRIBUTABLES, and "applets" incorporated into the SOFTWARE PRODUCT) and any copies of the SOFTWARE PRODUCT are owned by Microsoft or its suppliers. The SOFTWARE PRODUCT is protected by copyright laws and international treaty provisions. Therefore, you must treat the SOFTWARE PRODUCT like any other copyrighted material **except** that you may install the SOFTWARE PRODUCT on a single computer provided you keep the original solely for backup or archival purposes. You may not copy the printed materials accompanying the SOFTWARE PRODUCT.

4. **U.S. GOVERNMENT RESTRICTED RIGHTS.** The SOFTWARE PRODUCT and documentation are provided with RESTRICTED RIGHTS. Use, duplication, or disclosure by the Government is subject to restrictions as set forth in subparagraph (c)(1)(ii) of the Rights in Technical Data and Computer Software clause at DFARS 252.227-7013 or subparagraphs (c)(1) and (2) of the Commercial Computer Software—Restricted Rights at 48 CFR 52.227-19, as applicable. Manufacturer is Microsoft Corporation/One Microsoft Way/Redmond, WA 98052-6399.

5. **EXPORT RESTRICTIONS.** You agree that you will not export or re-export the SOFTWARE PRODUCT, any part thereof, or any process or service that is the direct product of the SOFTWARE PRODUCT (the foregoing collectively referred to as the "Restricted Components"), to any country, person, entity, or end user subject to U.S. export restrictions. You specifically agree not to export or re-export any of the Restricted Components (i) to any country to which the U.S. has embargoed or restricted the export of goods or services, which currently include, but are not necessarily limited to, Cuba, Iran, Iraq, Libya, North Korea, Sudan, and Syria, or to any national of any such country, wherever located, who intends to transmit or transport the Restricted Components back to such country; (ii) to any end user who you know or have reason to know will utilize the Restricted Components in the design, development, or production of nuclear, chemical, or biological weapons; or (iii) to any end user who has been prohibited from participating in U.S. export transactions by any federal agency of the U.S. government. You warrant and represent that neither the BXA nor any other U.S. federal agency has suspended, revoked, or denied your export privileges.

6. **NOTE ON JAVA SUPPORT.** THE SOFTWARE PRODUCT MAY CONTAIN SUPPORT FOR PROGRAMS WRITTEN IN JAVA. JAVA TECHNOLOGY IS NOT FAULT TOLERANT AND IS NOT DESIGNED, MANUFACTURED, OR INTENDED FOR USE OR RESALE AS ON-LINE CONTROL EQUIPMENT IN HAZARDOUS ENVIRONMENTS REQUIRING FAIL-SAFE PERFORMANCE, SUCH AS IN THE OPERATION OF NUCLEAR FACILITIES, AIRCRAFT NAVIGATION OR COMMUNICATION SYSTEMS, AIR TRAFFIC CONTROL, DIRECT LIFE SUPPORT MACHINES, OR WEAPONS SYSTEMS, IN WHICH THE FAILURE OF JAVA TECHNOLOGY COULD LEAD DIRECTLY TO DEATH, PERSONAL INJURY, OR SEVERE PHYSICAL OR ENVIRONMENTAL DAMAGE.

DISCLAIMER OF WARRANTY

NO WARRANTIES OR CONDITIONS. MICROSOFT EXPRESSLY DISCLAIMS ANY WARRANTY OR CONDITION FOR THE SOFTWARE PRODUCT. THE SOFTWARE PRODUCT AND ANY RELATED DOCUMENTATION IS PROVIDED "AS IS" WITHOUT WARRANTY OR CONDITION OF ANY KIND, EITHER EXPRESS OR IMPLIED, INCLUDING, WITHOUT LIMITATION, THE IMPLIED WARRANTIES OF MERCHANTABILITY, FITNESS FOR A PARTICULAR PURPOSE, OR NONINFRINGEMENT. THE ENTIRE RISK ARISING OUT OF USE OR PERFORMANCE OF THE SOFTWARE PRODUCT REMAINS WITH YOU.

LIMITATION OF LIABILITY. TO THE MAXIMUM EXTENT PERMITTED BY APPLICABLE LAW, IN NO EVENT SHALL MICROSOFT OR ITS SUPPLIERS BE LIABLE FOR ANY SPECIAL, INCIDENTAL, INDIRECT, OR CONSEQUENTIAL DAMAGES WHATSOEVER (INCLUDING, WITHOUT LIMITATION, DAMAGES FOR LOSS OF BUSINESS PROFITS, BUSINESS INTERRUPTION, LOSS OF BUSINESS INFORMATION, OR ANY OTHER PECUNIARY LOSS) ARISING OUT OF THE USE OF OR INABILITY TO USE THE SOFTWARE PRODUCT OR THE PROVISION OF OR FAILURE TO PROVIDE SUPPORT SERVICES, EVEN IF MICROSOFT HAS BEEN ADVISED OF THE POSSIBILITY OF SUCH DAMAGES. IN ANY CASE, MICROSOFT'S ENTIRE LIABILITY UNDER ANY PROVISION OF THIS EULA SHALL BE LIMITED TO THE GREATER OF THE AMOUNT ACTUALLY PAID BY YOU FOR THE SOFTWARE PRODUCT OR US$5.00; PROVIDED, HOWEVER, IF YOU HAVE ENTERED INTO A MICROSOFT SUPPORT SERVICES AGREEMENT, MICROSOFT'S ENTIRE LIABILITY REGARDING SUPPORT SERVICES SHALL BE GOVERNED BY THE TERMS OF THAT AGREEMENT. BECAUSE SOME STATES AND JURISDICTIONS DO NOT ALLOW THE EXCLUSION OR LIMITATION OF LIABILITY, THE ABOVE LIMITATION MAY NOT APPLY TO YOU.

MISCELLANEOUS

This EULA is governed by the laws of the State of Washington USA, except and only to the extent that applicable law mandates governing law of a different jurisdiction.

Should you have any questions concerning this EULA, or if you desire to contact Microsoft for any reason, please contact the Microsoft subsidiary serving your country, or write: Microsoft Sales Information Center/One Microsoft Way/ Redmond, WA 98052-6399.

Register Today!

Return this
Programming Components with Microsoft® Visual Basic® 6.0
registration card today

mspress.microsoft.com

OWNER REGISTRATION CARD   **1-57231-966-6**

PROGRAMMING COMPONENTS WITH MICROSOFT® VISUAL BASIC® 6.0

FIRST NAME	MIDDLE INITIAL	LAST NAME

INSTITUTION OR COMPANY NAME

ADDRESS

CITY	STATE	ZIP

	( )
E-MAIL ADDRESS	PHONE NUMBER

U.S. and Canada addresses only. Fill in information above and mail postage-free.
Please mail only the bottom half of this page.

**For information about Microsoft Press®
products, visit our Web site at
mspress.microsoft.com**